NEGOTIATING THE POWER OF NGOs

This book focuses on the socio-political environment that allows for the impactful work of NGOs through their proximity to local communities. The book showcases how this space has helped South African women's rights NGOs to bring about crucial legal reforms, which are quite relevant to women's lived realities. Recognising its limitations, the South African state encourages NGOs to work freely on the ground and with state institutions to ameliorate the conditions for women's rights. The outcome of this state–NGO dynamic can be seen in the numerous human rights gains achieved by NGOs in general, and by women's rights organisations specifically. In addition, vulnerable communities such as women living under customary law have a significantly better chance to access justice. The book then demonstrates the opposite scenario, using Egypt as a case study, where NGOs are viewed as a national threat, and consequently operate under restrictive rules.

REEM WAEL is a social science researcher with a geographic focus on the Middle East and Africa. She co-founded the first gender consulting firm in the Middle East to focus on research and policy, trainings and media; she worked on numerous research projects on gender cross-cutting with health, education, data and information, law, and violence. In her most recent full-time position, Reem was the Executive Director of HarassMap, an NGO based in Egypt, using an online–offline integrated approach to end social acceptability of sexual harassment in Egypt. She holds a PhD from the University of London, where she conducted socio-legal analysis on gender-based violence in South Africa.

CAMBRIDGE STUDIES IN LAW AND SOCIETY

Founded in 1997, Cambridge Studies in Law and Society is a hub for leading scholarship in socio-legal studies. Located at the intersection of law, the humanities, and the social sciences, it publishes empirically innovative and theoretically sophisticated work on law's manifestations in everyday life: from discourses to practices, and from institutions to cultures. The series editors have longstanding expertise in the interdisciplinary study of law, and welcome contributions that place legal phenomena in national, comparative, or international perspective. Series authors come from a range of disciplines, including anthropology, history, law, literature, political science, and sociology.

A list of books in the series can be found at the back of this book.

NEGOTIATING THE POWER OF NGOs

Women's Legal Rights in South Africa

Reem Wael

HarassMap, Egypt, Africa

CAMBRIDGE
UNIVERSITY PRESS

CAMBRIDGE
UNIVERSITY PRESS

Shaftesbury Road, Cambridge CB2 8EA, United Kingdom

One Liberty Plaza, 20th Floor, New York, NY 10006, USA

477 Williamstown Road, Port Melbourne, VIC 3207, Australia

314–321, 3rd Floor, Plot 3, Splendor Forum, Jasola District Centre, New Delhi – 110025, India

103 Penang Road, #05–06/07, Visioncrest Commercial, Singapore 238467

Cambridge University Press is part of Cambridge University Press & Assessment, a department of the University of Cambridge.

We share the University's mission to contribute to society through the pursuit of education, learning and research at the highest international levels of excellence.

www.cambridge.org
Information on this title: www.cambridge.org/9781108464840

DOI: 10.1017/ 9781108566339

First published 2019
First paperback edition 2026

A catalogue record for this publication is available from the British Library

Library of Congress Cataloging-in-Publication data
Names: Wael, Reem, author. | HarassMap (Organization)
Title: Negotiating the power of NGOs : women's legal rights in
South Africa / Reem Wael, HarassMap, Egypt, Africa.
Other titles: Negotiating the power of non-governmental organizations
Description: Cambridge [UK]; New York, NY: Cambridge University Press, 2019. |
Series: Cambridge studies in law and society | Includes bibliographical references.
Identifiers: LCCN 2018048888 | ISBN 9781108475136 (hardback) |
ISBN 9781108464840 (paperback)
Subjects: LCSH: Non-governmental organizations – Law and legislation – South Africa. |
Women, Violence against – South Africa. | Sexual harassment – Law and legislation – South
Africa. | Women's rights – South Africa. | Justice, Administration of – South Africa.
Classification: LCC KTL522.W34 2019 | DDC 345.68/0253082–dc23
LC record available at https://lccn.loc.gov/2018048888

ISBN 978-1-108-47513-6 Hardback
ISBN 978-1-108-46484-0 Paperback

CONTENTS

ACKNOWLEDGEMENTS

The book would have not been possible without the generosity of nongovernmental organisations in South Africa, and in Egypt. After working in the nonprofit section in Egypt, I truly understand the time and resource constraints on staff members, and therefore I appreciate the people who gave me some of their valuable resources.

This project is rooted in my doctoral dissertation, for which I am forever indebted to Professor Fareda Banda, my mentor and supervisor at the School of Oriental and African Studies. Her involvement in my work continues, and has provided some invaluable insights for this book.

I am eternally grateful to Ahmad Hegab and Hala Wael, who helped me structure and edit this book, and bring it to life. Their personal and professional support is priceless. My editor Tom Randall was remarkably helpful and attentive throughout the publishing process.

On a personal level, no one has given me more than my parents Nabila and Wael who have supported me in a prosperous career, and continue to do so.

TABLE OF CASES

The following table is a list of selected cases and laws relevant to the topic on the local, regional and international level, many of which are used in the book.

South African Cases

(*continued*)

South African Cases

Minister of Health *v.* Treatment Action Campaign [2002] (10) BCLR 1075 (CC), 123, 170

Minister of Home Affairs and Another *v.* Fourie and Another [2006] (3) BCLR 355 (CC), 41

Naidoo *v.* Minister of Police (20431/2014) [2015] ZASCA152 (2 October 2015), 193

National Coalition for Gay and Lesbian Equality *v.* Minister of Justice [1998] (12) BCLR 1517 (CC), 41, 176

Omar *v.* Government of the Republic of South Africa and Others [2006] (2) BCLR 253 (CC), 131, 170

Orr *v.* Minister of Law and Order ECD 25 September [1985] case no. 2507/85 (unreported), 123

Rikhoto *v.* East Rand Administration Board [1983] (4) South Africa 278 (W), 123

S *v.* Baloyi [2000] (1) BCLR 86 (CC), 31, 147

S *v.* Egglestone (482/07) [2008] ZASCA 77; [2008] 4 All South Africa 207 (SCA); 2009 (1) SACR 244 (SCA), 146

S *v.* Ferreira and Others [2004] 4 All SA 373 (SCA), 145

S *v.* Jackson [1998] (4) BCLR 424 (SCA), 145–146

S *v.* Jordan [2002] (11) BCLR 1117 (CC), 150, 151

S *v.* Marais [2010] (12) BCLR 1223 (CC), 149, 150

S *v.* Mokoena, S *v.* Phaswane [2008] (5) SA 578 (T), 42, 112, 133, 135

S *v.* Mvamvu [2005] 1 All SA 435 (SCA), 75, 80, 92

S *v.* Zuma [1995] (4) BCLR 401 (SA), 148

Shilubana & Others *v.* Nwamitwa [2009] (9) BCLR 914 (CC), 77, 78, 80

Sonke Gender Justice Network *v.* Malema (2010 (7) BCLR 729 (EqC)) [2010] ZAEQC 2; 02/2009 (15 March 2010), 136, 146, 169, 170, 177

Teddy Bear Clinic for the Abused Children and Another *v.* Minister of Justice and Constitutional Development and Another [2013] (73300/10) ZAGPPHC 1, 125, 137, 143, 144

Regional and International Cases

Egyptian Initiative for Personal Rights and Interights *v.* Egypt (2006) Comm. No. 232/06, (African commissions for Human and people's rights), 18

Maria da Penha *v.* Brazil (16 April 2001) Case 12.051, Report No. 54/01 (Inter-American Court of Human Rights), 167

Matter of Kasinga, 21 I. & N. 357 (United States of America: Board of Immigration Appeals 1996), 159

MC *v.* Bulgaria [2003] Case 39272/98 European Court of Human Rights, 39

(*continued*)

Regional and International Cases

Other Jurisdictions

Bangladesh

Botswana

India

Nigeria

United Kingdom

Zambia

PRIMARY SOURCES: SOUTH AFRICAN, INTERNATIONAL, REGIONAL AND GLOBAL LAW

South African Legislation

Bantu Education Act No 47 1953
Black Administration Act 38 of 1927
Black (Bantu) Authorities Act No 68 of 1951
Child Justice Act 75 of 2008
Children's Act No 38 of 2005
Commission of Gender Equality Act No 39 of 1996
Constitution of the Republic of South Africa Act No 108 of 1996
Correctional Services Act No 8 of 1959
Council of Traditional Leaders Act No 10 of 1997
Council of Traditional Leaders Amendment Act No 85 of 1998
Criminal Law (Sentencing) Amendment Act No 37 of 2007
Criminal Law (Sexual Offences) Amendment Bill B50–2003 (published in Government Gazette No. 25282 of 30 July 2003)
Criminal Law Amendment Act No 105 of 1997
Criminal Procedure Act No 51 of 1977
Domestic Violence Act No 116 of 1998
Fund-raising Act 107 of 1978
Group Areas Act No 41 of 1950
Immorality Amendment Act No 5 of 1927
Independent Police Investigative Directorate Act No 1 of 2011
Independent Police Investigative Directorate Bill B-15B of 2010
Industrial Conciliation Act No 28 of 1956
Interim Constitution of the Republic of South Africa, Act 200 of 1993
Intestate Succession Act No 81 of 1987
Labour Relations Act No 66 of 1995
Legal Aid Act 22 of 1969 (1969) (South Africa)
Marriage Act No 25 of 1961
Medical Schemes Act No 131 of 1998

(continued)

South African Legislation

National House of Traditional Leaders Act No 22 of 2009

National House of Traditional Leaders Amendment Act No 20 of 2000

National Instruction 3/2008 on Sexual Offences (Published in the Government Gazette No 865, 15 August 2008)

Native (Black) Administration Act No 38 of 1927

Native Building Workers Act No 27 of 1951

Native Labour (Settlement of Disputes) Act No 48 of 1953

Nonprofit Organisations Act No 71 of 1997

Police Act No 68 of 1995

Police Service Act No 68 of 1995

Prevention of Family Violence Act No 133 of 1993

Prohibition of Mixed Marriages Act No 55 of 1949

Promotion of Equality and Prevention of Unfair Discrimination Act No 4 of 2000

Recognition of Customary Marriages Act No 120 of 1998

Reservation of Separate Amenities Act No 49 of 1953

Security Officers Act No 92 of 1987

Sexual Offences Act No 23 of 1956 (Previous title: Immorality Act)

Sexual Offences and Related Matters Amendment Act No 32 of 2007

South African Development Community (SADC), Protocol on Gender and Development (2008) available at www.sadc.int/documents-publications/show/803

The Republic of South Africa Traditional Courts Bill 2008 (Published in the Government Gazette No. 30902 of 27 March 2008)

The Peace of Vereeniging Treaty (Pretoria 31 May 1902)

Traditional Leadership and Governance Framework Amendment Act No 41 of 2003

International Instruments

Charter of the United Nations (26 June 1945) 59 Stat. 1031

Convention on the Elimination of All Forms of Discrimination against Women (1979) 12

Convention on the Rights of the Child (1989) UN Doc A/44/49

Declaration on the Elimination of All Forms of Intolerance and of Discrimination Based on Religion or Belief (1981) UN Doc A/36/684

Declaration on the Elimination of Violence against Women (1993) UN Doc A/48/49

(continued)

International Instruments

Declaration on the Elimination of Violence against Women (20 December 1993) A/RES/48/104

Immigration and Nationality Act, 27 June 1952, last amended March 2004, (United States of America)

Optional Protocol to the Convention on the Elimination of all Forms of Discrimination Against Women (2000) UN Doc A/54/49 (Vol. I)

Universal Declaration of Human Rights (1948) UN Doc A/810 at 71

UNTS 13

Regional Instruments

African Charter on Human and Peoples' Rights (adopted 27 June 1981, entered into force 21 October 1986), 1520 UNTS

African Charter on the Rights and Welfare of the Child (1990) OAU Doc. CAB/LEG/TSG.Rev.1HR

African Commission on Human and People's Rights (25th Ordinary Session) res.38 (XXV) 99 (Bujumbura, Burundi 26 April to 5 May 1999)

African Union, Decision on the Protocol to the African Charter on Human and Peoples' Rights Relating to the Rights of Women, Assembly/AU/Dec.14 (II) art 18 (Africa's Women's Protocol)

Convention for the Protection of Human Rights and Fundamental Freedoms (1953) 213 UNTS 222

Convention on Preventing and Combating Violence against Women and Domestic Violence adopted by Council of Europe, CETS No 210 Istanbul November 2011

Protocol on the Prevention and Suppression of Sexual Violence Against Women and Children, adopted at the International Conference on the Great Lakes Region in Nairobi in December 2006 and entered into force in June 2008

Other Jurisdictions

Egypt

Bylaws to law 178/2002 (Arab Republic of Egypt)

Constitution of the Arab Republic of Egypt

Law regulating non-governmental organisations, 70/2017 (Arab Republic of Egypt)

Law regulating non-governmental organisations, 84/2002 (Arab Republic of Egypt)

Penal Code (Arab Republic of Egypt)

Presidential Decree No. 128 of 2014 (Arab Republic of Egypt)

(continued)

Other Jurisdictions

Presidential Decree Promulgating Law No 11/2011 (Arab Republic of Egypt)
Presidential Decree No 90 of 2000 (Arab Republic of Egypt)

Other African Jurisdictions

Constitution of Botswana (1966)
Constitution of the Republic of Nigeria (1999)
Constitution of Zambia (Act no 1, 1991)
NGO Coordination Act 1996 (Kenya)

India

Foreign Contribution Regulation Act of 1976

USA

Immigration and Nationality Act, 27 June 1952, last amended March 2004

ABBREVIATIONS

ADEW	Association for the Development and Enhancement of Women
ADR	alternative dispute resolution
ANC	African National Congress
ANCWL	ANC Women's League
BIA	Board of Immigration Appeals
BNWLA	Bangladesh National Women Lawyers Association
CALS	Centre for Applied Legal Studies
CBOs	community-based organisations
CEDAW	Convention on the Elimination of all Forms of Discrimination against Women
CEWLA	Centre for Egyptian Women's Legal Assistance
CGE	Commission on Gender Equality
CPA	Criminal Procedure Act
CRC	Convention on the Rights of the Child
DVA	Domestic Violence Act
DRC	Democratic Republic of the Congo
ECHR	European Court of Human Rights
EGP	Egyptian Pounds
FGM	female genital mutilation
FSAW	Federation of South African Women
GBV	gender-based violence
ICCPR	International Covenant on Civil and Political Rights
ICD	Independent Complaints Directory
ICESCR	International Covenant on Economic, Social and Cultural Rights
IJS	informal justice systems
IPID	Independent Police Investigative Directorate
JASA	Justice Alliance of South Africa
JSC	Judicial Service Commission
KZN	Kwazulu-Natal

LAB	Legal Aid Board
LRC	Legal Resource Centre
MOSS	Ministry of Social Solidarity
NCW	National Council for Women
NGO	nongovernmental organisation
NPO	Nonprofit Organisations Act
PIL	public interest litigation
PO	Protection Order
RAPCAN	Resources Aimed at the Prevention of Child Abuse and Neglect
SAA	South African Airlines
SADTU	South African Democratic Teachers' Union
SALC	South African Law Commission
SAPS	South African Police Service
SCA	Supreme Court of Appeals
SOA	Sexual Offences and Related Matters Amendment Act 2007
TAC	Treatment Action Campaign
TLAC	The Tshwaranang Legal Advocacy Centre
UK	United Kingdom
UN	United Nations
USA	United States of America
USD	United States of America Dollars
VAW	violence against women
WLC	Women's Legal Centre
WNC	Women's National Coalition

CHAPTER 1

INTRODUCTION

In January 2013, Andrew Harding, the correspondent for BBC Africa, wrote, 'Will South Africans ever be shocked by rape?' After investigating violence against women (VAW) in South Africa, Harding highlighted the casual attitude taken towards rape that was dominant in society. He reported an incident that had happened at the end of 2012. The police had arrested a rapist at a bar shortly after he had 'attacked and raped a 17-year-old girl at his table, but apparently considered the incident so trivial that he had not even tried to flee... Nor had anyone else in the bar, besides the alleged victim, thought of contacting the police'.[1]

As much as every South African woman has a well-founded fear of violence, it has become normalised in society. Many rape incidents lead to public outrage forcing the government to make promises or amend policies, many of which are implemented. However, the reactions of the public eventually fade and violence remains a real threat in women's daily lives. Activists wonder why the South African public does not react to horrendous episodes of rape in the same way that the Indian public reacted to the bus gang-rape incident in December 2012.

> At a time when Indians are re-examining their society in the light of a single, horrific incident of gang rape, South Africa seems numb – unable to muster much more than a collective shrug in the face of almost unbelievably grim statistics – seemingly far worse than India's.[2]

[1] Andrew Harding, 'Will South Africans ever be shocked by rape?', BBC World News, 10 January 2013, accessed 17 July 2018 at www.bbc.co.uk/news/world-africa-20971240

[2] Ibid.

Despite the immense resources dedicated to combat VAW, there has been an absence of collective outrage from the public that is persistent enough to recognise VAW as a grave violation against society. The one segment of society that has consistently attempted to tackle gender-based violence (GBV) is the nonprofit sector.

Scanning the development of women's rights in South Africa in the last two decades since the Constitution was enacted, it is evident that we cannot discuss GBV without putting nongovernmental organisations (NGOs) at the centre. While there is considerable research conducted on GBV in South Africa, there is a remarkable gap in the literature on the work of NGOs in fighting GBV at the local level, specifically focusing on the spaces and opportunities available for them in a young democracy like South Africa. This book aims to fill this gap, exploring the socio-legal space in which NGOs work to end GBV as mediators, advocates, lobbyists, service providers to GBV victims,[3] counsellors, lawyers and *amicus curiae* (friends of the court). Undertaking this work, NGOs close the gap between the law and local communities – a journey in which they develop complex relationships with both parties: state institutions and beneficiaries. This is the other side of the arguments explored in this book. While the research is primarily focused on VAW, NGO activism on the topic frequently overlaps with GBV, and therefore the terms will be used interchangeably.

This book argues that the legal and political space for discussing, negotiating and developing laws and policies on violence against women is quite liberal and open in South Africa, leading to significant accomplishments. Nongovernmental organisations play a central role in directing the movement against VAW by adopting multidimensional approaches and building constructive partnerships.

In the last two decades, VAW has been recognised as a global problem, attracting significant debate at the international and local levels. Under international human rights law, violence against women is defined as 'violence that is directed against a woman because she is a woman or that affects women disproportionately. It includes acts that inflict physical, mental or sexual harm or suffering, threats of such acts, coercion and other deprivations of liberty'.[4] Some forms of VAW, such as rape

[3] Women subjected to GBV are often referred to as either victims or survivors. This research will use the term 'victim' referring to a situation of victimisation – a victim in comparison to the offender. However, it remains at the woman's discretion to identify herself as victim or survivor.

[4] CEDAW Committee, General Recommendation No 19 on Violence Against Women, (1992), UN Doc A/47/38, para. 6.

and domestic violence are universal, while other forms are specific to geographic and cultural contexts. For example, female genital mutilation (FGM) is common in some African cultures, and the practice of dowry deaths is prevalent in India. Consequently, laws and policies have been designed to eradicate VAW at the international, regional and domestic levels.[5] However, VAW is reinforced by the social, political and economic inequalities that women bear, which necessitates the development of multifaceted approaches to combat it.

I GENDER-BASED VIOLENCE IN SOUTH AFRICA: SETTING THE CONTEXT FOR RESEARCH

A Research Objectives

Violence has prevailed throughout the social and political history of South Africa for centuries. The apartheid system that was formally promulgated in 1948 and lasted for four decades segregated racial groups, ensuring that white people received the best services. By the 1990s, negotiations were taking place between political parties, leading to the first democratic elections in 1994. In addition, an interim Constitution was drafted in 1994 to make the transition from minority rule to democracy. In 1996, it was replaced by the final Constitution. Currently, South Africa has one of the most progressive human rights systems in the world, coupled with some of the highest VAW statistics globally.

The contrast between law and society inspired this research, which aims to answer the following questions:

- What are the enabling factors within a socio-legal environment that affect the work of NGOs in fighting for women's rights in law and society?
- How do NGOs negotiate the threshold of human rights and state responsibility, specifically in the case of violence against women?
- How do NGOs, as third parties, affect women's access to justice when they are subjected to violence?

These questions will be answered in this socio-legal qualitative study, which is supported by primary research conducted in South Africa between 2010 and 2012. Additional fieldwork was undertaken in 2018

[5] See UN Department on Economic and Social Affairs, Handbook for the Legislation on Violence against Women, (New York, 2010) UN Doc ST/ESA/329. Also see UN Department on Economic and Social Affairs, Supplement to the Handbook for Legislation on Violence against Women (New York, 2011) ST/ESA/331.

in South Africa to capture updates and add a comparative component to the research. In the final chapter, the author will use the case of Egypt to compare the socio-legal space available to NGOs working on gender issues. Fieldwork included interviews with NGO employees, victims of VAW, and GBV shelter staff. This methodology is inspired by Hutchinson's reasoning that social science methods can be used by lawyers to identify the gap between legal theory and practice, as well as to explore the impact of law on society.[6] Similarly, social scientists study law to understand its background, evaluate its impact and suggest reforms.[7]

B Research Structure

This research argues that NGOs in South Africa operate in a plural socio-legal environment that encourages openness and partnerships. This space allows NGOs to play a pivotal role translating international human rights into local principles and initiatives to fight GBV using a variety of methods. Nongovernmental organisations design and implement programmes to engage with institutions of formal law and GBV victims, as well as institutions of customary law, traditional leaders and local communities. The nature and dynamic of this engagement are the core of this book. Acting as cultural translators, NGOs convey human rights principles to local communities and, simultaneously, NGOs provide the state with invaluable insights on the relevance of laws and policies to women's lived realities. Essentially, NGOs seek to close the gap between women and the law.

This introductory chapter will give an overview of the research project and a brief discussion of the literature on VAW globally; this will be followed by a review of the methodology.[8] Chapter 2 will discuss relevant domestic legislation and South Africa's obligations under international human rights law, demonstrating the liberal values enshrined in the formal legal system, paving the way for an open and engaging socio-legal environment. Recognising the limitations of law and institutions of formal justice, Chapter 3 will focus on the channels of informal justice, introducing customary law in South Africa, and locating it within formal law. The chapter will also identify the role of

[6] Terry Hutchinson, *Researching and Writing in Law* (Pyrmont, NSW: Lawbook, 2006), p. 89.

[7] Sayed Hassan Amin, *Research Methods in Law* (Glasgow: Royston Publishers, 1992) p. 61.

[8] The term 'women's movement' will be used to refer to a national, regional or international group of non-governmental organisations who form networks for women's rights.

NGOs as mediators, offering women an option other than official and customary law. Chapter 4 will track the women's movement in South Africa in the last few decades and analyse its relationship with the state, demonstrating a functional yet imperfect dynamic, with the two parties moving towards the same goals: advancing women's rights and fighting GBV. Chapter 5 will zoom in on the judiciary, first looking at its gender composition and then presenting the practice of cause lawyering. The chapter aims to showcase courts as a space for identifying and negotiating the limits of human rights and state responsibility, with the contribution of all concerned parties: litigants, the state, and NGOs; this will be exemplified by some case analyses. Chapter 6 will take a closer look at the value of cause lawyering, pinpointing some enabling factors and indicators of success. Chapter 7 will analyse the role of NGOs in facilitating women's access to justice, and whether this leads to empowerment. Chapter 8 is the comparative component added to the research in South Africa; to demonstrate the value of an open socio-legal and political environment that guarantees the freedom of NGOs to work on women's rights. This chapter will present Egypt as an opposite example, where the freedom of NGOs is curtailed in a shrinking public space, and where their work is therefore jeopardised. Chapter 9 presents a conclusion.

C Research Methods

This research is based on multiple theoretical backgrounds so as to honour its multidisciplinary approach: namely, feminist theory and legal pluralism theories, as well as theoretical perspectives on power and mediation.

South Africa was chosen as a case study for several reasons. First, in the pluralist nature of South African society, various ethnic and racial groups adopt different customs and informal normative orders, yet they are subject to one Constitution. The different procedures by which formal and informal legal systems operate under the same jurisdiction warrant an investigation of their responses to GBV. Second, alarming levels of GBV prevail despite the enactment of progressive laws that exceed the standards of international human rights law, which raises important questions about enforcement. Third, despite the persistent high levels of violence, the South African state prioritises this issue and recognises its limitations to curb GBV, giving space to NGOs to practise their expertise on the topic. This position opens up a crucial space of collaboration between NGOs and state institutions on many fronts.

As a result, South Africa has a civil society not only active in service provision, but also in law and policy development and in improving the capacity of state institutions to fight GBV. The methodology section towards the end of this chapter will give more details on the project, and present the research respondents.

II GENDER, RACE AND VIOLENCE IN THE SOUTH AFRICAN CONTEXT

A Tracing Violence to Apartheid

Researchers and academics have been trying to trace the growing normalisation of violence in South African society, which has created a suitable environment for VAW to flourish. Anglin states, 'it is not that human beings are inherently violent, but rather that certain contexts and social formations seem to produce violence'.[9] The violent history of South Africa, especially during the apartheid era, induced VAW. Moffett argues that sexual violence in contemporary South Africa is rooted in the inequalities lived in South African history and society. Apartheid legitimised violence in both public and private spheres as members of the white minority group exercised various forms of violence against the black[10] majority.[11]

While Roman Dutch law, the common law of South Africa, was discriminatory towards women, Andrews considers that African women living under customary law were more vulnerable.[12] This is because customary law treated women as minors who did not have rights. Furthermore, customary law was based on the collective interest of the community, and consequently, women were reluctant to challenge the system.[13] This bias prevails in South Africa today, as will be discussed in Chapter 3. Through a review of case law, Banda shows that 'a few' women 'challenge patriarchal laws and attitudes' because the social

[9] Mary K Anglin, 'Feminist perspectives on structural violence' (1998) 5 *Identities: Global Studies in Culture and Power*, 2, 146.

[10] The terms 'black', 'white' and 'coloured' are commonly used in South Africa (in official documents and by the population at large) to describe racial groups. See IV. Methodology and Data.

[11] Helen Moffett, 'These women, they force us to rape them: rape as narrative of social control in post-apartheid South Africa' (2006) 32 *Journal of Southern African Studies*, 1, 129.

[12] Penelope Andrews, 'Violence against women in South Africa: the role of culture and the limitations of law' (1998–1999) 8 *Temple Political & Civil Rights Law Review*, 430.

[13] Southern African Research and Documentation Centre, *Beyond Inequalities: Women in South Africa* (Southern African Research and Documentation Centre, 1997).

cost is often high, especially for women who depend on familial financial support.[14] Moreover, African women have had to endure racism and sexism, in addition to poverty and poor living conditions, which has made them more vulnerable than women from other racial groups. Living conditions during apartheid perpetuated GBV, particularly against black women. Black people were required to live in townships that were crowded, 'lawless, isolated, and impoverished'.[15] Therefore, women had neither privacy nor protection.[16]

Women rarely reported violence to the apartheid police. On the one hand, the police did not attend to VAW victims because their mandate was to control the political opposition;[17] to 'protect whites from blacks, not to protect black communities from crime'.[18] On the other hand, the community did not encourage the reporting of VAW. In fact, reporting rape was considered a betrayal, specifically by black women, because the police 'were seen as enemies of the community who often violated the victim further'.[19] Moreover, sexual violence was frequently used as a tool for political control. Black women were particularly targeted and abused by members of the police and military as they were obliged to carry passes, unlike women of other races.[20] In addition, female political prisoners were constantly threatened with rape and sexual abuse.[21] Unsurprisingly, the apartheid government did not respond to the high rates of GBV. Wojcicki also notes that the low conviction rates and lenient sentences for rapists were tolerated,[22] in part due to the narrow

[14] Fareda Banda, 'Women, law and human rights in Southern Africa' (2006) 32 *Journal of Southern African Studies* 13, 20.

[15] Helen Wells and Louise Polders, 'Anti-gay hate crimes in South Africa: prevalence, reporting practices, and experiences of the police' (2006) 2 *Agenda*, 3, 25.

[16] Lorenzo Di Silvo, 'Correcting corrective rape: Carmichele and developing South Africa's affirmative obligations to prevent violence against women' (2011) 99 *Georgetown Law Journal*, 5, 1476.

[17] Michelle J. Anderson, 'Rape in South Africa' (1999–2000) 1 *Georgetown Journal of Gender and the Law* 789, 791–792. Also see Jacklyn Cock, *Women and War in South Africa* (London: Open Letters, 1992) p. 18.

[18] Wells and Polders, 'Anti-gay hate crimes' 25; Penal Reform International, *Access to Justice in Sub-Saharan Africa: The Role of Traditional and Informal Justice Systems* (UK: Penal Reform International, 2000), p. 45.

[19] Matlhogonolo Maboe, 'Strategies to tackle rape and violence against women in South Africa' in Center for Women's Global Leadership ed., *Gender Violence and Women's Human Rights in Africa* (New Brunswick, NJ: Douglass College, Center for Women's Global Leadership, 1994), p. 31.

[20] Wells and Polders, 'Anti-gay hate crimes', 24. Also see Cock, *Women and War*, pp. 1–26.

[21] Wells and Polders, 'Anti-gay hate crimes', 24.

[22] Janet Maia Wojcicki, 'She drank his money: survival sex and the problem of violence in taverns in Gauteng Province, South Africa' (2002) 16 *Medical Anthropology Quarterly*, 3, 271.

definition of rape.[23] Under common law, rape was limited to an act of intentional sexual intercourse committed by a man against a woman without her consent.[24]

By 1990, negotiations between political leaders started on the transitional process. It was decided that all policemen and women would resume their roles in the new South African Police Service (SAPS).[25] The transformation of the role of the police from 'protectors of apartheid' to 'protectors of the community' was challenging[26] because of the resentment that the community felt towards members of the police. The government, therefore, introduced the Police Act in 1995,[27] which established Community Police Forums. These forums were supposed to provide space for communication between the police and the community, in an attempt to resolve their differences.[28] However, conflict arose between the two parties, particularly due to disagreements over priority issues. Schärf elaborated, 'when some communities in poor residential areas expressed the view that rape constituted the crime that worried them most, the police were floored, seeing that rape, and any form of sexual or domestic assault was considered entirely peripheral to the interests of the police'.[29] This disagreement increased the gap between local communities and the police.

In South African history, women's issues were never prioritised. During the transition to democracy, the hardships faced by women, including GBV, were redefined in terms of race. For example, the issue of rape was 'subsumed in narratives about race or class, not gender'.[30] Moffett refers to cases where anti-rape activists were accused of racism, not only by nationalists but also by society.[31] Gender issues therefore presented a threat to the national project in South Africa.

[23] Ibid.

[24] South African Law Commission, Sexual Offences: The Substantive Law (Discussion Paper 85, 1999).

[25] Wilfried Schärf, 'Community justice and community policing in post-apartheid South Africa' (2001) 32 *IDS Bulletin*, 1, 74.

[26] Human Rights Watch, *Violence Against Women in South Africa: State Response to Domestic Violence and Rape*, research report (Human Rights Watch, 1995).

[27] Police Act 68 of 1995 (South Africa).

[28] Ibid., s. 18.

[29] Schärf, 'Community justice', 76.

[30] Moffett, 'These women', 135.

[31] Ibid., 133–135.

B Gender-based Violence in Contemporary South Africa

In contemporary South Africa, gender issues have received a fair amount of attention; however, violence prevails. While women in South Africa experience many forms of violence, rates of rape and domestic violence are particularly alarming. One study conducted in 2004 by the Medical Research Council in South Africa found that every six hours, a woman is murdered by her intimate partner.[32] Reported rapes have increased annually since 1994, when official records showed that the 44,751 rapes reported in 1994–1995 grew to 71,500 in 2008–2009.[33] This was estimated to be 1–15 per cent of the actual number.[34] In a survey conducted with 2600 South African men in 2016, 56 per cent admitted that they had either beaten or raped a woman in the previous 12 months.[35] Another study showed that the services available to victims of sexual assault in South Africa are inadequate, criticising the poor quality of medical services, lack of privacy during examination, long waiting times and incompetent healthcare providers who treat victims of sexual assault.[36] Research also revealed that GBV can be reinforced by social myths, which is an additional challenge to the movement against GBV. For example, the myth that raping a virgin cures HIV[37] and the myth that raping a lesbian 'corrects' her sexual orientation perpetuate violence against women and girls. Social attitudes reflecting pervasive sexism exacerbate increases women's vulnerability to violence; in 2007, a prohibition against wearing trousers was imposed on women in Umlazi, a township in Kwazulu-Natal. The news on the ban went nationwide when one woman who defied the ban was stripped of her trousers in public as punishment.[38]

[32] Shanaaz Mathews et al., 'Every six hours a woman is killed by her intimate partner', Policy Brief (Medical Research Centre, 2004).

[33] South African Shadow Report submitted to the CEDAW Committee, 48th Session (17 January–4 February 2011), para. 3.1.3.9.

[34] Ibid., para. 3.1.3.2.

[35] Sonke Gender Justice, 'Wits-Sonke study reveals alarming levels of women's violence against women in Diepsloot', press release, 28 November 2016, accessed 17 July 2018 at http://genderjustice.org.za/news-item/wits-sonke-study-reveals-alarming-levels-mens-violence-women-diepsloot/

[36] Nicola Christofide et al., 'The state of sexual assault services: findings from a situation analysis of services in South Africa', research report (The South African Gender-based Violence and Health Initiative, 2003).

[37] Report to the CEDAW Committee, South Africa (24 March 2010) CEDAW/C/ZAF/2–4 (hereinafter, South Africa CEDAW report 2010), pp. 167–169.

[38] 'Anger at South Africa woman trouser "ban"', BBC News, 26 July 2007, accessed 28 June 2018, at http://news.bbc.co.uk/2/hi/africa/6917332.stm

III FEMINIST MOVEMENTS AND THE LAW

Sidelining women's issues is not limited to South Africa, it is global. Women's rights are considered peripheral at the local, regional and international levels. It is commonly argued that this is because the law, legal institutions and policy-making bodies are comprised of men, and therefore they reflect male priorities.[39] This section will discuss critiques of the gendered nature of law and institutions, reflecting the prevalence of gender-biased norms across borders.

A The Global Nature of Gender-based Violence

Gender-based violence includes sexual violence, physical violence, emotional and psychological violence, harmful traditional practices and socio-economic violence (such as discriminatory access to economic and social services).[40] The consequences of GBV on women include 'depression, sexually transmitted diseases, substance abuse, and sometimes murder'.[41] A plethora of literature has been devoted to investigate the causes, repercussions and eradication of GBV. Charlesworth and Chinkin demonstrate the indiscriminate nature of GBV, which affects women globally. They write:

> Battery is the major cause of injury to adult women in the United States, where a rape occurs every six minutes. In Peru, 70 percent of all crimes reported to police involve women as victims. In India, 80 percent of wives are victims of violence, domestic abuse, dowry abuse or murder. In 1985, in Austria, domestic violence against the wife was given as a factor in the breakdown of marriage in 59 percent of 1,500 divorce cases. In Australia, a recent survey indicated that one in five men believed it acceptable for men to beat their wives; while surveys by the Papua New Guinea Law Reform Commission found that up to 67 percent of wives had suffered marital violence.[42]

In 2013, research conducted by the World Health Organization (WHO) showed that 35.6 percent of women globally have experienced one or

[39] See Doris Buss and Ambreena Manji (eds.), *International Law: Modern Feminist Approaches* (Oxford: Hart, 2005).

[40] For more information and statistics see K Gibbons and T Johnson, *Integrated Approaches to Eliminate Gender Based Violence* (London: Commonwealth Secretariat, 2003).

[41] Jennifer Ulrich, 'Confronting gender-based violence with international instruments: is a solution to the pandemic within reach?' (2000) 7 *Indiana Journal of Global Legal Studies*, 2, 634.

[42] Hilary Charlesworth and Christine Chinkin, 'The gender of jus cogens' (1993) 15 *Human Rights Quarterly*, 1, 71–72.

more forms of sexual and physical violence.[43] In 2017, UN Women gathered information on the forms of violence experienced by women across the world. This includes high rates of sexual harassment on public transport in the United States of America (USA), early marriage in West and Central Africa, and FGM in numerous countries.[44]

Gender-based violence is reinforced by patriarchal social norms as well as traditional and religious beliefs.[45] Pagelow relates private forms of violence to the gender power dynamic within families. She explains that when men are oppressed in the public sphere, they direct their anger towards women, who are viewed as their subordinates in the private sphere.[46] Bunch also links 'power' to public forms of violence. She argues that VAW is meant to divert females from the public space, and therefore, maintains the gender power dynamic in both public and private relations.[47] She adds that men perceive women's bodies as their property, and therefore, women must reclaim this ownership so as to protect themselves from violence. As an example, she refers to the 'intensity of resistance to laws and social changes that put control of women's bodies in women's hands: reproductive rights, freedom of sexuality whether heterosexual or lesbian, laws that criminalize rape in marriage, etc'.[48] Ertürk, the UN Special Rapporteur on VAW, locates GBV in the socially constructed perceptions of gender that view women as subordinate and inferior to men.[49] She identifies enabling factors, such as poverty, labour exploitation, inequalities and exclusion from the decision-making process.[50] Likewise, Pickup argues that gender discrimination and GBV are interconnected; economic, social and political discrimination stimulate VAW and in return, VAW hinders women's access to resources such as social capital and labour.[51] Therefore,

43 Claudia Garcia-Moreno et al., 'Global and regional estimates of violence against women: prevalence and health effects of intimate partner violence and nonpartner sexual violence', report (World Health Organization, 2013), p. 20.

44 See 'Facts and figures: ending violence against women' UN Women, last updated August 2017, available at www.unwomen.org/en/what-we-do/ending-violence-against-women/facts-and-figures

45 Gibbons and Johnson, *Integrated Approaches*, p. 6.

46 Mildred Daley Pagelow, *Family Violence* (New York, Westport, CT and London: Greenwood Publishing Group, 1984).

47 Charlotte Bunch, 'Women's rights as human rights: toward a re-vision of human rights' (1990) 12 *Human Rights Quarterly*, 4, 491.

48 Ibid., 492.

49 Yakin Ertürk, Report by the Special Rapporteur on the Promotion and Protection of all Human Rights' (27 May 2009) UN Doc A/HRC/11/6/Add.5.

50 Ibid.

51 Francine Pickup et al., *Ending Violence Against Women* (Oxford: Oxfam, 2001), pp. 46 and 68.

research on GBV shows that the 'physicality' and 'everydayness' of violence must be considered 'from the vantage point of complex political economic processes'.[52] Responding to those complexities, Ertürk asserts that GBV must be approached with comprehensive strategies.[53]

International, regional and domestic legal institutions must therefore adopt gender-sensitive approaches, responding to the different inequalities to which women are exposed. This is the main criticism in feminist scholarship addressing the persistence of gender inequalities, which will be discussed in the next section.

B The Global Women's Movement

The international women's movement is a huge global network. The emergence and development of the movement were related to the United Nations, where 'chronologies of the international women's movement are largely a litany of UN meetings: Mexico, Copenhagen, Nairobi, Vienna, Cairo, Beijing'.[54] At the First World Conference on Women that took place in Mexico City in 1975,[55] the UN declared the Decade of Women (1976–1985). Follow-up conferences were held in Copenhagen in 1980,[56] Nairobi in 1985[57] and Beijing in 1995.[58] The meetings legitimised women's issues because they opened up a space for women from all backgrounds to identify common concerns and share information.[59] Moghadam argues that those conferences created a 'transnational feminist identity', and demonstrated that women could make great contributions to national and international policies and institutions.[60]

52 Anglin, 'Feminist perspectives', p. 146.

53 Ertürk, Special Rapporteur report, paras. 107–111.

54 International Council on Human Rights, *When Legal Worlds Overlap: Human Rights, State and Non-State Law* (Switzerland, Versoix: International Council on Human Rights, 2009), p. 168.

55 United Nations, 'Report of the World Conference of the International Women's Year' (Mexico, 19 June–2 July 1975) UN Doc A/CONF.66/34.

56 United Nations, Report of the World Conference of the United Nations Decade for Women: Equality, Development and Peace, (Copenhagen 14–30 July 1980) UN Doc A/CONF.94/35.

57 United Nations, World Conference to review and appraise the achievements of the United Nations Decade for Women: Equality, Development and Peace, (Nairobi 15–26 July 1985) UN Doc A/CONF.116/28/Rev.

58 United Nations, Report of the Fourth World Conference on Women, (Beijing 4–15 September 1995) UN Doc A/CONF.177/20/Rev.1.

59 International Council, *When Legal Worlds Overlap*, p. 169.

60 Valentine M. Moghadam, *Globalizing Women: Transnational Feminist Networks* (Baltimore and London: The Johns Hopkins University Press, 2005), p. 91.

However, with diverse political agendas and cultural backgrounds, it was challenging for NGOs to unite globally. Weldon explains that women found it difficult to overcome their differences,[61] with conflict arising particularly between organisations from the South and their counterparts from the North. The 1975 women's conference in Mexico witnessed the emergence of the conflict, in which Western (first world) feminists were accused of imposing their values on feminists from the global south (third world).[62] Nevertheless, there was consensus on an imminent need for a 'North-South sisterhood alliance' that could fight the patriarchal bond of governments across the world.[63] By uniting, women's organisations were able to make remarkable progress. For example, NGOs have since collectively lobbied on women's issues and successfully pressured governments to comply with their duties. As True explains, a united women's front provided 'dual entry points inside and outside institutional power for feminist activism to be successful', both at the global as well as the domestic level.[64] This was facilitated by the development of cyberspace, which was used by women's networks 'to grow, expand and come up with new ways to act and react to governmental policy and social norms'.[65] The movement also unanimously agreed on the urgency of addressing GBV and subsequently lobbied for the cause, which will be discussed in the next section.

The global women's movement organised separate campaigns to raise awareness of different forms of GBV such as rape and domestic violence. In addition, the movement advocated the recognition of 'violence against women' as a human rights violation and emphasised the power aspect embedded in all its forms.[66] Consequently, VAW became the most 'dynamic new international human rights concern'.[67] Those

[61] S Laurel Weldon, *Protest, Policy, and the Problem of Violence Against Women: A Cross-National Comparison* (University of Pittsburgh Press, 2002), pp. 59–60.

[62] Margaret E Keck and Kathryn Sikkink, *Activists Beyond Borders: Advocacy Networks in International Borders* (Ithaca, NY: Cornell University Press, 1998), p. 170.

[63] Sara Hlupekile Longwe, 'Breaking the patriarchal alliance: governments, bi-laterals, and NGOs' (1994) 2 *Gender and Development*, 3, 63.

[64] Jacqui True, 'Gender specialists and global governance' in Sandra Grey and Marian Sawer (eds.), *Women's Movements: Flourishing or in Abeyance* (London: Routledge, 2008), p. 92.

[65] C J Rowe, 'Cyberfeminism inaction' in Sandra Grey and Marian Sawer (eds.), *Women's Movements: Flourishing or in Abeyance* (London: Routledge, 2008), p. 129.

[66] Keck and Sikkink, *Activists Beyond Borders*, p. 172.

[67] International Council, *When Legal Worlds Overlap*, p. 166. Also see Christine Chinkin, 'Violence against women' in Marsha A. Freeman et al. (eds.), *The UN Convention on the Elimination of all Forms of Discrimination against Women: A Commentary* (Oxford: Oxford University Press, 2012), pp. 443–445.

developments at the international level were celebrated, yet international law and institutions remained predominantly 'male'.

C Feminist Critique of Law and Legal Institutions

The first step in eradicating GBV is developing appropriate legislation. However, the law has a limited impact on social problems that affect women. This is because law, legal institutions and policy-making bodies reflect male interests. Mackinnon explains: 'the law sees and treats women the way men see and treat women. The liberal state coercively and authoritatively constitutes the social order in the interest of men as a gender – through its legitimating norms, forms, relation to society and substantive policies. The state's formal norms recapitulate the male point of view on the level of design'.[68] Women therefore exist in the private sphere. The law fails to address the 'deepest, simplest, quietest, and most widespread atrocities of women's everyday lives'.[69] Legislation related to GBV such as sexual assault laws or domestic violence laws are non-existent, non-applicable, or discriminately enforced.[70] As an example, Mackinnon refers to rape law, arguing that the perception of rape reflected in the law does not capture the experiences of raped women. In law, rape is considered sex forced upon a woman by a stranger using a weapon in a public space, where preferably the woman is white and the man is black.[71] In reality, women are more likely to be raped in private, by a known perpetrator, and without the use of weapons.[72] Thus, enforcing progressive legislation is neither an indication of the gender sensitivity of the law, nor a reflection that the law addresses the roots of the violation, which is 'power'. Smart similarly notes that translating violations into legal rights is insufficient to guarantee women's protection because 'rights oversimplify complex power relations', and therefore, acquiring a specific right may imply that the power struggle behind it has been resolved.[73] This means that the recognition of rights and the promulgation of laws will not eliminate GBV as long as institutions retain their biased gender power dynamics.

68 Catharine A Mackinnon, *Toward a Feminist Theory of the State* (Cambridge, MA: Harvard University Press, 1991), p. 159.

69 Catherine Mackinnon, *Women's Lives Men's Laws* (Cambridge, MA: Harvard University Press, 2005), p. 34.

70 Ibid., p. 34.

71 Ibid., p. 35.

72 Mackinnon, *Women's Lives*, p. 35. Also see Susan Brownmiller, *Against Our Will: Men, Women and Rape* (New York: Ballantine Books, 1994), pp. 210–254.

73 Carol Smart, *Feminism and the Power of Law* (Routledge, 1998), p. 144.

Similarly, gender inequalities persist in the representation of international legal and policy-making institutions.[74] For example, Edwards criticises the imbalances of gender representation in the treaty bodies that monitor the implementation of the International Covenant on Civil and Political Rights (ICCPR) and the International Covenant on Economic, Social and Cultural Rights (ICESCR), among others.[75] This is problematic for several reasons: first, it violates women's right to equality in representing their governments at the international level pursuant to the Convention on the Elimination of all Forms of Discrimination against Women (CEDAW), Article 8.[76] Commenting on the Article, Wittkopp asserts that states are responsible for guaranteeing that women have equal opportunities to be 'recruited, selected, and promoted to these positions and they must be assigned to deal with substantive matters including traditionally male-dominated areas'.[77] Second, the absence of women's voices means that decisions taken will not protect their interests; third, gender-biased appointments in international institutions contradict the principle of universality and indicates that geographic representation is more valued than gender equality; fourth, the participation of women in the decision-making process is essential to modifying gender stereotypes.[78] Therefore, referring to Article 8 of the United Nations Charter[79] that calls for equal access of men and women to the UN, Ulrich argues that affirmative action must be taken to respond to the gender bias in international institutions. This is echoed in CEDAW Article 4(1), directing states to use 'temporary special measures aimed at accelerating de facto equality between men and women'.[80]

While the participation of women in international legal and policy-making bodies is crucial, it changes neither the structure nor

[74] See Alice Edwards, 'Violence against women as sex discrimination: judging the jurisprudence of United Nations human rights treaty bodies' (2008) 18 *Texas Journal of Women and the Law*, 1–44.

[75] Alice Edwards, *Violence Against Women under International Human Rights Law* (Cambridge: Cambridge University Press, 2011), p. 89.

[76] Convention on the Elimination of All Forms of Discrimination against Women (1979) 12 UNTS 13 (hereinafter CEDAW), Article 8; CEDAW Committee 'General Recommendation No 23 on Political and Public Life' (1997), UN Doc A/52/38 addressing the duty of the state to promote equal participation between men and women in politics.

[77] Sarah Wittkopp, 'Article 8' in Marsha A Freeman et al. (eds.), *The UN Convention on the Elimination of all Forms of Discrimination against Women: A Commentary* (Oxford: Oxford University Press, 2012), 223.

[78] Edwards, *Violence Against Women*, pp. 102–107.

[79] Charter of the United Nations (26 June 1945) 59 Stat. 103.1.

[80] CEDAW, Article 4(1).

the agendas that sideline women's issues.[81] Kettel adds that 'the structure of the gender machinery is such that much of this work falls into a prevailing vacuum of lack of interest and avoidance'.[82] She refers to the CEDAW and the Beijing Platform for Action adopted after the 4th UN Women's conference to show that governments do not take their commitments towards women's rights seriously.[83] Furthermore, states have been allowed to derogate from fundamental provisions of the CEDAW. For example, many states with predominantly Muslim populations made reservations to provisions related to Sharia law including 'equal treatment in participation and marital relations and the obligation to modify social customs and practices'.[84]

D Women's Rights and Feminism in Africa

While Western feminism has made significant progress in addressing Western women's issues, it has fallen short in tackling the hardships faced by African women. In response, parallel feminist movements have emerged to address women's issues in specific regional and cultural contexts. Feminist movements emerging in Africa suffered from a conflict of ideologies. Adeleye-Fayemi distinguishes between African women who adopt Western feminist principles and African feminists who adopt a 'watered down agenda'.[85] African feminism is 'anti-imperialist, socialist-oriented and keenly aware of the implications of social injustices for society as a whole. It is also anti-racist because it challenges the institutionalised racism of global and regional structures that exploit the continent and undermine its progress'.[86] Not only are there tremendous variations between the agendas of Western and African feminists, there are also differences in experience; African

[81] Hilary Charlesworth, 'Talking to ourselves? Feminist scholarship in international law' in Sari Kouvo and Zoe Pearson (eds.), *Feminist Perspectives on Contemporary International Law* (Oxford: Hart, 2011), p. 30.

[82] Bonnie Kettel, 'Challenging the margin: gender equality and the UN reform process' (2007) 28 *Third World Quarterly*, 5, 872.

[83] Ibid., 879; Andrew Byrnes, 'The Convention on Elimination of all Forms of Discrimination against Women' in Wolfgang Benedek et al. (eds.), *Human Rights of Women: International Instruments and African Experiences* (London: Zed Books, 2002), pp. 133–136.

[84] Danish Institute for Human Rights, *Informal Justice System: Charting a Course for Human Rights Based Engagement* (UN Women, UNICEF and UNDP, 2012), p. 101.

[85] Bisi Adeleye-Fayemi, 'Creating and sustaining feminist space in Africa' in Luciana Ricciutelli et al. (eds.), *Feminist Politics, Activism and Vision: Local and Global Challenges* (London: Inanna Publications, 2004), p. 109.

[86] Ibid.

women must fight against a rigid patriarchal system, while enduring the numerous political and economic challenges on the continent.[87]

Gender-based violence is a central issue to African feminism. Tamale locates the source of GBV in the basic unit of society: the family. She argues that domesticity occupies the lives of African women, 'strictly abiding by the patriarchal order and the "artificial" public/private distinction'.[88] Similarly, Onyango asserts that 'the state is simply the family writ large',[89] where gender-biased power relations that operate at the micro levels extend to the macro level. African women, therefore, experience the same inequalities in the public and private space.

In addition to the theoretical recognition of women's rights, the African human rights system has much to offer, but is yet to deliver on its promise. Appointing a Special Rapporteur on the Rights of Women in Africa in 1999[90] was a positive step. Otherwise, efforts to implement instruments of women's rights on the continent have been negligible. For example, prior to the enactment of the Africa's Women's Protocol[91], the African Charter had provided some level of protection. Beyani suggested that the 'interaction of standards' of CEDAW and the African Charter enhanced the protection measures from the 'oppressive social and traditional practices' that are undertaken against women in Africa.[92] A combined reading established that the 'moral and cultural values must be consistent with human rights standards'.[93] Another promising instrument in the African system is the Protocol on the Prevention and Suppression of Sexual Violence against Women and Children, drafted at the International Conference on the Great Lakes Region. The Protocol captures some of the overlooked dimensions of

[87] Gwendolyn Mikell, *African Feminism: The Politics of Survival in Sub-Saharan Africa* (Pennsylvania: University of Pennsylvania Press, 1997), p. 2.

[88] Sylvia Tamale, 'Alternative leadership in Africa' in Luciana Ricciutelli et al. (eds.), *Feminist Politics, Activism and Vision: Local and Global Challenges* (London: Inanna Publications, 2004), p. 316.

[89] As quoted in ibid.

[90] Decision taken at the African Commission on Human and People's Rights (25th Ordinary Session) res.38 (XXV) 99 (Bujumbura, Burundi 26 April to 5 May 1999).

[91] African Union, Decision on the Protocol to the African Charter on Human and Peoples' Rights Relating to the Rights of Women, Assembly/AU/Dec.14 (II) Article 18 (hereinafter, Africa's Women's Protocol).

[92] Chaloka Beyani, 'Toward a more effective guarantee of women's rights in the African human rights system' in Rebecca J Cook (ed.), *Human Rights of Women: National and International Perspectives* (Pennsylvania: University of Pennsylvania Press 1994), p. 294.

[93] Ibid., pp. 292–293. Beyani cited an example from the Tanzanian High Court judgment on the conflict between customary law and the Bill of Rights regarding the right of women to sell land.

gender and sexual violence, including the emotional repercussions on victims during trial, because of which the Protocol allows victims to give testimonies through camera or video links.[94] Additionally, the Protocol recognises the importance of engaging with perpetrators of violence and enjoins states to establish a fund 'for sensitizing the perpetrators on the wrongfulness of their sexual behaviour'.[95] Furthermore, the Protocol calls on states to create a special fund for the purpose of providing comprehensive assistance to victims of gender and sexual violence.[96]

The protection provided by the African system is arguably rhetorical. The African Charter provides mechanisms for enforcing human rights by bringing cases forward to the African Commission. Even though the Charter guarantees freedom from discrimination on grounds of gender and enjoins the state to eliminate discrimination against women,[97] cases brought before the Commission mainly addressed civil and political rights, which were defined and treated according to male priorities.[98] It was not until 2013 that the African Commission ruled on a case about GBV, holding the state of Egypt responsible for failing to protect female protesters from assault.[99]

The difficulty of enforcing women's rights is reflected in the minimal efforts made for the implementation of those rights in Africa, confirming Banda's assertion that 'normative recognition of women's rights' is not a guarantee of the enjoyment of those rights.[100] Experiencing those inequalities at the domestic, regional and international levels, women have united and initiated movements to fight for their interests at all levels.[101]

[94] Protocol on the Prevention and Suppression of Sexual Violence Against Women and Children, adopted at the International Conference on the Great Lakes Region in Nairobi in December 2006 and entered into force in June 2008 (Great Lakes Protocol) Article 6(5); Fareda Banda, 'Protocol to the African Charter on the Rights of Women in Africa' in Malcolm Evans and Rachel Murray (eds.), *The African Charter on Human and Peoples' Rights: The System in Practice, 1986–2006*, 2nd edition (Cambridge: Cambridge University Press, 2008), p. 458.

[95] Great Lakes Protocol, Article 6(7).

[96] Ibid., Article 6(8). Also see Banda, 'Protocol to the African Charter', p. 458.

[97] African Charter on Human and Peoples' Rights (adopted 27 June 1981, entered into force 21 October 1986), 1520 UNTS, Articles 2 and 18(3).

[98] Karen Stefiszyn, 'The African regional response to gender-based violence' in Centre for Human Rights (ed.), *Gender Based Violence in Africa: Perspectives from the Continent* (Pretoria: University of Pretoria, 2010), p. 25.

[99] *Egyptian Initiative for Personal Rights and Interights* v.*Egypt* (2006) Comm. No. 232/06, African Commission on Human and Peoples' Rights.

[100] Banda, 'Protocol to the African Charter', p. 441.

[101] For a historical narrative on women's collective movements in Africa, with a focus on Sierra Leone, see Filomina Chioma Steady, *Women and Collective Action in Africa* (USA: Palgrave Macmillan, 2005).

E Localising International Rights

International human rights principles provide a foundation for constitutional jurisprudence and legal reform, but they are not influential at the grassroots level until they are localised.[102] This is the core of Merry's book, *Human Rights and Gender-based Violence: Translating International Law into Local Justice*. She holds that at the international level, NGOs adopt issues of concern based on theme or region, which become the basis of networks and pressure groups.[103] Afterwards, achievements at the international level are taken to the local level, to be used by NGOs either for advocacy[104] or for intervention strategies.

Based on her research in Asia and the Pacific regions, Merry finds that localising international human rights principles requires a compromise between local and international values; international law must be translated into domestically accepted principles by the host society. Taking VAW as an example, she suggests a system that includes NGOs, activists and government officials who cooperate to design 'programs and institutions that incorporate indigenous social institutions such as kinship systems, transnational models such as shelters and human rights ideas'.[105] International principles must therefore be 'packaged' in familiar language and accepted terms before they are presented to local communities.[106]

Localising human rights and adopting feminist agendas is usually undertaken by NGOs, whose impact depends on 'the place each organisation occupies within social space and the volume and structure of the economic, social, cultural and symbolic power at its disposal'.[107] This is the core of the work implemented by NGOs in South Africa – localising human rights. While it is a necessary strategy, it is only possible in a socio-political environment that allows for the domestication of international human rights law. As Joachim confirm, the impact of programmes is determined by the political opportunities available for NGOs and the ability of NGOs to maximise their resources.[108]

[102] Sally Engle Merry, *Human Rights and Gender Violence: Translating International Law into Local Justice* (Chicago: University of Chicago Press, 2006), p. 164.
[103] Ibid. p. 51.
[104] Ibid. p. 52.
[105] Ibid. p. 135.
[106] Ibid.
[107] Neve Gordon, 'Human rights, social space and power: why do some NGOs exert more influence than others?' (2008) 12 *The International Journal of Human Rights*, 1, 35.
[108] Jutta Joachim, 'Framing issues and seizing opportunities: the UN, NGOs, and women's rights' (2003) 47 *International Studies Quarterly*, 2, 247.

Others have called for a balance between international rights and local realities. Wendoh and Wallace evaluate NGO programmes in four African countries, arguing that initiatives work better when they are sensitive to community values and beliefs, and when they give the community the time and space to absorb new ideas.[109] Also, Rani rejects a one-size-fits-all model for intervention in domestic violence cases; instead, research on the different perceptions of intimate violence is necessary, on which programmes tackling domestic violence should be based.[110] Recognising the legitimacy of different normative orders, Faedi argues that a compromise must be reached between 'traditional' principles reflected in customary practices and 'modern' principles reflected the human rights doctrine.[111] This was echoed in a research study conducted in South Africa, which found that many women resorted to channels of informal justice to resolve domestic violence cases.[112] Driven by those concerns, Onyango suggests that local activists should resolve issues of an African nature instead of relying on 'international' methods.[113] This includes responding to endemic problems such as FGM. Also recognising the legitimacy of an 'insider', An-Na'im accepts the challenge to 'culture' that is inspired by international principles of human rights as long as it is initiated by a community member who is legitimate to the local population.[114] At the same time, the insider should be 'supported and encouraged by external allies'.[115]

Although fundamentally important, the work of NGOs is widely criticised. Onyango lists some common concerns, particularly

[109] Senorina Wendoh and Tina Wallace, 'Re-thinking gender mainstreaming in African NGOs and communities' (2005) 13 *Gender and Development*, 2, 70.

[110] Manju Rani, Sekhar Bonu and Nafissatou Diop-Sidibe, 'An empirical investigation of attitudes towards wife-beating among men and women in seven Sub-Saharan African Countries' (2004) 8 *African Journal of Reproductive Health*, 3, 116.

[111] Benedetta Faedi, 'Domestic violence as a human rights violation: the challenges of a regional human rights approach in Africa' in Emily Burrill et al. (eds.), *Domestic Violence and the Law in Colonial and Postcolonial Africa* (Ohio: Ohio University Press, 2010) p. 256.

[112] Rachel Jewkes et al, *'He Must Give Me Money, He Mustn't Beat me': Violence Against Women in Three South African Provinces* (Pretoria: Medical Research Council, 1999), p. 22.

[113] J. Oloka-Onyango, 'Modern-day missionaries or misguided miscreant? NGOs, the women's movement and the promotion of human rights in Africa' in Wolfgang Benedek et al. (eds.), *Human Rights of Women: International Instruments and African Experiences* (London: Zed Books, 2002), p. 289.

[114] Abdullahi An-Na'im, 'State responsibility under international human rights law to change religious and customary law' in Rebecca Cook (ed.), *Human Rights of Women: National and International Perspectives* (Pennsylvania: University of Pennsylvania Press, 1994).

[115] Ibid.

about NGOs in Africa, including the lack of collaboration between organisations even within the same country and vagueness of goals and agendas.[116] He also condemns the dichotomy between traditional human rights organisations, where men occupy leadership positions, and women's rights organisations, led by females.[117] This polarity leads to the 'ghettoization' of women's organisations because they refuse to engage in mainstream human rights issues such as freedom of association and speech, unless it directly affects their causes.[118]

This book builds on the ideas discussed in this section. Merry's book focuses on the 'interface between global and local activism, showing how ideas about violence against women as human rights violations are produced in global conferences in New York and Geneva and appropriated in local community centres in Hawai'i, Delhi, Beijing, Fiji and Hong Kong'.[119] This research will thoroughly analyse the work of NGOs at the local level in South Africa, shedding light on the local environments conducive to the translation of human rights. In contrast, women's rights organisations in Egypt struggle to implement international human rights principles because of numerous disabling factors in Egyptian law and society.

The following section will review the methodological basis of this research and present the fieldwork data that will be used consistently throughout the book.

IV METHODOLOGY AND DATA

The work of NGOs in both the social and legal realm is best understood through a qualitative socio-legal analysis. While case law and secondary sources provide great insights, it was necessary to get first-hand accounts from people working in NGOs, or using their services. These encounters provide intricate details and personal insights, which are hard to capture in secondary sources. Therefore, some ethnographic research was undertaken in Johannesburg and Pietermaritzburg in South Africa. In addition, two phone interviews were conducted with Cape Town-based organisations; for the comparative component with

[116] Onyango, 'Modern-day missionaries', p. 290.
[117] Ibid., p. 291.
[118] Ibid., p. 293.
[119] Merry, *Human Rights and Gender Violence*, p. 3.

Egypt, four in-person interviews were held with NGO staff members in Cairo.

This section will discuss important elements of the methodology and introduce the sample.

A Setting the Research Framework

Patton warns: 'always be suspicious of data collection that goes according to plan'.[120] This project diverted from the initial vision. Originally, the research aim was to look at women's preference for informal justice over the adversarial system. Preliminary research, however, did not fully support this hypothesis, but rather pointed to a key player in the field of women's rights in South Africa: NGOs. Victims of violence almost always use the services of NGOs when they engage with the legal system. These services address all aspects of the legal journey, such as law-making, legal representation, impact litigation and counselling. Nongovernmental organisations, therefore, became the centre of the amended research project, leading to a doctoral degree in 2014; the study focused on the relationship between NGOs and women in their legal journey.

A few years later, a new issue came to light when the author moved back to Egypt, started comparing the state of the women's rights movement in both countries, and evaluating the progress they had made on the legal and social fronts. Despite the social and historical differences between Egypt and South Africa, the determining factor that stood out was the socio-legal and political space open to the women's movement. Women in both countries have some common challenges and some differences; however, ultimately it was evident that when states open up the space for women's rights development and believe in the role of NGOs to advance these rights, NGOs are able to grow and create significant impact. However, when women's issues are marginalised and NGOs are regarded as a national threat, the women's movement will eventually die. Not only will NGOs struggle to survive, but sexism will continue to spread exponentially in law and society. Emphasising this open socio-legal and political space, and exploring its repercussions on state–NGO–women's relations, therefore, became the new project for this book, in which a chapter is dedicated to Egypt for comparative purposes.

[120] Michael Quinn Patton, *Qualitative Research and Evaluation Methods* (USA: Sage Publications, 2002) 207.

B Conducting Research on a Sensitive Issue in a Foreign Country

Prior to field research, the author spent some time living and working in South Africa, which allowed for some familiarisation with the nature of interactions within group members and between different groups, particularly related to racial perceptions and categorisations, reflecting the legacy of apartheid. Not only is it accepted, but also expected to see and identify others in terms of their race. Racial identification such as 'Indian', 'Black', 'White', 'Hindu' and 'Coloured' are used on a mundane, regular and daily basis.[121]

In the multicultural society of South Africa, many researchers are considered outsiders, either based on their ethnicity, race, economic background or language. Therefore, respondents in this project were used to interacting with people from different backgrounds, which facilitated access to the field. In addition, the author's detachment from local politics may have encouraged women to share sensitive information.[122] In this way, the position of the researcher as an outsider was of benefit. On the other hand, for interviews conducted in Egypt, the author was considered an insider, not only as a native, but also as a women's rights supporter. Considering the sensitive security situation in Egypt that creates significant barriers for outsiders, the position of the researcher as an insider in the field was an advantage.

C Research Sample

The research sample for South Africa was 14 NGOs and four domestic violence shelters, as well as 13 women who were litigating at the time of the interview. For Egypt, three women and one man were interviewed, all of whom work in the socio-legal field relating to violence against women.

For this research, the questions touched on NGOs' work with the state on VAW, and with beneficiaries; therefore, the only criterion for

[121] See Ray Suarez, 'Reporter's notebook: South African society shaped by racial identity, apartheid', PBS Newshour, 20 February 2009, accessed 20 July 2018 at www.pbs.org/newshour/health/health-jan-june09-sa4_0220; Eusebius McKaiser, 'Not white enough, not black enough', The New York Times, 15 February 2012, accessed 20 July 2018 at https://latitude.blogs.nytimes.com/2012/02/15/in-south-africa-after-apartheid-colored-community-is-the-big-loser/?_r=0; Dawn Nell, 'The rainbow nation and its strange racial terminology', MacMillan Dictionary Blog, 28 June 2010, accessed 20 July 2018 at www.macmillandictionaryblog.com/bastaard

[122] See Dudu Jankie, 'Tell me who you are: problematizing the construction and positionalities of "insider"/"outsider" of a "native" ethnographer in a postcolonial context' in Kagendo Mutua and Beth Blue Swadener (eds.), *Decolonizing Research in Cross-Cultural Context: Critical Personal Narratives* (New York: State University of New York Press, 2004), p. 100.

NGOs to be included in this study was working fully or partly in the socio-legal field of VAW. Shelters were either run by NGOs or registered as NGOs, and therefore they were included in the sample to capture the relationship developed between NGOs and women. However, shelter staff also develop some relationships with state actors, which will be covered in the book. The only criterion for female participants was either being a 'user of the law' or having tried to engage with the law in the past in relation to VAW issues. Even though the author sought participants from urban and rural areas, from all racial groups and ages, and from different social classes, it was impossible to have a representative sample. This is because of the complexity of South African social construction, the limited number of respondents and the access channels to the respondents which was mainly through NGOs and shelters. The majority of participants were African and Coloured women. Also, with some exceptions, most women belonged to a lower socio-economic class.

Geographically, Johannesburg and Kwazulu-Natal hosted most of the interviewed NGOs, and they were chosen to broaden the social context of research. This approach revealed the variations in the experiences and challenges between the urban-based and rural-based organisations. For Egypt's interviews, the sample focused strictly on organisations that work on women's rights, especially violence against women. NGOs who are not independent and work under the umbrella of the state were excluded.

Nongovernmental organisations interviewed were of different sizes, geographic locations, mandates and activities. For example, some NGOs worked on the grassroots level having daily interaction with local residents and were deeply involved in their personal affairs, while others operated on a national level, working in a formal environment. In addition, the range of activities undertaken by NGOs varied from single-service NGOs to NGOs with a wider array of service provision. Some NGOs were visited only once and others were visited multiple times for follow-up as well as additional interviews.

D Interviews

Interviews were mostly semi-structured, and they started with fixed questions; NGO and shelter employees were asked about their organisations' structures and programmes. This was followed by a question on the channels through which they were reached by beneficiaries. At that point, questions flowed in different directions. However, all NGO employees were asked about their relationship with state actors and institutions, including the police, courts, prosecutors, several government departments (such as the Department of Social Development), among others. All employees were also asked about partnering with other organisations and their policy on reporting violence.

Interviews with GBV victims took another direction, starting with a recounting of the violence they had encountered, followed by the channel through which they had reached the NGO. The following questions were personalised to their stories, but generally investigated women's experiences with and perceptions of the legal system and services, women's relationships with NGO employees, women's knowledge about their rights and the status of their cases, and the women's desires and future plans.

Interviews in Egypt focused on the current socio-legal climate, relationships with the state, perceptions of the shrinking social and political space, and the impact of these political developments on the advancement of women's rights. Participants were also asked about the development of NGO–state dynamics in previous years.

V INTRODUCING ETHNOGRAPHIC DATA

At the request of most NGO staff and all women interviewed names have been changed. Therefore, codes are used for NGOs and aliases are used for individual respondents (both staff members and GBV victims). Names of NGOs will only be mentioned when referenced in a publication.

A NGOs

Nongovernmental organisations are usually the 'first stop' for victims of GBV; they assess the needs of beneficiaries and either provide the required services if available, or refer women to other NGOs. This makes it easier for women seeking services as they only need to reach one NGO and are then advised accordingly. Most NGOs provide free services. NGO6 is the only one interviewed that charges women 'whatever they can pay', but includes the possibility of a free service.

Starting at the micro level, NGOs provide immediate services to distressed women, such as counselling, medical assistance and legal advice. In addition, long-term needs such as shelters, long-term counselling and legal assistance are considered. Both individual counselling and couple's counselling are common services. Some NGOs have law clinics that sponsor cases either for direct clients or referrals from other NGOs. Some NGOs provide a number of services attempting a holistic approach. For example, counselling, legal advice and a shelter for abused women are all provided by one of the NGOs in the study. Other NGOs provide more specific services. There is a one-stop-centre in Johannesburg; IkhayaLethemba, providing comprehensive services to victims of GBV, women and children. Some NGOs have offices there. Table A.1 in the Appendix gives details of the NGOs interviewed, specifically regarding their activities.

B Shelters

This study includes four GBV shelters, as detailed in Table A.2 of the Appendix. Resident women and staff members, including managers, housemothers and social workers were interviewed.

C Women's Stories

The stories of thirteen women interviewed for the research are referred to in this book. They are summarised in Table A.3 of the Appendix.

D NGOs in Egypt

By way of comparison, representatives from four NGOs in Egypt were interviewed for this research. Details are set out in Table A.4 of the Appendix.

E Terms and Concepts

The following terms and concepts were recurrently mentioned during the interviews:

- Protection order (PO): serves as a restraining order against a family member.
- Lobola: dowry paid by the family of the groom to the family of the bride.
- Ukuthwala:[123] the practice, most common among the Xhosa-speaking tribes, of abducting young girls to force them into marriage.[124]

[123] See Mill Lake, *Strong NGOs and Weak States: Pursuing Gender Justice in the Democratic Republic of Congo and South Africa* (Cambridge: Cambridge University Press, 2018), 175.

[124] Ericka Curran and Elsje Bonthuys, 'Customary law and domestic violence in South African communities' (2005) 21 *South African Journal on Human Rights*, 4, 615.

Sometimes families who prefer to save on wedding expenses tolerate it. Ukuthwala is now abused by older men who kidnap young girls, rape them and enslave them. The practice is sometimes used by teenagers to force their families to accept their marriage. They make up a story of kidnap and rape, prompting their families to accept the marriage so as to save the girl's honour.

VI CONCLUSION

This introductory chapter has discussed a feminist critique of the law, and set the context of this research including the local, regional and global nature of GBV. The chapter has also traced GBV to the contemporary history of South Africa, where racial favouritism in law and society has affected women's experiences of violence. The work of NGOs at the international level is echoed by domestic NGOs that localise international principles. The methodology was explained, and the research participants were introduced.

Violence against women has been covered extensively in the literature. Significant resources have been dedicated towards understanding the causes and remedies of violence. However, VAW prevails. It is therefore essential to identify the social context in which violence flourishes; this includes locating stakeholders and understanding their work, investigating people's experiences with the law, detecting the gap between progressive laws and social realities, and identifying the socio-legal context most favourable for women's human rights to be respected, protected, ensured and fulfilled.

CHAPTER 2

SOUTH AFRICA: FORMAL LAW AND THE CONSTITUTION

South Africa is often referred to as the youngest democracy, and its Constitution is one of the most progressive globally. The Constitution is a product of multiple interest groups coming together to negotiate equality and freedom after a painful history. The basis on which South African legislation is formed is therefore equality and freedom from discrimination pursuant to the international human rights framework.

This chapter will start by discussing the birth of democracy, highlighting the most important provisions of the Constitution and legislation for women's rights. The chapter will proceed with an analysis of South Africa's obligations to protect women from GBV under international human rights law, and the engagement of NGOs in monitoring the progress. Section IV will present some mechanisms set up by the state for gender-specialised services, such as the sexual offences courts and the Commission on Gender Equality (CGE). Finally, recognising the role of NGOs in South Africa, it is essential to review the legislation that governs NGO operations – the final section of this chapter.

I SOUTH AFRICA'S FORMAL LAW

The birth of democratic South Africa was highlighted by Nelson Mandela's release from prison in 1990. This was followed by negotiations between political parties that lasted for about four years and ended with the transition of power from the Democratic Alliance (the political party that maintained apartheid) to the African National Congress (ANC), headed by Nelson Mandela. An interim Constitution was drafted in 1993 and the first election to include all races was held in 1994, putting Nelson Mandela in the president's office. The interim Constitution was a groundbreaking document, reflecting progressive principles of human rights including equality,[1] freedom[2] and justice.[3] It also recognised customary law. The interim Constitution subjected both common law and customary law to the rights and freedoms enshrined in the Bill of Rights.[4]

A Constitution

The South African Constitution was approved by Parliament in 1996[5] to become one of the most progressive Constitutions globally.[6] The Bill of Rights includes a broad range of rights and freedoms that are not enshrined in most other Constitutions, such as social and economic rights as well as the freedom from discrimination on all grounds including sexual orientation.

The Constitution contains general provisions to protect women from all forms of inequalities, including freedom from violence. Section 9 states that 'equality includes the full and equal enjoyment of all rights and freedoms'. To promote the achievement of equality, 'legislative and other measures designed to protect or advance persons, or categories of persons, disadvantaged by unfair discrimination may be taken'.[7] This provision also includes the 'preeminent principle of equality',[8] which prohibits the state from discriminating against any person on one or more grounds, including race, sex, gender, religion or marital status.[9] Section 12 guarantees the 'freedom and security of the person'[10] addressing the right 'to be free from all forms of violence from either public or private sources'.[11] This is a progressive provision as it invokes

[1] Interim Constitution of the Republic of South Africa, Act 200 of 1993 (hereinafter, Interim Constitution) s. 8.

[2] Ibid., ss. 11–19.

[3] Ibid., ss. 22, 24 and 25.

[4] Ibid., s. 33(2) and (3).

[5] Constitution of the Republic of South Africa, Act No 108 of 1996 (hereinafter, Constitution).

[6] See Heinz Klug, *The Constitution of South Africa: A Contextual Analysis* (UK: Hart Publishing, 2010).

[7] Constitution, s. 9(2).

[8] Penelope E Andrews, 'From gender apartheid to non-sexism: the pursuit of women's rights in South Africa' (2001) 26 *North Carolina Journal of International Law and Commercial Regulation*, 699.

[9] Constitution, s. 9(3).

[10] Constitution, s. 12.

[11] Constitution, s. 12(c).

the positive state responsibility of due diligence which has been used frequently in litigation, as will be demonstrated in Chapter 5. The Constitution confirms South Africa's commitment to gender equality 'as reflected by the government's ratification 741of the … CEDAW'.[12] Section 10 protects human dignity and section 11 protects the right to life. Section 12 protects against torture as well as degrading and inhumane treatment,[13] which are both associated with GBV. Finally, section 26 and section 27 guarantee the right to housing[14] and the right to health[15] respectively; both are essential for women's freedom from violence. Therefore, the Constitution embodies provisions that protect women from GBV, which are either stated directly or inferred.

Scanning international human rights law, it is evident that the South African Constitution and legislation meet the international standards for the protection of women from violence, if not exceeding them.[16] This can be seen in the provisions of the Equality Act,[17] which echo the principles advocated by CEDAW. Article 4 of CEDAW directs states to adopt 'temporary special measures aimed at accelerating de facto equality between men and women'.[18] Similarly, CEDAW General Recommendation 25 calls for the construction of policies that cater for the 'biological as well as socially and culturally constructed differences' that deprive women of an equal start with men, as guaranteeing equal treatment is insufficient when there is historical structural discrimination.[19] In addition, the inclusion of gender as well as 'sex' in the non-discrimination provision in the Constitution is an acknowledgement of the importance of a transformational approach to gender equality.[20] One of the strongest impediments to women's rights in South Africa is pervasive sexism in culture. CEDAW directs states to 'modify the social and cultural patterns of conduct … with a view to achieving the elimination of prejudices and customary and all other practices which are based

[12] Andrews, 'From gender apartheid', 701.

[13] Constitution, s. 12(1)(d) and (e).

[14] Constitution, s. 26(1).

[15] Constitution, s. 27(1)(a).

[16] CEDAW.

[17] Promotion of Equality and Prevention of Unfair Discrimination Act 4 of 2000 (hereinafter, Equality Act).

[18] CEDAW, Article 23.

[19] CEDAW Committee, General Recommendation No 25 on Article 4 paragraph 1 on temporary special measures, (2004), UN Doc A/59/38, para. 8.

[20] Constitution, s. 9(3); Rikki Holtmaat, 'Article 5' in Marsha A Freeman et al. (eds.), *The UN Convention on the Elimination of all Forms of Discrimination against Women: A Commentary* (Oxford: Oxford University Press, 2012), pp. 141–167.

on the idea of ... stereotyped roles of men and women'.[21] Although the South African Constitution guarantees the right to culture, this right is limited to a manner consistent with the Bill of Rights,[22] thereby guaranteeing that culture cannot be used as an excuse for gender discrimination and inequalities.

B Relevant Legislation in South Africa

Not only are the rights enshrined in the Constitution progressive, but South Africa has also excelled in drafting legislation that protects women from violence in both the public and the private spheres. This has been a matter of progress over the years, and the interpretation and implementation of these laws is continuously revised.

1 Domestic Violence Law

In the early 1990s, with the optimism triggered by the imminent demise of apartheid, domestic violence was recognised as a serious violation.[23] In 1993, the Prevention of Family Violence Act[24] came into force after many years of pressure from NGOs that worked with abused women.[25] The Act provided protection for women and children from violence or the threat of violence and guaranteed some rights, including the right to live in the family home.[26] The Act also authorised judges and magistrates to issue arrest warrants for abusers.[27]

Prevention of Family Violence Act

The Prevention of Family Violence Act was invoked by the Constitutional Court in *S v. Baloyi*,[28] in which the appellant repeatedly assaulted his partner and their daughter. The wife laid a charge of assault against the appellant and obtained an interdict using section 2(1) of the Act. Afterwards, the police arrested the husband for violating the interdict and the magistrate court convicted him. The

[21] CEDAW, Article 5(a).

[22] Constitution, s. 30.

[23] Felicity Kaganas and Christina Murray, 'Law and women's rights in South Africa: an overview' (1994) 1 *Acta Juridica*, 1–38.

[24] Prevention of Family Violence Act, No 133 of 1993 (South Africa), s. 2(1)(a).

[25] Sheila Meintjes, 'The politics of engagement: women transforming the police process – domestic violence legislation in South Africa' in Anne Marie Goetz and Shireen Hassim (eds.), *No Shortcuts to Power: African Women in Politics and Policy Making* (London and New York: Zed Books, 2003) p. 144.

[26] Prevention of Family Violence Act, s. 2(1)(c).

[27] Ibid., s. 2(2)(a).

[28] S v. *Baloyi* [2000] (1) BCLR 86 (CC).

husband appealed to the High Court, which declared section 3(5) of the Act to be unconstitutional – it violates the applicant's constitutional right under section 35(3)(h), which entitles him to be presumed innocent until proven guilty beyond reasonable doubt. The High Court referred the case to the Constitutional Court, which had to answer the following question: does sentencing the appellant for breaking a civil order suggest a reverse onus? It held that it did not. The court recognised that intimate violence has a 'hidden' and 'repetitive character' and that it is a distinctive crime because of its 'immeasurable ripple effects on our society and, in particular, on family life'.[29] This was a remarkable recognition by the court of the impact of domestic violence that reaches beyond one victim and affects society. The court also recognised the universality of domestic violence, noting that it remains an endemic problem because it continues to go unpunished. Finally, the court did not find a violation of the constitutional rights of the appellant, basing the judgment on the constitutional principle of equality as well as South Africa's international obligations under international law.[30]

Domestic Violence Act

Although the Prevention of Family Violence Act was a breakthrough in GBV legislation, it was a weak instrument and provided limited protection for women and children. This is because it was hastily passed by the apartheid regime as a last attempt at legal reform to save face.[31] Criticism of the Act included the incomplete definition of violence, the failure of the Act to recognise domestic violence as emerging from the unequal gender power dynamic, and the negligence of fundamental issues such as custody, maintenance and economic dependence.[32] Therefore, one year after the enforcement of the Prevention of Family Violence Act, NGOs and 'legal experts in the area of battery and violence against women' started to pressure the government for reform.[33] In 1998 the Prevention of Family Violence Act was replaced by the

[29] Ibid., para. 11.

[30] Ibid., paras. 25 and 33. This was done through a joint reading of the Prevention of Family Violence Act, the Constitution and the Criminal Procedure Act No 51 of 1977 (South Africa) (hereinafter CPA), s. 170.

[31] Shereen Usdin et al., 'The value of advocacy in promoting social change: implementing the new Domestic Violence Act in South Africa' (2000) 8 *Reproductive Health Matters*, 16, 56.

[32] Meintjes, 'The politics of engagement', p. 150. Also see Joanne Fedler, 'Lawyering domestic violence through the Prevention of Family Violence Act 1993 – evaluation after a year in operation' (1995) 112 *South African Law Journal*, 231.

[33] Meintjes, 'The politics of engagement', p. 151.

Domestic Violence Act (DVA),[34] which showed major improvements for the protection of women and children, reflecting the rights in the Constitution to equality and to freedom and security of person. State responsibilities enshrined in the Act exceed the government's obligations under CEDAW and the UN Convention on the Rights of the Child (CRC).[35] The DVA defines violence as 'physical abuse; sexual abuse; emotional, verbal and psychological abuse; economic abuse; intimidation; harassment; stalking; damage to property; entry in the complainant's residence without consent'; and 'any other controlling or abusive behaviour towards a complainant, where such conduct harms, or may cause imminent harm to, the safety, health or wellbeing of the complainant'.[36] Notably, the DVA captures the subtle nature of intimate violence that inflicts grave physical, emotional and psychological hardships on women. Most evident is economic violence, which is still either absent or not fully recognised in other international human rights instruments.

The duties of the police towards domestic violence complainants are clearly outlined in the DVA. Upon witnessing or being made aware of an act of domestic violence, a member of the police should: report the incident, inform the complainant of their legal rights, assist the complainant to find safe residence and direct them to get medical treatment.[37] A Peace Officer can arrest a suspected offender, if there is reasonable belief that a domestic violence offence has been committed.[38] The complainant has the right to request a PO from the court and to receive legal advice.[39] The complainant can also file an assault claim against the perpetrator,[40] with the option to 'lodge a criminal complaint' if a criminal offence was committed.[41] This can include: 'common assault, assault with the intention of doing grievous bodily harm, indecent assault, rape, incest, attempted murder, malicious damage to property, pointing a firearm'.[42] The court must then

[34] Domestic Violence Act No 116 of 1998 (South Africa) (hereinafter DVA).

[35] DVA Preamble. Also see Convention on the Rights of the Child (1989) UN Doc A/44/49 (CRC).

[36] DVA, s. (v)iii.

[37] Ibid., s 2(a).

[38] DVA, s. 3.

[39] Ibid., s 4(1).

[40] Ibid., s. 4(2).

[41] DVA, s. 4(2)(b).

[42] Lillian Artz, 'Policing the Domestic Violence Act: teething troubles or system failure' (2001) 47 *Agenda* 47, 5.

consider if there is enough evidence to prove the use of violence or the risk of violence that will cause 'undue hardship' so as to issue an interim PO.[43] The PO must be served on the respondent.[44] If the respondent does not challenge the interim PO, the court must issue a permanent PO,[45] prohibiting the respondent or any contracted party from approaching the complainant; committing any act of violence against the complainant, and from entering the complainant's residence or workplace.[46] A PO is issued with a suspended arrest warrant conditional on the respondent's compliance.[47] Both the PO and the arrest warrant must be sent by the court to the police station of the applicant's choice to be delivered to the accused.[48] If arrested, the respondent faces criminal charges.

The Domestic Violence Act provides a solid legal foundation for the protection of women from intimate violence, as it asks the 'woman's question'.[49] The principles embedded in the Act capture the connection between the gender power dynamic and women's vulnerability to domestic violence. For example, due to structural inequalities, women have limited access to resources and therefore become financially dependent on men. The inclusion of 'economic harm' in the definition of violence responds to such systematic inequality. Moreover, recognising that women face a great risk of violence after reporting, the Act directs the police to find safe accommodation for abused women. However, evaluating the impact of GBV legislation is profoundly challenging. For example, an increase in reporting violence can indicate an increase in the rate of GBV, but it could also reflect an increase in the reporting rate. Nevertheless, there is some indication that the DVA responds to the needs of South African women. For example, shortly after the DVA was enforced, the number of interdicts requested by women radically increased due to the expanded definition of domestic violence.[50]

[43] DVA, s. 5(2)(a).

[44] Ibid., s. 5(3)(b).

[45] Ibid., s. 5(6).

[46] Ibid., s. 7(1).

[47] Ibid., s. 8(1).

[48] Ibid., s. 6(6).

[49] M Michelle Govender, 'Domestic violence: is South Africa meeting its obligations in terms of the women's convention?' (2003) 19 *South African Journal on Human Rights*, 4, 672.

[50] Lisa Vetten, *Addressing Domestic Violence in South Africa: Reflections on Strategy and Practice* (UN Division for the Advancement of Women in collaboration and UN Office on Drugs and Crime, 2005).

Critique of the Domestic Violence Act

While the DVA is progressive and reflective of women's realities, it is not free from criticism. Dissel and Ngubeni argue that the DVA fails to offer sufficient remedies.[51] They propose for example, that 'a victim offender conference, or an enquiry by the traditional authority, may be additional mechanisms that women may turn to for assistance'.[52] A focus on the offender's rehabilitation as a long-term solution was also addressed by Daly.[53] Smythe suggests that redress for abused women can be offered in the form of 'social welfare grants'.[54] Some respondents interviewed for this research voiced similar concerns. Charlene from NGO2 sees the Act as 'reactionary and not preventive'; for instance, the abuser's arrest is enforced only after the PO is violated.[55] Furthermore, under the DVA, intimate violence is treated as a civil matter unless an assault is committed. This is because resolving civil claims is speedier and cheaper than litigating criminal offences.[56] However, this delay may lead to the escalation of the abuse and severely harm women. Janet from NGO6 criticised the law for failing to capture the damaging effects of women's economic dependency and lack of networks. She elaborated that 'the legal remedy for domestic violence is to remove the woman from the marital home, to shelter her and to put the man in prison', leading to further alienation for the victim. She suggested rehabilitation programmes for both. These criticisms echo CEDAW General Recommendation 19 that enjoins states to respect the 'integrity and dignity of victims of GBV'. The CEDAW Committee has also recommended that states provide 'rehabilitation programmes for perpetrators of domestic violence'.[57]

[51] Amanda Dissel and Kindiza Ngubeni, *Giving Women Their Voices: Domestic Violence and Restorative Justice in South Africa*, research report (Center for the Study of Violence and Reconciliation, 2003), p. 3.

[52] Ibid.

[53] Kathleen Daly, *Conventional and Innovative Justice Responses to Sexual Violence*, research report no 12 (Australian Center for the Study of Sexual Assault, 2011), p. 11.

[54] Dee Smythe, 'South Africa's response to domestic violence' in Carin Benninger-Budel (ed.) *Due Diligence and Its Application to Protect Women from Violence* (Leiden and Boston, MA: Martinus Nijhoff Publishers, 2008), p. 168.

[55] Lisa Vetten et al., *The Right and the Real: A Shadow Report Analysing Selected Government Departments' Implementation of the 1998 Domestic Violence Act and 2007 Sexual Offences Act*, Research Report, (Tshwaranang Legal Advocacy Centre to End Violence Against Women, 2010), p. 5.

[56] Usdin, 'The value of advocacy', 60.

[57] CEDAW General Recommendation No 19, para. 24.

Preventive laws require financial resources that the government does not usually allocate. This is evident in the DVA for which the government does not budget.[58] Vetten referred to the expanded definition of domestic violence in the DVA, which led to a sharp increase in the number of PO applications. However, the number of court employees did not correspond to the growing demand of clients.[59] Enforcement of the DVA also remains a challenge, primarily because of the police's reluctance to properly implement it.[60] This will be further elaborated in Chapter 7, which will discuss women's legal journeys. Perhaps one of the most notable shortcomings of the Act is its failure to recognise the distinctive challenges faced by women living under customary law, mostly residing in rural areas.[61] Their vulnerability is emphasised in Article 14 of CEDAW.[62]

2 Rape Law

Until 2007, the common law definition of rape was 'unlawful, intentional sexual intercourse with a woman without her consent'.[63] In 2003, Parliament introduced the Criminal Law (Sexual Offences) Amendment Bill,[64] which dramatically reformed legislation for sexual offences. However, deliberations on the bill extended for years, delaying its promulgation. The delay left the court stranded in *Masiya* v. *S*,[65] where the common law definition of rape was not congruent with constitutional principles. Mr Masiye had anally penetrated a nine-year-old girl – a crime of indecent assault under common law, which restricted rape to vaginal penetration. The circuit court decided to expand the common law definition of rape to be congruent with the Constitution. The new definition was 'acts of non-consensual sexual penetration of the male sexual organ into the vagina or anus of another person',[66] and

[58] Smythe, 'South Africa's response', pp. 168–170.

[59] Vetten, *Addressing Domestic Violence*, p. 6.

[60] Artz, 'Policing the Domestic Violence Act', 11.

[61] Curran and Bonthuys, 'Customary law', 608.

[62] See CEDAW Committee, General Statement on the Elimination of Discrimination against Women on Rural Women (Adopted on 19 October 2011 during the 50th session).

[63] John Milton, *South African Criminal Law and Procedure*, 3rd edition (South Africa: Juta, 1996), p. 435.

[64] Criminal Law (Sexual Offences) Amendment Bill B50-2003 (South Africa), published in Government Gazette No. 25282 of 30 July 2003.

[65] *Masiya* v. *Director of Public Prosecutions Pretoria (The State) and Another* [2007] (8) BCLR 827 (CC) (hereinafter *Masiya* case).

[66] Ibid., para. 11.

Mr Masiya was convicted of rape. The proceedings of this case will be discussed in Chapter 5.

The Sexual Offences and Related Matters Amendment Act (SOA) was finally passed in 2007.[67] The definition of rape is, 'any person (a) who unlawfully and intentionally commits an act of sexual penetration with a complainant (b), without the consent of b, is guilty of the offence of rape'.[68] Consent means 'voluntary or uncoerced agreement' and 'penetration' also has a broad definition, which includes the full or partial penetration of a sexual organ as well as the mouth and anus.[69] Penetrate includes using a genital organ, any other organ of the body, or any object.[70] The SOA defines sexual assault, as any person who commits a 'sexual violation' against another person, or 'inspires the belief in a complainant that this will happen'.[71] Statutory rape criminalises a person who commits 'an act of consensual sexual violation with a child' under 16.[72]

Under the SOA, rape and sexual assault should not be justified by the relationship between the offender and the complainant.[73] In terms of sentencing, the court shall not consider the following factors: sexual history of the complainant, physical injury of the complainant, or any cultural or religious beliefs of the respondent concerning rape.[74] Victims of rape and sexual assault who are minors are entitled to testify through an intermediary in court if there is a risk of 'undue mental stress or suffering'.[75] Offenders of serious offences (including rape) are sentenced to life in prison if compelling circumstances for a lenient sentence have not been proved.[76]

Very limited criticism has been directed towards the Act. In fact, it has been widely praised as inclusive and highly protective of GBV victims.[77] One of the few criticisms is its failure to recognise some forms of 'non-contact sexual abuse that should also be considered

[67] Sexual Offences and Related Matters Amendment Act No 32 of 2007 (hereinafter, SOA).
[68] Ibid., s. 3.
[69] Ibid., s. 1.
[70] Ibid.
[71] Ibid., s. 5.
[72] Ibid., s. 15.
[73] Ibid., s. 56(1).
[74] Criminal Law (Sentencing) Amendment Act No 37 of 2007 (South Africa) s 3 (a).
[75] CPA, s. 170(a).
[76] Sentencing Amendment Act, s. 51.
[77] See Lisa Vetten, 'Paradox and policy in post-apartheid South Africa' in Nicole Westmarland and Geetanjali Gangoli (eds.), *International Approaches to Rape* (UK: The Policy Press, 2012), pp. 147–169.

child abuse' such as 'sexual comments to a child, fetishism and voyeurism'.[78] Respondents interviewed for this research expressed some concerns as well. One example is the failure of the Act to capture the 'hate' element in corrective rape against lesbians. Nomsa from NGO10 argued that the law discriminates against lesbians because it fails to make the connection between homophobia and rape. Both criticisms are concerned with vulnerable groups, reflecting the need for the law to be more sensitive to intersectional vulnerabilities. Mandy from NGO4 echoed the abovementioned criticism of the DVA: rape law fails to capture the influence of culture on GBV. She illustrated her point with the example of Story 4 in which a manager repeatedly raped an employee. She explained that the legal case was weak because the victim neither left the job nor reported the rape because she blamed herself; Nasreen was Muslim and unveiled, which is considered a violation of the Islamic doctrine, leading her to believe that her uncovered body had encouraged the rape.

Ten years after the promulgation of the Act, the Deputy Minister of the Department of Justice and Constitutional Development called for stakeholders to 'critically evaluate the implementation and impact of the Act since it came into operation, and to identify the challenges that continue to compromise its successful implementation'.[79] This included 50 civil society organisations, in addition to magistrates and representatives of other relevant state departments. One challenge noted by the group was the dependency of the Act on numerous stakeholders to do different roles that should ultimately come together to guarantee the successful implementation of the Act.[80] This is not necessarily a weakness, but a detail in design that complicates its implementation. Otherwise, the criticism centred on implementation challenges, including calling for more sensitivity on the part of some state officials, among other recommendations.[81]

3 *Reflections on Gender-based Violence Legislation*

South African statutory law is adequately responsive to rape. It meets both state obligations under the Constitution and international human

[78] Louise P Aucamp et al., 'A critical analysis of legislation pertaining to the sexual abuse of children' (2012) 13 *Child Abuse Research: A South African Journal*, 3.

[79] Kgomotso Ramotsho, 'Sexual Offences Act reviewed', De Rebus: Law Society of South Africa, 1 February 2018, accessed 25 June 2018 at www.derebus.org.za/sexual-offences-act-reviewed/

[80] Ibid.

[81] Ibid.

rights law. The legislation is the most progressive in Africa[82] and is also regarded and referenced as an example for other states to follow. This can be seen in the case MC v. *Bulgaria* before the European Court of Human Rights (ECHR).[83] The case involved a complainant claiming that Bulgarian law did not adequately protect her from rape and sexual abuse because it only prosecuted cases where the victim had expressed active resistance to rape.[84] Bulgarian legislation did not capture the nature and context of rape, where in many cases, there is no possibility for active resistance or it is impossible to prove it. Interights, a London-based human rights NGO, acting as *amicus curiae*, cited rape laws from Canada, Australia and South Africa to argue that 'lack of consent was the defining element of rape and sexual abuse in those countries and that proof of use of physical force by the perpetrator or of physical resistance by the victim was not required'.[85] The court found a violation of the complainant's rights, pursuant to Articles 3 and 8 of the European Convention on Human Rights[86] guaranteeing the freedom from torture, degrading and inhuman treatments as well as respect of privacy and family life.

One notable strength of the South African legal system is the ongoing diligence to identify gaps in the law and its implementation, and to strive to improve it. This was demonstrated in the abovementioned consultation by a state official who, of his own accord, invited stakeholders to review the SOA. Another notable development that deserves appraisal is amending section 18 of South Africa's CPA,[87] which identifies serious crimes that lapse after 20 years. The Constitutional Court struck down this provision as unconstitutional after hearing the case *Levenstein* v. *Ministry of Justice*.[88] The eight applicants had been sexually abused by the defendant as children, more than 20 years ago. However, section 18 of the CPA prevented them from litigating because the defendant's crime did not include rape and therefore fell out of the exceptions

[82] Smythe, 'South Africa's response'.

[83] Case 39272/98, MC v. *Bulgaria* [2003] European Court of Human Rights.

[84] Ibid.

[85] Ibid. para. 147.

[86] European Convention for the Protection of Human Rights and Fundamental Freedoms (1953) 213 U.N.T.S. 222.

[87] Section 18, CPA: 'the right to institute a prosecution for any offense, other than the offenses of — murder; treason committed when the Republic is in a state of war … shall, unless some other period is expressly provided for by law, lapse after the expiration of a period of 20 years from the time when the offence was committed'.

[88] *Levenstein and Others* v. *Estate of the Late Sidney Lewis Frankel and Others* (CCT170/17) [2018] ZACC 16 (hereinafter, *Levenstein* case).

listed in the provision. Declaring this clause as unconstitutional was highly praised; the said provision perpetuated the preconceived notion of the harm affecting women from different sexual offences, assuming that rape (and therefore penetration) is more traumatising than other forms of sexual violence. The founder of South African Male Survivors of Sexual Abuse stated, 'we are extremely happy with this ruling. This empowers male and female survivors with the opportunity of getting justice ... but also about putting the power in their hands to make the choice to lay charges or not. Prior to this, the choice was removed from them'.[89] The proceedings on this case will be detailed in Chapter 5, as it is considered the most recent success of impact litigation.

4 *Additional Vulnerability and Extra Protection*

When addressing GBV, it is important to recognise two of the most vulnerable groups: homosexual people and children. Gays and lesbians are targets of hate crimes, including rape. Lacking agency, children are also exceptionally vulnerable and are therefore prone to mental and psychological manipulation.

Homosexuality in the Law

Even though South Africa is host to many conservative cultures, it is one of few countries that protects the right to freedom from discrimination on grounds of sexual orientation.[90] Section 1 of the Equality Act protects from discrimination based on sexual orientation. Same-sex partnerships are recognised in other statutes, such as the Medical Schemes Act of 1998,[91] which defines 'dependent' to include same-sex partners. The DVA expands the definition of domestic relationships to include unmarried people and same-sex couples.[92] Recognition of the rights of homosexuals was a result of advocacy and impact litigation undertaken by NGOs. For example, in *Langemaat* v. *Minister of Safety and Security*,[93] the High Court decided that it was discriminatory to differentiate between same-sex and opposite sex partnerships

[89] Carl Collison, 'Concourt ruling offers sexual abuse survivors opportunity of "getting justice"', *Mail & Guardian*, 14 June 2018, accessed 28 June 2018 at https://mg.co.za/article/2018-06-14-concourt-ruling-offers-sexual-abuse-survivors-opportunity-of-getting-justice

[90] Constitution, s. 9(3).

[91] Medical Schemes Act No 131 of 1998 (South Africa), s. 1.

[92] DVA, s. 1(vii).

[93] *Langemaat* v. *Minister of Safety and Security* [1998] (3) South Africa 312 (T).

in policy. The applicant was a lesbian police employee who wanted to add her partner to her medical aid. Another example is *National Coalition for Gay and Lesbian Equality* v. *Minister of Justice*,[94] in which the Constitutional Court declared unconstitutional various provisions outlawing 'sodomy' in legislation such as the Sexual Offences Act of 1956,[95] the CPA of 1977,[96] and the Security Officers Act of 1987.[97] In *Minister of Home Affairs and Another* v. *Fourie and Another*,[98] the Constitutional Court declared the definition of marriage in the Marriage Act of 1961 to be unconstitutional because it discriminated against homosexual people.[99] In the three cases, NGOs acted either as litigants or *amicus curiae*, a line of advocacy which will be discussed in Chapter 5. Because of such progressive legal amendments, currently 'lesbians, gay men and, to a more limited extent, transgender people have achieved equality' before the law.[100] In this sense, South Africa has excelled in recognising the human rights of a group that remains criminalised based on their sexual orientation in 76 countries around the world,[101] where at least five of those countries impose the possibility of the death penalty on those found guilty.[102] Despite the legal protection of their rights, gays and lesbians remain vulnerable in South Africa. They are common subjects of hate crime and some extreme forms of violence such as 'corrective rape', which targets lesbians with the intention of 'curing' them from homosexuality. This was expressed as a grave concern by the CEDAW Committee in the concluding observations in response to a South Africa report of 2010.[103]

[94] *National Coalition for Gay and Lesbian Equality* v. *Minister of Justice* [1998] (12) BCLR 1517 (CC) (hereinafter, *National Coalition* case).

[95] Sexual Offences Act No 23 of 1956 (Previous title: Immorality Act) (South Africa).

[96] CPA, s. 269 was considered unconstitutional.

[97] Security Officers Act No 92 of 1987 (South Africa).

[98] *Minister of Home Affairs and Another* v. *Fourie and Another* [2006] (3) BCLR 355 (CC).

[99] Marriage Act No 25 of 1961 (South Africa).

[100] Human Rights Watch, *We'll Show You You're a Woman: Violence and Discrimination Against Black Lesbians and Transgender Men in South Africa*, research report (Human Rights Watch, 2011), p. 13.

[101] Human Rights Council, Discriminatory Laws and Practices and Acts of Violence against Individuals based on their Sexual Orientation and Gender Identity (17 November 2011) UN Doc A/HRC/19/41 2011, para. 40.

[102] Human Rights Watch, 'We'll show you', p. 45.

[103] CEDAW Committee, Concluding Observations of the Committee on the Elimination of Discrimination against Women, (5 April 2011) C/ZAF/CO/4, para. 39.

Children

Children are vulnerable because they do not have legal capacity and are therefore easy targets of sexual violence. South African legislation captures this vulnerability. Under the SOA, it is mandatory for anyone who has knowledge about a sexual offence committed against a child to report it. Failing to do so, a person becomes 'guilty of an offence and is liable on conviction to a fine or to imprisonment'.[104] The law also provides special measures for child witnesses so as to protect them from secondary victimisation and further distress. In any trial, any person under 18 is entitled to testify through an intermediary if direct testimony would cause stress or suffering.[105] This option is commonly used in sexual offences cases. As previously mentioned, a noted strength of the South African legal culture is the constant revision and reflection on existing laws. The impact of sexual offences trials on children was the subject matter of *S* v. *Mokoena* and *S* v. *Phaswane*[106] (hereinafter *Mokoena* case). These cases were jointly heard by the High Court and later by the Constitutional Court and they both involved the rape of minor girls for which the perpetrators were tried and convicted.

As for child offenders, they have rights under the Child Justice Act,[107] which was passed in 2008. Arrested children under ten years old go through an assessment by a probation officer who determines their ability to understand the proceedings and their charges and the danger they pose to themselves and others, among other factors.[108] Depending on the age of the child, their maturity and mental capacity as well as the crime for which they are charged, the child is tried in a children's court,[109] joins a youth centre or enrols in a counselling programme.[110]

II INTERNATIONAL LAW

A International Law in South Africa

The global women's movement has brought GBV to the attention of the international community and has successfully advocated for the

[104] SOA, s. 54(1)(b).
[105] CPA, s. 170(a).
[106] *S* v. *Mokoena*, *S* v. *Phaswane* [2008] (5) South Africa 578 (T) (hereinafter *Mokoena* case).
[107] Child Justice Act 75 of 2008 (South Africa).
[108] Ibid., s. 5.
[109] Ibid., s. 69(3)(a).
[110] Ibid., s. 27.

drafting and enactment of international instruments to respond to the various forms of violence affecting women across the globe. This section will discuss GBV in the international sphere, assessing South Africa's performance and the role of NGOs in monitoring the state's performance.

During apartheid, the South African government did not support human rights. South Africa was one of the eight abstentions in the vote to adopt the Universal Declaration of Human Rights.[111] Democratic South Africa, however, shows commitment to international human rights principles, not only as embedded in domestic legislation, but also as reflected in the signature and ratification of the major human rights conventions. Both international law and customary international law are recognised in the South Africa Constitution in section 233, where courts are directed to 'prefer any reasonable interpretation of the legislation that is consistent with international law over any alternative interpretation that is inconsistent with international law'.

South Africa has ratified regional and international human rights instruments that address women's rights. The post-apartheid government signed the CEDAW in 1994 and ratified it without reservations in December 1995.[112] The Optional Protocol to CEDAW, which gives the right to the CEDAW Committee to investigate violations of women's rights, was ratified in 2005.[113] The Protocol to the African Charter on the Rights of Women in Africa was signed and ratified in 2004.[114] South Africa made a reservation to Article 4, which prohibits states from applying the death penalty on pregnant and nursing women, because of the unconstitutionality of the death penalty.[115] The state also made a reservation to Article 6(d) that directs states to ensure that all marriages should be registered.[116] South Africa noted that this Article would discriminate against women who enter into unregistered customary marriage and that it also conflicts with the Recognition of Customary

[111] Universal Declaration of Human Rights (1948) UN Doc A/810, at 71.

[112] South Africa CEDAW report (2010), p. 6.

[113] Optional Protocol to the Convention on the Elimination of all Forms of Discrimination Against Women (2000) U.N. Doc. A/54/49 (Vol. I).

[114] African Union, Decision on the Protocol to the African Charter on Human and Peoples' Rights Relating to the Rights of Women, Assembly/AU/Dec.14 (II) art 18 (hereafter Africa's Women's Protocol).

[115] Africa's Women's Protocol, Article 4(2)(j). For South Africa's reservation and interpretative declarations, see Jamil Ddamulira Mujuzi 'Protocol to the African Charter on Human and People's Rights on the Rights of Women in Africa: South Africa's reservations and interpretative declarations' (2008) 12 *Law, Democracy and Development*, 2, 41.

[116] Africa's Women's Protocol, Article 6(d).

Marriages Act. This Act guarantees that the 'failure to register a customary marriage does not affect the validity of that marriage'.[117]

B South Africa's Obligations under International Human Rights Law

While South Africa is praised for signing and ratifying instruments that protect women's rights, implementation remains a problem. South Africa, like other states, has not prioritised its international obligations towards women's rights. Both reports to the CEDAW Committee were late and the second report, which was submitted in 2009, covered a period of ten years (1998–2008). South Africa was expected to submit a report in 2015, which the CGE presented to the Women in the Presidency Committee in the Parliament in March of that year.[118] The Committee discussed some issues of concern particularly regarding the persistence of harmful practices such as FGM among rural women and other concerns around domestic violence, such as a lack of statistics and negative social attitudes towards family violence.[119] However, the report was never submitted, and this was noted in the report of the Special Rapporteur on Violence against Women in June 2016.[120] South Africa submitted a combined report to the African Commission in August 2015 on its performance pursuant to the African Protocol on Human and People's Rights and the Protocol on the Rights of Women.[121]

In the first CEDAW report in 1998, South Africa noted the high rate of GBV against women from different backgrounds.[122] Despite prioritising GBV in the government's agenda, rates of rape, sexual abuse and domestic violence were rising.[123] However, South Africa reported some accomplishments, including the launch of awareness

[117] Recognition of Customary Marriages Act No 120 of 1998 (South Africa), s. 4(9).

[118] Briefing by Commission for Gender Equality to the Women in the Presidency Committee on CEDAW and Beijing +20 report to UN by South Africa: 3 March 2015, accessed 20 July 2018 at https://pmg.org.za/committee-meeting/20098/

[119] Ibid.

[120] Report of the Special Rapporteur on violence against women, its causes and consequences on her mission to South Africa (14 June 2016) A/HRC/32/42/Add.2, p. 11. (hereinafter, Special Rapporteur report 2016).

[121] Combined Second Periodic Report under the African Charter on Human and People's Rights and Initial Report under the Protocol to the African Changer on the Rights of Women in Africa, South Africa (August 2015), accessed 20 July 2018 at www.achpr.org/files/sessions/58th/state-reports/2nd-2002-2015/staterep2_southafrica_2003_2014_eng.pdf

[122] Report to the CEDAW Committee, South Africa (25 February 1998) CEDAW/C/ZAF/1, p. 113.

[123] Ibid., p. 114.

campaigns that target gender violence and the introduction of victim support programmes.[124] In the 2009 report, South Africa reaffirmed its commitment to address gender violence and reported on the initiatives taken. For example, the Justice Crime Prevention Strategy was launched in 1999 to respond to issues relating to the victimisation of women and children, including domestic violence, trafficking and sexual offences.[125] It was implemented by the Sexual Offences and Community Affairs Unit that worked to design policy, build the capacity of service providers, raise awareness and provide training to officials who work with gender violence.[126] The state also referred to events such as the National 365 Day Action Plan to End Gender Violence, which addressed GBV in awareness campaigns and advocacy among other initiatives.[127] Women subjected to violence could also benefit from the victim programmes such as those at the Thuthuzela Care Centre, which offers a 24-hour one-stop service, where victims can access help, including medical assistance, court preparation advice and counselling.[128] The CEDAW Committee commended South Africa for the developments in legislation, but condemned the persistent gap between policy and practice. The Committee urged the government to take some measures to close this gap, such as ensuring women's effective access to justice, strengthening the linkages between different levels of government and providing gender-sensitive training for legal personnel.[129]

In its report to the African Union, South Africa reported on measures taken for the 'institutionalization of gender mainstreaming within state organs and government departments'.[130] Furthermore, the state reported on its work on GBV, particularly involving civil society and some of the measures already reviewed in this chapter such as establishing sexual offences courts and victim-friendly police stations. In addition, the report included two important measures: 'empowering prosecutors, police officers, magistrates and doctors with specialised skills' and 'keeping dangerous sexual offenders under long-term supervision on release from prison'.[131] The state also noted the strategy for

[124] Ibid., p. 115.
[125] South Africa CEDAW report (2010), p. 164.
[126] Ibid., p. 165.
[127] Ibid. p. 157.
[128] Ibid. p. 158.
[129] CEDAW Concluding Observations (2011), para. 19.
[130] South Africa combined report to African Union, p. 152.
[131] Ibid., p. 36.

eliminating violence based on sexual orientation committed against gays and lesbians.[132] Generally, the state rightly acknowledged the gender-related prevalent problems including the pervasive stereotypes 'rooted in the gender discourses of masculinity and femininity'.[133] In response, the Commission commended the state for instating the necessary laws, policies and various measures to promote the status of women.[134] However, the Commission expressed concern about the 'low representation of women at decision making levels and the Judiciary' in addition to the persistence of harmful practices, the failure to properly incorporate 'corrective rape' in the SOA, and the inadequacy of child marriage laws.[135]

C Monitoring the State: NGOs and Shadow Reports

At the international level, NGOs participate in the assessment of state performance by preparing shadow reports to the CEDAW Committee. In return, the CEDAW Committee appreciates the role of NGOs in the reporting process and has expanded their role by inviting them to attend the pre-sessional working groups and encouraging them to submit briefings and recommendations.[136] Since NGOs are more capable of assessing women's needs and realities, their evaluation of state performance is insightful. For example, the shadow report of 2011, responding to the 2009 government report, which was prepared by several NGOs,[137] suggested that the 365 Day Action Plan to End Gender Violence and the 16 Days of Activism Campaign, the only non-statutory measures to fight GBV undertaken, did not have a strong practical impact.[138] The report further stated that explanations on the part of the state for its the failure to implement successful programmes was unacceptable and asserted that 'it is necessary that the State interrogate the reasons for its ineffectiveness and indicate what it intends to do about any policy gaps, gaps between policy and practice, and gaps

[132] Ibid., p. 39.

[133] Ibid., p. 172.

[134] African Commission on Human and People's Rights, Concluding Observations and Recommendations on the Combined Second Periodic Report under the African Charter on Human and People's Rights and Initial Report under the Protocol to the African Changer on the Rights of Women in Africa (Adopted by the African Commission on Human and Peoples' Rights at its 20th Extra-Ordinary Session held from 9 to 18 June 2016, Banjul), pp. 9–10.

[135] Ibid., p. 19.

[136] See Byrnes, 'The Convention', p. 139.

[137] Centre for the Study of Violence and Reconciliation, People Opposing Women Abuse, Western Cape Network on Violence Against Women.

[138] South African CEDAW Shadow Report, 2011, para. 3.1.3.9.

between law and implementation'.[139] The state was also criticised for its failure to provide effective healthcare support, according to a study done by The Tshwaranang Legal Advocacy Centre (TLAC).[140] The report noted the government's failure to recognise the additional risk of violence faced by vulnerable women, such as indigenous women and refugees.[141] In addition, the link between HIV and GBV was not adequately addressed by the state.[142] The Concluding Observations of the CEDAW Committee showed that many of those points were noted.

A coalition of NGOs also submitted a shadow report to South Africa's report to the African Commission highlighting some important issues. For instance, the coalition pointed to the Traditional Leadership Framework Act that was still in deliberations, confirming that it 'entrenches patriarchy and subjugation of rural women'.[143] Other issues raised include the under-budgeting for GBV-related legislation such as the SOA, the barriers to the implementation of laws, and the additional hardships faced by migrant women.

III SPECIAL BODIES DESIGNED TO CATER FOR GENDER AND GENDER-BASED VIOLENCE

Realising that gender issues require special attention and expertise, the South African government has been diligent in designing both advisory and adjudicating bodies to oversee the most pressing gender-related problems. This section will review the sexual offences courts, Equality Courts and the Commission for Gender Equality (CGE). In addition, a brief overview of the Thuthuzela Care Centres which offer a one-stop shop to victims of violence will be given.

A Sexual Offences Courts

Perhaps most relevant to this research are the sexual offences courts. The South African government has been juggling with the idea since 1993. Nongovernmental organisations and the state agree that these courts are necessary and able to respond to the needs of sexual offences

[139] Ibid., para. 7.1.3.2.
[140] Ibid., para. 7.1.3.3.
[141] Ibid., para. 7.1.3.7.
[142] Ibid.
[143] Shadow Report on the South Africa State Report on the African Charter on Human and People's Rights and the Maputo Protocol by a Coalition of South African NGOs, 31 March 2016 (58th Ordinary Session of the ACHPR), p. 36.

victims. However, their financial demands are beyond the state's means; specialised courts add to judiciary logistical expenses, particularly because of all the special features required in sexual offences courts, such as video facilities and intermediaries. It has, therefore, been an unsettled matter for the last 15 years and remains to be so.

1 Inception

These courts were established for the prosecution of sexual offences as part of the project 'Justice Vision 2000', implemented by the Department of Justice and Constitutional Development.[144] The first court was set up in 1993 in Cape Town with the purpose of curbing the alarmingly high rape rates and preventing secondary trauma of rape victims. The courts had a threefold mission: to 'reduce the insensitive treatment of victims … to adopt a coordinated and integrated approach among the various role-players who deal with sexual offences; and to improve the investigation and prosecution'.[145] They employed specialised staff and provided adequate facilities for the victims.[146] In addition, they catered to both adult and child victims. For example, they had waiting rooms for victims to avoid perpetrators.[147] For children, they provided toys to create a relaxed atmosphere. In some cases, witnesses could give their statements via video link so as to prevent further trauma.[148]

The courts yielded some promising results. The two most notable advancements in litigating sexual offences are a higher conviction rate and a faster turnover period.[149] For instance, the conviction rate of rape was 20 per cent more in Sexual Offences Courts than in Regional Courts.[150] Walker and Louw studied the experiences and perceptions of victims, offenders and families of victims in the Court for Sexual Offences in Bloemfontein. All three groups still complained of a slow due process; however, they differed in their perceptions of the service. While the victims and their families viewed the courts in high regard

144 Human Rights Watch, 'We'll show you', p. 17.

145 Ministerial Advisory Task Team on the Adjudication of Sexual Offence Matters, Report on the Re-establishment of Sexual Offences Courts (Department of Justice and Constitutional Development, August 2013), p. 17.

146 Chineze J Onyejekwe, 'The interrelationship between gender-based violence and HIV/AIDS in South Africa' (2004) 6 *Journal of International Women's Studies*, 1, 37.

147 Department of Justice and Constitutional Development website www.justice.gov.za/about/sa-courts.html

148 Ibid.

149 Ministerial Advisory Task Team, Report on the Re-establishment, p. 24.

150 Ibid.

and felt treated with respect, the offenders believed that the courts were biased and that close involvement of female prosecutors in the cases clouded their judgement.[151]

2 *Moratorium*

In 2005, a moratorium was called by the Minister of Justice and Constitutional Development on the establishment of sexual offences courts in order to reassess the impact of the courts and revise their terms of reference.[152] In addition to their financial demands, a notable lack of legislation to establish the courts made them vulnerable to be 'closed at will';[153] a lack of training for court personnel, causing them to suffer trauma from the cases they encountered; and a missing monitoring and evaluation strategy were additional factors reinforcing the demise of the courts.[154] Consequently, the number of courts declined 'from an all-time high of 67 in 2005/06 to as few as 40 by October 2010'.[155] Although the government referred to the courts as an accomplishment in the CEDAW 2008 report, it neither gave an updated number nor provided an assessment of the success of the courts.[156] It also admitted that the demise of courts had led to a decrease in prosecutions.[157]

February 2013 witnessed a horrific gang rape incident that led to the death of a 17-year-old girl after she was severely beaten and mutilated.[158] This case led to an outcry across the country demanding the return of the sexual offences courts. In the following April, the Justice Department announced the reinstatement of the sexual offences courts and the establishment of 50 additional courts across the country, which

[151] See Stephen P Walker and Dap Louw, 'The court for sexual offences: perceptions of the victims of sexual offences' (May–June 2005) 28 *International Journal of Law and Psychiatry* 3; Stephen P Walker and Dap Louw, 'The court for sexual offences: perceptions of the families of the victims of sexual offences' (July–August 2005) 28 *International Journal of Law and Psychiatry* 4; SP Walker and D Louw, 'The court for sexual offences: perceptions of the perpetrators of sexual offences' (July–August 2005) 29 *International Journal of Law and Psychiatry* 4.

[152] Ministerial Advisory Task Team, Report on the Re-establishment, p. 23.

[153] Michelle Solomon, 'Claim that 58 sexual offences courts ready in SA by September looks untrue' Africa Check, 7 May 2013, accessed 4 June 2018 at www.africacheck.org/reports/claim-that-58-sexual-offences-courts-ready-by-september-looks-untrue/

[154] Ministerial Advisory Task Team, Report on the Re-establishment, p. 8.

[155] Vetten et al., *The Right and the Real*, p. 63.

[156] South Africa CEDAW report (2010), p. 51.

[157] Solomon, 'Claim that 58 sexual offences courts'.

[158] David Smith, 'South Africa searches for solution after teenage girl's gang rape and murder', The Guardian, 13 February 2013, accessed 20 July 2018 at www.guardian.co.uk/world/2013/feb/13/south-africa-rape-murder

were to gradually reach 90 courts by 2018.[159] His statement, however, raised doubt among the public since it was not followed by budget allocation or a clear framework for the plan.[160] In 2017, the Ministry announced a reduction of funds dedicated to sexual offences courts. They were to be replaced by alternative, less costly courts adjudicating on sexual offences to be launched in partnership with UNICEF.[161] This announcement was met by outrage from civil society organisations, and a concern that the already depleted resources dedicated to the issue are clearly not tackling the persistent rates of violence against women.[162] The Ministry, however, insisted that the reaction from civil society was overblown.[163]

3 *The Future of Sexual Offences Courts*

One positive development must be noted regarding the trial of sexual offences. In 2015, the Department of Justice and Constitutional Development prepared draft regulations relating to sexual offences courts and invited interested parties to submit commentaries regarding these regulations.[164] The draft included detailed plans for the courts, addressing both logistical and procedural issues such as waiting rooms, the availability and training of intermediaries, and testifying equipment. Some NGOs such as the Centre for Applied Legal Studies (CALS) submitted recommendations and suggestions.[165] In their submission in January 2018, the centre acknowledge that some elements of the draft need progressive realisation because of a budget deficit, but

159 'Sexual Offences Courts to Open Soon' News24, 18 April 2013, accessed 20 July 2018 at www.news24.com/SouthAfrica/News/Sexual-offences-courts-to-open-soon-20130418

160 Solomon, 'Claim that 58 sexual offences courts'.

161 Jeanette Chabalala 'Shock at moves to "spread resources" for sexual offences courts', News24, 18 May 2017, accessed 3 June 2018 at www.news24.com/SouthAfrica/News/shock-at-moves-to-spread-resources-for-sexual-offences-courts-20170518

162 Greg Nicolson, 'Gender-based violence: concerns raised over reduction in funding for sexual offences courts', Daily Maverick, 19 May 2017, accessed 4 June 2018 at www.dailymaverick.co.za/article/2017-05-19-gender-based-violence-concerns-raised-over-reduction-in-funding-for-sexual-offences-courts/#.WxlDj0iFPIU

163 Ibid.

164 Invitation for public comments, draft regulations relating to sexual offences courts: Criminal Law (Sexual Offences and Related Matters) Amendment Act, 2007 (Act No. 32 of 2007), General Notice, (Department of Justice and Constitutional Development, 2017), accessed 20 July 2018 at https://juta.co.za/media/filestore/2015/10/Draft_Regulations_relating_to_Sexual_Offences_Courts_2015.pdf

165 CALS, Submission to the Director-General: Justice and Constitutional Development on the Draft Regulations Relating to Sexual Offences Courts: Criminal Law (Sexual Offences and Related Matters) Amendment Act, 2007 (Act No. 32 of 2007) (January 2018).

it recommended temporary measures to avoid secondary victimisation – having separate waiting rooms for victims and offenders is one example.[166] The centre also suggested some gender-sensitive measures to lessen the trauma of transgendered victims.[167] The future of these courts remains blurry, but the conversation between the state and civil society on the way forward is happening, and some positive steps are evident.

B Equality Courts

Equality courts were created under the Equality Act of 2000 with the purpose of implementing section 9 of the Constitution, namely, as the Act states at its start, to 'prevent and prohibit unfair discrimination and harassment; to promote equality and eliminate unfair discrimination; to prevent and prohibit hate speech'. The courts were specifically designed to ensure a user-friendly environment that even illiterate people could navigate without assistance.[168] However, they remain relatively unknown and people have difficulty accessing these courts.[169] In fact, they have become more popular only after the *Malema* case,[170] which Sonke for Gender Justice brought against Julius Malema for inciting hate speech when he made sexist comments about Zuma's rape case during a political tour – a case that will be detailed in Chapter 5. The court had already ruled on a gender-related case in 2008, when a ban on wearing trousers was imposed on women in Umlazi. The court lifted the ban and ordered the attackers to apologise to the woman whom they had stripped naked as a punishment for defying the ban.[171] While it has not been fully utilised for gender litigation yet, Equality Courts show promising potential for adjudicating gender issues; they are 'flexible and informal', with a 'design that intends to enable cases to be processed without legal representation, with minimal cost, and within a quick time frame'.[172] In addition, these courts have discretion to pass innovative

[166] Ibid., para. 2.2.5.1.

[167] Ibid., para. 2.2.6.2.

[168] Dana Kaersvang, 'Equality Courts in South Africa: legal access for the poor' (2008) 15 *The Journal of the International Institute* 2, 8.

[169] Ibid.

[170] Bouwer Kobeli Morabe, 'The equality court explained', Polity, 19 May 2011, accessed 28 June 2018 at www.polity.org.za/article/the-equality-court-explained-2011-05-19

[171] 'Pants ban prohibited in Umlazi', News24, 9 April 2008, accessed 18 June 2018 at www.news24.com/SouthAfrica/News/Pants-ban-prohibited-in-Umlazi-20080409

[172] Emily N Keehn, *The Equality Courts as a Tool for Gender Transformation* (Cape Town: Sonke Gender Justice Network, 2010), p. 7.

and unorthodox judgments that are transformative in nature.[173] Despite their promise, however, they must be pursued with caution and with much-needed government and civil society 'oversights and efforts' as this is still a new venue for litigation.[174]

C Commission of Gender Equality

The Commission of Gender Equality (CGE) of South Africa was set up pursuant to section 187(1) of the Constitution, to 'promote respect for gender equality and the protection, development and attainment of gender equality'. The role of the commission is set out under The Commission of Gender Equality Act 1996.[175] The Act recognises women's disadvantaged position for historical and cultural reasons and prohibits unfair discrimination on the grounds of gender in relation to GBV and FGM, under section 8. Furthermore, the Act identifies the subtle and indirect forms that discrimination may take, such as inequalities resulting from gender division of labour.[176] The commission has additional roles under the Equality Act passed in 2000.[177]

The Gender Equality Act outlines the specific duties of the commission pursuant to section 11. This includes monitoring and evaluating policies and practices of state organs, public bodies and private businesses; in addition, it is tasked with evaluating any acts or laws that may jeopardise gender equality, including customary law.[178] Other responsibilities include developing and participating in education programmes to promote gender equality,[179] recommending laws or policies to uphold gender equality principles[180] and monitoring compliance with international human rights obligations.[181] The commission also has the power to receive complaints on any gender-related issue, or investigate gender-related issues of its own accord.[182] Chapter 5 has a section devoted to one of the most important complaints received and investigated by the commission, on the gender composition of the judiciary.

[173] Ibid.
[174] Ibid., p. 10.
[175] Commission of Gender Equality Act No 39 of 1996 (hereinafter, Gender Equality Act).
[176] Gender Equality Act, s. 8(i).
[177] Equality Act, ss. (20)(1)(f), 25(5)(b) and 32(c).
[178] Gender Equality Act, s. 11(a) and (c).
[179] Ibid., s. 11(b).
[180] Ibid., s. 11 (d).
[181] Ibid., s. 11 (h).
[182] Ibid., s. 11 (e).

Technically, the commission started out quite successfully adopting a 'consultative approach through information gathering and evaluation workshops', showing a commitment to its constituents.[183] However, since its inception, there was confusion over its ideology: internal disagreements ensued over the line of feminism to be followed, or whether it should act as a 'gender development agency'.[184] The commission was also faulted for failing to challenge the government on gender-related issues,[185] despite its core duty to represent women's interests within the government.[186] The CGE then moved towards 'a more general framework', retreating to first explore women's priority issues. Finding great challenges among poor rural women, the Commission took an interest in customary law and tradition,[187] in addition to other issues such as GBV, HIV, poverty and governance.[188]

Problems within the commission prevail, particularly related to its position as an independent body that is also located within the state's framework. However, it still does impactful work. One of the areas in which the commission is quite active is providing gender-related advice to courts in the role of *amicus curiae*. It has been involved in many cases, bringing the courts' attention to important gender issues.[189] Some of these cases will be discussed in Chapter 5.

D Thuthuzela Care Centres

The Thuthuzela Care Centres are another praiseworthy establishment aimed at speeding up the due process of law and preventing secondary victimisation. These centres offer a one-stop shop for sexual violence victims.[190] They were set up as a response to the low conviction rate of

183 Amanda Gouws, 'The state of national gender machinery: structural problems and personalised politics' in Sakhela Buhlungu et al. (eds.), *State of the Nation: South Africa 2005–2006* (Cape Town: HSRC Press, 2006), p. 151.

184 Gay W. Seidman 'Institutional dilemmas: representation versus mobilization in the South African Gender Commission' (2003) 29 *Feminist Studies* 3, 548.

185 Gouws, 'The state of national gender machinery', p. 152.

186 Seidman, 'Institutional dilemmas', 549.

187 Amanda Spies, 'The importance and relevance of amicus curiae participation in litigating on the customary law of marriage' (2016) 16 *African Human Rights Law Journal*, 253.

188 Gouws, 'The state of national gender machinery', p. 152.

189 For some case examples, see Rashida Manjoo 'Case study: the Commission for Gender Equality, South Africa: promotion and protection of gender equality – are separate structures necessary?' (July 2005) 14 *Griffith Law Review* 2, 275.

190 Department of Justice and Constitutional Development website. For details about the centre, see Thuthuzela Care Centre: Turning Victims into Survivors (The National Prosecuting Authority of South Africa) www.npa.gov.za/UploadedFiles/THUTHUZELA%20Brochure%20New.pdf; Also see Vetten, *The Right and the Real*, p. 60.

sexual violence crimes plaguing South Africa. So far, the centres show success indicators. They are located in hospitals and are able to receive victims directly from the police station by ambulance. Victims receive counselling in the ambulance and once they arrive at the centre, they are able to give their statements there rather than 'being shuttled around throughout the criminal justice system'.[191] As expected, there are mixed opinions on the quality of services provided, and an evaluation study done in 2015 showed that one third of NGOs involved in the centre had problems with the operations, while the others were either neutral or at the positive end of the spectrum.[192]

IV LAWS GOVERNING NGOs

NGOs are a huge asset to the state. They act as a liaison between state and society conveying women's lived realities to policymakers, they fill significant gaps in service provision and they also help the state to develop the legal culture of South Africa. This importance is reflected in the law governing the establishment and operations of NGOs.

The Nonprofit Organisations Act (NPO Act), passed in 1997, is the main instrument regulating the work of NGOs.[193] The Act recognises the role of NGOs in identifying and meeting the 'diverse needs of the population' and therefore directs government institutions to maintain a suitable environment in which NGOs can develop. The government is responsible, under section 2 of the NPO Act, for creating an environment 'within which the public may have access to information concerning registered nonprofit organisations'.[194] The Act recognises that the work of NGOs in service provision complements the government's initiatives, and states that the purpose of the Act is 'to promote a spirit of cooperation and shared responsibility within government, donors and non-profit organisations'.[195] The Act resonates with Article 4(p) of the UN Declaration on the Elimination of Violence against Women,[196] which highlights the important role of NGOs in

191 Thuthuzela Care Centres, UNICEF, accessed 6 June 2018 at www.unicef.org/southafrica/hiv_aids_998.html

192 Lisa Vetten, *'It Sucks' / 'It's a Wonderful Service': Post-Rape Care and the Micro-Politics of Institutions*, research report (Actionaid/Shukumisa, 2015), p. 11.

193 Nonprofit Organisations Act No 71 of 1997 (South Africa) (hereafter NPO Act), s. 3.

194 Ibid., s. 2(c).

195 Ibid., s. 2(e).

196 Declaration on the Elimination of Violence against Women (20 December 1993) A/RES/48/104.

fighting VAW.[197] In return, under the NPO Act, NGOs are obliged to maintain high standards of 'governance, transparency and accountability'[198]; submit annual financial reports;[199] abide by the Constitution and the law;[200] and implement transparency measures. The objectives of the Act demonstrate the government's appreciation and recognition of the civil society.[201]

NGOs have not always operated smoothly in South Africa. Chapter 8 will discuss the different relationships likely to develop between states and NGOs based on the political climate and the threat that NGOs pose to the longevity of the regime. Under the apartheid government, NGOs were considered a threat, and therefore the state used the law to shrink their working space and impose restrictive rules for operation. For instance, the state used brutal tax laws on companies to discourage corporate sponsorships;[202] the apartheid state also passed the Fund-raising Act[203] to curb foreign funding from flowing to NGOs. As expected, anti-apartheid NGOs circumvented the regulations by developing 'a range of administrative measures that would camouflage their funding sources' because they primarily depended on external funding.[204] The post-apartheid government was aware of these difficulties when reforming legislation and adopted a 'light touch' approach to avoid using controlling mechanisms with NGOs that resembled the apartheid era.[205] Currently, the relationship between NGOs and the state is a fruitful one, and will be discussed in Chapter 4.

V CONCLUSION

The law is a powerful tool; it can be used to put society on the right track for the implementation of human rights values or to institutionalise and regulate discrimination. South Africa has lived both realities

197 Ibid., Article 4(p).
198 NPO Act, s. 2.
199 Ibid., s. 18(1)(a).
200 Ibid., s. 20(1)(a)(i).
201 Bhekinkosi Moyo, 'Regulation or strangulation? NGO laws in Africa, part 1: South Africa', Mail & Guardian, 5 October 2008, accessed 20 July 2017 at www.thoughtleader.co.za/bhekinkosimoyo/2008/10/05/regulation-or-strangulation-ngo-laws-in-africa-part-1-south-africa
202 Adam Habib and Rupert Taylor, 'South Africa: anti-apartheid NGOs in transition' (1999) 10 *Voluntas: International Journal of Voluntary and Nonprofit Organization*, 1, 75.
203 Fund-raising Act 107 of 1978 (South Africa).
204 Habib and Taylor, 'South Africa: anti-apartheid NGOs', 75.
205 Richard Batley, 'Engaged or divorced? Cross-service findings on government relations with non-state service-providers' (2006) 26 *Public Administration and Development*, 3, 246.

in its recent history. There is no doubt that the post-apartheid state takes pride in the Constitution and has thrived to develop legislation that echoes the principles enshrined in the Bill of Rights. However, laws are as good as their implementation, and therefore there is still a long way to go for the progressive laws to echo in society.

This chapter has reviewed the most important legislation in democratic South Africa, in addition to South Africa's key international human rights obligations. The chapter has also presented some mechanisms developed by the state to reinforce the implementation of human rights for the most vulnerable groups, including, most relevant to this research, women. The next chapter will move to informal justice, looking closely at the legal pluralism that shapes South African society.

CHAPTER 3

INFORMAL JUSTICE: A FAVOURABLE ALTERNATIVE?

Perfectly drafted legislation does not guarantee effective implementation. The limits of formal law[1] and the complex ethnic composition of South Africa drive many South Africans to seek alternative channels of justice. Consequently, multiple normative orders operate simultaneously, making South Africa a truly pluralist society.

This chapter will discuss the nature and operation of the informal justice systems (IJS), starting with some theoretical perspectives of legal pluralism. This will be followed by an analysis of official and living forms of customary law. The chapter will then track the role of customary law in institutionalising discrimination in South Africa's history, and locate customary law in the current formal legal system. This includes a discussion on the functions and power of traditional leaders. Section V will move to adjudication, exploring how customary laws are negotiated in state courts; also, the section will look at the process of adjudication in customary courts. The chapter will then question if the process of justice provided by both systems responds to the needs of the community, especially women. NGOs will be presented as a possible favourable alternative to dispute resolution.

Taking a pluralist approach to the law provides valuable insights for GBV analysis, causes and remedies. Manji argues that it is necessary to see GBV through both pluralist and feminist lenses, so as to shed light on the gendered power structure in different social settings.[2]

1 See Antony Allott, *The Limits of Law* (London: Butterworths, 1980).

2 Ambreena S Manji, 'Imagining women's 'legal world': towards a feminist theory of legal pluralism in Africa' (1999) 8 *Social Legal Studies*, 4, 439.

I A PLURALIST ANALYSIS

Moore questions the power of 'formal legal institutions'. She argues that those institutions can only exercise 'legitimate use of force' as they do not have 'effective coercion or effective inducement'.[3] Multiple theories of legal pluralism attempt to untangle the mélange of different normative orders in society. Chiba developed a 'three level structure of law' theory, in which he coined the terms 'legal postulate', 'official law', and 'unofficial law'.[4] While official law refers to statutory law, informal law embodies the rules that are created out of consistent public behaviour and consent, even if they are not codified by the state; the definition of legal postulate is 'the system of values and ideals' on which unofficial law is founded.[5] Another significant contribution to legal pluralism is Teubner's 'autopoietic theory' in which he suggests that we should revise our understanding of law 'from function to code', while defining legal pluralism as 'a multiplicity of diverse communicative processes that observe social action under the binary code of legal/illegal'.[6] The autopoietic theory also perceives the legal system to be in a constant state of development because of the dynamic nature of its different elements.[7]

Santos's theory of legal pluralism is based on the perception that a set of rules is 'never exercised in a pure exclusive form'; therefore, it is necessary to evaluate normative orders in relation to others.[8] Santos identifies international, statutory and customary law as the most important normative frameworks; they intermingle in the legal space, and have a particular impact on people, depending on each person's location in the legal sphere.[9] He further develops the idea of interlegality, which refers to the impact of a plural legal system on people's 'legal experiences, perception and consciousness' in their daily affairs.[10] Looking at legal

[3] Sally Falk Moore, *Law as Process, an Anthropological Approach*, 2nd edition (Oxford: James Curreys, 2000), p. 56.

[4] Masaji Chiba, *Legal Pluralism: Toward a General Theory through Japanese Legal Culture* (Tokyo: Tokai University Press, 1989), p. 138.

[5] Ibid., p. 139.

[6] Gunther Teubner, 'Autopoiesis in law and society: a rejoinder to Blankenburg' (1984) 18 *Law and Society Review* 2, 292.

[7] Ibid., 356.

[8] Boaventura De Sousa Santos, 'Law: a map of misreading: toward a postmodern conception of law' (1987) 14 *Journal of Law and Society*, 3, 283.

[9] Ibid.

[10] Ralph Michaels, 'Re-Statement of non-state law: the state, choice of law and the challenge from global legal pluralism' (2005) 51 *Wayne Law Review*, 1211.

pluralism from another angle, Fitzpatrick's concept of 'integral plurality' emphasises the impact of social norms on formal law; formal laws are developed 'in relation to a plurality of social forms'.[11] However, he explains that social forms are always contradictory to each other by nature[12] and that state law 'stands in opposition to and in asserted domination over social forms that support it'.[13]

To conclude, pluralist theories see law as a dynamic process, in which different normative orders are constantly competing. The 'social forms' affect formal laws, but are also subject to them. Legal experiences are determined by the choices that people make and the opportunities available to them. In essence, the doctrine of legal pluralism recognises the norm-making institutions parallel to formal law, and how they intermingle to determine legal choices and shape legal realities of people.

II INSTITUTIONS OF INFORMAL JUSTICE

Some structures of informal justice, such as customary law, predate formal law.[14] The demand for adjudication in IJS grew dramatically at the end of the 1970s with the emergence of 'embryonic professional groups offering institutionalised help for party negotiations away from the surveillance of the courts and legal profession'.[15]

Systems of informal justice vary in terms of principles, procedures and structures. First, the formality of IJS depends on the recognition of the system by state law, the accountability of rulers, the availability of case records, the appointment of judges and the procedures implemented for monitoring and supervision.[16] Second, IJS are shaped by the ideologies on which they are based, including, 'the perception of justice, conformity of outcomes with legal norms as opposed to ad hoc solutions, individual v. communal justice provision, different objectives of the IJS, the level of compliance with human rights standards'.[17] Third, the legitimacy of the IJS depends on the equal treatment of subjects, the

[11] Moore, *Law as Process*, p. 883.

[12] Peter Fitzpatrick, 'Law and societies' (1984) 22 *Osgoode Hall Law Journal*, 1, 116.

[13] Ibid.

[14] See Simon Roberts and Michael Palmers, *Dispute Processes: ADR and the Primary Forms of Decision-Making*, 2nd edition (Cambridge: Cambridge University Press, 2005), pp. 11–13.

[15] Ibid., p. 65.

[16] Danish Institute, *Informal Justice System*, p. 34; Roberts and Palmers, *Dispute Processes*, p. 10.

[17] Danish Institute, *Informal Justice System*, p. 34.

legitimacy of judges, 'the level of internal coherence', and the 'guarantees of impartiality'.[18]

A Nature of Informal Justice Systems

Informal justice systems can be a reflection of the 'failure on the part of governments to take adequate comprehensive action' in responding to people's needs.[19] Institutions of informal justice could also emerge out of necessity, when 'spontaneous law' evolves and operates in parallel to official law.[20] These structures develop to prevent conflict by providing 'a new social contract, between the state and citizens or between different groups of citizens'.[21] For example, Dagnino refers to internally displaced communities, migrants abroad and communities that moved from their original environments as examples of groups that create platforms of informal justice to settle their disputes.[22]

South Africa has witnessed the emergence of different forums of informal justice. For example, at the beginning of the twentieth century, when the first townships and squatter camps were set up, street committees started operating in the Cape Town area.[23] These committees prevailed throughout the twentieth century, mainly because the apartheid police neglected the rising crime in townships that was linked to marginalised youths.[24] Another forum of informal justice was developed between 1984 and 1986; people's courts operating as disciplinary committees, 'were used to refer to courts that prefigured a post-apartheid vision of local justice… These courts were subsequently discredited and from 1988 onwards' they were known as community courts.[25] In all cases, inaccessibility to formal justice due to a variety of barriers is the push factor for people to seek other channels for dispute resolution.[26]

[18] Ibid.

[19] Julie Stewart, 'Arenas of anguish – tracking multiple perpetuation trauma in HIV/AIDS and gender-based violence intersections' in Centre for Human Rights (ed.), *Gender Based Violence in Africa: Perspectives from the Continent* (Pretoria: University of Pretoria, 2010), p. 121.

[20] Francesca Dagnino, 'Expanding access to justice in Africa' in Ayesha Kadwani Dias and Gita Honwana Welch (eds.), *Justice for the Poor: Perspectives on Accelerating Access* (Oxford: Oxford University Press, 2009), p. 420.

[21] International Council, *When Legal Worlds Overlap*, p. 11.

[22] Dagnino, 'Expanding access to justice', p. 420.

[23] Penal Reform, *Access to Justice*, p. 40.

[24] Ibid., p. 45.

[25] Ibid., p. 20.

[26] Conceicao Osório, 'The justice delivery system: a crossroads', WLSA, July 2003, accessed 30 June 2018 at www.wlsa.org.mz/article-the-justice-delivery-system-a-crossroads/

B Customary Law

There is no longer, if there ever was, a 'pure' informal justice that is entirely separate from formal systems of law.[27] In some jurisdictions, customary law is recognised as part of the official legal system. However, the institutions that make and enforce customary laws are highly informal. The community develops customary norms, which are eventually legitimised by common practice. Disputes are resolved either by family members, community elders or traditional leaders (chiefs) under vastly different concepts of formal justice which is based on impartiality, informally as:

> traditional arbitrators are not strangers to the disputants and cannot be said to be disinterested parties, they cannot be regarded as impartial in the formal sense… Furthermore their personal knowledge of the community, the dispute, the nature of previous settlements, and the disputants – including personal histories and reputations – is vital to [the arbitrators'] ability to resolve the case and they are expected to use it in doing so. For the effective restoration of social harmony, it is important that there is genuine acceptance of any ruling.[28]

These factors, in addition to the characteristics of IJS discussed in the previous section, put customary law under the auspices of informal justice.

1 Official versus Living Customary Law, and Customs

Social perceptions and interpretations of customary law are widely debated in scholarship. Bennett locates customary law between rule and fact.[29] In the legal doctrine, rules are based on authoritative texts, while facts are proved by evidence.[30] Customary law is created when a common practice becomes widely accepted, replicated and ultimately transformed into 'fact'. Customary law could refer to either official customary law or living customary law, as defined by Himonga and Bosch.[31] Official customary law is a kind of 'legal positivism'; it is fairly

[27] Andrew Woolford and R S Ratner, *Informal Reckonings: Conflict Resolution in Mediation, Restorative Justice and Reparations* (London: Routledge-Cavendish, 2008), p. 37.

[28] Penal Reform, *Access to Justice*, p. 25.

[29] TW Bennett, *Customary Law in South Africa* (Juta, 2004), p. 44.

[30] Ibid.

[31] See Chuma Himonga and Craig Bosch, 'The application of African customary law under the Constitution of South Africa: problems solved or just beginning?' (2000) 117 *South African Law Journal* 306. Also see Alice K Armstrong, *Struggling over Scarce Resources: Women and Maintenance in Southern Africa* (Harare: University of Zimbabwe Publications, 1992), pp. 31–34.

easy to ascertain because it can be found in 'statutes and decisions of the courts, and also because it 'can be enforced by state law enforcement machinery'.[32] On the other hand, norms of living customary law are dynamic and subject to constant change as they are created and developed from common practices;[33] therefore living customary law is neither known nor experienced by the outsider.[34] Oomen writes:

> Lessons offered by customary law studies are, again, pertinent: culture cannot be understood outside of its context of social interaction and power relations, and the best that researchers can do is to map out this whole fluctuating landscape... this can only be done by taking a non-essentialist approach where 'law is whatever people identify and treat through their social practices as law'.[35]

Customary laws often overlap with customs as the line between them is quite thinly drawn. Both customary norms and mere customs are behaviours widely exercised by the community.[36] Although violations of both are criticised, repercussions for the violator are different. On the one hand, violating a custom may upset members of the community, but it does not bear serious consequences for the violator. On the other hand, the pressure to abide by customary law is enormous and the punishments for violators are severe. This is because group members usually perceive customary law as binding and the fact that a few members of the group reject it does not undermine its legitimacy.[37]

2 *Customary Law and Formal Law: Procedure and Structure*

Differences between the structures and procedures of customary law and common law are flagrant, as they are primarily based on different ideologies. Kamau explains that the purpose of dispute resolution in customary law is the 'restoration of harmony in the community with emphasis on reciprocal obligations and duties'.[38] Customary trials, therefore, aim to compensate victims, prevent further crime and reintegrate both

[32] Himonga and Bosch, 'The application of African customary law', 329.

[33] Barbara Oomen, *Chiefs in South Africa: Law, Power and Culture in the Post-Apartheid Era* (USA: Palgrave 2005), p. 201.

[34] Bennett as quoted in Werner Menski, *Comparative Law in a Global Context: the Legal Systems of Asia and Africa* (Platinum, 2000), p. 422.

[35] Oomen, *Chiefs in South Africa*, p. 31.

[36] Himonga and Bosch, 'The application of African customary law', 321.

[37] Ibid.

[38] Winifred Kamau, 'Law, culture and dispute resolution: prospects for alternative dispute resolution in Africa (2009) 15 *East African Journal of Peace and Human Rights*, 2, 340.

victim and offender into the community.[39] On the other hand, formal law emphasises the 'vindication of individual's rights'.[40] In customary law, for which Elias uses the term 'African law', there is no distinction between civil and criminal offences. Serious crimes such as murder and theft 'are generally treated as matters for private redress by the wronged party or group rather than by the state as the custodian of public safety and welfare'.[41] Thus, in customary law, fines and compensation are directed to the aggrieved party, whereas in formal law, fines imposed by the courts are paid to the state.[42] In terms of procedure, customary trials provide a platform for members of the community to discuss matters of custom and customary law; therefore, both parties in the dispute and their supporters are involved in the decision-making process, and the judgments are based on 'compromise rather than strict rules of law'.[43]

Both systems have advantages and disadvantages that shape people's preferences. Litigation is cheaper in customary tribunals than in formal courts;[44] customary courts are more accessible to marginalised communities; traditional court trials are conducted in languages familiar to the community; and the administration of justice is faster in customary courts because there is no case backlog.[45] Customary law is usually preferred by poor communities because the compensation is directed to the injured party rather than the state.[46] Perhaps the most important reason for the preference of informal justice is that it gets to the '"real" underlying cause of the problem(s)'.[47] However, mere reliance on customary law is dangerous; because adjudicators are rarely held accountable, which may lead to serious human rights violations.[48] In addition, decisions made in traditional courts are not usually monitored or recorded.[49] Most important for this research, customary systems tend to favour males and

[39] Ewa Wojkowska, *Doing Justice: How Informal Justice System Can Contribute*, research report (Oslo: United Nations Development Programme, 2006), p. 17.

[40] Kamau 'Law, culture and dispute resolution', 340.

[41] Taslim Olawale Elias, *The Nature of African Customary Law* (Manchester: Manchester University Press, 1956), p. 110.

[42] Minneh Kane et al., *Reassessing Customary Law Systems as a Vehicle for Providing Equitable Justice for the Poor*, research paper (New Frontiers of Social Policy, Arusha, December 2005), p. 12.

[43] Penal Reform, *Access to Justice*, p. 15.

[44] Kane et al. *Reassessing Customary Law*, p. 9. For further comparison between formal and informal justice systems see Woolford and Ratner, *Informal Reckonings*, pp. 19–39.

[45] Kane et al., *Reassessing Customary Law*, p. 9; Wojkowska, *Doing Justice*, p. 17.

[46] Kane et al., *Reassessing Customary Law*, pp. 10–11; Wojkowska, *Doing Justice*, p. 17.

[47] Roberts and Palmers, *Dispute Processes*, p. 10.

[48] Kane et al., *Reassessing Customary Law*, p. 13; Wojkowska, *Doing Justice*, pp. 22, 23. Kane et al., *Reassessing Customary Law*, p. 11; Wojkowska, *Doing Justice*, pp. 22, 23.

[49] Kane et al., *Reassessing Customary Law*, p. 12.

'stack the system against youths, women, the poor, ethnic minorities and groups who were traditionally discriminated against'.[50]

III CUSTOMARY LAW IN THE HISTORY OF SOUTH AFRICA

A brief overview of South Africa's history shows the pluralist nature of South African society that has existed for centuries. Unsurprisingly, gender bias has been persistent.

A Settlement and Hegemony

Historically, South Africa was a tempting conquest as it connected European colonial powers to their colonies in Asia.[51] Dutch people were the first European settlers in the seventeenth century, followed by the British who conquered the Cape in 1795.[52] This led to a period of conflict between two colonial powers, the British and the Boers (the descendants of the Dutch). The final battle was the Second Anglo-Boer war in 1899 that lasted for three years and ended with the defeat of Boer troops and the union of South Africa under British rule.[53] A unity government was formed,[54] which decided to keep the Roman Dutch legal system. However, English legal practice has a strong influence on the formation of contemporary South African law. This includes the influence of doctrine, precedent, the organisation of courts and judicial procedures as well as the formation of statute and judgment.[55]

B Segregation and Separation

Racial and ethnic divisions have persisted for centuries, reinforcing the pluralist nature of South African law and society. Racial segregation started in early colonial history when the Dutch settlers determined the legal status of people based on their race, imposing oppressive laws on the indigenous population, known as 'natives'.[56] In the following few

[50] Kane et al., *Reassessing Customary Law*, p. 13; Wojkowska, *Doing Justice*, p. 20.

[51] Robert Ross, *A Concise History of South Africa* (Cambridge: Cambridge University Press, 1999), p. 22.

[52] Ibid. p. 35.

[53] The Peace of Vereeniging Treaty (Pretoria 31 May 1902) (South Africa).

[54] Nigel Worden, *The Making of Modern South Africa: Conquest, Apartheid, Democracy* (Oxford: Blackwell, 2007), p. 36.

[55] Martin Chanock, *The Making of South African Legal Culture 1902–1936* (Cambridge: Cambridge University Press, 2001), p. 32.

[56] Worden, *The Making of Modern South Africa*, p. 75.

decades leading to apartheid in 1948, rules and policies were gradually enforced to restrict the movement and activity of the natives.[57]

1 *Separate Laws*

The British colonised many countries in Africa. Due to the tribal nature of African societies, the dilemma of regulating multiple legal systems led the colonial powers to impose the 'indirect rule' system, which was initially developed and strongly advocated by Fredrick Lugard in Nigeria.[58] Indirect rule promoted the authority of chiefs and traditional leaders, as long as peace was maintained, and designed a chain of command that had the governor general as the final arbiter.[59] The government also appointed some traditional leaders in the colonial administration,[60] in an attempt to control the affairs of the indigenous communities.[61]

Indirect rule was applied in South Africa from the 1850s.[62] Initially, the colonial powers rejected the codification of customary law, because it was regarded as inferior to 'modern law'.[63] In 1927, the government passed the Native Administration Act, which recognised the authority of traditional leaders over the indigenous populations.[64] The Act gave discretion to 'the courts of Native Commissioners in all suits or proceedings between Natives involving questions of customs'.[65] Traditional courts were allowed to resolve civil matters and try some non-serious criminal offences. However, they were not allowed to rule on serious crimes such as 'treason, sedition, murder, culpable homicide, rape, arson, robbery'.[66]

The Native Administration Act did not rejuvenate African traditions, but it reaffirmed racial segregation of law, land and society.[67] It therefore reinforced the oppression of the native population under

[57] For details and examples, see ibid., pp. 76–82.
[58] See Nkiru Uwechia Nzegwu, *Family Matters: Feminist Concepts in African Philosophy of Culture* (New York: State University of New York Press, 2006), pp. 63–89.
[59] See Toyin Falola, *Colonialism and Violence in Nigeria* (Bloomington and Indianapolis: Indiana University Press, 2009).
[60] Jason C Myers, *Indirect Rule in South Africa: Tradition, Modernity and the Costuming of Political Power* (New York: University of Rochester Press, 2008), p. 1.
[61] J C Bekker et al. (eds.), *Introduction to Legal Pluralism in South Africa*, 2nd edition (Durban: LexisNexis Butterworths, 2006), p. 119.
[62] Myers, *Indirect Rule in South Africa*, p. 1.
[63] Chanock, *The Making of South African Legal Culture*, p. 273.
[64] Bekker et al., *Legal Pluralism*, p. 120.
[65] Native (Black) Administration Act No 38 of 1927 (South Africa), s 11(1).
[66] South African Law Commission, *Harmonisation of the Common Law and Indigenous Law: Traditional Courts and the Judicial Function of Traditional Leaders* (Discussion Paper 82, 1999), p. 27.
[67] Ibid., p. 10.

a localised system. This arrangement was favourable to the colonial administration because they did not have to interact with the natives and yet they could control native affairs. This was because the colonial government had the right to appoint and relegate traditional leaders,[68] while the natives had no influence on colonial institutions.[69] Indirect rule also meant that the chiefs who did not serve the interest of the apartheid government were usually expelled.[70] The Native Administration Act was not well received by the black population since it 'increased the power of appointed chiefs at the expense of elected leaders'.[71]

2 *Separate Lives: Apartheid*

In 1948, the Herenigade Nasionale Party (HNP) came to power in South Africa, using the system of apartheid as a means to unite white voters.[72] Apartheid was enforced by a series of Acts that regulated the public and private affairs of people, based on the principle of racial segregation.[73] The most important statutes included: the Immorality Amendment Act,[74] which prohibited Europeans from having sexual intercourse with people of other races; the Prohibition of Mixed Marriages Act;[75] the Bantu Education Act,[76] which segregated educational facilities based on race; the Reservation of Separate Amenities Act,[77] which segregated public facilities; and a series of other Acts restricting the economic activities of the natives and prohibiting strikes.[78] Perhaps the most important was the Black Authorities Act of 1951,[79] which divided land

[68] Thandabantu Nhlapo, 'Indigenous law and gender in South Africa: taking human rights and cultural diversity seriously' (1995) 13 *Third World Legal Studies*, 50.

[69] Worden, *The Making of Modern South Africa*, p. 109.

[70] Prince Mashele, 'Traditional leadership in South Africa's new democracy' (2004) 31 *Review of African Political Economy*, 100, 349.

[71] Laurence Boulle, *South Africa and the Consociational Option: A Constitutional Analysis* (Johannesburg: Juta, 1984), p. 90.

[72] Worden, *The Making of Modern South Africa*, p. 99.

[73] John C Mubangizi, *The Protection of Human Rights in South Africa: A Legal and Practical Guide* (Juta, 2004), p. 38.

[74] Immorality Amendment Act No 5 of 1927 (South Africa). The Act enacted in 1927 prohibited extra-marital sex between white and black people, but in 1950 it was amended to fully prohibit sexual intercourse between Europeans and non-Europeans.

[75] Prohibition of Mixed Marriages Act No 55 of 1949 (South Africa).

[76] Bantu Education Act No 47 of 1953 (South Africa).

[77] Reservation of Separate Amenities Act No 49 of 1953 (South Africa).

[78] See Native Building Workers Act No 27 of 1951 (South Africa), Native Labour (Settlement of Disputes) Act No 48 of 1953 (South Africa) and Industrial Conciliation Act No 28 of 1956 (South Africa).

[79] Black (Bantu) Authorities Act No 68 of 1951 (South Africa).

among the different racial groups and appointed native leaders to rule the territories assigned to the black population. The Act was intended to gradually create independent legal jurisdictions based on ethnicities.

Under apartheid, all offenders of serious crimes were tried under formal law, but the application of the law was discriminatory. Courts were perpetuating racial favouritism, giving black people the most severe punishments, as opposed to minor punishments given to Europeans.[80] Some laws were exclusively designed to control black people, such as the pass offences law, which required them to carry identity books when they left their designated areas.[81] The police were equally biased and only engaged with black people when they were trespassers or pass offenders.[82]

C Gender in the History of South African Law

1 Gender Under Customary Law

Gender stratification is a common feature of the customary legal systems. Burman noted the example of Sesotho law, where men had full authority over extended family members and women were considered perpetual minors.[83] The gendered division of labour entitled men to control economic resources, most importantly, cattle. The legal system was designed to perpetuate gender inequalities by stressing the priority of the homestead, at the expense of individual freedoms.[84]

The patriarchal nature of customary systems was sustained by the colonial powers that supported chiefs in return for their loyalty. Recognition and support of the colonial administration granted traditional leaders the legitimacy to enforce gender-biased customary norms. Therefore, women were fighting both a patriarchal discriminatory system and a colonial one.[85] Chanock wrote:

> The state's production of a customary law was a fundamental and powerful intervention in the way in which African life could and would develop under white rule. African tribal authorities and family heads

[80] Raymond Suttner, 'The ideological role of the judiciary in South Africa' in John Hund (ed.), *Law and Justice in South Africa* (Rondebosch: Centre for Intergroup Studies, 1988), p. 89.

[81] Ibid., p. 90.

[82] Ibid.

[83] Sandra Burman, 'Fight a two-pronged attack: the changing legal status of women in Cape-ruled Basutoland, 1872–1884' in Cherryl Walker (ed.), *Women and Gender in Southern Africa to 1945* (Cape Town and London: David Philip Publisher, 1990), p. 55.

[84] Ibid., p. 55.

[85] See Oyeronke Oyewumi, *The Invention of Women: Making an African Sense of Western Gender Discourses* (Minneapolis and London: University of Minnesota Press, 1997).

> in the countries around South Africa, and inside it, needed the weight of state power to enforce the customary family law. Without this power the practices of young men and women, of divorcees and widows, all of whom struggled against aspects of the maintained patriarchy, would be clearly visible as custom.[86]

Despite their inferior status, Weir warned about generalisations regarding the subordination of women in pre-colonial South Africa. She argued that women's contributions were not codified because writers and narrators of history were predominantly male, who preferred to ignore women's positive roles.[87] She specifically looked at the role of women in the history of Kwazulu-Natal (KZN), showing that they were active members in society. Women had undertaken leadership initiatives, sometimes military but 'more often economic and religious'.[88] Living customary law was also useful for women at times. Based on some empirical studies conducted during colonial and apartheid South Africa, Bennett shows that traditional leaders were more likely to give sympathetic hearings to women because they were more responsive to social and cultural developments than the codified system of official customary law.[89]

The early decades of the twentieth century witnessed the mobilisation of women who participated in political movements.[90] Gasa mentioned some of their most impressive contributions, such as the anti-pass protest in Bloemfontein in 1894 and others in 1913.[91] Women's mobilisation for political causes built the foundation for the South African women's movement that would become an essential force in the resistance movement against apartheid, and remains active in South Africa today.

86 Martin Chanock, 'Law, state and culture: thinking about "customary law" after apartheid' (1991) *Acta Juridica*, 55.

87 Jennifer Weir, 'Chiefly women and women's leadership in pre-colonial Southern Africa' in Nomboniso Gasa (ed.), *Women in Southern African History: They Remove Boulders and Cross Rivers* (Cape Town: Human Science Research Council, 2007), p. 5. Also see Oyewumi, *The Invention of Women*, pp. 121–122 and 146–148.

88 Weir, 'Chiefly women', p. 4. For narratives on Igbo women in Nigeria during colonial rule see Nzegwu, *Family Matters*, pp. 89–102.

89 T W Bennett, *Human Rights and African Customary Law under the South African Constitution* (Cape Town: Juta, 1995), p. 85.

90 Nomboniso Gasa, 'Let them build more goals' in Gasa N (ed.), *Women in Southern African History: They Remove Boulders and Cross Rivers* (Cape Town: Human Science Research Council, 2007), p. 29.

91 Ibid. pp. 133–139.

2 *Gender in the Roman Dutch Law*

The impediments faced by African women during apartheid were a reflection of a sexist society that affected all women negatively, albeit differently. Just like their native counterparts, white women were subjected to discriminatory provisions under Roman Dutch law, which became the common law of the land. Roman Dutch law was based on conservative ideologies regulating gender roles and duties. In marriage, white women were considered legal minors.[92] The law did not only give a husband guardianship over the spouse's property, but also over their person.[93] The husband was obliged to financially support his wife in return for her obedience, which 'presumably included yielding to his sexual demands' as the definition of marriage included the 'lawful use of each other's bodies'.[94] Citing different cases in the 1970s, Kaganas and Murray showed that marital rape was not punished under Roman Dutch Law, and that judges were reluctant to label sexual acts between a husband and wife as rape. They therefore sentenced perpetrators of marital rape based on indirect assault, a lesser charge.[95]

IV CUSTOMARY LAW IN CONTEMPORARY SOUTH AFRICA

A Customary Law in the Constitution

Customary law 'de facto ... governs the domestic affairs of three quarters of the South African population'.[96] It is therefore fundamental for the human rights discourse in South Africa to guarantee cultural rights and recognise customary law and traditional leaders in the Constitution.

The Constitution honours the right to culture in section 31, which states that 'every person shall have the right to use the language and to participate in the cultural life of his or her choice'.[97] Both customary law and the rule of traditional leaders are recognised in section 211 of the Constitution. Courts are expected to 'apply customary law when that law is applicable, subject to the Constitution and any legislation that

[92] Chanock, *The Making of South African Legal Culture*, p. 201.

[93] Felicity Kaganas and Christina Murray, 'Rape in marriage – conjugal right or criminal wrong' (1983) *Acta Juridica*, 126.

[94] Ibid.

[95] Ibid., 125.

[96] T W Bennett, 'The equality clause and customary law' (1994) 10 *South African Journal on Human Rights*, 1, 122.

[97] Constitution, s. 31.

specifically deals with customary law'.[98] Some customary matters are addressed in specific legal instruments, such as customary marriages,[99] or the rule of traditional leaders, which is regulated by multiple Acts that will be discussed shortly. Himonga and Bosch argue that section 31 and section 211 taken together indicate that the Constitution endorses 'living customary law'. They write:

> At the very least, since the right to culture is conferred on individuals and on cultural groups, it is the law generated by the cultural communities that is recognised by the Constitution. It is not the law created by the state and its institutions, or stated by academics whose writings are based on official records... the right to culture implies the entrenchment of the living customary law as opposed to official customary law.[100]

B Traditional Leadership

Even though traditional leaders enjoy legitimacy in their community, chieftaincy is highly criticised in law and politics; this was evident in the conflict between the post-apartheid government and chiefs during the Constitution drafting process. Recovering from decades of institutionalised discrimination, there was a general consensus between the parties drafting the Constitution of the importance of establishing a modern nation-state that adopted human rights principles. Particular emphasis on the right to 'equality before the law' contradicted the premises of chieftaincy that 'suggested both hereditary and patriarchal privilege'.[101] In addition, chiefs assume the three roles of the government,[102] which clearly contradicts the premise of the modern nation-state that is based on the separation of powers. It was essential to regulate the position and operations of traditional leaders, still a reality in South African legal culture.

1 Law Regulating Traditional Leadership

The appointment of traditional leadership is regulated by a series of Acts that are occasionally amended to keep up with social and political developments.[103] The National House of Traditional Leaders was

[98] Constitution, s. 211 (3).
[99] Recognition of Customary Marriages Act.
[100] Himonga and Bosch, 'The application of African customary law', 331.
[101] Myers, *Indirect Rule in South Africa*, p. 98.
[102] Bennett, *Customary Law*, p. 125.
[103] This includes Council of Traditional Leaders Act No 10 of 1997 (South Africa), which was amended by the Council of Traditional Leaders Amendment Act No 85 of 1998 (South Africa). Also see National House of Traditional Leaders Amendment Act No 20 of 2000 (South Africa)

founded in 1997 as the National Council of Traditional Leaders and renamed in 1998[104] with the mission of representing 'the aspirations of traditional communities by playing a meaningful role in cooperative governance'.[105] The Governance Framework Act, which was passed in 2003, recognises the gender bias inherent in customary norms; therefore, it promotes the participation of women at all levels of governance (local, provincial and national). For example, traditional communities must establish a council to oversee customary affairs, according to provincial legislation; and one-third of the members must be female.[106] However, the Act also permits deviation from this rule, if qualified female candidates are not available.[107]

Several governmental bodies and Acts regulate customary matters. The National House of Traditional Leaders Act, passed in 2009, regulates the appointment of chiefs and monitors their conduct.[108] The Commission of Traditional Leadership Disputes and Claims identifies rightful leaders and resolves disputes regarding chieftaincy.[109] The Commission is also responsible for resolving disputes about customary law or customs within a community or between two communities.[110] The National Council of Traditional Leaders is divided into the National House and provincial houses, in which the latter have more power and authority. Provincial houses can evaluate any parliamentary bill on customary law or traditional leadership and provide recommendations; however, consideration of their contribution is at the legislature's discretion.[111] Also, local houses of traditional leaders work with government agencies in local communities, focusing on customary law matters, but also participating in development initiatives for the community.[112]

and Traditional Leadership and Governance Framework Amendment Act No 41 of 2003 (South Africa) (hereinafter, Governance Framework Act).

[104] National House of Traditional Leaders, Budget Review Report 2007–2008, accessed 20 July 2018 at http://pmg-assets.s3-website-eu-west-1.amazonaws.com/docs/080311nhtl.htm

[105] Ibid.

[106] Governance Framework Act, s. 3(2)(a).

[107] Ibid., s. 3(2)(d).

[108] National House of Traditional Leaders Act No 22 of 2009.

[109] South African Government website, Commission on Traditional Leadership Disputes and Claims Announcement, accessed 20 July 2018 at www.gov.za/commission-traditional-leadership-disputes-and-claims-announcement

[110] Governance Framework Act, s. 21.

[111] Bennett, *Customary Law*, p. 118.

[112] South African Government website, Traditional leadership, accessed 20 July 2018 at www.gov.za/about-government/government-system/traditional-leadership

2 The Right of Traditional Leaders to Adjudicate

Pursuant to the Governance Framework Act, 'national government or a provincial government, as the case may be, may, through legislative or other measures, provide a role for traditional councils or 10 traditional leaders in respect of … administration of justice'.[113] However, the government agency allocating the role must ensure that both the allocation and the administration of the role[114] are consistent with the Constitution. Until 2005, the Native Administration Act was enforced, giving chiefs power to hear and try cases, although many of its provisions have since been amended or repealed as they were found to be unconstitutional. Under the Act, customary courts only had jurisdiction 'to hear and determine civil claims arising out of Black law and custom' brought before them 'by Blacks against Blacks resident within [their] area of jurisdiction'.[115]

The resurgence of a Traditional Courts Bill[116] in 2012 that was dismissed by Parliament in 2008 was the latest attempt to reinstate the rule of traditional leadership. The 2008 bill was widely criticised for giving traditional leaders immense power. The bill failed to:

> recognise customary dispute-resolution processes at the local levels where the system works best and provides no role for the community councils, which are the bedrock of the system. Instead it vests power exclusively in 'senior traditional leaders' as presiding officers… [It] provided traditional leaders with the unilateral power to create and enforce customary law within the bounded jurisdictional areas it confirms. Instead of focussing on what unites people, it reinforced the constructs of ethnic difference and insider-outsider status that can only further divisions in our country.[117]

Furthermore, the bill would have, 're-imposed' the tribal identities prevalent during apartheid, force 18 million South Africans to fall

[113] Governance Framework Act, s. 20.

[114] Ibid., ss. 20(2)(c) and 20(3).

[115] South African Law Commission, Harmonisation of the Common Law and the Indigenous Law: The Application of Customary law: Conflict of personal Laws (Issue paper 4 1996), para. 3.9.

[116] The Republic of South Africa Traditional Courts Bill 2008 (published in the Government Gazette No 30902 of 27 March 2008) (hereinafter, Traditional Courts Bill).

[117] Aninka Claassens, 'What's wrong with the Traditional Courts Bill', Mail & Guardian, 2 June 2008, accessed 30 June 2018 at www.mg.co.za/article/2008-06-02-whats-wrong-with-the-traditional-courts-bill

under a 'second-class justice system', and exclude women from shaping and developing customary laws.[118]

The bill was proposed to Parliament again in 2012, calling for an expansion of the role of traditional courts. According to the Bill, traditional courts would be able to resolve civil and some criminal disputes arising out of customary law.[119] These do not include constitutional matters, divorce, marriage, custody of minor children and interpretation of a will, among others.[120] The bill specifies a ceiling to the sentences that traditional courts would be able to impose.[121] Outrage in the South African civil society and human rights organisations erupted over this bill as it jeopardised the human rights of vulnerable groups. This led to the formation of the Alliance for Rural Democracy, a network of NGOs aiming to promote the voice of the people they serve in rural communities.[122] Furthermore, women specifically opposed the bill, contending that 'it would legalise and entrench current discrimination'.[123] Other minority groups would have been seriously harmed by the provisions of the bill, such as the LGBT community.[124] Eventually, in 2014 the bill was dismissed from consideration in parliament – an event perceived as a great victory for both rural women and civil society.[125]

In 2016, an improved and updated version of the bill was reintroduced. The Deputy Justice Minister argued that some kind of regulation for customary adjudication is necessary because it is a fact, and not a choice. While he acknowledged that the updated version will not please everyone, he hoped that it would at least be satisfactory.[126]

118 Sithuthukile Mkhize, 'A victory for the rights of women in rural South Africa', Open Society Foundations, 7 May 2014, accessed 30 June 2018 at www.opensocietyfoundations.org/voices/victory-rights-women-rural-south-africa

119 Traditional Courts Bill, s. 5(1).

120 Ibid., s. 5(2).

121 Ibid., s. 10.

122 'Twists and turns in Traditional Courts Bill proceedings', Sonke Gender Justice, 1 November 2012, accessed 30 June 2018 at www.genderjustice.org.za/article/sordid-twist-to-traditional-courts-bill-proceedings/

123 Alliance for Rural Democracy, 'Traditional courts bill is dead!', Land and Accountability Research Centre, 21 February 2014, accessed 30 June 2018 at www.customcontested.co.za/traditional-courts-bill-dead/

124 Graeme Reid, 'The traditional courts bill threatens LGBT South Africans', Human Rights Watch, 29 May 2012, accessed 30 June 2018 at www.hrw.org/news/2012/05/29/traditional-courts-bill-threatens-lgbt-south-africans

125 Mkhize, 'A victory for the rights of women'.

126 Thulani Gqirana, 'New traditional courts bill "everyone can live with"', News24, 23 January 2017, accessed 30 June 2018 at www.news24.com/SouthAfrica/News/new-traditional-courts-bill-everyone-can-live-with-20170123

Some improvements in the bill included reaffirming voluntarism to customary law adjudication. The bill also gave women and other vulnerable groups the right to fully participate before the courts;[127] however, women may choose to refrain.[128] The bill, therefore, addressed some of the concerns, but hung on to other provisions such as not allowing official legal representation to act in such capacity before the court. Griffin argues that this is neither negative nor unorthodox. Pursuant to the bill, litigants can receive help from anyone in court; however, legal practitioners are not to act in their official capacity so as to maintain these courts as 'speedy, cheap and accessible' options for people. He adds that, 'the nature of this provision is not new in South African law, as both the Small Claims Court and Commission for Conciliation, Mediation and Arbitration… hearings do not allow for legal representation'.[129]

It has taken ten years to draft the bill and the delay is frustrating all parties involved. The opt-out clause in the revised bill was the subject matter of unpleasant debate, and a source of grievance among traditional leaders, who called it 'a carry-over of colonial systems'.[130] Whether agreement can be reached remains to be seen. The debates around this bill demonstrate the conflict between formal and customary justice. This conflict is prevalent in court proceedings, as will be discussed in the following section.

V COURTING CUSTOMARY LAW

The Constitution directs courts to apply customary law in relevant cases. The South African Law Commission suggests guidelines for this application. First, both parties to the conflict must agree on the set of customary laws to be enforced, which is usually the set of laws prevalent in the resident area of either party.[131] If the parties cannot agree, the

[127] Sindiso Mnisi Weeks, 'South Africa's Traditional Courts Bill 2.0: improved but still flawed', The Conversation, 4 April 2017, accessed 30 June 2018 at www.theconversation.com/south-africas-traditional-courts-bill-2-0-improved-but-still-flawed-74997

[128] Gqirana, 'New traditional courts bill'.

[129] Richard Griffin 'The Traditional Courts Bill: Are they getting it right?', Helen Suzman Foundation, 14 February 2017, accessed 30 June 2018 at www.hsf.org.za/publications/hsf-briefs/the-traditional-courts-bill-are-they-getting-it-right

[130] Marianne Merten, 'Parliament: Opt-out, Traditional Courts Bill supporters' most hated clause', Daily Maverick, 19 March 2018, accessed 30 June 2018 at www.dailymaverick.co.za/article/2018-03-19-parliament-opt-out-traditional-courts-bill-supporters-most-hated-clause/#.WzhCmNIzbIU

[131] South African Law Commission, *Harmonisation of the Common Law*, p. 85.

Court must investigate the most appropriate customary law system,[132] based on criteria such as the context of the case or the cultural background of the parties.[133] As a last resort, the court should apply the defendant's customary law system.[134] This is, however, quite challenging to balance while upholding human rights.

The boundaries between gender, customary law and formal law have been tested in the Constitutional Court on several occasions. After reviewing multiple cases heard by South African courts, Nhalpo concludes that courts consider living rather than official customary law. However, the difficulty remains within courts to untangle customary law and bring it in line with the Bill of Rights.[135]

A South African Courts Engaging with Customary Law

1 Customary Law Regulating Personal Affairs

In S v. *Mvamvu*,[136] the Supreme Court of Appeals ruled on the disagreement between a man and a woman about their marital status. The complainant argued that according to customary law, they were divorced and therefore, she was a victim of rape. The accused believed that they were still married, also based on customary law, which gave him the right to sex on demand. He was convicted of rape by the magistrate court, but was given a reduced sentence of five years.[137] The leniency was based on the defendant's perception that he was having sex with his wife.[138] The sentence was appealed in the Supreme Court, which replaced it with a harsher one.

This case demonstrates how matters of customary law are perceived and practised by the community. The accused and the complainant had known each other since childhood and had entered into a customary marriage in 1995, when the complainant was 15. Four years later, they had marital problems and the complainant obtained an interdict against the accused. The complainant also moved into her brother's house and was permitted by the family of the accused to remove her traditional

[132] Ibid., p. 30.

[133] Bekker et al. *Legal Pluralism*, p. 25.

[134] South African Law Commission, *Harmonisation of the Common Law*, p. 86.

[135] Thandabantu Nhlapo, 'Customary law in post-apartheid South Africa: The vexed question of cultural diversity, women's rights, "living law", and appropriate law reform' (2014) New York Law Review, accessed 20 July 2018 at www.nylslawreview.com/wp-content/uploads/sites/16/2014/11/Nhlapo.pdf

[136] S v. *Mvamvu* [2005] 1 All SA 435 (SCA) (hereinafter *Mvamvu* case).

[137] Criminal Law Amendment Act No 105 of 1997 (South Africa), s. 51(1) and (3)(a).

[138] *Mvamvu* case, para. 10.

wedding attire – a customary sign of separation. On the other hand, the accused believed that they were still married because, according to customary law, divorce is not finalised until family members attempt to reconcile the partners, and also until lobola is returned; none of these conditions were fulfilled.[139] After the interdict was issued against the accused, he abducted the complainant for three days, during which he raped her six times. Two weeks later, when the accused was wanted for rape, he showed up at the complainant's residence and raped her again.[140]

In his mind, based on customary law that governs family affairs, the accused was acting on his rights. For the complainant, who had obviously resorted to formal law to obtain an interdict, the marriage was clearly over. In both scenarios, however, there was an act of sexual violence involved, rape, which should not be subject to customary law. This was the basis on which the Supreme Court imposed a harsher sentence, but refrained from imposing the maximum sentence. Echoing the Magistrate Court, the Supreme Court held that the actions of the accused, although 'a consequence of male chauvinism' were not meant to harm the complainant, but were merely an expression of his desire to reconcile the marriage.[141] This was based on the testimony of Reverend Ngesi, an expert witness on their customary practices. The court stated:

> It is clear from his evidence (Reverend Ngesi) that at the time of the incidents the accused honestly (albeit entirely misguidedly) believed that he had some 'right' to conjugal benefits. His actions, though totally unacceptable in law, might well be (albeit only to a limited extent) explicable given his background… which was not completely strange to the complainant… His actions were shaped and moulded by the norms, beliefs and customary practices by which he lived his life.[142]

In this case, the court adopted a gender-biased stance. Criticising the judgment, Terblanche argued that the Court had overemphasised the importance of customary norms when there was a clear violation of the complainant's rights; a domestic violence interdict was issued against the accused before the first rape incident and the police were searching for him before the second rape incident. These two facts indicate that the accused was fully aware of the violations before he had

[139] Ibid., para. 4.
[140] Ibid., para. 5.
[141] Ibid., para. 16.
[142] Ibid.

committed them.[143] Furthermore, the court gave significant weight to the intention of the accused to win his wife back. Considering personal intentions may open the space for men to abuse customary law so as to maintain the gender power dynamic.

2 *Primogeniture and Female Leadership*

Two of the most common grievances experienced by women living under customary law surround the right to inheritance and the ability to rule, both of which have been heard by courts in South Africa. *Bhe and Others* v. *Khayelitsha Magistrate* and *Shibi* v. *Sithole and Others*[144] were jointly heard by the Constitutional Court. The cases sought the confirmation of orders of constitutional invalidity made by two High Courts. With both cases, the South African Human Rights Commission and the Women's Legal Trust brought forward a class action on behalf of all women and girls prevented from inheritance, with the CGE acting as *amicus curiae*. The court condemned customary practices that are contrary to the Constitution and recognised the 'hardship which this caused for women and children', stressing that developments of customary law that are congruent with the Constitution should be supported.[145] Subsequently, relevant sections of the Black Administration Act and the Intestate Succession Act were repealed[146] and a new interim regime regulating the intestate succession for black estates was ordered. This case demonstrates the importance of Article 5 of CEDAW, which directs states to 'modify the social and cultural patterns' that promote prejudice and discrimination against women.

Shilubana v. *Nwamitwa*[147] highlights the importance of the *amici* contributions to the court – a common strategy used for impact litigation, to be analysed in Chapter 5. Nongovernmental organisations, acting as *amici*, argued for the development of customary law to meet the constitutional rights of women. The applicant Ms Shilubuna was the daughter of a chief who died in 1968 without a male heir. Since customary law restricted chieftaincy to males, the position was passed to the chief's brother. In 1996–1997, inspired by the gender equality clause in the Constitution, the Council of Traditional Authorities in

143 Stephan Terblanche, 'Case reviews; sentencing' (2005) 18 *South African Journal of Criminal Justice*, 3, 394.

144 *Bhe and Others* v. *Khayelitsha Magistrate* [2005] (1) BCLR 1 (CC).

145 Curran and Bonthuys, 'Customary law', p. 628.

146 Black Administration Act 38 of 1927; Intestate Succession Act No 81 of 1987 (South Africa).

147 *Shilubana and Others* v. *Nwamitwa* [2009] (9) BCLR 914 (CC).

the community decided that Ms Shilubana would succeed her uncle. After the death of Ms Shilubana's uncle, her cousin legally challenged her to chieftaincy, arguing that as the eldest son of the last chief, he was the legitimate successor. Both the High Court and the Supreme Court of Appeals ruled in his favour. The case was then taken to the Constitutional Court, where the CGE, National Movement of Rural Women and the Congress of Traditional Leaders acted as *amici*. The *amici* supporting the claimant argued that the court must support the community's initiative to develop customary law when the said changes honour the constitutional principle of non-discrimination[148] and aim to remedy past discrimination.[149] On the other hand, the Congress of Traditional Leaders contended that the development of customary law should be supported by the whole community and not by a privileged few, questioning the legitimacy of the Council of Traditional Authorities who supported Shilubana.[150] In its consideration of the merits, the Court encouraged local communities to develop their customary laws in line with current social and political norms.[151] In addition, the court asserted that the position taken by the Council of Traditional Authorities to honour constitutional principles should be welcomed, even if the Council did not have the right to make such a decision.[152] The court finally revoked the orders of the High Court and the Supreme Court and ruled in favour of Ms Shilubana.

This case demonstrates that customary law should not be immune from external judgment, particularly by the state,[153] and confirms that the Bill of Rights must override cultural principles and practices that are discriminatory. This is because 'as long as most traditional customary chiefs are male, they are likely to perpetuate the exclusion of women, and any reform effort will probably need to start with the government body exercising some influence in the selection process'.[154]

B African Courts Engaging with Customary Law

Mojekwu and others v. *Ejikeme and others* dealt with a conflict in Nigeria between customary law and women's rights regarding both the law of

[148] Ibid., para. 33.
[149] Ibid., para. 37.
[150] Ibid., para. 38.
[151] Ibid., para. 45.
[152] Ibid., para. 60.
[153] The *Shilubana* case served as precedent for other cases. See *Mayelane* v. *Ngwenyama and Another* [2013] (4) South Africa 415 (CC).
[154] Danish Institute, *Informal Justice System*, p. 103.

succession and women's freedom. The case was essentially about a conflict in inheritance where both parties claimed customary right to property. There was agreement that women were not entitled to inherit if the deceased was not survived by male relatives except when the Nnewi custom of Nrachi had been performed for one of his daughters, who then becomes entitled to inherit.[155] This custom allowed a man with no male heirs to prevent one of his daughters from marriage and keep her in his household. The disagreement in this case was about the daughter for which the custom had been performed, and consequently the offspring entitled to inherit. The appellants claimed that Nrachi had been performed for their mother/grandmother and therefore they had a right to inherit their great-grandfather's property. The respondents claimed that the Nnewi custom was performed for another daughter who died childless; therefore, the deceased had no male lineage to inherit, which directs the inheritance to them.[156] The trial judge focused the ruling on the alignment of customary law with the Constitution, ruling in favour of the appellants based on the fact that these customs are in contradiction of constitutional rights to equality and freedom from discrimination.[157] The Court of Appeals agreed that both customs discriminate against women and go against natural justice by putting unrealistic conditionality on women to get their rightful inheritance. In this landmark case, the court bravely re-evaluated the customs, a move from which Nigerian courts have previously shied away.[158] In addition, the Court recognised the Nigerian state's obligation under international law, particularly to modify social and cultural practices that are harmful to women, and asserted that if the legislature fails to do so, the courts will have to take action.[159]

[155] A custom that allowed men to keep an unmarried daughter in their home to raise his children, especially males. In this case, a woman is treated like a son and is entitled to inherit.

[156] *Mojekwu and others* v. *Ejikeme and others* (2000) 5 NWLR 402.

[157] Nigerian Constitution (1999), section 42: 'A citizen of Nigeria of a particular community, ethnic group, place of origin, sex, religion or political opinion shall not, by reason only that he is such a person (a) be subjected either expressly by, or in the practical application of, any law in force in Nigeria or any executive or administrative action of the government, to disabilities or restrictions to which citizens of Nigeria of other communities, ethnic groups, places of origin, sex, religions or political opinions are not made subject; or (b) be accorded either expressly by, or in the practical application of, any law in force in Nigeria or any such executive or administrative action, any privilege or advantage that is not accorded to citizens of Nigeria of other communities, ethnic groups, places of origin, sex, religions or political opinions.'

[158] Francis O. Anaeme, 'Reducing gender discrimination and violence against women through library information services' (2012) *Library Philosophy and Practice*, 765.

[159] CEDAW, Article 5; Mune Ndulo, 'African customary law, customs, and women's rights' (2011) 11 *Indiana Journal of Global Legal* Studies, 1, 87–120.

Botswana saw a similar case[160] regarding a dispute over the right to inheritance concerning the property of a deceased man. The High Court struck down the Ngwaketse rule of customary law that prohibited women from inheriting a father's property, which went to the youngest living son. In this case, the three daughters lost in customary court, as well as the appeal, to their nephew who claimed entitlement to the property pursuant to customary norms. Therefore, the applicants took the case to state courts to argue that this customary rule is inconsistent with their constitutional right to equality under section 3 of the Constitution of Botswana.[161] The Court struck down the decision of the Customary Court of Appeals and ruled that the customary norm of Ngwaketse contravenes the Constitution. This case clearly set straight the legal hierarchy in which customary courts are subject to constitutional principles. The appellants were supported by the South African Litigation Centre to treat this as a test case and frame the issue as a women's rights and constitutional issue.

In the reviewed cases dealing with customary laws in both South Africa and other African jurisdictions, courts were confident in ruling against customary law when it failed to meet constitutional principles, although in S v. *Mvamvu* the Court was lenient. Lehnert sees the relationship between customary law and the judicial system as a 'check and balance one'. Courts monitor the development of customary law to ensure its conformity with constitutional principles. This keeps customary law relevant to people[162] and also encourages local communities to accept human rights principles as they become integral to the legal system with which they are familiar.[163] Similarly, the Association of Rural Women, which acted as *amicus curiae* in the *Shilubana* case, warned courts against 'ascertaining the content of customary law from the written records' specifically from 'apartheid-era administrators, legislators and courts'.[164]

While theoretically formal law must override customary law, this is far from guaranteed. Cases that penetrate through to reach the

[160] *Mmusi and Others* v. *Ramantele and Others* [2013] AHRLJ 11.

[161] Botswana Constitution, s. 3: 'every person in Botswana is entitled to the fundamental rights and freedoms of the individual, that is to say, the right, whatever his race, place of origin, political opinions, colour, creed or sex, but subject to respect for the rights and freedoms of others and for the public interest'.

[162] Wieland Lehnert, 'The role of the courts in the conflict between African customary law and human rights' (2005) 21 *South African Journal on Human Rights*, 2, 251.

[163] Ibid., 255.

[164] *Shilubana and Others* v. *Nwamitwa*, para. 35.

Constitutional Court are the exception, rather than the rule. These situations are exceptional; cases are strongly supported by NGOs working on broader causes and the perseverance of specific women allows for a case to blow up. However, in daily affairs, conservative gender practices prevail, which NGOs have to address on a smaller scale, as will be discussed shortly.

C Justice in Customary Courts

Chieftaincy is acquired by lineage. Bekker refers to the South-Eastern Bantu-speaking people as an example to demonstrate how chiefs are appointed. Chiefs are usually the most senior male members of the community. The position of the chief as 'the central authority figure in the community is determined by his place in the line of descent within the ruling lineage and is passed on to his successor in accordance with the rules of succession observed by the community concerned'; this is usually the eldest son of the first (and main) wife.[165]

1 Chiefs as Adjudicators

The chief is a respected figure in the community and possesses power and authority, assuming a key role in dispute resolution. In his role as adjudicator, the chief may consult several advisory boards.[166] Procedures of dispute resolution vary among different customary law systems, some more structured than others. For example, Comaroff and Roberts describe the precise steps that should be taken for conflict resolution in the Tswana communities. First, parties to the dispute must try to resolve it amicably. If those attempts fail, the parties 'must seek the advice and help of senior agnates and matrilineal kin – fathers, brothers, and paternal and maternal uncles'.[167] At this stage, the headman of the ward must be consulted if the conflict is still unresolved. If all these attempts fail, only then can the chief hear the case.[168]

The following examples demonstrate the administration of informal justice. Bennett uses Bhaca Warheard's Tribunal in 1960 as an example of a traditional court. He writes:

> Cases were heard near the wardhead's homestead, normally in the open, in the shade of an accommodating tree, and usually at a time when

[165] Bekker et al. *Legal Pluralism*, p. 115.

[166] Ibid., p. 117.

[167] John L. Comaroff and Simon Roberts, *Rules and Processes: The Cultural Logic of Dispute in an African Context* (Chicago: University of Chicago Press, 1981), p. 108.

[168] Ibid.

> members of the community were free to attend… the proceedings were quite casual. Women were expected to remain silent, unless asked to speak and if a woman wished to present a case, she had to be assisted by a male relative. Otherwise, all adult males were free to participate.[169]

Oomen demonstrates another example of a dispute in the Sekhukhune area in 1999. Men, women, the school governing body, parents, teacher, two chiefs, a competing school forum and the ANC branch as well as many villagers in the area were present. The case concerned a strike organised by female teachers to protest a policy that had been passed by the school principal, forbidding female teachers from wearing trousers. The discussion was led by the school principal. Some of the comments reported by Oomen included allegations that wearing trousers solicits rape and contradicts social norms.[170]

Those examples provide some insights into the administration of justice under customary law. First, customary norms are dynamic and open to interpretation and debate. The fluidity of customary norms are often used to restrict women's freedom and reinforce sexist norms. Second, deliberations in customary trials are conducted in a relaxed and casual atmosphere. Third, both examples show gender bias in the procedure of the hearings. Nevertheless, traditional courts enjoy legitimacy among many South Africans, with limited criticism, from those such as the 'Rural Women's Movement which called for the total abolition of traditional courts'.[171]

Because of gender stratification in customary laws, adjudication in customary courts is unsurprisingly gender biased. This is exacerbated when chiefs step out of their jurisdiction to adjudicate serious offences such as rape.[172] The following section will elaborate on the impact of the proceedings in customary courts on women's access to justice.

2 *The Administration of Justice in Customary Courts*

The gender issue remains at the core of the conflict between customary law and formal law, as shown in the debate regarding the aforementioned traditional courts bill, introduced in 2008 and debated until 2016, unresolved. This is because justice under customary law, particularly for women and minority groups, is undermined by both the

[169] Bennett, *Customary Law*, p. 166.
[170] Oomen, *Chiefs in South Africa*, p. 204.
[171] Ibid., p. 99.
[172] Bekker et al., *Legal Pluralism*, p. 137.

content and implementation of rules. Referring to Uganda, Kane and others write:

> To the extent that the local context may remain insensitive to the concrete situation of significant sectors of the population such as women and other marginalized groups, then there are serious issues of access to justice that arise simply from the content of the substantive (statute or customary) law sought to be applied.[173]

Lack of awareness of women's rights by both 'users and providers' of informal justice is alarming.[174] In addition, channels for obtaining such information are usually inaccessible to women.[175] Banda asserts that even if women have access to customary courts, the rulings may violate women's rights, especially in cases of death or divorce.[176] Procedures of IJS are gender biased and inevitably hinder women's access to justice, particularly because they are not monitored or appealed. In customary courts, women are not permitted to file complaints independently; they can only appear in courts with the 'intervention of senior male family members'[177] to represent them. Therefore, they are effectively discouraged to bring forward cases that challenge traditional gender ideologies through male relatives, and before male judges. One of Oomen's respondents had questioned, 'how do you expect old, uneducated men without any woman present, to come up with fair judgement?'[178] Women are also likely to be surrounded by a group of men during trial. This setting undermines women's confidence and ability to argue their cases.[179] Furthermore, traditional courts run without strict procedural rules, and hearings are likely to take place without lawyers. Faundez writes:

> It is undeniable that many community justice institutions are far from embodying the ideal models of liberal legality and they often commit serious violations of international human rights. In procedural terms, these violations relate to the absence of due process safeguards as their decisions are biased, often inconsistent and not subject to any form of

[173] Kane et al., *Reassessing Customary Law*, p. 20.

[174] Danish Institute, *Informal Justice System*, p. 106.

[175] Ibid.

[176] Fareda Banda, 'Women and access to justice' in Ayesha Kadwani Dias and Gita Honwana Welch (eds.), *Justice for the Poor: Perspectives on Accelerating Access* (Oxford: Oxford University Press, 2009), p. 142.

[177] Curran and Bonthuys, 'Customary law', 633.

[178] Oomen, *Chiefs in South Africa*, p. 165.

[179] Curran and Bonthuys, 'Customary law', 633.

> review. Moreover, the accused often does not have a chance to be.... adequately represented.[180]

Since customary law focuses on reinstituting peace and harmony in the community, remedies offered often carry grave violations of women's human rights. Enyew exemplifies societies such as Beni-Shangul Gumuz where women are often unwillingly offered in marriage to another family to restore harmony and maintain peace between the two parties.[181]

It is worth noting that IJS are sometimes useful for women, particularly in cases that do not involve grave violations. Access to IJS might also be favourable when it is the only option available to women. However, the socio-economic and cultural contexts of traditional societies may force women to accept unfavourable settlements because they are dependent on their families.[182]

A restructuring of the institution of customary justice is highly unlikely because, as Nhlapo explains, in 'African societies' male elders have the power of political leadership and decision-making and, therefore, they make the rules that concern women and children.[183] However, women theoretically have the option to challenge the system, either renouncing these rules through litigation in formal courts, or abandoning the system altogether and resorting to other forms of adjudication. This may be formal courts, but can also be NGOs.

VI FORMAL LAW, INFORMAL SYSTEMS OF JUSTICE OR NGOs?

With the gender-biased nature of customary law and the inaccessibility of formal law (the subject matter of Chapter 7) can NGOs provide a favourable alternative to women? Traditional communities usually prefer alternative dispute resolution (ADR) methods over pursuing formal channels of justice. In addition to the reduced cost and speedier trials, informal justice recognises the sociocultural environment and

[180] Julio Faundez, 'Community, justice institutions and judicialization: lessons from rural Peru' in Ayesha Kadwani Dias and Gita Honwana Welch (eds.), *Justice for the Poor: Perspectives on Accelerating Access* (Oxford: Oxford University Press, 2009), p. 107; see also Danish Institute, *Informal Justice System*, pp. 106–128.

[181] Endalew Lijalem Enyew, 'Ethiopian customary dispute resolution mechanisms: forms for restorative justice?' (2014) 14 *African Journal on Conflict Resolution* 1, 144.

[182] Banda, 'Women and access to justice', p. 143.

[183] Thandabuto Nhlapo, 'Cultural diversity, human rights and the family in contemporary Africa: lessons from the South African Constitutional debate' (1995) 9 *International Journal of Law and the Family* 2, 208, 211.

takes into account the 'nonmaterial interests of the disputants'.[184] Alternative dispute resolution is common in numerous countries such as Pakistan and Afghanistan,[185] and among many African communities. Nongovernmental organisations get involved in various ways such as offering mediation and paralegal services which promise great success.[186] For instance, undertaking mediation in Bangladesh has proved to be 'an effective model of justice provision'.[187]

A Mediation: An Alternative to Adjudication

The most common form of informal justice is mediation, which can be offered by different parties. Roberts identifies three types of mediation.[188] Minimal intervention indicates an attempt to revive 'a flow of conversation' between two parties that has been obstructed by a conflict. In directive intervention, the mediator's opinion determines the direction of the mediation process, where the mediator provides new information that affects the final decision to be reached by the parties. Therapeutic intervention is the third approach to mediation and it resembles formal adjudication, where the 'joint decision-making on specific issues is postponed in favour of an examination of the relationships that have broken down'.[189] In those cases, the mediator investigates the actions of the parties and searches for the deeply rooted problems behind the dispute.[190] This process requires the mediator to have knowledge of the local context, but also flexibility and innovation to reach agreeable remedies. It is not expected that all parties would be content with these remedies, but they would be able to survive amicably following the resolution of the dispute. Felstiner elaborates:

[184] Leonard L Riskin, 'Mediation and lawyers' (1982) 43 *Ohio State Law Journal*, 29, 34.

[185] Thomas Barfield et al., *Clash of Two Goods: State and Non-State Dispute Resolution in Afghanistan*, research report (USA: United States Institute of Peace, 2006), p. 15. Joy Watson, *The Role of the State in Addressing Sexual Violence: Assessing Policing Service Delivery Challenges Faced by Victims of Sexual Offences*, Policy Brief (Cape Town: APCOF, 13 August 2015).

[186] Mette Lindorf Nielsen, 'From practice to police, and back: emerging lessons from working with community-based justice mechanisms in Helmand, Afghanistan' in Peter Albrecht et al., (eds.), *Perspectives on Involving Non-State and Customary Actors in Justice and Security Reform* (Rome: International Development Law Organization, 2011), p. 151.

[187] Craig Valters and Ferdous Jahan, *Getting to Grips with Power: Can NGOs Improve Justice in Bangladesh?* research report (Overseas Development Institute, March 2017), p. 27.

[188] Simon Roberts, 'Three models of family mediation' in Robert Dingwall and Jon Eekelaar (eds.), *Divorce Mediation and the Legal Process* (Oxford: Oxford University Press, 1988), pp. 144–149. Also see Roberts and Palmer, *Dispute Processes*, p. 91, where they provide a mediation spectrum 'of progressively increasing intensity'.

[189] Roberts, 'Three models', p. 145.

[190] Ibid.

> Since successful mediation requires an outcome acceptable to the parties, the mediator cannot rely primarily on rules but must construct an outcome in the light of the social and cultural context of the dispute, the full scope of the relations between the disputants and the perspectives from which they view the dispute. Mediation, then, flourishes where mediators share the social and cultural experience of the disputants they serve, and where they bring to the processing of disputes an intimate and detailed knowledge of the perspectives of the disputants.[191]

In the African context, mediation is more fluid and less clearly delineated than in the Western context.[192] Mediation discussed in this book refers to the third type as identified by Roberts: therapeutic intervention. Nongovernmental organisations offering mediation services, therefore, may completely replace the role of formal justice, echoing the theories of pluralism reviewed earlier in this chapter.

B Gender and Dispute Resolution in South Africa

A decade before the end of apartheid, NGOs had been in demand for dispute resolution primarily through mediation services. The Independent Mediation Service of South Africa was one of the earliest initiatives. A number of NGOs followed, and with some significant donor funding, they started implementing 'mediation and community reconciliation programmes to help manage and control community tension, resolve neighbourhood disputes, train community leaders in negotiation and conflict management techniques and establish neighbourhood justice centres'.[193] NGO mediation is based on norms relevant to local cultures and the procedures are convenient to members of the community.

While ADR is preferred by both women and men, 'women gave higher marks to mediation than did men'.[194] This is because of their social vulnerabilities that may be exacerbated by prolonged trials, and the failure of the formal legal system to offer relevant remedies that are likely to be

[191] William Felstiner, 'Influences of social organization on dispute processing' (1974) 9 *Law and Society Review*, 1, 74.

[192] See James Ptacek (ed.), *Restorative Justice and Violence against Women* (Oxford: Oxford University Press, 2009). The authors discuss the use of restorative justice (informal intervention) in VAW cases in the United States, Canada, Australia and New Zealand. Also see Roberts and Palmer, *Dispute Processes*, pp. 66–67.

[193] A A Okharedia, 'The emergence of alternative dispute resolution in South Africa: a lesson for other African countries', 6th IIRA African Regional Congress of Industrial Relations, Lagos Nigeria (January 2011), p. 5.

[194] Gilat J. Bachar and Deborah R. Hensler, 'Does alternative dispute resolution facilitate prejudice and bias? We still don't know' (2017) 70 *SMU Law Review*, 4, 830.

implemented in their traditional communities.[195] Moult conducted a study looking at 'justice' as administered by NGOs. Her findings suggest that for conflict resolution, women prefer ADRs for their simplicity and familiarity, speed and relevance, all of which are conditions that are hardly met by the formal legal system.[196] NGOs attend to cases shortly after they receive them, whether those cases involve payments of outstanding maintenance or 'mediation-style interventions'.[197] Resorting to NGOs, specifically community-based organisations (CBOs), reduces the cost of transport for women as meetings are conducted near the litigants' houses; NGOs do not have specific working hours and therefore attend to cases swiftly and at any time; finally, the language and procedures used by NGOs are familiar to the community.[198] Victims can tell their stories in their own words while avoiding traumatising memories, and feeling support and comfort throughout the process.[199] Further, NGOs have guaranteed women's active involvement in the justice sector and provided women with support and a voice. One study found that 'in community mediation, where the NGO plays a significant role, women are able to attend and represent themselves, and they are given time to state their case'.[200] Similarly, in the Shalish community in Bangladesh, NGOs were able to support disputants to get fairer outcomes by providing timely, clear and respectful support to disputants.[201] The only exception where formal law is preferred is to fulfil a strong desire to punish the offender.[202]

Engaging in the adjudication of informal justice was a service offered by all NGOs working in rural communities in the research conducted for this book. NGO6 provides mediation services to women as a substitute for family courts or lawyers. The NGO has set-up divorce clinics to assist government efforts and also to ease the transition for couples who want to divorce amicably. As expected, the NGO confirmed that women specifically prefer amicable resolution over lengthy trials,

[195] Tanja Chopra and Deborah Isser, 'Women's access to justice, legal pluralism and fragile states' in Peter Albrecht et al. (eds.), *Perspectives on Involving Non-State and Customary Actors in Justice and Security Reform* (Rome: International Development Law Organization, 2011), p. 26

[196] Kelley Moult, 'Providing a sense of justice: informal mechanisms for dealing with domestic violence' (2005) 12 *South Africa Crime Quarterly*, 1, 20.

[197] Ibid., p. 22.

[198] Ibid., p. 23.

[199] Judith Lewis Herman, 'Justice from the victim's perspective' (2005) 11 *Violence Against Women* 5, 574.

[200] Valters and Jahan, *Getting to Grips with Power*, p. 24.

[201] Ibid., p. 9.

[202] Moult, 'Providing a sense of justice', 20.

especially in family law matters. In fact, upon the community's request, NGO12 set up a similar clinic to resolve domestic violence and other family and community disputes amicably. In addition, the NGO has trained coordinators on the nature of intimate violence and the gender power dynamic, so that they would adopt a gender-sensitive approach when mediating gender issues. This service was reported as successful, particularly because it produced decisions that were sensitive to each individual case. For example, regarding cases of intimate violence, Jabu from NGO13 recounted a case in which a man failed to pay child support. After an investigation, the coordinator discovered that the man did not have access to his pension fund and was therefore unable to pay. She helped him with the pension, which consequently resolved the child support issue. In this case, the NGO worked on an issue indirectly related to the main mediation complaint – a step that the formal justice system is quite unlikely to take. Another example mentioned by Joyce from NGO12 concerned a woman who was HIV positive and constantly subjected to intimate violence. After several mediation sessions, the client reported that the marriage had significantly improved due to the counsellor's help. This was reflected in the woman's improved health and the positive change in her husband's abusive behaviour.

Preference for mediation in family violence cases resonates with the debate on the best route for domestic violence, and whether the law truly responds to women's needs and desires. Winick's therapeutic jurisprudence explores the question of mandatory arrests of an abusive husband without considering the wife's wishes. She argues that this could be a 'paternalistic practice that does not take sufficient account of the preferences of the victim, depriving her of control over significant aspects of her life and reinforcing feelings of powerlessness'.[203] Goldfarb also questions the restricted response of the law towards domestic violence and calls for revising the methods with which the issue is resolved.[204] Customary resolutions in domestic violence cases were also preferred in Moult's research. She reported that the mediators

[203] Bruce Winick, 'Applying the law therapeutically in domestic violence cases' (2000–2001) 69 *University of Missouri-Kansas City Law Review*, 1, 72. Similarly, Miller argues that mandatory arrest policies might victimise women. For more information, see Susan L. Miller, *Victims as Offenders: The Paradox of Women's Violence in Relationships* (New Brunswick, New Jersey and London: Rutgers University Press, 2005); Gill Hague et al., *Is Anyone Listening: Accountability and Women Survivors of Domestic Violence* (London: Routledge, 2003). The authors criticise the fact that battered women are not consulted on the policies regarding domestic violence.

[204] Sally F Goldfarb, 'Reconceiving civil protection orders for domestic violence: Can law help end the abuse without ending the relationship?' (2008) 29 *Cardozo Law Review*, 4.

she interviewed confirmed that 'almost all abusers accept the invitation to attend a meeting', primarily due to the 'close social networks that exist in townships and rural areas'.[205] When abusers refused to attend, interveners fetched them from their houses and simply reminded them that the NGO was only trying to help, 'particularly as an alternative to the (less appropriate) criminal justice system'.[206]

The solutions to women's problems are therefore not necessarily found within the law. Nongovernmental organisations are able to dig deep into the socio-economic, political and cultural domains to determine the causes of women's hardships and provide relevant remedies.

C The Power and Position of Mediators

Moult's research shows that NGOs can offer both convenient procedures for the administration of justice and speedy (albeit temporary) relief to urgent problems. For example, during one of the field visits to a CBO in a Johannesburg township, a teenage girl was sleeping at the NGO premises because she was homeless. The girl was an orphan and had been living with family friends for a while before she was evicted. She was sleeping at the NGO premises while alternative housing was arranged and the dispute was resolved. This kind of help can only be provided by CBOs. The head of the organisation explained that community members fetched her from her house when they needed her help at any hour. This example demonstrates that the proximity of NGOs to the community enables NGOs to recognise and respond to the multidimensional nature of women's hardships, despite their limited financial resources.[207]

In some cases, the parties to the dispute consider the NGO's decision as binding. One of the mediation sessions observed in the course of research for this volume was conducted by Arriera, head of NGO1. The dispute was between two families that had been in conflict for years and had gone to court several times to no avail. The session included discussion for about 45 minutes, during which some family members were enraged. However, Arriera had a strong presence in the room and was therefore in full control. They expected her to pass a 'judgment' at the end of the session, which they considered binding. In this case, formal law did not resolve the conflict and the NGO's intervention was the last

[205] Moult, 'Providing a sense of justice', p. 21.
[206] Ibid.
[207] Ibid., p. 23.

chance for peace. Arriera, however, expected conflict to arise again in the future, and was prepared for it.

The abovementioned examples show that mediators do not have the power to enforce decisions, just to facilitate reaching an agreement.[208] However, disputants give them legitimacy by accepting the ruling even if it is not in their favour.[209] This position gives NGOs significant power and prestige facilitating their work on justice; 'many NGOs use this perception to convince disputants to attend mediation, or to maintain an agreed resolution'.[210] One noted problem, however, is that men often question women's authority as mediators and adjudicators, particularly in cases that challenge men's power. In her study, Moult noted that some offenders were 'impossible to work with' – specifically when mediators are female; in these cases, NGOs have to postpone hearings until a male mediator becomes available.[211] Similarly, in Rajshahi, Bangladesh, female facilitators have been ridiculed and, in some rare cases, retaliated against by husbands of domestically abused women.[212]

VII ASSESSMENT OF INFORMAL JUSTICE SYSTEMS

A Is Legal Pluralism Useful for Women?

The impact of legal pluralism on women is debated. Referring to a study conducted on survivors of gender violence in Zimbabwe, Armstrong demonstrates the complexity of the situation: women prefer to consult chiefs and headmen about intimate violence as they are usually proactive; they advise men not to hit their wives, and they also urge the parents of the woman to intervene and protect their daughters.[213] However, they still try 'to impose traditional norms and try to preserve the marriage at all costs', which questions the root of their care and concern about women.[214] On the other hand, research has also shown that when justice is administered by informal institutions, women are at great risk of discrimination. After reviewing methods by which legal pluralism can accommodate the human rights discourse and Muslim

[208] Riskin, 'Mediation and lawyers'.
[209] Valters and Jahan, *Getting to Grips with Power*, p. 27.
[210] Ibid., p. 23
[211] Moult, 'Providing a sense of justice, p. 22.
[212] Valters and Jahan, *Getting to Grips with Power*, p. 25.
[213] Alice Armstrong, *Culture and Choice: Lessons from Survivors of Gender Violence in Zimbabwe* (Harare: AKA Distributer, 1998) p. 64.
[214] Ibid.

family law, Amien concluded that informal justice will inevitably work against gender equality.[215]

Oomen gives one of the most remarkable examples of the injustice that informal justice inflicts on women, highlighting the helplessness of women against such a rigid normative order. She recounts a story:

> A widowed Jehovah's Witness refused to follow the customary procedure of washing her hands and sprinkling herbs after her husband's death. When senior male community members, angered by her disregard for custom threatened to keep her locked up in the house for a year, her son called in the South African Human Rights Commission, who supported her claim by pointing to the constitutional freedom of movement. Even though the chief was publicly humiliated, it did not help the woman much. Not only had she already been locked in the house by the time the decision was made, she also faced expulsion by the traditional leader who lashed out at her 'disobedience,' stating: I don't know what makes this woman think that her rights will take precedence over those of the tribe.[216]

From this story, we can draw some observations. First, resorting to formal institutions, such as the South African Human Rights Commission, is time-consuming and not necessarily effective. Second, the chief's surprise that a woman would put her personal desire before the communal decision reflects the emphasis in customary law on social cohesion, which takes precedent over individual rights and freedoms. Third, it is evident that the rule of customary law overrode that of formal law. Fourth, such stories may discourage other women who might want to challenge discriminatory social norms.

It is difficult to make firm conclusions on the impact of informal justice on women as it usually depends on the case and the social factors around it. It also depends on the other options available to women, which may be rather limited.

B Making Legal Choices

Choosing a specific institution of justice does not restrict the usage of other channels. Dagnino argues that different normative orders are not exclusively followed and that people can be subject to different laws simultaneously depending on the 'interests at stake' in each situation.[217]

[215] Waheeda Amien, 'A South African case study for the recognition and regulation of Muslim family law in a minority Muslim secular context' (2010) 24 *Law, Policy and the Family*, 3, 361.

[216] Oomen, *Chiefs in South Africa*, p. 214.

[217] Dagnino, 'Expanding access to justice', p. 420.

This pluralist legal environment is common across the African continent, specifically for women, who 'very rarely live exclusively in terms of either "traditional" or "modern" identities'.[218] When Griffiths analysed family law disputes in Botswana, she recited narratives in which litigants used both systems of formal law and customary law interchangeably.[219] In *S v. Mvamvu*, discussed earlier in this chapter, the wife who was living under customary law and married according to its norms chose to resort to formal law for protection from domestic violence. Her case was ultimately heard by state courts. The mingling of justice systems is therefore possible and should be respected.

Findings of this research also show that women's legal pursuits shift between formal and informal justice, with the involvement of NGOs. For example, victims of domestic violence request POs from courts, without intending or wanting their partners to be arrested. The head of an urban NGO specialising in GBV, who was interviewed for this research, estimated that 80 per cent of women who sought the services of the NGO for domestic violence did not want to leave their partners, but they wanted the law to remedy the relationship. This is usually the choice for economically dependent women,[220] and will be further discussed in Chapter 7 alongside other women's legal decisions. Not only do women consciously make the decision to resort to NGOs, they expect NGOs to act against their partners if the PO was violated. This scenario is confirmed by Jewkes's research, in which she notes that, 'whilst the majority of women went to the police wanting an interdict or for the man to be prosecuted, nearly half of the women reported that they were actually seeking other forms of intervention from the police when they reported the abuse'.[221]

The key in this issue is choice, as objective as possible. Ideally, women must have the choice of various channels of justice from which they can choose depending on the relevance and convenience in each different case. In reality, however, it is common for informal justice systems to be imposed on the woman. For example, in Baluchistan and Afghanistan, women who engage with institutions of formal justice are considered traitors who taint family honour.[222] In this way, formal law is sometimes

[218] Curran and Bonthuys, 'Customary law', 614.

[219] Anne Griffiths, *In the Shadow of Marriage: Gender and Justice in the African Community* (Chicago: University of Chicago Press, 1997), pp. 118–122.

[220] Moult, 'Providing a sense of justice', p. 23.

[221] Jewkes et al., *'He Must Give Me Money'*, p. 19.

[222] Danish Institute, *Informal Justice System*, p. 107.

regarded as a threat to the 'ideology and existence' of informal justice systems.[223]

Choosing to adopt a specific framework of customary norms may suggest 'cultural voluntarism', a term coined by Eekelaar; he emphasises the impossibility of knowing the extent to which an individual voluntarily adopts a set of norms. He therefore asserts that 'as a minimum … respecting voluntary behaviour requires institutional means, supported by, but not identical with, the state that allow the individual voice to be heard against group interests, whatever they may be, and to adjudicate the competing claims'.[224]

Examples of court cases mentioned earlier in this chapter shed light on the choices that are often available to women living under customary law. Taking their cases to court obviously reflects rejection of these customary norms; however, not every woman who is unsatisfied with the normative order under which she is living will be able to follow suit. The role of state law in this 'choice' is indisputable: if these women choose to challenge customary norms and resort to the formal legal system, the state must provide the channel, without giving weight to women's customary law or culture. Women's desire to invoke their legal rights must be upheld. This is why any law regulating the adjudicating power of chiefs, such as the aforementioned Traditional Courts Bill, must include an opt-out clause for community members who prefer to use formal law.

VIII CONCLUSION

Formal justice is only one way to resolve conflict. Societies have traditionally followed other channels of conflict resolution at some point throughout history, and some societies still follow these alternative methods today. These are highly pluralist societies, in which people following different sets of norms and rules must coexist amicably. Conflict does and will continue to happen; however, formal states with democratic institutions find various ways to interweave all sets of norms in a manner that promotes the human rights values of inclusion and equality. To achieve this, South Africa set guidelines in the Constitution and legislation regarding overriding rights, and left the debate to the courts based on individual cases.

[223] Ibid.

[224] John Eekelaar, 'From multiculturalism to cultural voluntarism: a family-based approach' (2010) 81 *The Political Quarterly*, 3, 353.

This chapter discussed legal pluralism theory that sees the different normative orders in a combination of conflict and harmony. Even in countries where the constitution overrides customary law, 'the issue of customary law and the arbitrariness of rulings by traditional authorities remains a major source of concern for women's rights activists'.[225] Because of their patriarchal history and tendencies, general perceptions as well as rulings of traditional leaders are often gender biased, prioritising community over individual's (especially women's) rights.

Women have a lot at stake, faced with a situation where their access to formal justice is limited, and their likelihood of finding justice in customary courts is curtailed. As institutions that work closely with local communities, and are, therefore, aware of their needs, NGOs in South Africa have engaged in informal justice, especially by offering alternative forms of dispute resolution that may be preferable to women, so as to provide a compromise between the expensive and unreachable institutions of formal justice, and the gender-discriminatory institutions of customary law.

[225] Aili Mari Tripp, 'Women's movements and Constitution making after civil unrest and conflict in Africa: the cases of Kenya and Somalia' (2016) 12 *Politics and Gender*, 1, 103.

CHAPTER 4

FROM POLITICS TO LAW-MAKING: NGOs AND THE STATE IN SOUTH AFRICA

NGOs work across various spheres and engage with different stakeholders – a diversity that strengthens their impact. Relationships between the state and NGOs, however, have not been always amicable and remain shaky at times. However, the birth of democracy unified the goals of some stakeholders, including NGOs and the state, with a central focus on equality and eliminating discrimination.

This chapter will focus on the women's movement, its relationship with the state, and its role in law-making at the dawn of democracy and afterwards. It will start by tracking the rise and development of the South African women's movement throughout apartheid, and into the negotiations for transitional democracy. The remainder of the chapter will centre on the role of NGOs in democratic South Africa including contributions to the most important GBV instruments, working in partnerships with the state, and taking significant burdens away from state institutions.

I WOMEN'S MOVEMENT IN SOUTH AFRICA: FROM HISTORY TO DEMOCRATIC TRANSITION

A Inception and Identity

1 Women Rising

South African women played a limited role in politics until 1943, when the ANC Women's League (ANCWL) was founded.[1] The league's mission was to advocate women's interests within the national movement. However, racial equality and nationalism remained the

[1] Gisela Geisler, 'Parliament is another terrain of struggle: women, men and politics in South

main focus of the liberation movement. For example, the Freedom Charter,[2] which the ANC and its allies drafted, called for 'equality' based on 'colour, race, sex or belief'. However, the provisions of the Charter suggested that it prioritised racial equality in statements such as 'South Africa belongs to all who live in it, black and white' and 'we, the people of South Africa, black and white together equals, countrymen and brothers adopt this Freedom Charter'.[3]

Gradually, women became politically active and therefore mobilised for different causes. The 1950s witnessed the emergence of political activism at the grassroots level[4] and the establishment of the Federation of South African Women (FSAW) within the Congress Alliance.[5] The FSAW included members of different institutions, such as trade unions and political organisations, who participated in drafting the Freedom Charter in 1955.[6] The FSAW later adopted the Women's Charter,[7] which became its manifesto.[8] The Charter denounced the discrimination faced by all South African women. In addition, the Women's Charter recognised that development would only be possible through the unity of men and women and that national liberation must be prioritised. It also highlighted hardships that African women experienced because of custom, such as the denial of the 'right to own, inherit or alienate property'.[9]

2 *Identity: Race Versus Gender*

Even before apartheid had been formally instituted, it was widely recognised that the experiences of white and black women had some commonalities, but the 'privileged racial group' to which white women belonged 'softens the impact of gender discrimination'.[10] Locating black women's experiences was still challenging as it lay in the 'intricate

Africa' (2000) 38 *The Journal of Modern African Studies*, 4, 608.

[2] African National Congress, Freedom Charter (Adopted at the Congress of the People at Kliptown, 26 June 1955).

[3] Ibid.

[4] See Cock, *Women and War*, pp. 46 and 51.

[5] Catherine Albertyn, 'Women and the transition to democracy in South Africa' (1994) *Acta Juridica* 43.

[6] Anne Marie Goetz, 'Women in politics and gender equity in policy: South Africa and Uganda' (1998) 25 *Review of African Political Economy*, 76, 246.

[7] African National Congress, Women's Charter (Adopted in Johannesburg, 17 April 1954).

[8] Albertyn, 'Women and the transition', 43.

[9] ANC Women's Charter.

[10] Cherryl Walker (ed.), *Women and Gender in Southern Africa to 1945* (Cape Town: New Africa Books, 1990), p. 2.

interrelationship of gender, race and class', possibly linked to the noted absence of their voices from history.[11]

The difficulty of uniting women on the gender front increased with apartheid. Native women were sceptical of the idea of unity when their lives were significantly different from their white counterparts who enjoyed various privileges.[12] Nationalism was therefore prioritised over the gender cause. This is a recurrent trend in historical narratives, including the civil rights movement in the USA,[13] the Mozambique national liberation movement[14] and the Indian national liberation movement.[15] For example, during the Indian independence movement, Nehru stated that, 'in a national war, there is no question of either sex or community. Whoever is born in this country ought to be a soldier'.[16] The ANCWL similarly prioritised race over gender issues. For example, the representative of the ANC women's secretariat in 1979 made a speech confirming that women in South Africa never asked for ... African and other oppressed people of our country first'.[17] At the 1985 UN Nairobi Conference on Women, the ANC delegation agreed that it would be 'suicidal' to adopt feminist ideas at the time, explaining that advocating for women's rights would deplete the resources of the women's movement when their main focus should be the abolishment of apartheid. Similar trends persisted in the private sphere, where 'discussions of apartheid's impact on black women have tended to emphasize the destabilization of African households rather than gender-based inequalities within those households'.[18]

[11] Ibid.

[12] Anne McClintock, 'No longer in a future heaven: women and nationalism in South Africa' (1991) 51 *Transition*, 118; Georgina Waylen, *Engendering Transitions: Women's Mobilization, Institutions, and Gender Outcomes* (Oxford: Oxford University Press, 2007), Waylen argues that it is possible for women to make specific gains post a national movement under certain conditions.

[13] Bell Hooks, *Feminist Theory: From Margin to Center*, 3rd edition (New York and London: Routledge, 2014).

[14] K Sheldon, 'Women and revolution in Mozambique' in Tetreault M (ed.), *Women and Revolution in Africa, Asia and the New World* (University of South Carolina Press, 1994), p. 41.

[15] Kumari Jayawardena, *Feminism and Nationalism in the Third World* (London: Zed Books, 1986), pp. 73–98. For discussions on the debate of race and gender, see Haleh Afshar and Mary Maynard (eds.), *The Dynamics of Race and Gender: Some Feminist Interventions* (London: Taylor and Francis, 1994).

[16] Jayawardena, *Feminism and Nationalism*, p. 98.

[17] Mavis Nhlapo as quoted in Judy Kimble and Elaine Unterhalter, '"We opened the road for you, you must go forward": ANC women's struggles, 1912–1982' (1982) 12 *Feminist Review*, 13.

[18] Gay W Seidman, '"No freedom without the women": mobilization and gender in South Africa, 1970–1992' (1992) 18 *Signs* 2, 295.

The priority given to the national project that lasted throughout apartheid, in addition to the challenge of uniting women, meant that the 'gender revolution' had to be postponed, directing women's efforts to the 'fulfilment of black peoples' aspirations'.[19] Additionally, the South African women's movement rejected Western feminism, as did other women's movements in developing countries; this is because Western feminist movements ignored issues of urgency to women of the global south, such as matters of survival, and instead, focused on issues considered irrelevant at the time, such as lesbian rights.[20]

3 *State Relations*

The state generally harassed all NGOs that did not support the apartheid system during the 1970s. This, in addition to depleted resources, ensured that NGOs 'really served as a sideshow to the more formal contest and engagement within civil society and between civil society and the state'.[21] Since the women's movement did not have a clean separation from the national movement under apartheid, its relationship with the state was similar to that of the nationalist movement, with repression at its core.[22]

4 *Towards Democracy*

The women's movement in the 1980s continued to shy away from associating with feminism to describe their goals and ideologies, which contributed to their weak ideological foundation.[23] This is because activists were trapped between Marxism and feminism where an 'analyses of racial capitalism were by definition predicated on race and class; the issue became how to "add gender" to these analyses without leaving the paradigm'.[24] This is a common stance among women's rights activists in Africa who believed in feminist values and adopted feminist agendas but refused to associate with the terminology.[25]

[19] Geisler, 'Parliament is another terrain', 609.

[20] Cock, *Women and War*, p. 47.

[21] Adam Habib, 'State-civil society relations in post-apartheid South Africa' (2005) 72 *Social Research* 3, 674.

[22] Seidman, '"No freedom without the women"', 296.

[23] Shireen Hassim, '"A conspiracy of women": the women's movement in South Africa's transition to democracy' (2002) 69 *Social Research* 3, 694.

[24] Patricia Van Der Spuy and Lindsay Clowes, 'Accidental feminists? Recent histories of South African women' (2007) *Kronos* 33, 212.

[25] Ronit Frenkel, 'Feminism and contemporary culture in South Africa' (2008) 67 *African Studies*, 1, 2.

However, women's activism continued, if not in political parties, then in other institutions, such as trade unions.[26] By the 1980s, community organisations at the local level began to re-emerge and reorganise to address women's issues that did not constitute a threat to the movement against apartheid. For example, the FSAW was reconstituted in 1985 and developed programmes to address GBV and to help female political prisoners.[27] Some organisations focused on both political and developmental issues, such as the Natal Organisation of Women and the Federation of Transvaal Women.[28] Connell explains that these organisations enjoyed autonomy to run social, economic and cultural programmes; in addition, workshops and seminars raised awareness of issues affecting women, such as GBV.[29] The transitional period intensified gender activism. For example, women took to the streets throughout the country in February 1990 to march against rape.[30]

Women's activism notably declined towards the end of apartheid as the focus increasingly diverted to maintain the anti-apartheid movement. This was exacerbated when many women's organisations formed alliances with the ANCWL, which generated 'ideas into gender debates', but impeded the attempt by the women's movement to cut the cord from the national movement.[31] The tables truly turned during the democratic negotiations thanks to 'the new political opportunities offered by the transition from apartheid to democracy, the creation of an autonomous organization for representing the women's movement, and the consolidation of the notion of equality within the African National Congress'.[32]

B Women's Movements in South Africa's Democratic Transition

By the end of 1980s and early 1990s, negotiations between the apartheid government and the ANC (the party that would win the 1994 elections) had begun. During this period, women's issues were politicised.[33] McClintock argues that it was not until the early 1990s that 'women's

[26] Cherryl Walker, *Women and Resistance in South Africa* (Cape Town and Johannesburg: David Philip Publishers, 1991), pp. 57–58.

[27] M Bahati Kuumba, *Gender and Social Movements* (Jaipur: Rawat Publications, 2003), p. 128.

[28] Dan Connell, 'Strategies for change: women and politics in Eritrea and South Africa' (1998) 25 *Review of African Political Economy*, 76, 197.

[29] Ibid.

[30] McClintock, 'No longer in a future heaven', 121.

[31] Hassim, '"A conspiracy of women"', 694.

[32] Ibid.

[33] Kuumba, *Gender and Social Movements*, p. 129.

empowerment came to be seen as a separate, independent, and indispensable element of the full social transformation of the nation'.[34]

1 Movement Building

The South African women's movement is perhaps one of the few examples in history where women were able to insert 'gender equality concerns into the heart of democratic debates'[35] at the time of political negotiations. Foreseeing the imminent Constitution-making process, South African women started organising. Nongovernmental organisations arranged a series of workshops and meetings to discuss lobbying strategies, and to agree on priorities that would effectively protect their rights in the Constitution.[36] By 1991, there was a clear need for a women's movement that was broader than the members of the ANC, sharing a wider vision focused on gender,[37] and by 1992, the Women's National Coalition (WNC) was formed.[38] It included women from different political parties and interest groups with the common goal of bringing women's rights into the national dialogue.[39] The Coalition worked as a pressure group in the Constitution-making process and simultaneously launched grassroots programmes to mobilise and educate women.[40] This period also witnessed a mobilisation of 'local, nongovernmental and governmental structures' that addressed specific women's issues such as health, poverty and domestic violence.[41] The success of the WNC was rooted in its ability to show feminists the possibility of adopting a non-racial feminist agenda and in its success in recognising diversity without overriding the collective feminist purpose.[42]

Women's mobilisation had a strong impact during the transition process. Most notably at the official level, the first Parliament (elected in 1994) included 111 women, over one-quarter of all seats.[43] Women's

[34] McClintock, 'No longer in a future heaven', 117.

[35] Hassim, '"A conspiracy of women"', 693.

[36] Brigette Mabandla, 'Women in South Africa and the Constitution-making process' in Julie Peters and Andrea Wolper (eds.), *Women's Rights, Human Rights: International Feminist Perspectives* (New York: Routledge, 1995), p. 68.

[37] Hassim, '"A conspiracy of women"', 699.

[38] See Geisler, 'Parliament is another terrain', 613.

[39] Mabandla, 'Women in South Africa', p. 68.

[40] Geisler, 'Parliament is another terrain', 613.

[41] Kuumba, *Gender and Social Movements*, p. 129.

[42] Sheila Meintjes, 'The women's struggle for equality during South Africa's transition to democracy' (1996) 30 *Transformation*, 49.

[43] Geisler, 'Parliament is another terrain', 607.

emancipation was one of the four issues on the ANC campaign manifesto, in addition to housing, education and employment.[44] This recognition showed that women's issues had become a national concern. It also indicated that the women's movement had power, which created an opportunity to campaign for other gender issues.[45] While the women's movement made progress on the national level, women reported conflicting experiences on the personal level. Geisler gives two examples: on the one hand, in May 1995, Frene Ginwala, the speaker in Parliament, was referred to as 'Mr Speaker' 34 times in one speech. However, Brigitte Mabandla, a member of Parliament, reported that, one year into her post, she had recognised significant improvement in male attitudes towards women, reflecting less resentment and uncertainty.[46]

Meaningful gains were limited to the macro level. Social and political obstacles had jeopardised women's participation, their unity and their image in the media.[47] Even in Parliament, the gender bias of public institutions still limited women's contributions.[48] For example, meetings went on into the late hours of the night infringing upon women's traditional roles; in addition, women were excluded from informal decision-making.[49] Goetz argues that this bias is inevitable and is likely to continue, adding that 'voice does not easily and simply lead to better outcomes for women'.[50]

2 *Constitutional Negotiations*

The drafting of the Constitution was the key moment for women in the transitional phase, as it set the framework under which gender issues would be treated for many years to come. The negotiation process was long and tiresome, described as 'protracted multi-party negotiations', ultimately leading to the Interim Constitution.[51] The WNC acted as

[44] Goetz, 'Women in politics', 247.

[45] Ibid.

[46] Geisler, 'Parliament is another terrain', 618.

[47] Denise Walsh, 'The liberal movement: women and just debate in South Africa 1994–1996' (2006) 32 *Journal of Southern African Studies*, 1, 90.

[48] Anne Marie Goetz, 'Women's political effectiveness: a conceptual framework' in Anne Marie Goetz and Shireen Hassim (eds.), *No Shortcuts to Power: African Women in Politics and Policy Making* (London and New York: Zed Books, 2003), p. 35.

[49] Walsh, 'The liberal moment', 91.

[50] Goetz, 'Women's political effectiveness', p. 35.

[51] Jacklyn Cock, 'Engendering gay and lesbian rights: the equality clause in the South African Constitution' (2002) 26 *Women's Studies International Forum* 1, 37.

'a gender watchdog during the period of constitutional negotiations', pushing for the demands and desires of women from all backgrounds.[52]

Common concerns for the women's movement at this time included issues related to poverty, employment, housing and violence; however, most importantly, women expressed apprehension about customary norms that treated all females as 'perpetual minors', limiting their rights to inheritance, and severely undermining their rights.[53] This was addressed by the WNC, which had mobilised 'a broad consensus to lobby for the reform of customary law', but it 'was met head-on by traditional leaders, for whom an equality clause was anathema'.[54] Traditional leaders saw gender equality as a threat to their rule and longevity; in the constitutional negotiations, they demanded the endorsement of their status and power in the Constitution, and they claimed exclusive ruling power over communities falling under customary law.[55]

Traditional leaders labelled gender equality as a foreign idea – a common argument used by conservative states to maintain the gender power dynamic. It is also an excuse repeatedly used by states to derogate from upholding the right to gender equality, criticising the 'individualism implicit in Western human rights thought' that contradicts the emphasis on community interest prevalent in African societies.[56] This resonates with the stance taken by many countries with Muslim majorities that have derogated from specific provisions of CEDAW that they perceive as contradictory to Sharia.[57] Responding to traditional leaders in South Africa, the women's lobby argued that excluding women living under customary law from the equality clause essentially legitimised discrimination against the most vulnerable and isolated women.[58] Finally, traditional leaders withdrew and were satisfied with a guarantee of 'cultural rights' in the Constitution.[59]

The contribution of the women's movement to the Constitution-making and its impact on the rights and freedoms enjoyed by women for the following decades is undeniable. Tripp noted, 'countries that have gone the furthest in advancing women's constitutional rights were

[52] Kuumba, *Gender and Social Movements*, p. 129.
[53] Ibid.
[54] Hassim, '"A conspiracy of women"', 719.
[55] Mabandla, 'Women in South Africa', p. 69; Hassim, '"A conspiracy of women"', 719.
[56] Ronald Thandabantu Nhlapo, 'International protection of human rights and the family: Africa variations on a common theme' (1989) 3 *International Journal of Law and Family*, 1, 4.
[57] Danish Institute, *Informal Justice System*, p. 101.
[58] Nhlapo, 'International protection', 69.
[59] Albertyn, 'Women and the transition', 60.

generally places where women's movements were most active around these issues'.[60]

3 *Post-apartheid Hardships*

With the birth of democracy in South Africa, NGOs suffered the loss of both funding and employees. Many staff members left NGOs and joined government institutions so as to contribute to the transitional process from within the system. This move had mixed repercussions; negatively, 'this loss of expertise and staff was difficult for the NGO world, which was grappling with its place and relationship with the new regime'.[61] However, on the positive side, NGO staff members who had always considered the government as the enemy became open to the possibility of cooperation for the first time when some of their former colleagues joined government institutions.[62] Therefore, after working in opposition for decades, NGOs and the government started cooperating and coordinating to raise awareness on gender issues and provide services, especially addressing GBV.[63] Britton explained that 'although they have become the primary contract agents for the government, many women's groups remain thwarted by the complexities of their new bureaucratic relationship with the same government institutions they used to oppose during apartheid'.[64]

Women's organisations were not the only ones forced to revisit their roles and identities in South African politics and society. The whole NGO sector faced an unexpected crisis shortly after apartheid ended. For example, the Legal Resource Centre (LRC) was one of the main and first providers of legal aid in South Africa,[65] but had to change its mandate under the new democracy. During apartheid, the Centre focused on litigation concerning racial discrimination. However, after apartheid, the Centre shifted its interest to 'constitutional litigation, developmental work and law reform' and 'is now concerned with

[60] Tripp, 'Women's movements and Constitution making', 86.

[61] David Cote and Jacob Van Garderen, 'Challenges to public interest litigation South Africa: external and internal challenges to determining the public interest' (2011) 27 *South African Journal on Human Rights*, 1, 168.

[62] Ibid., 169.

[63] Hannah Britton, 'Organising against gender-based violence in South Africa' (2006) 32 *Journal of Southern African Studies*, 1, 147.

[64] Ibid.

[65] David McQuoid-Mason, 'Access to justice in South Africa' (1999) 17 *The Windsor Yearbook of Access to Justice*, 237. For impact litigation regarding pass laws undertaken by LRC during apartheid, see Richard L Abel, *Politics by Other Means: Law in the Struggle Against Apartheid, 1980–1994* (New York and London: Routledge, 1995), pp. 24–33.

constitutional issues; land, housing and development; environmental issues; and gender issues'.[66] Some organisations changed their structure rather than their agenda, such as Black Sash – an NGO founded during apartheid to work on issues regarding the Constitution and racial discrimination.[67] After participating in the Constitution drafting process, Black Sash faced the same dilemma:

> the very foundations of South Africa began to change, the Black Sash too began to consider what its new role should be. Gradually, and at times painfully, it moved away from being an organisation that was member driven, and almost entirely made up of white women volunteers. By the end of 1995, the Black Sash had evolved into its current structure of a professionally staffed non-governmental organisation, led by a National Director, and accountable to a Board of Trustees.[68]

Nongovernmental organisations also redefined their mandates and agendas when foreign donors redirected their funds to the post-apartheid government, leaving women's organisations to compete for limited resources.[69] Funding restraints forced NGOs to scale down operations, going from offering broad and general legal advice to focusing on specific legal issues; this was an attempt on the part of NGOs to show their expertise in specialised areas of law in order to attract donor funding.[70]

II NGOs IN DEMOCRATIC SOUTH AFRICA

After their short-lived ordeals, NGOs flourished in the new democracy; a decade after the end of apartheid, there were 85,000 registered NGOs,[71] reaching an estimated 100,000 in 2013.[72] The relationship between women's organisations and the state became more amicable and cooperative.[73] The state recognised the importance of NGOs and

[66] McQuoid-Mason, 'Access to justice', 237.

[67] Black Sash 'Our History', accessed 20 July 2018 at www.blacksash.org.za/index.php/our-legacy/history-of-the-black-sash. For examples of cases sponsored by Black Sash during apartheid see Abel, *Politics by Other Means*, pp. 27–54.

[68] Black Sash 'Our history'.

[69] Britton, 'Organizing against', 145.

[70] Cote and Garderen, 'Challenges to public interest litigation', 169.

[71] James Taylor, ' Struggles against systems that impoverish: South African civil society at the crossroads' (2013) 23 *Development in Practice*, 5/6, 620.

[72] Lauren Stuart, 'The South African nonprofit sector: struggling to survive, needing to thrive', NGOPulse, 9 April 2013, accessed 7 July 2018 at www.ngopulse.org/article/south-african-nonprofit-sector-struggling-survive-needing-thrive

[73] Britton, 'Organizing against', 147.

their contribution to development and therefore gave NGOs significant political and legal space to operate.

A The Power and Reach of NGOs

In democratic South Africa, cooperation between NGOs and the state created a divide between NGOs and CBOs; NGOs moved to policy-making[74] and CBOs were linked to local communities. At that point, 'NGOs were challenged as not having the legitimacy of being mandated by the people, and accused of being agents of foreign agendas'.[75] Both national NGOs and CBOs, however, provided an invaluable source of information for the state on women's lived realities,[76] which led to a constructive partnership, as will be discussed in the following section.

Differences in the scope of work of NGOs and CBOs gradually became valuable to both as they worked on critical and complimentary spheres. Looking at strategies adopted by women's organisations to influence government policy, Connolly found that NGOs frequently form partnerships with organisations that work on the same interest.[77] This was echoed and further elaborated by Sandy, a participant in this research study, whose organisation primarily works on legal support and development. She explained the importance of creating partnerships with CBOs in order to enable lawyers to understand the issues that are important to the people. She elaborated that lawyers have academic and intellectual interests that can direct policy change. However, advocating issues that are unimportant to the public is fruitless, and therefore her NGOs maintain close ties with CBOs so as to be grounded and know how people want the law to help them. This is aimed at developing a bottom-up approach to influence policy.[78]

B NGOs in Law-making

After apartheid, tackling VAW became a priority for the state and, as a result, a number of partnerships formed between NGOs and government institutions. Because of these spaces, 'women's organizations

[74] Llewellyn Leonard, 'Characterising civil society and its challenges in post-apartheid South Africa' (2014) 40 *Social Dynamics* 2.

[75] Taylor, 'Struggles against systems', 622.

[76] Tinus Kruger et al., *Making South Africa Safe: A Manual for Community-Based Crime Prevention*, research report (The Council for Scientific and Industrial Research, 2016), p. 32.

[77] Sarah Connolly, *Assessing the Successes of and Challenges Facing Civil Society Organizations in South Africa, in Influencing Gender-Based Violence Policy*, research report (SIT Graduate Institute, 2017), p. 31.

[78] Ibid., p. 34.

have been influential in shaping law on violence against women, both domestic violence and sexual violence, around a feminist agenda'.[79] For instance, while parliament debated the sexual offences bill, NGOs united through the National Working Group on Sexual Offences, 'bringing rape to the forefront of public consciousness'.[80]

The drafting of the two most important legislative instruments combatting VAW included contributions from NGOs. For the DVA, the TLAC was quite involved in the drafting process and its director was a member of the South African Law Commission's (SALC) committee on domestic violence.[81] Contributions by TLAC can be summarised as follows:

> The TLAC made several submissions to the SALC, and many of its recommendations were eventually incorporated in the 1998 legislation… TLAC also conducted research to identify the services that women currently used in connection with gender-based violence and how responsive these services were to their needs. The study assessed the use of the criminal justice system, the health system, and the services provided by TLAC. After examining 942 records of domestic violence, including hospital charts from the local hospital, the study found that the majority of women sought help from the police[82]

The same research study shed light on how the public health system was failing victims of domestic violence, as it found that a miniscule number of victims who were treated by healthcare providers were referred to the police or a social worker.[83]

Similarly, various NGOs have contributed to different parts of the SOA based on their expertise. For instance, there was some debate on the treatment clause in the SOA: even though the Law Commission had proposed the provision of free treatment to victims of sexual offences, the Cabinet determined that the financial obligation would be too high on the state and therefore scrapped the provision from the

79 Shereen W Mills, 'Consent and coercion in the law of rape in South Africa: a feminist transformative approach' (2010) 28 *Canadian Women's Studies*, 1, 84.

80 Shereen W Mills, 'Reforming the law of rape in South Africa' in Clare McGlynn and Vanessa E Munro, (eds.), Rethinking Rape Law: International and Comparative Perspectives (London: Routledge, 2010), p. 254.

81 Liesl Gerntholtz and Jennifer MacLeod, 'Gender and socio-economic rights: the case of gender-based violence and health' in Malcolm Langford et al, (eds.), *Socio-economic Rights in South Africa: Symbols or Substance* (Cambridge: Cambridge University Press, 2014), p. 375.

82 Ibid.

83 Ibid.

draft.[84] After appeals from 'concerned NGOs', an updated version of the draft, released in 2006, included a compromised stance giving the right for a victim to receive a PEP test at designated hospitals if the attack triggered a risk of HIV.[85] Similarly, based on a submission by the NGO, Resources Aimed at the Prevention of Child Abuse and Neglect (RAPCAN), the Committee changed its stance on child perpetrators of rape.[86] Even in the sentencing clause, NGOs made contributions towards the understanding of how gender stereotypes feed myths on women's consent.[87]

III NGOs ENGAGING WITH THE STATE

NGOs and governments are mutually dependant, and yet they monitor each other. In fact, 'there is a variety of emerging relations between governance from above and below, at local, regional, national and global levels' involving NGOs that work 'with and against the state'.[88] Mercer argues that NGOs in the global south have remarkable influence because they are able to reach the masses, particularly the poorest and most marginalised communities,[89] which is often challenging to governments. States who realise this power and do not see it as a threat can share the heavy burden of development with NGOs, who are involved and concerned partners. Although NGOs sometimes provide certain services that overlap with the government, Lea and Stemson warn that this should not be read as a withdrawal or weakness of the state. Rather, it represents 'a re-ordering or re-articulation of relations between state and non-state actors'.[90]

Working on GBV in South Africa, NGOs must engage with legal institutions and government agents. In the course of this engagement,

[84] Stefanie Roehrs, 'Half-hearted HIV-related services for victims' in Lillian Artz and Dee Smythe (eds.), *Should We Consent? Rape Law Reform in South Africa* (Cape Town: Juta, 2008), p. 180.

[85] Ibid., p. 181.

[86] Jacqui Gallinetti and Daksha Kassan, 'Children and sexual offences' victims' in Lillian Artz and Dee Smythe (eds.), *Should We Consent? Rape Law Reform in South Africa* (Cape Town: Juta, 2008), p. 172.

[87] Yonina Hoffman-Wanderer, 'Sentencing and management of sexual offenders' in Lillian Artz and Dee Smythe (eds.), *Should We Consent? Rape Law Reform in South Africa* (Cape Town: Juta, 2008), p. 228.

[88] John Lea and Kevin Stemson, 'Security, sovereignty and non-state governance "from below"' (2007) 22 *Canadian Journal of Law and Society*, 2, 10.

[89] Claire Mercer, 'Reconceptualizing state-society relations in Tanzania: are NGOs "making a difference"?' (1999) 31 *Area*, 3, 247.

[90] Lea and Stemson, 'Security, sovereignty', 10.

a relationship develops, characterised by mutual dependence with moments of conflict. Generally, the amicability between the state and NGOs depends on the kind of work undertaken by the organisation or the kind of services they need from each other. Conflict is unlikely to arise if NGOs only ask for assistance and support from law enforcement agents, or offer guidance and insights. However, when NGOs monitor, challenge and criticise the government, issues of authority and territoriality may create conflict. These relations are the subject matter of Chapter 8.

A NGOs and State Institutions: Cooperation

Implementing state–NGO partnerships needs an open channel of communication and an understanding that all parties are moving towards the same goals.[91]

1 Nationwide Projects

There are two levels of cooperation between the state and NGOs. On a macro level, NGOs can create partnerships for large-scale projects with different government departments. In Ikhaya Lethemba, staff members from Teddybear Clinic and Lifeline, in addition to 'doctors and nurses from medico-legal services, prosecutors from the National Prosecuting Authority, forensic police officers from SAPS and social workers from the Department of Social Development', all work together to provide comprehensive services for victims of violence, includes a shelter for abused women.[92] Some partnerships are project-based with specific objectives and time frames. Gender Links occasionally works with the government and other NGOs to conduct research and campaigns on 'societal ills' such as HIV and AIDS.[93] The government also often uses NGOs as consultants on environmental concerns.[94] Public national campaigns such as the 16 Days of Activism are also implemented through collaboration between NGOs and the state.[95]

[91] Kruger et al., *Making South Africa Safe*.

[92] Center for the Study of Reconciliation and Development, *Mapping Local Gender-based Violence Prevention and Response Strategies in South Africa*, research report (April 2016), p. 5.

[93] Ibid., p. 10.

[94] Jacklyn Cock and David Fi, 'The impact of globalisation on environmental politics in South Africa, 1990–2002' (2001) 5 *African Sociological Review*, 2, 19.

[95] Center for the Study of Reconciliation and Development, *Mapping Local Gender-based Violence*, p. 4; Mothibi A Kholofelo, 'Challenges and achievement with regard to woman and child abuse prevention by the South African Police Services' (2016) 4 *Sociology and Anthropology*, 1, 9.

2 Training

Training is one of the major joint activities that is not only necessary but also reflective of the government's acknowledgement of NGOs' expertise. Stop Trafficking of People linked up with the Limpopo police in a partnership where the NGO trained police to identify human trafficking victims.[96] In a research study, a staff member from LRC noted that the kind of direct contact they have with law enforcement agents during training is quite influential as it develops a fruitful relationship afterwards, one where trainees can ask for and receive help and advice any time. She added, 'we almost changed their mindsets'.[97] Similarly, both NGO8 and NGO10 in this research study have previously provided training to the police on the nature of child abuse and homosexuality, respectively.

3 Community-based Partnerships

Community-based organisations are involved with state agents on a grassroots level, for instance providing direct assistance in police stations. The SAPS Victim Empowerment programme is one example. It is based on a broader partnership set up by SAPS with the Community Police Forums to work with NGOs and CBOs to establish 'victim friendly facilities and volunteer networks at all police stations… to improve services to victims of crime and violence'.[98] This programme engages with and trains local volunteers to contribute to these services.[99] Similarly, a few participants in this research were originally trained by the state to volunteer on court premises, but eventually launched their own community initiatives. For example, Arriera of NGO1 was originally trained to work at a Magistrate Court, assisting victims of violence with advice and simple tasks such as filling out PO forms. She was selected for the training based on her leadership skills and reputation in the community. When her contract with the court ended, she set up NGO1 on police station premises in the township where she lived, and resumed her work with the community independently. NGO3 provides a similar example in which the head of the NGO, Katrina, was trained

[96] 'Police, NGO team up to fight human trafficking', News24, 4 October 2016, accessed 7 July 2018 at www.news24.com/SouthAfrica/News/police-ngo-team-up-to-fight-human-trafficking-20161004

[97] Connolly, *Assessing the Successes*, p. 45.

[98] SAPS, 'Victim empowerment service in the South African police service', SAPS website, accessed 7 July 2018 at www.saps.gov.za/resource_centre/women_children/amended_victim_empo_service.pdf

[99] Ibid., p. 16.

by the government about a decade ago, under a programme developed specifically to facilitate access to justice for women. The founders of NGO3 later decided to become independent and set up the NGO with the mission of providing services to rural communities.

In this way, these NGOs and CBOs 'fill a gap in service provision at stations, by providing sensitive support and additional information to survivors that can help them on their journey to healing'.[100] Located on police premises, NGO13 enjoys a mutually beneficial relationship with the police. One notable benefit of proximity to the police, as Jabu explained, is to alleviate the trauma for GBV victims. Jabu and a policewoman agreed that rape victims would give their statements only once at the NGO trailer, with both of them present, so as to avoid repetition of traumatic events. In addition, the policewoman responsible for social crime helps with Jabu's transportation for field visits; she also transfers victims to hospitals and safe houses in police cars. Similarly, in the Democratic Republic of the Congo (DRC), NGO staff members accompany legal investigators in sexual violence cases to offer counselling and support to victims, promoting a sensitive investigative process.[101]

4 *Referrals*

This research found that police and courts frequently refer cases to NGOs for specialised assistance. For example, NGO8 staff members who work on child abuse cases maintain productive relationships with prosecutors. They meet every two months to discuss updates and new business. Simultaneously, the police refer cases of sexual abuse against children to the NGO for assessment and recommendations. Similarly, staff members from NGO1 and NGO10 reported that they receive court preparation referrals from the police and courts. In addition, the police refer women to NGOs for administrative assistance, such as filling out PO forms. Government and NGOs often provide similar services, but these are not to be confused as duplicated services. There may be slight differences that improve relief for victims of violence. For instance, NGOs and the state saw 'slightly different populations of rape survivors. State facilities attended to large numbers of victims who had been recently raped and were, therefore, most likely to be experiencing the acute stage of trauma, while organisations with office-based services

[100] Shukumisa, *Monitoring the Implementation of Sexual Offences Legislation*, research report (Tshwaranang Legal Advocacy Centre and others, 2013–2014), p. 34.

[101] Lake, *Strong NGOs and Weak States*, p. 167.

were also seeing women seeking help with historical experiences of rape, who had typically not reported the attack at the time it occurred'.[102]

The SAPS Victim Empowerment programme includes a referral system by local police stations to NGOs and shelters, specifying different services to which victims can have access.[103] This is a mutually beneficial relationship since the police can resort to NGOs for support, but at the same time, NGOs can receive better services from the police, especially CBOs, which are often engaged in dispute resolution in their area or that work in dangerous fields. In this research, all shelters personally knew the police as they often needed to call them when the shelter premises were attacked by angry partners of residents. Beth reports that the first time she summoned the police to Shelter1 was when a resident's husband had attacked the shelter. All residents and staff hid in their rooms until the intruder gave up and left. While hiding, Beth called the police, but to no avail. Afterwards, she built a relationship with the station head and communicated with him directly when similar attacks happened, which are common occurrences for domestic violence shelters.[104] Similarly, Bridget from Shelter 4 commended the police in the area and confirmed that the relationship between them was solid. She explained that the police promptly responded to her calls when partners of the residents attacked the crisis centre. In return, the police brought abused women to the safe house or the shelter when they needed urgent accommodation. There were some cases in which the police did not assist women, but this was usually resolved as soon as shelter staff members interfered.

These examples show that the state trusts the knowledge and expertise of NGOs, and realises their key role in upholding human rights. Ayanda Dlodlo, South Africa's Deputy Minister of Public Service and Administration, stated in an interview, 'The South African Government is alive and engaged with the matter of finding innovative ways to work in partnership with non-governmental stakeholders to improve accountability'.[105]

[102] Vetten, '*Its Sucks/ It's a Wonderful Service*', p. 10.

[103] SAPS, 'Victim empowerment service', p. 16.

[104] For instance, see Pam Belluck, 'Shelters for women disclosing their locations, in spite of risks', *The New York Times*, 10 August 1997, accessed 20 July 2018 at www.nytimes.com/1997/08/10/us/shelters-for-women-disclosing-their-locations-in-spite-of-risk.html

[105] 'South Africa looking for innovative ways to work with NGOs – interview with minister', Open Government Partnership, 12 September 2012, accessed 5 July 2018 at www.opengovpartnership.org/stories/south-africa-looking-innovative-ways-work-ngos-interview-minister

5 *Court Summons for Expert Assistance*

The following chapter will discuss cases in which courts have requested submissions from NGOs on their topics of expertise. Sandy, a participant in this study who works on impact litigation explained that courts may either issue an open call for submissions so that any interested party can contribute, or send direct requests to specific NGOs with the required expertise. For instance, the court in the *Mokoena* case[106] issued an open call for interested parties to make submissions on the procedures of sexual offences trials affecting children victims and witnesses. For Sandy, calling for assistance is an encouraging indication that 'the court knows what it does not know'. She added, 'I would rather the court asks for extra assistance than try to rely on its own knowledge that it does not have'. Similarly, in 2013, the Department of Justice and Constitutional Development had amended some regulations at the sexual offences courts, and invited interested parties to comment and advise.[107] These invitations are usually directed at NGOs, and the feedback is seriously considered by the state. The CALS, in its submission as a response to the invitation, thanked the Department of Justice and Constitutional Development on its 'inclusion of many suggestions made by individuals and organisations dealing with gender based violence in the previous round of comments on the Draft Regulations of 2015'.[108]

Participants in this research reported contributing to the court as well, either in the form of submissions or as expert witnesses. For example, Linda from NGO9 occasionally gives testimony in her expert field: battered women's syndrome. Moreover, the government has sought the expertise of NGOs in monitoring and evaluation. In one case, a magistrate court invited Linda from NGO9 to monitor the implementation of the DVA as the NGO was working on a related project. The next chapter will zoom in on the methods used by courts to diversify their sources of information.

B State and NGOs: Moments of Conflict

It is rare that an open public conflict between NGOs and the state occurs in South Africa. There are some ideological conflicts and NGO criticism of public institutions is often not appreciated. For instance, in 2012, the South African Democratic Teachers' Union (SADTU) were

[106] *Mokoena* case, para. 13.

[107] Invitation for public comments, 2017.

[108] CALS, Submission to the Director-General: Justice and Constitutional Development on the Draft Regulations Relating to Sexual Offences Courts.

outraged by NGO criticism. They accused NGOs of enforcing a neo-liberal agenda and receiving foreign funding, to which a human rights lawyer responded by highlighting the need for cooperation between civil society and SADTU instead of 'launching an offensive'.[109] There was also an issue with state funding to NGOs in 2013, which prompted the Department of Social Development to deregister 36,488 NGOs for not conforming to financial regulation – a move which lead to some hiccups in the relationship.[110] Similarly, in terms of GBV, rather than 'conflict' there are some imperfections in the NGO–state relationship.

When NGOs are perceived to be interfering with or questioning the work of the police or courts, this is not always received lightly. The current mechanism for the accountability of the police is the Independent Police Investigative Directorate (IPID) unit, regulated by the Independent Police Investigative Directorate Act.[111] While Vetten expressed scepticism about this unit's potential when the bill[112] was introduced in Parliament, she noted that it promised 'at least one favourable outcome – the creation of a civil society reference group slated to meet on a quarterly basis' with the Civilian Secretariat for Police 'to address issues of policing in relation to women and children'.[113] NGO5 uses the IPID[114] to report police misconduct and finds this effective.

The strong research skills of NGO staff members and their ability to evaluate the social foundation behind the law enable NGOs to gather valuable information regarding the quality of service provision. In a study conducted in 2006–2007, the TLAC revealed that only 6.7 per cent of domestic violence victims pressed charges and were therefore counted in formal statistics.[115] The Shukumisa campaign ran a similar research project jointly undertaken by a coalition of NGOs to evaluate the compliance of the police with the SOA. While most policemen were willing to assist the monitors without any difficulty, in some stations, researchers were denied access and assistance for several reasons. In some cases, monitors had to return several times to the

[109] Victoria John, 'Sadtu warns it will go after NGOs', Mail & Guardian, 2 November 2012, accessed 7 July 2018 at www.mg.co.za/article/2012-11-02-sadtu-warns-it-will-go-after-ngos
[110] Stuart, 'The South African nonprofit sector'.
[111] Independent Police Investigative Directorate Act No 1 of 2011 (South Africa) (hereinafter IPID Act).
[112] Independent Police Investigative Directorate Bill B-15B of 2010.
[113] Vetten et al., *The Right and the Real*, p. 22.
[114] IPID website www.ipid.gov.za/
[115] Vetten et al., *The Right and the Real*, p. 31.

station and negotiate with the police for access and information.[116] Other stations did not accept monitors without written permission from SAPS.[117] These projects may be seen as inviting conflict between the states and NGOs; at the same time, they are also reflective of the openness of state institutions to be monitored by NGOs.Shortcomings in police conduct that affect women's access to justice will be the subject matter of Chapter 7.

NGOs are not the only parties to reveal state derelictions. A leaked government report, published by the South African *Mail & Guardian* newspaper, revealed that a meagre 9 per cent of all reported cases of child rape in 2000 resulted in conviction.[118] Statistics in South Africa reflect a universal problem of attrition. Regan and Kelly attribute low attrition rates to the government's persistent neglect of rape and sexual assault,[119] a universal problem that also persists in the UK, where they conducted their research. Another study compared the attrition rate in five countries with developed legal systems to confirm this conclusion.[120] The only positive outcome of the study was the decreasing weight given to circumstantial factors such as the character and credibility of the victims, as well as the relationship with the stranger, which have traditionally been at the centre of rape trials.[121] However, attrition remains low.

One noted grievance of NGOs is the lack of and/or slow action on the part of the state. While the state listens to NGO suggestions on policy reform, they do not necessarily implement them, especially in a timely manner.[122] This is often a motivation for NGOs to litigate in the public interest against specific state departments. One such example is the *Child Law* case that NGOs filed against the Ministry of Education regarding the quality of schools in the Eastern Cape.[123]

Occasional conflict does not automatically lead to deteriorating relationships between the two parties. One research participant,

[116] Shukumisa, *Sexual Violence, Calling the System to Account*, research report (Tshwaranang Legal Advocacy Centre and Others, 2010), p. 8.

[117] Ibid.

[118] Deborah Ewing, 'Rape, gender and the justice system' (2003) 56 *Agenda*, 54.

[119] Linda Regan and Liz Kelly, *Rape: Still a Forgotten Issue*, briefing document (Europe: Rape Crisis Network, 2003), p. 4.

[120] Kathleen Daly and Brigette Bouhours, 'Rape and attrition in the legal process: a comparative analysis of five countries' (2010) 39 *Crime and Justice*, 1, 565–650.

[121] Ibid.

[122] Connolly, *Assessing the Successes*, p. 51.

[123] *Centre for Child Law* v. *Government of the Eastern Cape Province*, Eastern Cape High Court, Bisho, case no 504/10 (settled by a memorandum of understanding signed 4 February 2011).

Sandy, works on impact litigation, which means that she is constantly up against different state departments in court. However, she confirms that this does not affect the relationship out of court, explaining that her NGO spends an inordinate amount of time talking to the state and making recommendations. They also understand that the state fears NGO criticism and therefore they try to help as much as possible. Connolly found similar trends in her research. One of her respondents noted, 'in working with the government, our success has depended on the department that we are trying to influence. We have had some success with the Department of Health (DOH) and the Department of Labor, but less so with the Ministry of Women and the Presidency'.[124] Sandy also asserts that different units and staff in the same state department may have various levels of readiness to cooperate with NGOs.

IV 'PUSHING THE BURDEN' ONTO NGOs

The collaboration between NGOs and government agencies benefits many women. However, it 'may also leave space for "quackery" and ineffective remedies to which individuals fall prey'.[125] One possible negative impact of an increasingly active NGO scene is teaching the state to be ineffective in service provision. This sometimes happens in South Africa, as the government relies too heavily on NGOs to assist and provide resources to victims, and therefore relaxes state services in these areas.[126] For instance, law enforcement agents are often over-dependent on NGOs. Arriera from NGO1 reported that the police always refer GBV victims to her, including victims of rape and assault. Referrals take place before cases are opened so that court preparation, guidance on the administration of the law and mediation between family and community members. can all be addressed first.

Law enforcement agents are more likely to refrain from intervening or to postpone intervention when IJS are available. Research on informal justice in other countries echoes this trend. For example, police in the Gambia delay investigation to allow 'non-formal peacemakers' to intervene, taking the initiative to reconcile the parties in the dispute or to refer the cases to 'respected elders'.[127] Moult similarly found that on

[124] Connolly, *Assessing the Successes*, p. 32.
[125] Stewart, 'Arenas of anguish', p. 121.
[126] Bronwyn Pithey et al., 'Gender-based violence in South Africa: a submission to the Universal Periodic Review' (Shukumisa, 2016).
[127] International Council, *When Legal Worlds Overlap*, p. 47.

many occasions, women are denied assistance in police stations if they have not approached informal justice mechanisms first.[128] This practice seriously curtails justice and deprives women of their legal agency – a disadvantage of legal pluralism. Research in Kyrgyzstan also found that the availability of customary courts encourages both the police and courts to send citizens directly to this form of informal justice, without their consent.[129] Similarly, the police in Fiji have encouraged the community to resort to bulubulu for rape cases. This is an informal system of dispute resolution under which the liability of rape shifts from the offender to his kin group.[130] Thus, remedies for rape include an apology and some offerings from the offender, which the victim is pressured to accept, and consequently to forgive the offender.[131] Not only do ADR channels save state resources, they also protect state agents from complex and sensitive social matters that they may prefer to avoid.

This shift in responsibilities encourages the community to expect NGOs to carry the burden, reducing state accountability to curb VAW. Because of a lack of public resources, the availability of more specialised services at NGOs and the inability of the government to reach all members of the community, women are likely to have better experiences approaching NGOs. For example, when there was a shortage of staff to implement the DVA, NGOs replaced government institutions, performing specific tasks related to the DVA.[132] This situation is also favourable to the state, 'since there are so many South African NGOs focused on preventing and responding to GBV', state resources are better invested elsewhere.[133]

V CONCLUSION

The unique history of South Africa has strangely allowed for a women's movement to be quite effective at the greatest time of need. The women's movement rose with remarkable power after decades of repression of the women's agenda for the sake of the national movement. Matters could have gone in the wrong direction for women's rights had

[128] Moult, 'Providing a sense of justice'.
[129] International Council, *When Legal Worlds Overlap*, p. 78.
[130] Ibid., p. 79.
[131] Merry, *Human Rights and Gender Violence*, p. 113.
[132] Vetten, *Addressing Domestic Violence*, p. 7.
[133] Connolly, *Assessing the Successes*, p. 43.

the women's movement been relegated from the democratic transition process, as they have been in countless other countries.

The gains that women made two decades ago, and the relationship that developed with the state afterwards, provide a strong foundation for women's legal rights, significantly improving the experiences of women seeking relief from violence, starting with drafting legislation, which was discussed in this chapter, to the actual channels to access justice which are covered throughout the book. This includes the role of NGOs in informal justice, access to channels of formal justice and impact litigation. The foundation presented in this chapter paved the road for all the other gains. Imperfections are inevitable; however, this book aims to show that NGOs and the state get over these hurdles and focus on the common goal.

CHAPTER 5

THE JUSTICE SYSTEM: SPACE FOR NEGOTIATING HUMAN RIGHTS

In the pluralist legal system of South Africa, the judiciary plays a pivotal role in developing and maintaining a stable legal culture. Between balancing conflicting human rights, developing law to eliminate de jure and de facto inequalities, and domesticating international human rights law, South African jurisprudence is one of the richest globally. The plurality of the legal culture offers a suitable environment for cause lawyering – a practice that allows the state, judiciary and NGOs (representing the public) to negotiate and redefine human rights and state responsibility.

This chapter demonstrates how a judiciary can foster the growth and development of women's rights, and human rights in general. Coming out of the darkest times in history, the state was determined to create a space for justice that people can trust. Therefore, it has been open to reflecting on and revising not only the law, but also internal practices of the justice system. Moreover, the judiciary is keen to develop law in a direction that relates to people's lived realities. Therefore, analysing case law, one can see strong consideration given to the impact of court judgments on society, the socio-economic background and conditions of litigants, and the precedent created by judgments. In striving to close the gap between law and society, this legal space provides the perfect environment for NGOs to direct legal developments in a way that would improve the lives of women.

The chapter will first introduce cause lawyering and its birth in South Africa. It will proceed to discuss the gender composition of the judiciary – a matter of debate in South Africa over the last few years.

The discussion will move to case law where a variety of cases will be presented, highlighting the human rights discussions and negotiations taking place between litigants, the state and the judiciary, and leading to legal developments. This section will include case law related to GBV, in addition to some human rights cases. These negotiations are based on varied input from NGOs, global research, international human rights law, and expert opinions. They do not necessarily lead to legal gains, but they introduce important topics to the public sphere and lead to the development of necessary laws and policies. Finally, the chapter will provide snippets from impact litigation in selected countries to crystallise landmark decisions for women's rights.

I INTRODUCING CAUSE LAWYERING

A Public Interest Litigation, Impact litigation and Strategic Litigation

Cause lawyering is used to advocate for social and political change by engaging with courts. There is a slight difference between the two most common forms of cause lawyering: impact litigation and public interest litigation (PIL). Perelman explores PIL taking the Legal Resource Centre as an example. The centre has a 'constitutional litigation unit' and a network across the country to scan cases with potential to generate 'meaningful public interest impact ... either through the media attention they attract or as legal precedent'.[1] For PIL, NGOs select any cases with merit as long as they fall within their overall strategy[2] so as to press for legal reform in the direction they desire.[3] Impact litigation is a more focused approach; it is exercised for public interest but using a different methodology. Nongovernmental organisations invest their resources in one or a few cases that are likely to create precedent and make a huge impact for a specific cause.

Strategic litigation and impact litigation are used interchangeably in the literature; both are practised to identify legal gaps or highlight violations in state obligations under international human rights law.[4] Sandy, from NGO14, specialising in cause lawyering, sheds some light

[1] Jeremy Perelman, 'The way ahead? Access-to-justice, public interest lawyering and the right to legal aid in South Africa' (2005) 41 *Stanford Journal of International Law*, 2, 371.

[2] Cote and Garderen, 'Challenges to public interest litigation', 179.

[3] Margareth Etienne, 'The ethics of cause lawyering: an empirical examination of criminal defense lawyers as cause lawyers' (2005) 95 *Journal of Criminal Law and Criminology*, 4, 1243.

[4] Cheryl Thomas et al., *Working with the Justice Sector to End Violence Against Women and Girls*, research report (UN Women December, 2011), p. 91.

on further slight differences between the two terms. She explains that the three most obvious goals of litigation are: making, amending or repealing problematic laws. Some cases, however, may not have significant impact but carry strategic value. For instance, NGOs can undertake litigation which they know will fail, in a strategic attempt to put an issue for the first time before a court.[5] Another line of strategic litigation can bring forward 'regular' cases that the court sees every day, with a strategic value in the social background of the case. One example of this line of lawyering can be seen in a recent damages case brought forward by Jade September, yet to be heard by the Equality Court. The transgendered applicant was put in a male prison, leading to her constant humiliation that pushed her to attempt suicide, because of which, she is suing for damages.[6] The case carries significant strategic value, highlighting a problematic procedure in prisons. It also reflects Sandy's assertion that because the precedent system is already established, it is important to contribute to the body of case law. In this way, 'change is not always aimed at the legal or policy-level, but sometimes at enforcement and practice or raising the visibility of an issue and changing attitudes'.[7] Since cause lawyering often has non-legal goals, some cases are litigated because they raise a 'social debate' on a specific topic.[8] In any case, it is often difficult to draw the line between impact litigation and strategic litigation, but with practice, lawyers excel at dealing with each case based on its unique components and extracting the maximum benefit from the facts; this is described by Sandy as 'the art of litigation', inspiring the title of the following chapter.

B The Judiciary Position in Cause Lawyering

Cause lawyering rests on the role of the judiciary to promote 'the observance and the attainment of human rights' with regards to the

[5] Ibid.

[6] See Carl Collison, '"I didn't want to die" – queers battle prison', Mail & Guardian, 18 January 2018, accessed 11 July 2018 at www.mg.co.za/article/2018-01-18-i-didnt-want-to-die-queers-battle-prison-wardens

[7] Tamar Ezer and Priti Patel, 'Being strategic about strategic litigation: four things we've learned from a public health context', Human Rights Funders Network, 28 July 2016, accessed 11 July 2018 at www.hrfn.org/community-voices/being-strategic-about-strategic-litigation-four-things-weve-learned-from-a-public-health-context/

[8] Lawyers without Borders, *Strategic Litigation of Human Rights Abuses: A Guidebook for Legal Practitioners from the Commonwealth Caribbean* (Quebec City and Kingston: Lawyers without Borders, 2014), p. 23.

appropriate boundaries of the judicial power in law-making.[9] This is perhaps the area of adjudication that requires judges to mostly consider the socio-economic circumstances behind the facts of the case.[10] This point is the centre of the debate on 'judicial activism' – a term, often perceived as negative, and used for judges who rule on causes. The opposition to judicial activism is even stronger regarding socio-economic rights that are directly related to budgetary considerations and therefore lie within the power an elected body – parliament.[11] Public interest litigation can thus be seen as interference in extra-judicial matters in relation to a specific political position. South African senior politicians have previously accused courts of taking an oppositional role in reference to some unfavourable court judgments against the state.[12]

Cause lawyering, however, has become a reality, forcing the judiciary to embrace their role in law-making – an increasingly popular practice globally and specifically within African states.[13] This approach is used 'to try and effect a legal change which the other organs of democratic governance – legislative and executive – are unable or unwilling to do'.[14] The cause may be related to democracy or the rule of law, but it usually addresses more profound issues concerning unequal distribution of power, de facto discriminatory legislation, developing social and customary norms, or sending strong messages to society on the importance of human rights.[15] The emergence of cause lawyering in developing

[9] *International Standards of Judicial Independence* (International Association of Judicial Independence and World Peace, 2008), s. 1.2.1.2.

[10] K C Andrew and S C Nyirenda, 'The role of the judiciary in protecting the rights of vulnerable groups in Malawi' in Anneke Meerkotter (ed.), *Using the Courts to Protect Vulnerable People: Perspectives from the Judiciary and Legal Profession in Botswana, Malawi, and Zambia* (Southern Africa Litigation Centre and others, 2015), p. 4.

[11] Priti Patel, 'Realising the full potential of civil and political rights for marginalized populations in African Countries' in Anneke Meerkotter (ed.), *Using the Courts to Protect Vulnerable People: Perspectives from the Judiciary and Legal Profession in Botswana, Malawi, and Zambia* (Southern Africa Litigation Centre and others, 2015), p. 42.

[12] Venita Govender and Rachel Killean, *Lawyers, Conflict and Transition: South Africa*, research report (Economic and Social Research Council, December 2016), p. 20.

[13] B K Oagile and J Dingake, 'The role of the judiciary and the legal profession in protecting the rights of 18 vulnerable groups in Botswana' in Anneke Meerkotter (ed.), *Using the Courts to Protect Vulnerable People: Perspectives from the Judiciary and Legal Profession in Botswana, Malawi, and Zambia* (Southern Africa Litigation Centre and others, 2015), p. 23.

[14] Aidan O'Neill, 'Strategic litigation before the European Courts' (2015) 16 *ERA Forum*, 4, 496.

[15] Frank Munger, 'The cause lawyer's cause' in Stephen Ellman et al. (eds.), *For Martin Chanock: Essays on Law and Society* (Annandale, NSW: The Federation Press, 2010), p. 98; Carrie Menkel-Meadow, 'The causes of cause lawyering' in Austin Sarat and Stuart Scheingold (eds.), *Cause Lawyering, Political Commitments and Professional Responsibilities* (Oxford: Oxford University Press, 1998), pp. 31–61.

countries proves that 'law's compelling ideals are taking hold in the Global South'.[16] In fact, the judiciary is not only developing common law, but also customary law, as well as domesticating international human rights principles and state obligations, as will be seen in this chapter.

C A History of Cause Lawyering in South Africa

Tools for public interest litigation during apartheid were limited; there was no progressive Constitution to guarantee the adjudication of rights, and the judiciary was adamant in strictly applying the law despite their personal convictions of the embedded injustice.[17] However, the apartheid state upheld the judiciary as an honourable rank as they needed to keep a firm grip on the law, the main force keeping apartheid alive. This opened some space for activists to find loopholes in the law and use the legal system against the regime through PIL.[18] Lawyers showed remarkable courage representing poor black South Africans and NGOs started directing their resources to this line of work.[19] The LRC, for example, a rights-based NGO founded in 1979, litigated issues of concern for the disadvantaged South Africans in different legal areas.[20] The Centre for Applied Legal Studies also launched in 1979 as a legal research unit at Wits University to work primarily on legal reform and access to justice.[21]

Organisations undertaking PIL during this time focused on government process and regulations.[22] Their approach was smart and strategic; knowing that it was a lost cause, they did not challenge the apartheid system, but they challenged the government's use of excessive force in implementing the law.[23] They started by providing the much-needed free legal services in pass courts. Their contribution had a 'dramatic impact' as lawyers 'challenged the prosecution on process

[16] Munger, 'The cause lawyer's cause', p. 97. For information on PIL in India, see Hans Dembowski, *Taking the State to Court: Public Interest Litigation and the Public Sphere in Metropolitan India* (Oxford: Oxford University Press, 2001). Also see Surya Deva, 'Public interest litigation in India: a critical review' (2009) 28 *Civil Justice Quarterly*, p. 19.

[17] Steven Budlender et al., *Public Interest Litigation and Social Change in South Africa: Strategies, Tactics and Lessons*, research report (The Atlantic Philanthropies, 2014), p. 6.

[18] Govender and Killean, *Lawyers, Conflict and Transition*, p. 10.

[19] C J Arup, 'Educating cause lawyers in Australia after South Africa' in Stephen Ellman et al. (eds.), *For Martin Chanock: Essays on Law and Society* (Annandale, NSW: The Federation Press, 2010), p. 113.

[20] McQuoid-Mason, 'Access to justice', 237.

[21] Center for Applied Legal Studies website at www.wits.ac.za/cals/about-us/

[22] Yoseph Mulugeta, 'Public interest litigation as practiced by South African human rights NGOs: any lessons for Ethiopia' LLM Thesis (University of Pretoria, 2005), p. 35.

[23] Ibid.

and substantive concerns, significantly slowing down the processing rate, generating delays and blockages and frustrating the courts' operability'.[24] The most notable litigation gains secured by NGOs at this time related to housing and evictions, employment abuses, pass laws and police brutality.[25] In these instances, despite the oppressiveness of the system, the law was used quite creatively.[26] In the last few decades, cause lawyering has shifted its approach and efforts, addressing the most pressing social needs at any given time. Initially, it focused on civil and political rights, but with the end of apartheid, socio-economic litigation took priority due to rampant poverty.[27]

D Cause Lawyering in Practice

Today, cause lawyering is one of the main tools used by NGOs to advocate for legal and social change. Impact litigation gradually became more favourable than PIL, driven by funding constraints as well as the assumption that the state is more reluctant to provide legal assistance for cases that could create further state obligations.[28] Some NGOs focus on a broad issue or interest group, such as reproductive rights or homosexuality, while others prefer to direct their resources towards one focus area. For instance, the Centre for Child's Law litigates test cases related to children in, or affected by, the criminal justice system.[29]

Impact litigation entails NGOs either litigating directly or acting as *amicus curiae* (friends of the court). The first approach is more costly and time-consuming whether the NGO directly litigates or sponsors an ongoing case.[30] Intervening as *amici* is therefore a preferred choice. The role of *amicus curiae* was spelled out by the Constitutional Court as drawing 'the attention of the court to relevant matters of law and fact to which attention would not otherwise be drawn' in addition to the duty to 'provide cogent and helpful submissions that assist the court'.[31] Information submitted by *amici* should be different from the arguments

[24] Govender and Killean, *Lawyers, Conflict and Transition*, p. 11.

[25] Fayeeza Kathree, 'Public interest law: its continuing role in South Africa' (2002) 15 *Advocate*, 3, 33; *Orr* v. *Minister of Law and Order* ECD 25 September 1985 case no. 2507/85 (unreported); *Rikhoto* v. *East Rand Administration Board* 1983 (4) South Africa 278 (W).

[26] Mulugeta, 'Public interest litigation', p. 35.

[27] Kathree, 'Public interest law', 33.

[28] Ibid., 34.

[29] *Strategic Impact Litigation for Children's Rights*, research report (Centre for Child Law, 2011), p. 5.

[30] Spies, 'The importance and relevance of amicus curiae', 252.

[31] *Minister of Health* v. *Treatment Action Campaign* [2002] (10) BCLR 1075 (CC), p. 5 (hereinafter, TAC case).

of the two parties in a given case.[32] The Constitutional Court also identified *amici* as 'not a party to litigation' but the outcome of the case will affect its interests.[33]

NGOs, as any interested party, are able to apply for *amicus* status under rule 10 of the Constitutional Court rules.[34] In the application to be admitted as *amicus*, the party must explain the interest in the case and the position to be taken.[35] There are different strategies that NGOs undertake in the role of *amicus*; all require expertise on the issue of adjudication. One approach is to provide an argument much more radical than the applicant's so as to change the direction of litigation. This is risky because if accepted, the case may have a much greater benefit to society than the limited impact on the direct litigant, but if rejected, the applicant will lose the case.[36] In other cases, NGOs may receive an invitation from the court to provide submissions on novel and emerging matters. Courts generally consider *amici* impartial, trusted and reliable.[37] In this case, NGOs provide clarity for the court on cases with difficult facts and legal issues, or if the arguments provided by the two parties do not capture the core of the case.[38] *Amici* can also have minimal intervention, which usually occurs when an important legal issue has been left out of the argument, for instance introducing the international human rights law position on the legal matter.[39]

NGOs have brought cases to alternative adjudicating bodies, although most of the impact litigation work remains in High Courts. The Women's Legal Centre (WLC), a women's rights organisation in South Africa, brought the case of 'constructive dismissal after sexual harassment'[40] before the Commission for Conciliation, Mediation and Arbitration.[41] The case involved a police officer who was mistreated and harassed by her colleagues because she filed a rape claim against her

[32] *Strategic Impact Litigation*, p. 4.

[33] *Hoffmann* v. *South African Airways* [2000] (11) BCLR (CC) 1235, para. 63 (hereinafter, *Hoffman* case).

[34] Rules of the Constitutional Court, 460 Regulation Gazette (Department of Justice and Constitutional Development, 31 October 2003).

[35] Ibid. s. 10(6).

[36] Budlender et al., *Public Interest Litigation*, p. 137.

[37] Obonye Jonas, 'The participation of the amicus curiae institution in human rights litigation Botswana and South Africa: a tale of two jurisdictions' (2015) 59 *Journal of African Law* 2, 339.

[38] Budlender et al., *Public Interest Litigation*, p. 139.

[39] Ibid., p. 140.

[40] Women's Legal Centre Newsletter, volume 1 (Women's Legal Centre, 2008), p. 7.

[41] The Commission for Conciliation, Mediation and Arbitration is a dispute resolution body established under the terms of the Labour Relations Act No 66 of 1995 (South Africa).

manager. She therefore quit her job and sought compensation with the assistance of WLC and other organisations. The WLC supported the case to emphasise the need for strict policies to curb sexual harassment against female employees in the workplace.[42]

South Africa has also seen some strategic litigation attempts to reinforce conservative norms. In *Teddy Bear Clinic v. Minister of Justice and Constitutional Development*,[43] the Justice Alliance of South Africa (JASA) supported the state in opposing the decriminalisation of sex for children under 18. In this case, the Teddy Bear Clinic sought to remove the minimum legal age for consensual sex, but JASA submitted eight expert reports and affidavits in an attempt to convince the court that lowering the legal age for sex has negative psychological effects and is likely to spread HIV, among other sexual transmitted diseases.[44] While the Court ruled in favour of the Teddy Bear Clinic, JASA's intervention had exhausted significant resources of the Clinic in the process.[45]

II A CLOSE LOOK AT THE JUDICIARY

A liberal, plural judiciary sets the stage for cause lawyering. This openness, diversity and plurality must emanate from within the institution, which warrants a look inside the South African judiciary. Unsurprisingly, historical structural discrimination compromises the possibility of maintaining a judiciary that truly reflects the social composition of South African society.

A Commission for Gender Equality Investigating Women on the Bench

The underrepresentation of women on the bench was the core of the case brought by the Democratic Governance and Rights Unit and Sonke for Gender Justice against the President of South Africa and the Minister of Justice before the CGE in 2012.

The case questioned the slow pace with which the gender transformation of the judiciary is taking place. Applicants cited section

[42] Women's Legal Centre Newsletter.

[43] *Teddy Bear Clinic for the Abused Children and Another v. Minister of Justice and Constitutional Development and Another* [2013] (73300/10) ZAGPPHC 1 (hereinafter, *Teddy Bear* case).

[44] 'JASA assembles experts to oppose bid to lower age of sexual consent', Gateway News, 14 December 2011, accessed 2 June 2018 at www.gatewaynews.co.za/jasa-assembles-experts-to-oppose-bid-to-lower-age-of-sexual-consent/

[45] Budlender et al., *Public Interest Litigation*, p. 20.

174 of the Constitution, which directs the appointment of judges to be in line with the gender and racial composition in the country; in 2009–2012, out of 110 appointed justices, only 24 were women, despite the fact that there were more female graduates and female admitted attorneys than male, and that there were 561 female practising advocates at this time. Applicants argued that this amounted to a violation of the right to equality in the Constitution[46] and the right to be free from discrimination under the Promotion of Equality and Unfair Discrimination Act,[47] in addition to violations of international law provisions that South Africa had ratified.[48] In defence, the Judicial Service Commission (JSC) revealed their selection process and the gender division of applicants versus the gender division of accepted candidates.[49] The data showed expected progress since 1994 when there were 165 judges including 160 white men, three black men and two white women. However, the progress is not fast enough. By 2003, the number of black judges went up to 34 per cent and female judges up to 12 per cent.[50] The excuse that 'women do not apply for the positions' or 'not enough women are qualified' is quite redundant and unconvincing, and it essentially blames women for the impediments they face.[51] No consideration or responsibility was taken by any of the stakeholders concerned for the structural sexism or gender stereotypes that unsurprisingly create a glass ceiling for women and, instead, they opted to deflect blame onto each other.

B The Importance of Investigating the Issue of Female Judges

While statistics reflect alarming structural difficulties for South African women to advance in the judiciary, this is a universal problem persistent in some of the most developed legal systems.[52] In fact, the statistics are quite embarrassing for other countries such as the United Kingdom

46 Constitution, s. 9(3) and (4).

47 Equality Act, s. 8(h) and (i).

48 Including Article 2 and Article 9(2) of the Africa's Women's Protocol, and Article 7(f) of the SADC Protocol on Gender and Development.

49 See François Du Bois, 'Judicial selection in post-apartheid South Africa' in Kate Malleson and Peter H Russell (eds.), *Appointing Judges in an Age of Judicial Power – Critical Perspectives from Around the World* (Toronto: University of Toronto Press, 2006), p. 12.

50 Ibid., p. 11.

51 Ulrike Schultz and Gisela Shaw (eds.), *Gender and Judging* (Oxford: Hart Publishing, 2013), p. 20.

52 Gender Equality Commission, *Balanced Participation of Women and Men in Decision-Making*, analytical report (Council of Europe, 2016), p. 13.

(UK) where women occupy just 16.6 per cent of the all-white Supreme Court.[53]

It is therefore commendable that this conversation is happening in South Africa, engaging different stakeholders as well as the public. The JSC agreed that gender bias remains a problem; however, it contended that there are no shortcuts to solutions that entail joint efforts from all parties including the CGE, academia and women's NGOs.[54] This investigation allowed the CGE to dig deeper into the problem, addressing other stakeholders. For instance, CGE communicated with institutions such as the Black Lawyers Association and the South African Chapter of the International Associate of Women Judges to question their roles in prepping women for these positions.[55] They highlighted some social barriers to explain the discrepancy between the high numbers of female law graduates and practitioners, and the low number of applicants and appointments. For instance, some obstacles include the social and family responsibilities burdening women.[56] It was also reported that the interview process is 'brutal' to female candidates.[57] Furthermore, gender equality may take a backseat to racial equality in the process of reforming the judiciary.[58] This confirms that social impediments affecting women's upward mobility are a recurrent problem, one that female judges also face.

This CGE complaint investigation is a pivotal development in the contemporary legal history of South Africa. It shows that the CGE was dedicated for years as the case proceeded until 2016; it undertook a profound investigation attempting to reach the core of the problem, while involving multiple stakeholders so as to understand the parameters of the solution. This investigation provided the country with an opportunity to pause after almost 15 years since the end of apartheid, and re-evaluate the progress made in the internal structure of the judiciary.

[53] Stephen Clear, '2018 must be the year that we reimagine judicial diversity' The Conversation, 3 January 2018, accessed 2 June 2018 at www.theconversation.com/2018-must-be-the-year-that-we-reimagine-judicial-diversity-89593

[54] Commission for Gender Equality (CGE), *Lack of Gender Transformation in the Judiciary*, investigative report, Complaint Ref No: WC/DRGU and Sonke/2012/KL (2016), p. 30 (hereinafter CGE report).

[55] Ibid., p. 47.

[56] CGE report, p. 49; Also see Ruth B Cowan, 'Women's representation on the courts in the Republic of South Africa' (2006) 6 *The University of Maryland Law Journal of Race, Religion, Gender and Class*, 308.

[57] CGE report, p. 50.

[58] Cowan, 'Women's representation', 309.

The complaint was brought by two civil society organisations, but paved the way for many more to start The Judges Matter coalition[59] – dedicated to being a watchdog for the selection of judges, and the causes that they follow and sponsor.[60] The debate regarding this matter did not only flood civil society, but it found its way into public debate with massive media coverage, discussed in the next chapter.

C The Importance of Women on the Bench

Obviously, female judges want to be appointed on merit, and not gender.[61] However, the 'visibility' of women on the bench is of the utmost importance, especially because female judges have reported that they feel 'invisible and excluded by male judges and lawyers'.[62] Furthermore, a strong presence of women on the bench can 'feminise' the judiciary. Dawuni studied the impact of increasing the number of female judges in Ghana and concluded that their presence on the bench has 'actualized the principle of gender equality before the law'.[63] One of the participants she interviewed confirmed that she chose to join the bench after an inspirational talk by a Justice that she admired and respected; others have noted that the appointment of the first female Chief Justice has completely changed the landscape for the judiciary and encouraged women to move up the system.[64] Visibility is therefore important, especially in creating a critical mass where the image of female judges is normalised and respected[65]

Focusing on South Africa, Cowan explains that in addition to inspiring women to join the bench, female judges encourage more women to approach the court through their jobs as well as their

[59] Michelle Korte, 'Judges matter: transforming the judiciary', GroundUp, 15 July 2014, accessed 20 June 2018 at www.groundup.org.za/article/judges-matter-transforming-judiciary_1999/

[60] www.judgesmatter.co.za/

[61] Mai Swart, 'Gender reform in the judiciary is still skin deep', Mail & Guardian, 24 July 2015, accessed 20 June 2018 at www.mg.co.za/article/2015-07-23-gender-reform-in-the-judiciary-is-still-skin-deep

[62] CGE report, p. 32.

[63] Josephine J Dawuni 'To "mother" or not to "mother": The representative roles of women judges in Ghana' (2016) 60 *Journal of African Law*, 3, 425.

[64] Ibid., 426.

[65] The issue of gender differences in judging has been discussed in some literature globally. See Schultz and Shaw, *Gender and Judging*; Gretchen Bauer and Josephine Dawuni (eds.), *Gender and the Judiciary in Africa: From Obscurity to Parity?* (New York: Routledge, 2015); Nienke Grossman, 'Sex on the bench: do women judges matter to the legitimacy of international courts' (2011–2012) 12 *China Journal of International Law*, 2, 647–683; Erika Rackley, *Women, Judging and the Judiciary: From Difference to Diversity* (Oxon: Routledge, 2013); Sally J. Kenney, *Gender and Justice: Why Women in the Judiciary Really Matter* (New York: Routledge, 2013).

volunteer work. She also suggests that in cases with a strong element of women's rights or reflective of women's lived experiences, the opinion of females may have influenced their male colleagues.[66] Female judges also take the socio-economic background of litigation quite seriously without jeopardising their unbiased stance.[67] While more women are needed in the judiciary, more feminist judges are needed as well – judges who always ask the 'woman question'.[68]

III NEGOTIATING HUMAN RIGHTS – NGOs, LITIGANTS, STATE AND COURTS

This chapter has so far discussed the practice of impact litigation and showed how it was used, even to question judicial practice. This section will move the discussion to court proceedings, zooming in on the negotiations on human rights and state responsibility between courts, litigants, NGOs and the state. The section aims to show that genuine apolitical discussions and negotiations over the human rights discourse are reflective of a plural and liberal judiciary; these negotiations are responsible for the development of human rights in South Africa. Most cases are focused on gender, but the section also includes other cases with important human rights elements.

A Violence and Gender Issues

1 Protection from Violence

In *Carmichele* v. *Minister of Safety and Security*,[69] the discussion centred around the limits of the duty of the state to protect women from violence, and the duty of the courts to develop these limits to align with Constitutional rights. The CALS acted as *amicus curiae*. Mr Coetzee had a history of sexual violence including molestation and indecent assault for which he had received a suspended sentence. At the time of the attack on the appellant, Mr Coetzee had been arrested and released on a charge of rape, and sent for psychiatric evaluation which came

[66] Ruth Cowan, 'Do women on South Africa's Courts make a difference', Courting Justice, June 2011, accessed 20 June 2018 at www.courtingjustice.com/DoWomen-MD.html

[67] Dawuni, 'To "mother"', 428; Winfred Kamau, 'Women judges and magistrates in Kenya: challenges, opportunities and contributions' in Ulrike Schultz and Gisela Shaw (eds.), *Gender and Judging* (Oxford: Hart Publishing, 2013), pp. 167–190.

[68] Schultz and Shaw, *Gender and Judging*, p. 38.

[69] *Carmichele* v. *Minister of Safety and Security* [2001] (10) BCLR 995 (CC) (hereinafter, Carchmichele case).

back normal.[70] He was later found guilty of both offences and sentenced to 17 years' imprisonment combined. However, the applicant sought damages from the Minister for Safety and Security and the Minister of Justice and Constitutional Development for failing to protect her from the violent attack.

The applicant argued that the authorities had enough information to deem the offender dangerous and not release him on bail: the police were aware of his violent history and were also warned by a family friend about the threat that Coetzee presented, but they refrained from taking the initiative to investigate.[71] Both the High Court and the Supreme Court of Appeals (SCA) dismissed the applicant's claim. When balancing the Constitutional right of the applicant against the state responsibility to protect her, the SCA used a test from court precedent. The SCA held that the legal duty to protect depends on various circumstances in each individual case, ultimately asking 'is it reasonable to expect of the defendant to have taken positive measures to prevent the harm?'[72] In this case, the SCA found two duties, one of the police to provide the prosecutor with sufficient history of Coetzee to inform the decision of release, and the duty of the prosecutor to decide on the release based on the information provided by the police.[73] The Court found no fault on the police as they had provided the prosecution with the history of Mr Coetzee, but asserted that even though the 'state may be vicariously liable for an omission by a prosecutor in exercising a discretion', more probing into the conditions of bail must be considered.[74] The facts of the case did not convince the SCA that the prosecutor had enough reason to suspect Coetzee of repeating violent behaviour. Furthermore, the Court contended that prosecutors at this time had just received a memo noting that if they decided to reject a release on bail, they must prove danger to the community.[75]

In this case, both the court and the prosecutor completely disregarded the social context of violence against women that plagues the country. This context should have prompted the prosecutor to deny bail so as not to risk future victims by releasing a man who obviously had a violent past; in addition, with the rampant rates of VAW in South Africa, the court could have applied a higher threshold on prosecution. In

[70] Ibid., para. 2
[71] Ibid., para. 15.
[72] Ibid., para.7.
[73] Ibid., para. 15.
[74] Ibid., para.17.
[75] Ibid., paras. 18–19.

this sense, both the judiciary and the prosecution had failed to protect women from violence.[76] Furthermore, in the judgment, the SCA undermined the issue of violence against women, contending that just like everyone is subject to burglary, all women are subject to rape and therefore there was insufficient evidence for the state to treat the applicant any differently from other women.[77]

The Constitutional Court approached the topic from a broader perspective guided by the CALS as *amicus curiae*; it asserted that the trial judge and the SCA conducted the right tests. However, their duty under the Constitution was much broader. Insufficient legislation at the time of the trial should not entail an exoneration from the court *a quo*, but should rather impose a duty on courts to develop common law to protect the constitutional rights of the applicant.[78] When the case reached the Constitutional Court, CALS challenged the manner in which the SCA has trivialised violence against women as any other crime, and convinced the Constitutional Court that 'sexual violence and the threat of sexual violence goes to the core of women's subordination in society. It is the single greatest threat to the self-determination of South African women', adding precedent[79] to show that courts have the obligation to send a firm message to society that VAW will not be tolerated. Not only was this litigation a success, but it was a groundbreaking case emphasising the positive obligations on the state to eliminate GBV.[80]

In *Omar* v. *Government of the Republic of South Africa and Others*, the Court ruled on the constitutionality of Article 8 of the DVA, which allows the court to issue a suspended arrest warrant with the Protection Order. The CGE acted as *amicus curiae*. In this case, the Court measured the rights of women under the DVA against the Constitutional rights of the claimant. The applicant argued that issuing two orders simultaneously violated his constitutional rights 'to freedom and security of the person, a fair trial and access to courts'.[81] Among his various arguments,

[76] Rebecca H. Rittenhouse, *The Due Diligence Obligation to Prevent Violence Against Women: The Case of Pakistan*, legal report (New York: Human Rights Foundation, 22 December 2011), p. 6; *Vertido* v. *Philippines* (2010) CEDAW/C/46/D/18/2008: even if the offender is prosecuted eventually, the state can still be held liable and so can the judiciary.

[77] *Carmichele* case, para. 21.

[78] Ibid., para. 28.

[79] *Grant Chapman* v. *The State* [1997] 3 All South Africa 277 (A) (hereinafter, *Chapman* case).

[80] This case was used as precedent in other cases such as *Ghia Van Eeden* v. *Minister of Safety and Security*, [2002] 4 All South Africa 346 (SCA).

[81] *Omar* v *Government of the Republic of South Africa and Others* [2006] (2) BCLR 253 (CC), para. 1 (hereinafter, *Omar* case).

the applicant submitted that the broad definition of domestic violence in the Act read with section 8 may encourage a 'malicious and vindictive complainant ... cause an innocent respondent to be arrested'.[82] This argument has been exhausted; it attempts to maintain the gender power dynamic in law and society by keeping the private sphere in the control of men, who are expected to decide on remedies for domestic violence.[83] In weighing these contradictions, the Court discussed the nature and history of domestic violence, asserting that any law or Act can be manipulated. However, this does not automatically render it unconstitutional. Taking into consideration the history of domestic violence in South Africa as well the gender power dynamics in intimate relationships, the Court stated that 'the possibility of the Act being maliciously manipulated is by far outweighed by its potential to afford protection by the police to the victims of domestic violence, against the background of a history in which this protection was sadly withheld'.[84] The court further highlighted the vulnerability of women and children in violent homes and recognised that the emphasis on the privacy of family affairs is what often leaves women and children unprotected in the face of violence with the 'justification for non-interference'.[85] The court's argument here mirrors earlier feminist critique of the masculinity of the law that has called for keeping the state out of 'private' domestic affairs – an argument used by many states opposed to domestic violence laws.[86] Therefore, the issuance of a suspended arrest warrant is merely a method of ensuring the protection of women from further violence and demonstrating the seriousness of the crime to the offender.[87]

2 *Criminal Procedures in Sexual Violence Cases Involving Children*

NGOs were invited by the High Court to make submissions on whether several provisions of the Criminal Procedure Act of 1977[88] and the

[82] Ibid., para. 58.

[83] See R L McNeely and Gloria Robinson-Simpson, 'The truth about domestic violence: a falsely framed issue' (1987) 32 *Social Work*, 6, 485–490; Kristin L Anderson and Debra Umberson, 'Gendering violence: masculinity and power in men's accounts of domestic violence' (2001) 15 *Gender and Society* 3.

[84] *Omar* case, para. 60.

[85] *Omar* case, para. 18.

[86] An example is Lebanon, which eventually passed a poor domestic violence law in 2014, but had used the public/private argument until then. See Marla Swanson, 'The fight to criminalize violence against women in Lebanon' Open Society Foundations, 6 May 2011, accessed 6 June 2018 at www.opensocietyfoundations.org/voices/fight-criminalize-violence-against-women-lebanon

[87] *Omar* case, para. 27.

[88] Provisions regarding oath, intermediaries and open trials.

Criminal Law Amendment Act of 1997[89] are in the best interests of the child, pursuant to section 28(2) of the Constitution. These provisions were mainly regarding the courts' discretion to appoint intermediaries in sexual violence cases involving children, the possibility of child victims and witnesses to testify without a counsellor or advisor and putting children under oath. The Court also considered whether expected delays in the litigation process may cause additional trauma to children who have to repeatedly testify, recounting their traumatic experiences possibly for years. These issues were brought to the attention of the High Court after receiving the *Mokoena* and *Phaswane* cases for confirmation and sentencing. Both cases concerned the rape of minor girls. The details of the proceedings prompted the Court to investigate procedural issues relating to children involved in sexual offences trials, reaching out to various ministries and NGOs to advise.[90]

The Centre for Child Law, the Centre for the Study of Violence and Reconciliation and the TLAC in addition to others responded to the court's call. Submissions centred on the impact of proceedings on children. One matter brought up by the Centre for Child Law and recognised by the court is the complication of the legal language, especially with vulnerable children who are 'by their very nature ill-equipped to deal with a confrontational and adversarial setting in which adults dictate the subject matter, the nature and the style of the conversations'.[91] The case raised another important issue related to the South African judicial system's infrastructural capacity. The National Prosecuting Authority submitted that only 14 per cent of South African Courts have access to intermediaries and are equipped with devices allowing child victims and witnesses to testify out of court.[92] On the other hand, the counsel for the accused raised concerns about the impact of 'child sensitive' measures on the right to fair trial of the defendant, particularly in terms of cross examination and the ability to challenge evidence. Most importantly, counsel pointed to the conflict between the emphasis on shielding the child from further harm, and the right of the defendant to be presumed innocent. The court recognised these challenges and contended that judges are expected to 'weigh up' the evidence and take into account the limitations facing the accused in their defence.[93]

[89] Criminal Law Amendment Act 105 of 1997 (South Africa), s. 52(2) and (3)(d) and (e).

[90] *Mokoena* case, paras. 3–4.

[91] Ibid., para. 12.

[92] Ibid., para. 26.

[93] Ibid., para. 15.

The conflict between balancing the child's wellbeing and the rights of the accused is an unsettled global dilemma. Some research suggests that a tremendous fear experienced by children in court is meeting the defender, and this fear has often paralysed victims and affected their testimonies.[94] Similar research in the USA shows that repeated testimonies confuse children and often lead to inconsistencies in their stories.[95] Swedish courts have also been found to hold children's testimonies to unrealistic expectations. For instance, their testimonies were expected to be rich in detail and spontaneous, among other criteria.[96] In the aftermath of 'controversy about the justice system's fairness toward abuse victims', Justices in Canada have been cautioned from expecting specific conduct and behaviour from children subjected to sexual violence.[97] Similar concerns arose in Australia in 2017, where a judge noted how cross-examination 'damages vulnerable witnesses'; since their testimonies are often the only evidence against the accused, lawyers are determined to discredit the victims, which puts too much pressure on children.[98] South Africa has been facing the same challenges; the court has used the two said cases to revise procedural roles and examine their conformity with the Constitution, with the help of NGOs and relevant state institutions.

In the two said South African cases, the court's stance was impressive, echoing similar concerns raised globally and taking a remarkably progressive stance. Similarly, the engagements between all parties of the case demonstrate their diligence to reach the most favourable conditions for children, while upholding the right to fair trial of the accused. More importantly, this case is the product of the court's diligence; of its own accord, the Court sensed inadequacies in the administrative procedures that may jeopardise the constitutional rights of a vulnerable group and

[94] See Gail S Goodman et al., 'Testifying in criminal court: emotional effects of child sexual assault victims' (1992) 57 *Monographs of the Society for Research in Child Development*, 5.

[95] Edward H Weiss and Regina F Berg 'Child victims of sexual assault: impact of court procedures' (1982) 21 *Journal of the American Academy of Child Psychiatry*, 5, 515.

[96] See Emilie Ernberg et al., 'Court evaluations of young children's testimony in child sexual abuse cases', Legal and Criminological Psychology, 7 February 2018, accessed 6 June 2018 at www.onlinelibrary.wiley.com/doi/epdf/10.1111/lcrp.12124

[97] See Sean Fine 'Sexual assault myths at centre of important Supreme Court case', The Globe and the Mail, 8 Febraury 2018, accessed 6 June 2018 at www.theglobeandmail.com/news/national/sexual-assault-myths-at-centre-of-important-supreme-court-case/article37916188/

[98] Calla Wahlquist 'Court system is unfair and traumatic for child sexual abuse victims, inquiry chair says', *The Guardian*, 2 August 2017, accessed 6 June 2018 at www.theguardian.com/australia-news/2017/aug/02/court-system-is-unfair-and-traumatic-for-child-sexual-abuse-victims-inquiry-chair-says

consequently sought advice from all expert parties. The court eventually found he said sections of the CPA to be unconstitutional and referred the matter to the Constitutional Court for confirmation.[99] Appreciation of the *amici* submissions was noted on several occasions; first, the Court directly praised the thorough and comprehensive research conducted by the *amici*; and second, the court recognised that the *amici* 'had the interests of the children involved ... at heart'.[100] This case reemphasised the fundamental role that NGOs play in vindicating the rights of victims, and the expected diligence of courts to continuously recognise and revise both legal and administrative matters that may undermine justice.

In *Director of Public Prosecutions, Transvaal* v. *Minister of Justice and Constitutional Development*,[101] the Constitutional Court was asked to confirm the ruling of the High Court in the abovementioned cases, and again the Court invited NGOs to provide submissions on the matter. The Centre for Child Law, together with Childline, submitted reports in support of the High Court ruling, confirming the necessity of the appointment of intermediaries for all children, closing court proceedings to the public when there are children involved and using simple language with children such as not forcing them to give oath but rather to 'tell their story'.[102] Looking at the facts from another perspective, the Constitutional Court found no violation of section 28(2) of the Constitution. The Court asserted that if any procedures are deemed harmful to children, then an application can be made to the judge who is expected to interpret the law in the closest manner to align with the Constitution,[103] noting that this is probably what happened in the *Phaswane* case. The Court found 'competing interests' between 'the right to open justice and, on the other hand, protecting children and the identity of witnesses' and asserted that 'discretion is a tool which enables courts to mediate between these competing interests'.[104]

While this could be considered a litigation loss, this case brought forward crucial matters for discussion such as the abovementioned conflict of rights – issues that are still unsettled in countries with developed

[99] CPA, ss. 153(3) and (5), 158(5), 164(1) and 170A(1) and (7) were inconsistent with s.28(2) of the Constitution.

[100] *Mokoena* case, para. 15.

[101] *Director of Public Prosecutions, Transvaal* v. *Minister for Justice and Constitutional Development and Others* [2009] (7) BCLR 637 (CC) (hereinafter, *Transvaal* case).

[102] *Strategic Impact Litigation*, p. 7.

[103] *Transvaal* case, para. 139.

[104] Ibid., para. 150.

justice systems. More importantly, the case was the epitome of how deficit in funding can affect the constitutional rights of children. Litigation before the trial court was prolonged due to a lack of intermediaries, the decreasing number of Sexual Offences Courts and the poor training of prosecutors who could deal with child witnesses.[105] While striking down the decision of the High Court, the Constitutional Court ordered the Director-General for the Department of Justice and Constitutional Development to submit information on all the reported administrative shortages, and the steps taken to remedy this problem.[106]

3 *Reinforcing Gender Stereotypes*

The Equality Court has taken a progressive stand towards holding officials accountable for their words. In *Sonke Gender Justice Network* v. *Julius Malema*, the Equality Court had to decide whether Malema's words before students at the Cape Peninsula University of Technology during a campaign trail were considered hate speech and/or harassment under the Equality Act. When Malema was asked about the Zuma rape trial, he defended Zuma by explaining that women who hang around in the morning, ask for breakfast and money for a cab have enjoyed sex, and therefore were not raped. Those who did not enjoy sex (i.e. raped) leave early in the morning and do not ask for taxi money. Sonke argued that Malema's words constituted hate speech[107] and cumulatively harassment,[108] asserting violations of sections 9, 10 and 16 of the Constitution and some provisions of the Equality Act. The Court questioned whether Malema's words were based on one or more of the prohibited grounds in the Constitution, and whether they could be considered hurtful or harmful to a reasonable person. The Court further stipulated that the law does not examine his intention, only the impact of his action.[109]

The respondent argued that none of the audience members present on this day felt offended by his words; however, the Court stipulated that as a public figure, Malema's influence goes far beyond the audience; even more concerning to the Court was Malema's influence on a vulnerable

[105] Ibid., paras. 191–197.
[106] Ibid., para. 206.
[107] Equality Act, s. 11.1.
[108] Equality Act, s. 11.
[109] *Sonke Gender Justice Network* v. *Malema* (2010 (7) BCLR 729 (EqC)) [2010] ZAEQC 2; 02/2009 (15 March 2010), para. 14 (hereinafter, *Malema* case).

group – youth[110] – who are more susceptible to internalise and adopt sexist attitudes.[111] In this sense, the Court's judgment considered factors beyond the law, looking at the impact of speech on a specific segment of society that would play an important role in either perpetuating or challenging gender stereotypes in the future of South Africa. The broad perspective of the Court indicates a genuine understanding of the injury that sexism can cause.[112] Malema's words have done the harm by influencing the perceptions of young men's expectations from women they sleep with, and of young's women's expectation of their own behaviour. Any remedies other than legal liability at this point is what Johnson calls 'unringing the bell'.[113]

4 *Delayed Disclosure of Sexual Offences*

The most recent example of successful impact litigation on matters of gender and violence received a judgment in June 2018. The Constitutional Court ruled on the constitutionality of section 18 of the Criminal Procedure Act,[114] which states that the right to institute a prosecution for any offence shall lapse after 20 years, with the exception of serious crime including murder, rape and crimes against humanity.[115] In 2016, Levenstein and seven other applicants brought a claim against Mr Frankel for sexual abuse that had happened over 20 years ago when they were between the ages of six and fifteen. They also challenged the constitutionality of section 18, which lists rape as the only sexual offence enjoying an exemption from the section. The applicants, with the Teddy Bear Clinic and CALS acting as *amicus curiae*, argued that this exception indicates a preconceived notion of the impact of sexual offences against women. It assumes that the impact of rape is far greater than that of other sexual offences including prolonged sexual abuse and child molestation, among others.

The proceedings before the High Court initiated a dialogue over important legal amendments pertaining to the impact of sexual offences on victims and the conditions for disclosure. While all parties

[110] See Rosemary Sword and Phillip Zimbardo, 'The Trump effect: an update: The toxicity is spreading', Psychology Today, 30 January 2018, accessed 20 June 2018 at www.psychologytoday.com/us/blog/the-time-cure/201801/the-trump-effect-update

[111] *Malema* case, para. 17(b)(x).

[112] Sara Mills, *Language and Sexism* (Cambridge: Cambridge University Press, 2010), p. 36.

[113] Robert Mark Simpson, 'Un-ringing the bell: McGowan on oppressive speech and the asymmetric pliability of conversations' (2013) 91 *Australasian Journal of Philosophy*, 3.

[114] *Levenstein* case.

[115] CPA, s. 18.

of litigation agreed that the section is unconstitutional, they disagreed on the reform. The state and the applicants suggested adding 'indecent assault against children' to section 18, whereas the *amici* rejected the limitation of the section to children; they demanded expanding the provision to sexual offences committed against victims of all ages.[116] The disagreement between the *amici* and the applicants reflects the different drives behind litigation: the applicants focused on their stories and sought their direct legal victories. They even used precedent to convince the Court to stay focused on the facts of the case and not make broader rulings.[117] On the other hand, the *amici* targeted a broader legal gain to benefit all victims of sexual offences. They contended that section 18, in its current form, reflected patriarchal connotations; it puts more emphasis on the form of sexual violence that includes penetration, assuming that it causes greater trauma to victims compared to other forms of sexual violence. On this matter, the High Court sided with the *amici*, noting that legislative history never distinguished between adult and child victims regarding the impact of violence. Creating a distinction for this law would be an 'artificial restriction'.[118]

This case is an important reminder to challenge social perceptions on injury. For instance, sexual violence is categorised by type rather than by 'frequency and severity' which may be stronger indicators to impact.[119] The Court ruled on the unconstitutionality of the section and gave Parliament 24 months to amend the law.

B Human Rights Litigation

This section will discuss a broader range of human rights issues brought before the court. Since the emphasis of this chapter is on the space provided by the justice system for dialogue between litigants, the state and the court, it is necessary to highlight other cases where conflicting human rights were discussed.

1 Housing Rights

In *Dladla* v. *City of Johannesburg*,[120] the CALS and the Centre for Child Law acted as *amici*. In this case, the Constitutional Court struck down a

[116] *Levenstein* case, para. 11.

[117] The applicants cited the *Masiya* case in which the court debated the reform of the definition of rape to include anal penetration, but chose to remain silent on the gender neutrality of the law as it did not relate to the facts of the case.

[118] *Levenstein* case, para. 20.

[119] *Levenstein* case, para. 54.5.

[120] [2017] ZACC 42 (hereinafter, *Dladla* Constitutional Court).

decision of the SCA, on the constitutional rights under sections 10, 12 and 14 regarding the rights to privacy, to human dignity and to freedom and security of the person. The applicants were residents of Ekuthuleni Shelter to which they moved after they were evicted from a dilapidated building. Based on a Constitutional Court decision, the City was obliged to provide suitable temporary accommodation, and therefore it struck a deal with the shelter to house the residents. However, some of the rules of the shelter were problematic and raised the legal issues in this case: the lockout rule and the family separation rule.[121] The former severely restricted residents' presence in the shelter, and the latter prohibited heterosexual partners from sleeping in the same room, as the shelter imposed sex-segregated sleeping arrangements. The case went to the High Court that ruled in favour of the applicants, the Supreme Court that struck down the decision and ruled in favour of the City, and finally the Constitutional Court that confirmed the constitutional violations of the said rules.

This case is a great example of negotiations on the limits of state responsibility, on which three courts have disagreed. While all courts agreed that the said rules counted as violations of constitutional rights, they disagreed on whether the limitations of these rights could be justified. The SCA looked at the reasonable measures undertaken by the City to temporarily accommodate people, vis-a-vis the size of the problem and the financial burden it entails. It found justification in the ban on heterosexual couples from sharing the same room, asserting that people in temporary accommodation should not expect the same freedoms as people in their homes.[122] Further, the Court saw these rules as a method of discouraging dependent behaviour and encouraging residents to move out.[123] On the other hand, the Constitutional Court looked at the state's duty to progressively realise the right to adequate housing enshrined in the Constitution, and whether conditions for this right may be waived in temporary housing situations. In their submission as *amicus curiae*, the CALS steered the discussion to women's rights, noting that access to adequate housing is a prerequisite to the enjoyment of other human rights, particularly because women are responsible for taking care of the house, and are more vulnerable to domestic violence when domestic conditions are unstable. They

[121] Ibid., para. 10.

[122] *City of Johannesburg* v. *Dladla* (403/15) [2016] ZASCA 66 (18 May 2016), para. 23 (hereinafter, *Dladla* High Court).

[123] Ibid., para. 23.

are also the first to carry the burden of any disruption in family life because of unequal gender power dynamics in intimate relations.[124] The Constitutional Court finally found constitutional violations in the rules, noting that the 'Constitution confers the rights guaranteed by sections 10, 12 and 14 on everyone, regardless of where they are at a given time'.[125]

Housing rights were also the subject of litigation in *Government of the Republic of South Africa* v. *Grootboom*.[126] In this case, the *amici* altered the course of litigation by introducing a radical argument when the case went to the Constitutional Court. The case concerned the eviction of members of a community who had unlawfully occupied land belonging to the municipality. The High Court found no violation in the right to adequate housing in the Constitution because this right is a progressive one, obliging the state to take reasonable measures to achieve it. The Court referred to the Soobramoony's judgment regarding the 'difficult decisions' that the state has to make when realising socio-economic rights.[127] The Court, however, noted a violation of section 28 of the Constitution – protecting the rights of children– which is not a progressive right. In an attempt to balance between state obligation, state resources and constitutional rights, the Court was wary about setting such a precedent that could possibly trigger dependency on state resources and encourage squatter residents to make similar claims demanding that their children be housed, and for them to accompany their children. Therefore, the court clearly stated that the *Grootboom* case related to the wellbeing of these specific children, confirming that housing is the primary responsibility of parents, and therefore, 'the same may not always be the case with children who belong to and live with squatter families'.[128]

When the case reached the Constitutional Court, the LRC (with the Human Rights Commission and the Community Law Centre) got involved as *amici* directing the court to focus on the 'cause' of housing rights, raising the issue of 'minimum core obligations' even for

[124] *Dladla* Constitutional Court, para. 29.

[125] Ibid., para. 44.

[126] *Government of the Republic of South Africa* v. *Grootboom* [2000] (11) BCLR 1169 (CC) (hereinafter, *Grootboom* Constitutional Court). Also see Geoff Budlender, 'Access to justice, lessons from South Africa land reform program' in Yash Ghai and Jill Cottrell (eds.), *Marginalized Communities and Access to Justice* (Abingdon and New York: Routledge, 2010), pp. 23–37.

[127] *Grootboom and Others* v. *Oostenberg Municipality and Others* (6826/99) [1999] ZAWCHC 1 (17 December 1999), p. 7.

[128] Ibid., p. 19.

progressive rights. They directed the Court to read the Constitution alongside the International Covenant of Social and Economic Rights, which clarifies the steps that the state should take to realise those rights.[129] The Court agreed with the *amici*, but clarified that housing responsibilities fall on numerous parties, including citizens. The court added that 'a co-ordinated state housing programme' should be a working plan between the state's three branches with adequate legislation, and that each party should accept responsibility for its part of the plan.[130] The judgment formed the basis of numerous future cases, as it introduced some guidelines for states to realise progressive Constitutional rights. As noted by Calmore, this is a common repercussion of cause lawyering where clients are seen as a 'social group', and their personal ailments are deemed as public issues.[131]

The two previous cases essentially brought to life the constitutional right to housing, identifying the boundaries of state responsibility and the limits of the constitutional right. Court proceedings reflect the 'thinking process' of judges and the manner in which they balance different rights and responsibilities. Furthermore, the *Grootboom* case sheds light on the role of NGOs in litigation, and the value of their input in these negotiations. Albie Sachs, a constitutional judge in this case wrote:

> This amicus intervention swung the debate dramatically. Most of the preceding arguments had failed to really look socio-economic rights in the eye. There had been technical arguments and attempts to frame the case in terms of children's rights, but Geoff forced us to consider what the nature of the obligations imposed by these rights.[132]

2 Freedom from Discrimination

In *Hoffmann* v. *South African Airways*, the Constitutional Court relied on the evidence submitted by the *amicus curiae* to make a judgment. The respondent, South African Airlines, had prohibited the employment of people who were HIV positive as cabin attendants. The defendant argued that those measures were for the protection of passengers, adding that it would be difficult for Hoffmann to get the requisite inoculations, such as yellow fever. In this case, the Court balanced the rights of an

[129] *Grootboom* Constitutional Court, para. 27.

[130] Ibid., para. 40.

[131] John O. Calmore, 'A call to context: the professional challenges of cause lawyering at the intersection of race, space and poverty' (1998–1999) 67 *Fordham Law Review*, 5, 1937.

[132] Albie Sachs, 'Concluding comments on the panel discussion' (2007) 8 *ESR Review*, 1, 18.

individual person against the benefits on the wider community, asking, what are the risks that Mr Hoffmann's condition would pose on others in his work environment? The Witwatersrand High Court found a stronger weight in the SAA argument and ruled that the discrimination was justifiable. However, the litigation lacked important medical evidence until the Aids Law Project applied and was granted leave to act as *amicus curiae*.[133] The new evidence concerned the 'nature of the HIV disease, its progression, treatment and transmission… the ability of people living with HIV to be vaccinated against yellow fever',[134] in addition to an employee's ability to perform work duties.[135] This evidence 'altered the course of argument',[136] prompting the Constitutional Court to uphold the appeal and assert that commercial safety cannot be used as an excuse to impose policies that reinforce prejudice and discrimination.[137]

The negotiations in this case were essentially on the situations when discrimination is justifiable. The court recognised that a safe working environment may be considered grounds for derogation, and even cited a case from the UK for reference. In *Dhinsa* v. *Serco*,[138] the employment tribunal found that the safety of the work environment (a prison) superseded the claimant's right to maintain a religious practice; the case, however, was specific to the person's work environment and religious rituals. However, in Hoffmann's case, the employer used generalisations to justify discrimination and this was the court's red flag. The Court held that not all HIV cases impose the same risk to the surrounding environment, and the ability to receive inoculation is also different for each individual case. The court also made broader statements on the social impact of using such generalisations to disqualify a candidate from a job. In a country where HIV is rampant and patients are stigmatised, people are reluctant to reveal their condition for fear of discrimination. Consequently, members of this vulnerable group do not get the necessary treatment and the cycle of stigma prevails. This is the practice that the court hoped to defy.[139]

[133] Gilbert Marcus and Steven Budlender, *A Strategic Evaluation of Public Interest Litigation in South Africa*, research report (The Atlantic Philanthropies, 2008), p. 58.

[134] *Hoffmann* case, para. 13.

[135] Ibid., para. 15.

[136] Ibid., para. 40.

[137] See Albie Sachs, *The Strange Alchemy of Life and Law* (Oxford: Oxford University Press, 2009), p. 195–197.

[138] *Dhinsa* v. *Serco* and another ET/1315002/09.

[139] *Hoffmann* case, para. 28.

3 *Sexual Conduct of Minors*

In *Teddy Bear Clinic* v. *Minister of Justice and Constitutional Development*, litigants challenged the constitutionality of sections 15, 16 and 56(2)(b) of the SOA. The case was brought forward by the Teddy Bear Clinic (an NGO specialising in violence against children) and RAPCAN. The provisions criminalised consensual sex between children (under 16). The WLC, TLAC and JASA acted as *amicus curiae* – with JASA supporting the respondent. This case demonstrated a battle between liberal and traditional ideologies. The applicants argued that criminalising sexual activity, a normal part of adolescence, is detrimental because it is likely to limit the access of teenagers to reproductive healthcare resources and expose adolescents to unnecessary distress by labelling them as criminals and sex offenders.[140] They relied on expert opinions to demonstrate the impact of constraining such 'natural' acts and argued that these prohibitions violate the human dignity of children – a constitutional right. The respondents, however, contended that social stigma associated with sexual conduct is rooted in social norms and not in the said laws.

The Court found the provisions unconstitutional and against the best interests of the child.[141] It settled this matter by pointing to the relationship between law and society: criminalising an act necessarily stigmatises it,[142] and therefore the Court found the respondent's argument that the stigma is rooted in society as ill-founded. Even if the enforcement of these laws is rare, their mere existence places a negative connotation on sexual activity, and consequently stigma.[143] In this case, the Court's judgment primarily rested on the privileged position of the NGOs that guarantees their proximity to the public and provides them with updated knowledge of norms and values among adolescents. The court stated:

> The deponents are all involved with young people and the difficulties they experience, especially those of a sexual nature… It becomes clear from a study of this evidence that everyone seems to accept the need to be open and honest about teenage sexuality and to allow young people

[140] *Transvaal* case, para. 6.3.
[141] *Teddy Bear* case, para. 53.
[142] See Aziza Ahmed, 'Criminalising consensual sexual behaviour in the context of HIV: Consequences, evidence, and leadership' (2011) 6 *An International Journal for Research, Policy and Practice*, 3.
[143] *Teddy Bear* case, para. 55.

> to make truly informed choices as to when they will start exploring and eventually having sex.[144]

This victory is an important one; it highlights the privileged position of NGOs, allowing them to understand lived realities of people. Research for this book echoed this position, highlighting the possible effect of the said laws on female teenagers. For example, one of the respondents, the head of an NGO, explained that these provisions had been used against pregnant teenage girls – pregnancy is proof that they had sex, which was illegal. Males could threaten females with this clause to force them to conceal the pregnancy or abort it. She added that the police had sometimes used those provisions to take revenge against girls (or were bribed by someone to do so). Parents had also abused this law when they disapproved of their children's relationships. Finally, the provisions provided an easy escape for rapists who were under 16. For instance, another interviewee recounted a case with which the NGO was involved. A boy who was under 16 years old raped two girls, of 13 and 16. After the school disciplinary board investigated the case, the boy hired a lawyer and admitted to have had intercourse with both of them. However, he argued that the first girl was under 16, and therefore, she was also guilty pursuant to section 15 of the SOA. He also claimed that the older girl had raped him, based on their ages. Consequently, both girls were intimidated into dropping their cases because of those legal technicalities.

The provisions were also problematic because they were in contradiction of the Child Protection Act.[145] This Act secured the right of the child to take oral contraceptives and guaranteed the right to abortion without the consent of parents from the age of 14.

C Fostering a Liberal Judiciary: Diversifying Sources of Information

NGOs are not the only source of information that inform legal proceedings. Seeking insights from multiple sources is a strong reflection of the plurality of the South African justice system. This section will review several of the numerous cases where expert input introduced the court to new dimensions of the facts.

[144] *Teddy Bear* case, para. 58.

[145] Children's Act No 38 of 2005 (South Africa).

1 Experts and Research Input in Court Proceedings

In *S* v. *Ferreira*, the applicant had murdered her husband and alleged that she committed the crime in self-defence as she was a victim of domestic violence. To understand the implication of intimate violence on the victim, the Supreme Court of Appeals cited foreign research. The Court consulted an expert on the impact of abuse on women, who confirmed that abused women suffer from low self-esteem and they may find that the only escape from violence is to take the partner's life.[146] Moreover, the court referred to the huge body of international literature that explores the causes and consequences of partner abuse, particularly citing Dr Lenore E Walker's 'The Cycle Theory of Violence.'[147] The court ultimately reduced the life sentence to six years. In this case, the court made practical use of academic research, an overlooked benefit of research.[148] Using academic research as evidence reflects openness and trust in professional opinions; judges understand that academics have more time and space to research specific topics, and more importantly research provides 'social science evidence to examine the "legislative fact" that underpins legal rules'.[149]

Similarly, foreign research was used as evidence in *S* v. *Jackson*.[150] The SCA struck down the cautionary rule[151] that was regularly used in rape cases. In this case, the complainant appealed against a sentence passed by a regional court convicting him of attempted rape and sentencing him to 18 months' imprisonment conditionally suspended for five years. The complainant argued that the trial court did not fully consider the cautionary rule. State counsel asserted that the rule was not only discriminatory against women but also 'increases the burden of proof resting on the State'.[152] The Court rejected the appeal and expressed concern over the leniency of the sentence. The Court considered the

[146] S v. *Ferreira and Others* [2004] 4 All South Africa 373 (SCA).

[147] Ibid., para. 37. See Lenore Walker et al., 'Beyond the juror's ken: battered women' (1982) 7 *Vermont Law Review* 1; Lenore E A Walker, *The Battered Women's Syndrome*, 3rd edition (New York: Springer, 2009).

[148] See Sandra M Nutley et al., *Using Evidence: How Research Can Inform Public Services* (Bristol: Policy Press, 2007), p. 11.

[149] Russell Smyth, 'Academic writing and the courts: a quantitative study of the influence of legal and non-legal periodicals in the High Court' (1999) 166 *University of Tasmania Law Review*, 2, 167.

[150] S v. *Jackson* [1998] (4) BCLR 424 (SCA).

[151] For background on the cautionary rule, see Alice Armstrong, 'Evidence in rape cases in four Southern African countries' (1989) 33 *Journal for African Law*, 2, 172–184.

[152] S v. *Jackson*, para. 10. Also see Human Rights Watch, *The State Response to Domestic Violence and Rape*, research report (Human Rights Watch, 1995).

difference in size and abilities of the appellant and the victim, in addition to the offender's job as a policeman and his status as a friend, which understandably made the victim trust him.[153] The Court used comparative jurisprudence[154] and cited relevant academic research, specifically an article by Armstrong where she stated that:

> There is absolutely no evidence that women are less truthful than men, or that they fantasise more or that they are naturally vengeful and spiteful. Such a suggestion is misogynistic, and should be dismissed out of hand. Therefore the cautionary rule is based on a principle which is discriminatory towards women, and inappropriate in countries committed to equal rights for men and women, and the rule should be prohibited on this ground alone. The cautionary rule has been called a lingering insult to women.[155]

Not only did this judgment challenge the gender stereotype, it also opened space for further discussion on the perceptions of women in court. In *S* v. *Egglestone*,[156] the SCA used this precedent to define the relationship between applying the cautionary rule and the duty of the prosecution to prove guilt beyond reasonable doubt. The SCA held that while the defendant is to be treated as innocent unless proven guilty beyond reasonable doubt, gender stereotypes of women's truthfulness cannot be used in arguments by either party. Even shaky evidence may call for a cautionary approach, but not a cautionary rule.[157]

Lisa Vetten, a women's rights activist, was invited as a witness in the *Sonke* v. *Malema* case, an invitation that the defendant did not welcome and even challenged. The respondent questioned her formal qualifications in reference to her knowledge on rape. She responded by citing her many years of work in the civil society, her training as a counsellor and her extensive research on rape, which provide her with the necessary understanding of the nature of the crime – a response that satisfied the court.[158] Vetten's testimony did not only condemn Malema's position, but also pinpointed its repercussions on society. She accurately explained how Malema's actions were more detrimental

[153] *S* v. *Jackson*, paras. 10 and 23.

[154] For example, the court cited reform law in the United Kingdom specifically from *R* v. *Hester* [1973] AC 296 and *Director of Public Prosecutions* v. *Kilbourne* [1973] AC 729.

[155] Armstrong, 'Evidence in rape cases', 183.

[156] *S* v. *Egglestone* (482/07) [2008] ZASCA 77; [2008] 4 All South Africa 207 (SCA); 2009 (1) SACR 244 (SCA).

[157] Ibid., para. 12.

[158] *Malema* case, para. 17(b)vi.

than mere words. Men continuously set strict expectations to women's behaviour, and hold women responsible to meet these standards. These sexist expectations are so deeply entrenched in society that women often start internalising them and abiding by them, triggering guilt and self-blame.[159] Malema had decided how women should act when they are raped and made a public judgment on Zuma's case based on his perception; his actions confirm that 'myths and stereotypes are typically created by groups dominant in society'.[160] The involvement of Vetten in this case directed the court to see the depths of the impact of Malema's words. It is easy, and was probably expected, to discard his rant as political talk and claim negligence; however the impact is everlasting.

2 *Referencing International Law in South African Jurisprudence*

International law is frequently used in courts to draw the boundaries of state responsibility. It is also a valuable tool for NGOs to negotiate women's rights in impact litigation. South African courts quite often refer to international law in their judgments, and sometimes it has even swayed the direction of litigation.[161] In *Carmichele* v. *The Minister of Safety and Security*, about the prison escapee who subsequently raped a woman, the Constitutional Court's judgment was strongly influenced by the state's international obligations, stating that 'South Africa also has a duty under international law to prohibit all gender-based discrimination that has the effect or purpose of impairing the enjoyment by women of fundamental rights and freedoms'.[162] Similarly, the Constitutional Court decision in *S* v. *Baloyi* was partially based on South Africa's international obligations to uphold human rights and fundamental freedoms. Emphasising the positive state responsibility of due diligence to eliminate VAW, the Court cited CEDAW, the Universal Declaration of Human Rights and DEVAW.[163]

The Constitutional Court in *Christian Education South Africa* v. *Minister of Education*[164] favoured an interpretation in line with

159 See Kelly L Lemaire et al., 'Labelling sexual victimization experiences: the role of sexism, rape myth acceptance and tolerance for sexual harassment' (2016) 31 *Violence and Victims*, 2; Amy Grubb and Emily Turner, 'Attribution of blame in rape cases: A review of the impact of rape myth acceptance, gender role conformity and substance use on victim blaming' (2012) 17 *Aggression and Violent Behavior*, 5, 443–452.

160 *Malema* case, para. 17(b)vii.

161 See *Grootboom* Constitutional Court, para. 27.

162 *Carmichele* case, para. 62.

163 *S* v. *Baloyi*, paras. 12–13.

164 *Christian Education South Africa* v. *Minister of Justice* [1998] (12) BCLR 1449 (CC).

international human rights law to resolve an ideological conflict between 'freedom of religion' and violence against children. Christian Education of South Africa, representing 196 Christian Schools, claimed that the South African Schools Act of 1996, which prohibited corporal punishment, violated the rights of the parents of the students to freedom of religion. The applicant argued that corporal punishment was part of their religious beliefs and practices. The respondent, the Minister of Education, held that inflicting corporal punishment upon children violates their constitutional rights to human dignity and freedom and security of person. In addition, allowing derogation for Christian schools would violate the children's right to equality.[165] Despite the dilemma of balancing cultural diversity against human rights, Justice Sachs rejected an exemption in this case because corporal punishment infringed on children's human rights. The judgment was primarily based on the constitutional rights of children, South Africa's obligations under the CRC, which require states to 'take all appropriate measures to protect the child from violence, injury or abuse';[166] and Article 5 of the Declaration on the Elimination of All Forms of Intolerance and of Discrimination Based on Religion or Belief,[167] which states that 'Practices of a religion or belief in which a child is brought up must not be injurious to his physical or mental health or to his full development'.

Comparative jurisprudence is also found in South African judgments.[168] In *S* v. *Zuma*, the court cited case law from Hong Kong[169] and the United States of America.[170] In *Masiya* v. *S*, the *amici* used the example of *SW* v. *United Kingdom*[171] before the ECHR to support their argument. These are just some of the numerous cases in which international law was a strong element in litigation; however, the trend is quite indicative of the value of international human rights law. South Africa has ratified all relevant international human rights

[165] Ibid., para. 10; Constitution, ss. 9, 10 and 12.

[166] CRC, Article 19.

[167] Declaration on the Elimination of All Forms of Intolerance and of Discrimination Based on Religion or Belief (1981) UN Doc A/36/684.

[168] See Ronald C Slye, 'International law, human rights beneficiaries and South Africa: some thoughts on the utility of international human rights law' (2001) 2 *Chicago Journal of International Law*, 1.

[169] *S* v. *Zuma* [1995] (4) BCLR 401 (SA), para. 31.

[170] Ibid., para., 20.

[171] *SW* v. *United Kingdom*; *CR* v. *United Kingdom* (1995) 21 Eur. H. R. Rep. 363.

instruments – the first sign of readiness to uphold the enshrined rights.[172] However, for various reasons, governments are not always eager to implement these obligations; international treaties then become a great resource for litigation – a tool that can be used by NGOs and activists to domesticate international human rights and by courts to diversify their references and resources. This approach is only possible in countries with independent and developed progressive justice systems; it reflects a genuine interest of courts to have the required diligence to revise and develop domestic human rights.[173]

D The Gains in Litigation Losses

The purpose of a liberal and plural legal system is not to always rule against the state – a victory is not always guaranteed, and nor should it be. In fact, the term public interest law 'does not imply that the side represented by the public interest lawyer is always right as a matter of law, policy or even morality'.[174] Cause lawyering is therefore about defining human rights, the limits of these rights and the socio-economic cost to the best ability of the court. Lost litigation for NGOs does not mean a lost cause.

1 *Battered Women's Syndrome*

In *Marais* v. *S*,[175] the argument of the *amici* altered the path of litigation by directing the court to consider a murder case in the context of domestic violence. The complainant was appealing a life sentence that she had received for the contract murder of her abusive husband. Ms Marais argued that she was a victim of domestic violence, as she was assaulted and raped on multiple occasions. She alleged that she had planned to set up the murder as a charade. The High Court rejected this argument and found that she was not a battered woman and that she had committed a 'calculated murder motivated by financial greed'.[176] Mrs Marais took the case to the Constitutional Court arguing that her right to fair trial has been violated; she claimed that she was not aware that the High Court had rejected her domestic violence defence, and that she was ready to present more evidence.[177] The Constitutional Court saw this case to be merely about

[172] Beth A. Simmons, *Mobilizing for Human Rights: International Law in Domestic Politics* (Cambridge: Cambridge University Press, 2009), p. 12.

[173] Ibid., p. 14.

[174] Kathree, 'Public interest law', 32.

[175] S v. *Marais* [2010] (12) BCLR 1223 (CC).

[176] Ibid., para. 6.

[177] Ibid., para. 14.

a disagreement with the High Court on its fact-finding and this, alone, does not reflect a constitutional issue. The Constitutional Court therefore dismissed her application.[178] This can be considered a litigation failure, especially because civil society got involved in the case at a late stage when the TLAC submitted an application for *amicus curiae*, so as to present the court with expert evidence on the reality of domestically abused women. Despite the litigation failure, NGOs accepted the due course of law, with the director of the WLC explaining that 'this judgment was positive as it showed the law could be developed so that Battered Woman Syndrome could be used as a defence in the correct circumstances' – the argument, however, needs to be introduced earlier in the case.[179]

2 Sex Work and Gender Stereotyping

De facto discrimination that perpetuates gender stereotypes was the main issue raised by the *amici*, CALS and the CGE, among others, in *S* v. *Jordan*.[180] The case questioned the constitutionality of several provisions of the Sexual Offences Act,[181] relating to prostitution and brothel ownership. The appellants and *amici* argued that the prostitution provisions de facto discriminated against women because they only criminalised selling sexual services, predominantly undertaken by women, whereas male clients were considered accomplices. They also argued against the constitutionality of the brothel ownership provisions. The High Court had already ruled that the brothel ownership provisions were constitutional, but that the prostitution provisions were unconstitutional. The appellants therefore asked the Constitutional Court to revise the first matter and confirm the second.

The approach of the majority of judges 'lacked gender sensitivity',[182] asserting that the provisions did not violate constitutional rights. Most importantly, the majority judgment saw the prostitution provision as non-discriminatory because it was applicable to both men and women who sell sexual services. They further contended that cutting

[178] Marais later won an appeal on sentencing and had her sentence reduced to 20 years instead of a life sentence. See Leila Samodien, '"Black widow" wins appeal against sentence', IOL, 23 December 2011, accessed 20 June 2018 at www.iol.co.za/capetimes/black-widow-wins-appeal-against-sentence-1203843

[179] 'Husband killer loses bid for appeal', IOL, 22 September 2010, accessed 20 June 2018, at www.iol.co.za/news/south-africa/western-cape/husband-killer-loses-bid-for-appeal-680850

[180] *S* v. *Jordan* [2002] (11) BCLR 1117 (CC) (hereinafter, *Jordan* case).

[181] Sexual Offences Act 23 of 1956, s. 20.

[182] Ashley Martabano and Michelle O'Sullivan, 'Three steps forward, two steps back: legal activism for women's rights in South Africa' (2004) 60 *Agenda*, 56.

the 'supply' was a common strategy to curb prostitution.[183] The stigma attached to prostitutes was seen as rooted in the 'social product of their occupation and not a legal consequence of gender discrimination' and, therefore, women who took the profession of sex workers were expected to know the stereotypes attached to it.[184] This assumption was unsurprisingly criticised by civil society – the judgment was understood to say that if one knows the stereotypes attached to a profession yet chooses to take it, then they 'must surely fit the stereotype'.[185]

Dissident judges also stressed that it is inappropriate for the court to answer a constitutional claim by suggesting that the discrimination lies in society and not in the law 'when the law serves to foster those values'.[186] Sachs and O'Regan were among the minority judges who considered the provisions to be discriminatory. They adopted a gender-sensitive approach to sex work, noting the disadvantages that push women to specific professions such as prostitution. They also adopted a practical approach, locating the solution in regulation rather than prohibition of sex work.[187] Furthermore, they repeatedly referred to the *amici* submission,[188] which urged the court to look beyond the law and to consider the negative impact that a stereotype embedded in a court judgment would have on women.[189] They stated:

> The female prostitute has been the social outcast, the male patron has been accepted or ignored. She is visible and denounced, her existence tainted by her activity. He is faceless, a mere ingredient in her offence rather than a criminal in his own right, who returns to respectability after the encounter. In terms of the sexual double standards prevalent in our society, he has often been regarded either as having given in to temptation, or as having done the sort of thing that men do. Thus, a man visiting a prostitute is not considered by many to have acted in a morally reprehensible fashion. A woman who is a prostitute is considered by most to be beyond the pale. The difference in social stigma tracks a pattern of applying different standards to the sexuality of men and women.[190]

[183] *Jordan* case, para. 51.

[184] Ibid., para. 16.

[185] Charlene May, 'Substantive gender equality, sex work and the assumptions of S v Jordan: in pursuit of equality in South Africa' in Mandivavarira Mudarikwa et al. (eds.), *Pursuit of Equality in South Africa* (Johannesburg: Synergetic Fast Services, 2017).

[186] *Jordan* case, para. 60.

[187] *Jordan* case, para. 45.

[188] Ibid., paras. 21–53, 77, 87.

[189] Ibid., para. 59.

[190] Ibid., para. 64.

The loss in this case was quite disappointing because it was the epitome of how law may look deceptively non-discriminatory. The gains from this case, however, centred on the movement it stirred around the meaning of de facto discriminatory laws,and the public dialogue it triggered on the issue of sex work. This includes academic analysis, NGO activism and the state's diligence to design a gender-sensitive treatment of sex work.

Kruger argues that stigmatising prostitutes affects their reporting rates on violent crimes, as they know their words will be poorly judged because of their profession.[191] This was confirmed by one of the respondents in this research: the head of an NGO who works on GBV. She reported that the NGO occasionally received sex workers who had experienced violence. These clients approach them to know their options, but usually refrain from reporting violence committed by policemen when they learn that they cannot make anonymous complaints. Similarly, in 2016, the report of the Special Rapporteur on violence against women noted 'evidence of police using the law against women in prostitution to commit abuses', which essentially impedes women's access to justice.[192] The decision in the *Jordan* case could also reinforce the legitimacy of violence against women who are seen as deviating from social norms.[193] Sachs locates the problem in the confusion over the relationship between law and society. He asks; is criminalising commercial sex necessary to reduce it, or does criminalising it provide a suitable environment for violence to flourish?[194] Academic critique similarly offered a comparative approach to the legality of prostitution. Fritz found that women in countries with loose controls over sex work enjoyed more sexual reedom, in comparison to women in countries where the practice was banned.[195]

On behalf of the state, the South African Law Reform Commission published a report in 2015 exploring the issue of legalising prostitution and its impact on society, particularly looking at its relation with VAW

[191] Rosaan Kruger, 'Sex work from a feminist perspective: a visit to the Jordan case' (2004) 20 *South African Journal on Human Rights*, 1, 144.

[192] Special Rapporteur report, 2016, p. 6.

[193] See Rikki Holtmaat, 'Preventing violence against women: the due diligence standards with respect to the obligation to banish gender stereotypes on ground of Article 5(a) of the CEDAW Convention' in Carin Benninger-Budel (ed.), *Due Diligence and Its Application to Protect Women from Violence* (Leiden and Boston, MA: Martinus Nijhoff Publishers, 2008), pp. 63–90.

[194] Sachs, *The Strange Alchemy*, p. 59.

[195] Nicole Fritz 'Crossing Jordan: constitutional space for (un)civil sex' (2004) 20 *South African Journal on Human Rights*, 2, 239.

and gender stereotypes.[196] The report provided legislative and non-legislative recommendations, and endorsed recommendations given by a WLC and SWEAT[197] project – both civil society organisations working with sex workers.[198] One of the most important findings of the report is the absence of a national plan to address sex work. The Commission urged the state to design a national strategy to complement the proposed legislative reform, offer an exit and alternative livelihood to sex workers and provide health, education and other economic support to truly empower people who wish to leave the profession. NGOs remain involved in the pursuit of a solution. In February 2018, CALS submitted a response to the Law Commission's report, urging the Commission to 'truly listen to and engage with the views and interests expressed by sex workers' and to be more sensitive with terminology, such as replacing the word 'prostitute' with sex worker.[199]

What started as a court case affecting a few people has ultimately pushed a critical discussion to the forefront of the public discourse. Regardless of the litigation outcome, the fact that the conversation has been ongoing for years and has maintained the attention of both state and civil society indicates a success for impact litigation.

2 *Developing the Definition of Rape*

Masiya v. *S* was not a total loss. Mr Masiya had anally penetrated a nine-year-old girl before the promulgation of the sexual offences bill. Rape under common law was restricted to vaginal penetration and therefore Mr Masiye should have been charged with indecent assault. The Magistrate Court, however, sensed the inadequacy in the law and determined that the sentence was unsuitable for the crime. Of its own accord, the Court developed the definition of rape, charged Mr Masiye with rape, and referred the case to the High Court for confirmation and sentencing. The Court further expressed not only the injustice, but the ludicrousness in considering Mr Masiye's actions as anything less than rape. The Judge stated:

196 South African Law Reform Commission, Project 107 on Sexual Offences: Adult Prostitution (2017).

197 SWEAT is an NGO working on advocacy related to sex workers in Africa; see www.sweat.org.za/

198 South African Law Reform Commission, Project 107, p. 5.

199 Sheena Swemmer and Vuyo Mntonintshi, *Response to the South African Law Reform Commission's Report on 'Sexual Offences: Adult Prostitution'* (Centre for Applied Legal Studies, 26 February 2018), para. 2.1.4.

> One's initial feelings of righteousness would however immediately rebel against such thought. Why must the unconsensual sexual penetration of a girl (or a boy) per anum be regarded as less injurious, less humiliating and less serious than the unconsensual sexual penetration of a girl per vaginam? The distinction appears on face value to be irrational and totally senseless… It therefore appears that the common law definition of rape is not only archaic, but irrational and amounts to arbitrary discrimination with reference to which kind of sexual penetration is to be regarded as the most serious, and then only in respect of women.[200]

This case highlights judges' role in applying justice rather than applying the law – a space that only a progressive and plural justice system would provide. The case, however, was referred to the Constitutional Court to rule on the constitutionality of the definition of rape under common law, and Mr Masiye's right to a fair trial.

Before the Constitutional Court, the CALS and TLAC, acting as *amicus curiae*, argued that vaginal and anal penetrations inflict the same psychological trauma upon the victim, and that rape is essentially about 'power', which should be the main consideration in the judgment.[201] The Constitutional Court agreed and expressed its awareness that the sexual offences bill was under parliamentary review. Notwithstanding, it asserted that it could not 'delay, defer or refuse to deal with an extension of the definition when the facts before it demand such an extension and when it is clearly in the public interest to do so'.[202] In this regard, the case was a success.

The Constitutional Court, however, ruled that charging the accused retrospectively with rape infringed on his right to a fair trial. Like the *Jordan* case, *Masiya* v. *S* stirred up an important discussion in law and society at a time when rape was narrowly defined before the promulgation of the SOA. Not only did it demonstrate the need for legal reform for sexual offences, but it also identified the gender power dynamic at the core of sexual violence. Furthermore, the case opened up a public discussion on the issue of male rape, and on the role of courts as legislators.[203]

[200] Ibid., para. 9.
[201] Ibid., para. 39.
[202] Ibid., para. 44.
[203] Ibid., para. 30; See Cowan, 'Do women', p. 6; Pierre De Vos, 'Male rape: what were the judges smoking?', Constitutionally Speaking, 10 May 2007, accessed 20 June 2018 at www.constitutionallyspeaking.co.za/male-rape-what-were-the-judges-smoking

This case demonstrates a wider problem in South Africa, and globally, regarding the roles of parliament and the court. Parliament takes a significant amount of time to process bills – time that victims of serious crimes cannot afford. The Sexual Offences Bill was introduced to the South African Parliament in 2003,[204] five years after 'discussions and debates' in the South African Law Reform Commission.[205] The Constitutional Court heard Masiye's case in 2007 and the bill was still not promulgated. The delays were not justifiable; they caused frustration among some members of parliament[206] and triggered public outrage. South Africa did not have the luxury of such delays when rape reports amounted to 150 per day at that time.[207] The Sexual Offences Bill was not the last delay in parliament, as this trend has frustrated the public for years after this case.[208]

Parliamentary delays put courts in a difficult position, as demonstrated by the *Masiya* case. Courts face litigants living with the problems embedded in the bills before parliament and these victims expect justice. Courts must sometimes engage in law-making; however, they remain conservative in this role so as not to 'encroach on the "legislative terrain"'.[209] Dynamics between the three state powers demonstrate the importance of maintaining and honouring the judiciary's limited but necessary role in law-making.

[204] Criminal Law (Sexual Offences) Amendment Bill B50–2003 (published in Government Gazette No. 25282 of 30 July 2003).

[205] 'Taking stock of the Sexual Offences Bill', University of Cape Town News, 4 June 2007, accessed 6 June 2018 at www.news.uct.ac.za/article/-2007-06-04-taking-stock-of-the-sexual-offences-bill

[206] Justice and Constitutional Development Portfolio Committee, Meeting Report, 18 May 2007, Criminal Law (Sexual Offences) Amendment Bill: Adoption of Report. Chairperson, Ms F Chohan-Khota.

[207] Clare Nullis, 'New rape laws to help protect victims', The Mail & Guardian, 14 December 2007, accessed 6 June 2018 at www.mg.co.za/article/2007-12-14-new-rape-laws-to-help-protect-victims

[208] See Sue Segar, 'Parliament may face court challenge if it delays language bill', IOL, 19 January 2012, accessed 6 June 2018 at www.iol.co.za/dailynews/news/parliament-may-face-court-challenge-if-it-delays-language-bill-1215868; Marianne Merten, 'Parliament: national minimum wage bill will not be rushed', The Daily Maverick, 23 March 2018, accessed 6 June 2018 at www.dailymaverick.co.za/article/2018-03-23-parliament-national-minimum-wage-bill-will-not-be-rushed/#.Wx_snkiFPIU

[209] Sheena Adams, 'Court finds men can't be raped', The Mercury, 11 May 2007, cited in the Committee meeting of Justice and Correctional service, accessed 20 June 2018 at https://pmg.org.za/committee-meeting/8049/

E Impact Litigation Globally

While South Africa is one of the global leaders of impact litigation, there has been some significant gains in women's rights in other countries. This section will present some of the landmark cases in other jurisdictions.

1 *Nationality Laws*

The *Attorney General of Botswana* v. *Unity Dow*[210] was about one of the legal rights that many women are still struggling to enjoy today – the right to pass citizenship to one's children. In this case, the complainant was a citizen of Botswana married to a foreigner and was unable to pass citizenship to her children because Botswanan law restricted this right to children of males or children born out of wedlock. The plaintiff argued that these provisions violated the Constitution. The High Court ruled in favour of the plaintiff and the Court of Appeals upheld the ruling.

The Court recognised the hardships that women face because of this discrimination. For instance, their children would be excluded from any government scholarships or subsidies available to citizens; also, the applicant would have to choose between her country and her family if her husband's residence permit was not renewed and he had to leave the country with her non-citizen children. Furthermore, the Court held that the said Act infringed the right to liberty of women as it limits their choices in marrying non-citizens. The Attorney General's arguments primarily rested on the claim that Botswana adopts a patrilineal system, which should not be disturbed.[211] For instance, if the husband was expelled from Botswana or wished to return to his home country with his children, the Attorney General stated, 'of course one would hope she, the applicant, would follow her husband'. The Judge, however, supported the plaintiff, asserting that the Attorney General may have felt 'that this answer would have appealed to the patriarchs of Biblical times'[212] but in reality, this restriction curtails the freedom of choice for women. For instance, if the spouses disagree and the applicant needs to

[210] *Attorney-General* v. *Dow* 1992 BLR 119 (CA) (Botswana) (hereinafter, *Dow* case).

[211] Also see Rebecca Cook, *Human Rights of Women: National and International Perspectives* (Pennsylvania: University of Pennsylvania Press, 1994), pp. 293–295.

[212] *Dow* case, p. 37.

return to Botswana, she will show up at the border without a residency permit for her children.[213]

Dow, as a lawyer, brought forward her case to test the limits of constitutional rights; in other words, conducting her own impact litigation. She knew 'at least 30 women' in her area with similar circumstances and countless women living in rural areas on the South African border, married to South African men who had no clue that their children were not considered citizens of Botswana.[214] The right to pass citizenship to women's children is still in heated debate in some countries around the world, many located in the Middle East.[215]

2 *Discrimination against Women*

In *Longwe* v. *Intercontinental Hotels*,[216] a female lawyer brought a case against the hotel chain in Zambia after she was refused entry to a hotel bar because she was unaccompanied by a male. The hotel set the rule because unaccompanied women have caused problems in the past. Longwe alleged an infringement of her constitutional rights pursuant to sections 11 and 23(2).[217] The respondent did not try to negate the facts or deny their policy, but rested their defence on the premise that as a private institution, they were entitled to set their own policies, and these should not be considered discrimination.[218] The Court ruled in favour of Ms Longwe and asserted that everyone is bound by the Constitution. Furthermore, the Court noted that all public institutions must be open to the public without any grounds of discrimination, and expressed 'amusement' that the hotel defence team was trying to convince the Court that private institutions were entitled to discriminate.[219] This

[213] Ibid., p. 37.

[214] Marsha Freeman, 'Women, law and land at the local level: claiming women's human rights in domestic legal systems' (1994) 16 *Human Rights Quarterly*, 3, 570.

[215] For example, Lebanon, Jordan, Saudi Arabic, Qatar, and the United Arab Emirates. See Fahmiyya Sharafeddine, 'Discrimination against women in the nationality law: its impact on Lebanese families and issues of national integration' (December 2017) 17 *The Peace Building in Lebanon*, 15; UNHCR, Gender, equality, nationality laws and statelessness, background note, (UNHCR 7 March 2014); Global Campaign for Equal Nationality Rights at https://equalnationalityrights.org

[216] *Longwe* v. *Intercontinental Hotels* (1993) 4 LRC 221 (Zambia) (hereinafter, *Longwe* case).

[217] Constitution of Zambia (Act no 1, 1991), ss. 11 and 23(2).

[218] Sara Hlupekile Longwe, 'Case study: legal action to stop hotels discriminating against women in Zambia' (2011) 15 *Feminist Africa*, 92.

[219] Ibid.; also see Robyn Emerton et al. (eds.), *International Women's Rights Cases* (New York: Routledge, 2016), p. 95.

case was a breakthrough because it held a private institution in violation of the Constitution; it also strongly referenced international law. The Court cited instruments such as the CEDAW and the African Charter, noting that Zambia's ratification without reservations indicates the state's full acceptance of the provisions.[220]

3 *Reproductive Rights*

Tysiac v. *Poland*[221] went to the European Court of Human Rights when the applicant sought to abort a pregnancy that was detrimental to her health, and which she had failed to do legally in Poland. The public hospital refused to perform the procedure, despite a medical note indicating the applicant's condition, which forced the applicant to carry to term. The case was a success as the ECHR found a breach in Article 8 of the European Convention on Human Rights: the state has failed in its duty to take positive measures to respect the applicant's rights under the said Article.[222] The ruling was based on the government's failure to adopt procedures to guarantee that women can appeal a state rejection of the termination of a women's pregnancy. The Court further specified that the state should enforce procedures allowing women to be heard in person, issue written documentation explaining the grounds for rejections, and give timely responses considering the time sensitivity element linked to pregnancy.[223] This case is significant in the movement promoting women's reproductive rights, representing a major shift in the ECHR stance towards the issue of abortion, almost creating 'a right to abortion'.[224] Furthermore, the applicant was supported throughout this process by two local NGOs, as well as international NGOs when the case went to the ECHR. It therefore exemplifies how strategic litigation cases can be found in the daily work of women's organisations.[225]

220 Lillion Mushota, International law, women's rights and the courts: a Zambian n using courts to protect vulnerable people, research paper, (Southern Africa Litigation Centre and others, 2004), p. 98.

221 *Tysiac* v. *Poland*, [2007] Case 5410/03, European Court of Human Rights (hereinafter, *Tysiac* case).

222 Ibid., para. 129.

223 Ibid., paras. 86–88.

224 Nicolette Priaulx, 'Testing the margin of appreciation: therapeutic abortion, reproductive 'rights' and the intriguing case of *Tysiąc v. Poland*' (2008) 15 *European Journal of Health Law*, 4, 361–379. This was also expressed in the opinion of the dissident judge in the case.

225 Gesine Fuchs, 'Using strategic litigation for women's rights: political restrictions in Poland and achievements of the women's movement' (2013) 20 *European Journal of Women's Studies* 1, 32.

4 *Female Genital Mutilation, Violence against Women and Claiming Refugee Status*

Matter of Kasinga[226] was a breakthrough case in which fleeing GBV was considered grounds for asylum. The case was heard by the Board of Immigration Appeals (BIA) in the USA after Ms Kasinga's lawyer stirred media and publicity in her direction. The applicant had fled Togo because of a threat to undergo female genital cutting and to enter a forced marriage. She applied for and was denied asylum as soon as she arrived in the USA and was imprisoned for a year. Her claim was based on the fact that the government of Togo knew about the FGM and would not have taken any steps to protect her.[227] However, FGM was a nationwide practice and Ms Kasinga was not individually targeted for it, which weakened her claim. A young lawyer working at a human rights clinic took the case while Ms Kasinga was in detention and immediately blew the story in the media.[228] In a matter of a few days Ms Kasinga was out of prison, and after a few months, the BIA granted her political asylum.

In this case, the BIA accepted the applicant's claim based on her membership of a 'social group' that triggers her fear of persecution. They defined persecution broader than the norm stating, 'persecution can consist of the infliction of harm or suffering by a government, or persons a government is unwilling or unable to control, to overcome a characteristic of the victim'.[229] The BIA also identified the group to which Ms Kasinga belonged as the young women from her tribe who have not had GFM and are opposed to the practice.[230]

In this case, the definition of asylum[231] had to be stretched to include the hardships faced by Kasinga. Defining and drafting human rights with a male-centric approach has always been a major critique

[226] *Matter of Kasinga*, 21 I. and N. 357 (United States of America: Board of Immigration Appeals 1996) (hereinafter, *Kasinga* case).

[227] Ibid., p. 359.

[228] Center for Gender and Refugee Studies, 'Matter of Kasinga' https://cgrs.uchastings.edu/our-work/matter-kasinga-1996

[229] *Kasinga* case, p. 365.

[230] Ibid., p. 365.

[231] Immigration and Nationality Act, 27 June 1952, last amended March 2004, (United States of America). The definition of a refugee in the Act resembles that of the UN Declaration of the Right of Refugees, identifying a refugee as a person unable to return to one's country because of 'persecution or a well-founded fear of persecution on account of race, religion, nationality, membership in a particular social group, or political opinion'. These are mostly men's concerns for men, although they sometimes apply to women. However, concerns that are unique to women such as the issue in Kasinga's case need to be fitted into the narrow definition of the Act.

of international law instruments,[232] and Kasinga's situation is a case in point.

IV CONCLUSION

It is important to remember and honour cases on which human rights lawyers and litigants tirelessly worked for years to show that the law can be gender discriminatory in theory and in practice. Nongovernmental organisations working for women's rights carry a significant burden, whether in litigating specific cases or in shifting the legal culture to be more gender sensitive. They need to:

> Get the courts to understand the context of women's lives and in particular... to persuade them to protect women by recognising their agency or decision-making capacity on the one hand, and on the other, the fact that women's choices are often constrained particularly in a context of endemic poverty. Without convincing courts to develop a contextual approach, we will not win cases.[233]

Fortunately, the justice system in South Africa provides the space for NGOs to fulfil the abovementioned role, bringing women's lived realities into the core of litigation. This chapter has demonstrated how a judiciary that is open to diversified sources of information can encourage dialogue and negotiations on the meaning and limitations of human rights. This includes balancing conflicting rights, setting the boundaries for state responsibility and assessing the compatibility of laws with people's social needs and realities.

Evaluating the openness of the legal culture also entails a closer look at the organisations making and applying the laws, including all arms of the state. These institutions are responsible for working together to respect, protect, ensure and fulfil human rights, through setting and executing national plans to meet the needs of the people. Nongovernmental organisations are at the core of these relations not only in defining and developing human rights as shown in this

[232] See Mackinnon, *Toward a Feminist Theory*; Melanie Randell, 'Refugee law and state accountability for violence against women: a comparative analysis of legal approaches to recognizing asylum claims based on gender persecution' (2002) 25 *Harvard Women's Law Journal*, 281–318; Mackinnon, *Women's Lives*; Smart, *Feminism and the Power of Law*.

[233] Martabano and O'Sullivan, 'Three steps forward', 60.

chapter, but in many other areas of work discussed throughout this book.

The process of cause lawyering explored in this chapter is a significant opportunity for negotiations on the balance between human rights and state responsibility. The next chapter will discuss other dimension of impact litigation.

CHAPTER 6

THE ART OF LITIGATION: TACTICS AND IMPACT

The judiciary has a key role in the development of laws and human rights principles in South Africa. The impact of this role, however, remains a matter of debate. It has been hailed as a speedier alternative to parliamentary law-making and criticised because of the lack of or delays in the implementation of judgments. This leaves us with the question, is impact litigation a useful tool for socio-legal change?

This chapter will provide some perspectives on the value of cause lawyering, shedding light on some techniques and enabling factors for positive impact. It will start by exploring the differences between cause lawyering and other fields of legal practice, proceeding to map the goals and challenges of impact litigation. Section III will focus on the role of NGOs in impact litigation, both in and out of courts. The chapter will end with some conclusions to wrap up the debate on impact litigation.

I CAUSE LAWYERING IN A BRIEF

A Lawyering Versus Cause Lawyering

Practising cause lawyering entails specific qualities that may contradict with mainstream lawyering. Schneider explains that lawyers who do cause lawyering face a dilemma; as lawyers, they are trained to distrust their instincts and detach themselves from their personal experiences,[1] whereas cause lawyering requires devotion and dedication to a cause.

[1] Elizabeth Schneider, 'Lesbians, gays and feminists at the bar: translating personal experience into effective legal argument – a symposium' (1988) 10 *Women's Rights Law Reporter*, 2, 115; Austin Sarat

Furthermore, lawyers have a 'duty of loyalty' to their clients but are expected to not get attached or accountable for their clients' decisions,[2] whereas the loyalty of cause lawyers is to a cause, and often they do not differentiate the client from the cause. While lawyers' competency is mostly important in courts, cause lawyers are expected to be 'competent in the public arena' as their jobs entail much more than legal arguments.[3] This is why cause lawyers need to follow strict rules and ethics. For instance, they should treat 'cause clients' and private clients with the same level of respect – they both have the final decision in the proceedings of their case.[4] Furthermore, they should never put a cause before a client.[5]

Human rights lawyers, working for nonprofit organisations are often the best candidates to undertake cause lawyering. This puts a huge burden and responsibility on them, a point noted by all participants in this research who worked on impact litigation. This is because 'feminist theory and feminist litigation have an incredibly important intellectual and transformative potential in the field of law',[6] as they bear the responsibility to help courts understand the women's lived realities, transforming the justice sector into a gender sensitive one.[7]

NGOs are the best candidates for this mission as they work on the multiple dimensions of women's realities, and are therefore able to challenge the traditional power relations that perpetuate gender inequalities. Also, unlike lawyer practitioners, lawyer activists see the broader impact in one legal victory, which may enhance their patience and perseverance. Although exhausting, cause lawyering is 'a rewarding, challenging, and stimulating experience' and provides an opportunity 'to be exposed to novel and difficult legal issues'.[8]

and Stuart Scheingold, 'Cause lawyering and the reproduction of professional authority: an introduction' in Austin Sarat and Stuart Scheingold (eds.), *Cause Lawyering, Political Commitments and Professional Responsibilities* (Oxford: Oxford University Press, 1998); Robert MacCrate, '"The lost lawyer" regained: the abiding values of legal profession' (1996) 100 *Dickinson Law Review*, 603–606.

2 Deborah J Cantrell, 'Sensational reports: the ethical duty of cause lawyers to be competent in public advocacy' (2007) 30 *Hamline Law Review*, 3, 570.

3 Ibid., 575.

4 Bettina E. Brownstein, 'Private practice and cause lawyering: a practical and ethical guide' (2009) 31 *University of Arkansas at Little Rock Law Review* 4, 607.

5 Michelle N Meyer, 'The plaintiff as person: cause lawyering, human subject research, and the secret agent problem' (15 July 2012) 119 *Harvard Law Review*, 5.

6 Schneider, 'Lesbians, gays and feminists', 115.

7 Martabano and O'Sullivan, 'Three steps forward', 60.

8 Brownstein, 'Private practice', 608.

B Environments Conducive to Impact Litigation

Assessing the impact of impact litigation calls for a consideration of both the goal of litigation and the legal and political climate in which litigation takes place. Roa and Klugman identify four conditions determining a favourable socio-legal climate for impact litigation, increasing the odds for genuine social impact. These are: an independent judiciary; a functional rights framework; strong civil society organisations that are able to re-frame social issues into legal issues and bring them forward to court; and a network that guarantees that the opportunities offered by impact litigation are not lost.[9] Budlender elaborates by pointing to a strong and independent legal culture, public information campaigns and grassroots social movements for legal education, accessible service provision and support for litigants.[10] Considering all these criteria, the South African socio-legal environment is definitely conducive to cause lawyering. The liberal nature of the judiciary and the constitutional provision on access to justice, 'coupled with the relaxed approach to standing in rights litigation has the aim of making the courts accessible to the ordinary citizen either by self-representation or through public interest groups and individuals'.[11] In addition, South Africa fosters a vibrant civil society working on all prerequisites of impact litigation such as legal awareness, service provision and media advocacy.

The state response to impact litigation also depends on the political conditions of the said country, the issue litigated and the state's consideration of international image and pressure. A report on strategic litigation for torture cases conducted by NGOs found a relationship between the political circumstances and the readiness of the country to acknowledge judgments resulting from cause lawyering. For instance, the Turkish government made remarkable progress in the 1990s for about a decade, coinciding with its attempts to join the European Union, but then escalated the use of torture again after the attempted coup in 2016.[12] In this case the state's stance changed towards impact litigation with the political motivations at different times.

[9] Mónica Roa and Barbara Klugman, 'Considering strategic litigation as an advocacy tool: a case study of the defence of reproductive rights in Colombia' (2014) 22 *Reproductive Health Matters*, 44, 31.

[10] Budlender et al., *Public Interest Litigation*, p. 96.

[11] Mulugeta, 'Public interest litigation', p. 36.

[12] Helen Duffy, *Strategic Litigation Impacts Torture in Custody*, research report (Open Society Foundations, 2017), p. 24.

II UNPACKING IMPACT LITIGATION

A Precedent

A legal victory guarantees a legal precedent, if not much else. Precedent is not only an important guide for judges, respecting it and following it is a reflection of the status of the court that created the precedent.[13] Furthermore, abandoning precedent and issuing unprecedented judgments undermines the concept of justice and creates 'splits in the law, yielding different outcomes'.[14]

Precedent can cross borders and positively impact cases in different jurisdictions; the previous chapter cited some foreign case law used as precedent in South African courts. Other global examples include *Bangladesh National Women Lawyers Association (BNWLA)* v. *Government of Bangladesh*,[15] which was strongly inspired by *Vishakha and Others* v. *State of Rajasthan*[16], India. Both cases were brought against the state for failing to take appropriate measures to protect women from sexual harassment at the workplace. The *BNWLA* case was brought forward almost a decade after the *Vishakha* case, but used it heavily as precedent. The Supreme Court of Appeals in Bangladesh referenced the *Vishakha* case to set some rules and guidelines on curbing sexual harassment at the workplace, 'to be followed and observed at all work places and educational institutions till adequate and effective legislation is made in this field'.[17]

However, it is important to refrain from exaggerating the impact of legal precedent. Despite the Kasinga victory, discussed in the previous chapter, gender-based asylum claims continued to be rejected by adjudicators.[18] The *Carmichele* case in South Africa was undoubtedly a legal gain; however, the cases that used this precedent years later suffered the same administrative delays for remedies, making Alix Carmichele 'one of many failed by law enforcement in South Africa'.[19] It is therefore

[13] See Mary Garvey Algero, 'The sources of law and the value of precedent: a comparative and empirical study of a civil law state in a common law nation' (2005) 65 *Louisiana Law Review* 2.

[14] William D Bader and David R Cleveland, 'Precedent and justice' (2011) 49 *Duquesne Law Review* 56.

[15] *Bangladesh National Women Lawyers Association* v. *Government of Bangladesh* SCA 5916/2008 (hereinafter *BNWLA* case).

[16] *Vishaka and others* v. *State of Rajasthan and others* (1997) 6 SCC 241.

[17] *BNWLA* case, para. 55.

[18] Center for Gender and Refugee Studies, https://cgrs.uchastings.edu/our-work/matter-kasinga-1996

[19] Dennis Davis and Michelle Le Roux, *Precedent and Possibility: The (ab)use of Law in South Africa* (Cape Town: Juta and Company Ltd, 2009), p. 174.

often argued that legal precedent may promote the concept of accountability but true justice and fair compensation remain illusory.[20]

B The Power of Court Conduct and Judiciary Decisions

While impact litigation is commonly criticised for mere 'symbolism', it is important not to undermine its social value. Court proceedings are 'listened to, accorded authority, transcribed and deliberated on'.[21] Legal gains are important because gender-insensitive court judgments essentially disempower women, which can have a ripple effect on society and discourage others from claiming their rights. This reflects the importance of collective forms of empowerment. Allen argues that the conduct of investigators sends a strong message to current and future victims about the repercussions of reporting sexual violence. Negative stories about women's experiences with the legal system indicate that the costs of reporting outweigh the benefits.[22] This is because positive stories do not resonate as negative ones. A Human Rights Watch Report gives some examples: Abigail, a lesbian, was raped by an acquaintance, and was sceptical about the justice system, especially after attending a hearing for another lesbian's rape case. Abigail was specifically discouraged by the judge's questions regarding personal issues, such as, 'are you a boy or a girl? Are you a lesbian? What do you do?'[23]

The Supreme Court of Appeals in *Chapman* v. *S* was quite aware of the 'symbolic power', as well as the ripple effect of gender-insensitive court judgments. In this case, the appellant was appealing his seven-year sentence for three counts of rape. The Supreme Court upheld the verdict and reaffirmed the atrocious nature of rape and its infringement on the rights of women to integrity, dignity and privacy. The court stated:

> Women in this country are entitled to the protection of these rights. They have a legitimate claim to walk peacefully on the streets, to enjoy their shopping and their entertainment, to go and come from work, and to enjoy the peace and tranquillity of their homes without the fear, the apprehension and the insecurity which constantly diminishes the quality and enjoyment of their lives. The appellant showed no respect for their rights... The courts are under a duty to send a clear message to

20 Ibid., p. 175.

21 Ronnit Redman, 'Litigating for gender equality: the amicus curiae role of the sex discrimination commissioner' (2004) 27 *University of New South Wales Law Journal* 3, 849.

22 W. David Allen, 'The reporting and underreporting of rape' (2007) 73 *Southern Economic Journal*, 3, 624.

23 Human Rights Watch, 'We'll Show You', p. 55.

> the accused, to other potential rapists and to the community: We are determined to protect the equality, dignity and freedom of all women, and we shall show no mercy to those who seek to invade those rights.[24]

The court clearly grasped the power of judicial decisions and the responsibility that judges carry towards the public that goes beyond the disputing parties. Furthermore, the Court accurately captured the reality of women's fear of rape that constrains their movement and curtails their daily activities. A lesbian woman interviewed by Human Rights Watch echoes the Court's statement in the *Chapman* case; she stated, 'I don't go out of home late now because [the men in the neighbourhood] keep promising to rape me'.[25]

Sending a message to society that violence against women will not be tolerated and excused by the court is therefore of the utmost importance, despite its symbolic nature. It sits at the core of the relationship between law and society in which the state sets the threshold of acceptable actions versus intolerable ones. This symbolism also reminds states of their responsibilities. For instance, in the *Tysiąc* case, the judgment was not directly about abortion, but the ECHR sent Poland 'an explicit reminder that they must provide fast, transparent and accessible procedures for complaints against a denial of legal abortion'.[26]

C Empowering Women

It took Alix Carmichele, who won the landmark case *Carmichele v. Minister of Safety and Security and Others*, ten years in court to achieve her legal victory. Before litigation, of her own accord, she did an impressive amount of research to understand why the police had not protected her from the sexual offender. She concluded that the negligence and the dereliction on the part of the police towards curbing VAW must not be condoned. Her mother warned her of litigation, stating 'you can waste half your life',[27] and yet Alix decided to proceed. With each court dismissing her case, Alix's perseverance grew stronger until she reached the Constitutional Court, finding solace in the fact that her case may protect future victims. It was a tough journey with all the probing into her life and personality by the media; in addition, the state resorted to

[24] *Chapman* case, para. 4. Also see *Maria da Penha* v. *Brazil* (16 April 2001) Case 12.051, Report No. 54/01 (Inter-American Court of Human Rights).

[25] Human Rights Watch, 'We'll Show You', p. 52.

[26] Fuchs, 'Using strategic litigation', 32.

[27] 'I am a Woman', Lauren Groenewald and Miki Redelinghuys of Plexus films, Season 1 episode 19 act 2 (5 August 2012).

some unprofessional methods to discredit her, by, for instance, claiming that she was litigating because she was after money.[28] However, years after the turmoil, Alix confirms that she would do it all over again.[29]

The *Dow* case, in which a Botswanan lawyer sought the right to pass her nationality to her children, demonstrated how prolonged litigation took a toll on the appellant. It put Unity Dow in a financial and emotional turmoil. She stated:

> On a personal level, that was hard. It wasn't just my case, my issue, but the focus was on me personally. At the time I was young and thought everything was possible but there was a real cost both financially and emotionally. I always say at the start I was driving a BMW and by the end of the case I was in a pick-up truck. I had to take my kids out of private school and put them in public school.[30]

Yet this case did not sink her. Her perseverance was evident in her future, as she became the first female judge in Botswana's High Court and had an incredibly successful career afterwards.

There is a strong case to argue that litigation in general empowers women, regardless of the outcome. The ethnographic research conducted in South Africa for this book reveals some of these examples. An NGO staff member argued that women want to engage with formal law, but do not have the tools, which they can acquire through awareness programmes provided by various NGOs. She explained that many women decide to access formal justice once they find a suitable portal. For instance, one participant had been subjected to many years of domestic violence in this study; she proactively and persistently sought legal redress once she became aware of her options through an NGO. While inadequacies in the law push women away from the legal system, some women still choose to pursue their cases in order to feel empowered. Another lawyer in this research had a client who was sexually harassed at work. She brought two cases to court against the harasser: a rape case and a civil claim for sexual harassment in the workplace. The perpetrator had offered to settle the labour case on condition that she withdrew the criminal case. However, the applicant insisted on taking her rapist to court. This adamant stance reshuffled the power

[28] Ibid., act 3.

[29] Ibid.

[30] Lucy Lamble, 'UN Women report: access to justice in Botswana', *The Guardian*, 6 July 2011, accessed 3 June 2018 at www.theguardian.com/global-development/poverty-matters/2011/jul/06/un-women-justice-botswana

dynamic in the applicant's favour. In another interview, an NGO staff member made an observation based on her years of work with victims of GBV. She believed that the desire to report reflects a sense of empowerment. This is because, as Pelad explains, women feel that they have taken back control of their decisions.[31] One study with domestic violence victims confirmed that legal redress gives women a sense of control over their affairs.[32] Litigation is therefore one method of acquiring agency, which Connell defines as any action taken by women to show some kind of resistance and self-determination, in an attempt to regain control of their lives.[33]

The outcome of *Sonke Gender Justice Network* v. *Julius Malema* empowered female activists collectively. Malema initially used various tactics to dismiss accusations. For instance, he initially tried to 'racialise' the case and then announced that he would not pay his fine on principle. However, in 2011, not only did Malema pay his 50,000 rand fine, he also issued a public apology to all women for his comments.[34] The appellant in this case sees it as a sign that politicians are taking responsibility.[35] When interviewed, Sandy, from NGO14, confirmed that any case that holds a public official accountable for sexist speech is definitely a legal gain, especially considering the pervasive sexism and homophobia in South African society that needs ironclad accountability measures.

At the start of litigation, Alicja Tysiąc[36] stayed covert and unknown to the public, probably because of the common social pressure and stigma consuming women who ask for the right to abortion. However, she gradually embraced her journey to demand her rights from the state and thus, 'in a process of exemplary personal empowerment, the claimant's perspective on the problem of denied abortions was also changed, with the process clearly politicizing and radicalizing her'.[37]

31 Einat Pelad et al., 'Choice and empowerment for battered women who stay: toward a constructive model' (2000) 45 *Social Work*, 1, 12.

32 Edna B Foa et al., 'Psychological and environmental factors associated with partner violence' (2000) 1 *Trauma, Violence and Abuse*, 1, 82.

33 Patricia Connell, 'Understanding victimization and agency: considerations of race, class and gender' (2008) 20 *Political and Legal Anthropology Review*, 2, 118.

34 'Malema pays R50 000 fine for rape remark', News24, 8 August 2011, accessed 20 June 2018 at www.news24.com/SouthAfrica/Politics/Malema-pays-R50-000-fine-for-rape-remark-20110808

35 Ibid.

36 *Tysiac* case.

37 Fuchs, 'Using strategic litigation', 31.

The 'empowerment' impact of litigation or the social messages confirmed by court judgments are not guaranteed, and nor should they be. This is the strength of impact litigation: it is a dynamic and complex process with unpredictable outcomes, aiming to reach a higher threshold for upholding human rights.

D Locating the Impact

Measuring the impact of litigation requires an understanding of the cause and the goals of litigation. While legal activism may yield direct changes, material changes or changes in jurisprudence and policy, it can also have a 'less quantifiable impact' such as changes in social attitudes and perceptions.[38] Some cases do not require significant financial resources or law/policy reform, such as *Sonke Gender Justice Network* v. *Julius Malema*. In this case, Malema paid the fine imposed by the court, and issued a public apology. In other cases, such as *Omar* v. *Government of the Republic of South Africa and Others*, which challenged the Constitutionality of the DVA, the judgment itself is considered a success. When the remedy includes policy reform, it may take some time. For instance, in *Levenstein and others* v. *Frankel*, the Constitutional Court gave parliament 24 months to rectify the defective law.[39]

Delays in implementing court judgments are usually associated with budget allocations, but progress is likely to occur even after delays. In *Centre for Child Law* v. *Government of the Eastern Cape Province*, in which the government was taken to court to address the issue of mud schools,[40] progress happened at a slow pace.[41] In *Minister of Health and Others* v. *Treatment Action Campaign and Others*,[42] the government restricted access to Nevirapine, a drug that prevents the transmission of HIV from mother to baby, to specific sites instead of opening it up to the public. The TAC took the state to court to order the roll -out of the service across the country based on the Constitutional right to health, and secured a legal victory in 2002. Not only were healthcare workers able to deliver the drug to expectant mothers who were HIV positive immediately after the judgment, starting April 2003, both budget and

[38] Duffy, *Strategic Litigation*, p. 25.

[39] *Levenstein* case

[40] *Child law* case. The memorandum of understanding between the parties was signed 2011–02–04.

[41] Ann Skelton, 'The role of the courts in ensuring the right to a basic education in a democratic South Africa: a critical evaluation of recent education case law' (2014) 46 *De Jure*, 1; Qingliu (Mary) Yang, 'Eradicating "mud schools" in South Africa' (2015) 54 *Columbia Journal of Transnational Law Bulletin*, 1.

[42] *TAC* case.

policy changes supported the roll-out of the treatment to all expectant mothers with HIV.[43] The drug was important specifically in light of South Africa's high infant mortality rate. In 1990, South Africa was one of four countries below the baseline set for the millennium development goals. Research that was conducted in 2013 on different data sets concluded that 'all models and data sources agree that the nation has achieved one of the fastest rates of child mortality reduction in the world', only exceeded by three other countries.[44] A notable component of this success is reducing the number of children born with HIV through the scaling up of government programmes to dispense the necessary medication.[45]

Impact litigation has had some notable successes globally as well. On 13 August 1997, the Supreme Court of India commissioned the Vishaka guidelines (in relation to the *Vishaka* victory), putting the burden on employers to guarantee and maintain a working environment for women where they are safe from sexual harassment. Another example is *Laxmi* v. *Union of India*,[46] which was about an acid attack victim who went to court attempting to regulate the sale of acid. Not only did the court rule in her favour, in 2013, it imposed some quite strict regulations on acid sales. Despite the emotional turmoil that Unity Dow went through during litigation, and the prolonged process of legal reform that followed the legal victory, 'even today young people come up to Dow, they owe their citizenship to her, and parents thank her too'.[47] Furthermore, the case opened up the space for more legal reforms for the benefit of women, particularly regarding rape and property law.[48] The *Longwe* case also eventually saw some positive impact. Despite the legal victory, hotels continued to discriminate against women in general. The hotel bar, the subject of the case, was opened to unaccompanied women as a result of the judgment; however, the casino at the same hotel posted

[43] Brian Honemann and Mark Heywood, 'A judgment that saved a million lives', The Star, 5 July 2012, accessed 17 June 2018 at www.iol.co.za/the-star/a-judgment-that-saved-a-million-lives-1334636

[44] Kate J Kerber et al., 'South African child deaths 1990–2011: have HIV services reversed the trend enough to meet Millennium Development Goal 4?' (2013) 27 *AIDS* 16, 2644; also see Rosie Burton et al., 'Prevention of mother-to-child transmission in South Africa: an ever-changing landscape' (2015) 8 *Obstet Med* 1.

[45] Kerber et al., 'South African child deaths'.

[46] *Laxmi* v. *Union of India and Ors*. [Writ Petition (C) No.129 of 2006 (India)].

[47] Lucy Lamble, 'UN Women report: access to justice in Botswana', *The Guardian*, 6 July 2011, accessed 3 June 2018 at www.theguardian.com/global-development/poverty-matters/2011/jul/06/un-women-justice-botswana

[48] Ibid.

a notice prohibiting unaccompanied women. The plaintiff's husband complained to the General Manager, citing the *Longwe* judgment and asserting that 'the ruling applied to all parts of the hotel, to all hotels in Zambia, and indeed to all public places in Zambia'. The notice was eventually removed.[49]

E Challenges of Impact Litigation

The most common criticism of impact litigation is the focus on the theoretical outcomes and not the practical benefits. Basically, the question of 'what happens after successful litigation?' sometimes has no definite answer.

Court judgments are not always implemented, and when they are, severe delays are expected. This is particularly prevalent in economic rights litigation as these judgments entail budgetary reallocations and calls on scarce resources. The most cited example of this failure to achieve results is Irene Grootboom. Despite the litigation victory on the right to housing, she died in 2008 'homeless and penniless', eight years after her landmark legal gain.[50] Furthermore, the 'comprehensive and co-ordinated' programme that the government had been instructed to prepare, has not been executed, 'leaving thousands homeless'.[51] In his reaction to her death, her legal representative in the landmark case contended that the courts and the legal system had failed Irene.[52] Similarly, in the long run, court judgments do not necessarily impact the lives of the vulnerable group. For instance, legal victories in impact litigation for the rights of refugees in South Africa did not improve the conditions for refugees and asylum seekers in the litigated areas.[53] There have also been reported delays in damages ordered by courts. 'Millions of rands' of financial claims from cases using the *Carmichele* precedent were pending for extended periods of time.[54]

Amit locates the problem in the inability of the courts to enforce their decisions. Of all three branches of the state, the judiciary is the

[49] Longwe, 'Case study', 96.

[50] Pearlie Joubert, 'Grootboom dies homeless and penniless', Mail & Guardian, 8 August 2008, accessed 10 June 2018 at www.mg.co.za/article/2008-08-08-grootboom-dies-homeless-and-penniless

[51] Francis Hweshe, 'Call for faster delivery after Irene's death', IOL, 5 August 2008, accessed 10 June 2018 at www.iol.co.za/news/south-africa/call-for-faster-delivery-after-irenes-death-411161

[52] Joubert, 'Grootboom dies'.

[53] Roni Amit, 'Winning isn't everything: courts, context, and the barriers to effecting change through public interest litigation' (2011) 27 *South African Journal on Human Rights*, 1, 10.

[54] Davis and Le Roux, *Precedent and Possibility*, p. 174.

weakest because it lacks enforcement mechanisms and 'budgetary power'.[55] Lawyers are equally guilty of neglecting the post-litigation stage, when the hype around the case fades.[56] In addition, the state employs some misleading tactics to avoid an unfavourable court ruling, which would create precedent that they cannot afford. For instance, some government departments tend to settle matters amicably at the last moment before a judgment, hindering 'proper jurisprudence to be built'.[57] Hurdles created by government tactics are coupled with government incompetence. Often, they are left clueless in court decisions, unable to decide how to rectify a violation, essentially limiting the 'transformative potential of strategic litigation on economic and social rights'.[58]

Another line of criticism is the symbolism of the legal victory with little regard to the impact on the litigants' life. The involvement of NGOs essentially shifts the focus of the case from the litigants' hardships, to the 'cause'.[59] This is demonstrated in *Levenstein* v. *Frankel*,[60] discussed in the previous chapter. There was disagreement between the litigants and the *amici* on framing the case. While the litigants focused on their hardships, NGOs argued for a wider legal gain. Similarly, Marcus and Budlender refer to the *Government of the Republic of South Africa* v. *Grootboom* to show that the involvement of the LRC 'took the focus away from the individual plaintiffs and their situation and focused on the government programme to the potential exclusion of individual relief'.[61] One participant in the study noted the substantial cost of litigation in high courts, which allows only a limited number of women to take this route. When NGOs sponsor cases, they are able to 'pick and choose' the ones to be litigated. In some of these cases, lawyers have the upper hand in the relationship.[62]

55 Amit, 'Winning isn't everything', 10.

56 Cote and Garderen, 'Challenges to public interest litigation', 181.

57 Budlender et al., *Public Interest Litigation*, p. 13.

58 'Strategic litigation with strong data drives better implementation of right-to-education ruling in South Africa', ESCR, 15 December 2017, accessed 4 June 2018 at www.escr-net.org/news/2017/strategic-litigation-strong-data-drives-better-implementation-right-education-ruling-south

59 Peter Margulies, 'Political lawyering, one person at a time: the challenge of legal work against domestic violence for the impact litigation/client service debate' (1996) 3 *Michigan Journal of Gender and Law*, 2, 495.

60 *Levenstein* case.

61 Marcus and Budlender, A *Strategic Evaluation*, p. 58.

62 Lynn Jones, 'The haves come out ahead: how cause lawyers frame the legal system for movements' in Austin Sarat and Stuart Scheingold (eds.), *Cause Lawyering, Political Commitments and Professional Responsibilities* (Oxford: Oxford University Press, 1998), p. 184.

NGOs may not be litigating enough. To achieve real impact, 'cases probably need to be run repeatedly to stamp both the principle and financial consequences upon criminal justice system practices'[63] – a strategy contradicting the core strategy of impact litigation, which aims to create a ripple effect from a single or a few legal victories. Nongovernmental organisations have limited funding and are unlikely to sponsor cases with the same issue once a precedent has been set. This was confirmed by several NGO employees interviewed for this study. Limited funding therefore jeopardises the impact of strategic litigation because achieving maximum social impact 'tends to require a series of cases brought on different but related issues over a substantial period of time. Earlier cases thus act as vital building blocks for more complex and difficult later cases'.[64]

III NGOs IN IMPACT LITIGATION

A Framing the Argument

Lawyers and NGOs must understand the power of the judiciary and suggest remedies accordingly.[65] The justice system in South Africa has changed over the years. Moving from a repressive apartheid regime to a new democracy, courts were eager to honour constitutional rights, which is reflected in some landmark decisions such as the *Grootboom* case. Sandy, from NGO14, explained that this eagerness gradually shifted to caution; courts are now more reserved with their judgments, 'pushing PIL lawyers to think differently about remedies'. NGOs are now more careful about asking the courts to interfere with executive discretion; however, they frame their remedies creatively so as to avoid this conflict. Sandy elaborated, 'instead of asking the court to order the executive power to build 20 domestic violence shelters, we rather say, 'we want the court to order the state to show us the plans on how to roll out shelters in the next period'. Therefore, remedies associated with impact litigation need to change with the political climate, and the readiness of the courts to pass unorthodox and unique judgments.

[63] Vetten, *Addressing Domestic Violence*, p. 9.

[64] Budlender et al., *Public Interest Litigation*, p. 115.

[65] Priti Patel and Tamar Ezer, *Advancing Public Health Through Strategic Litigation: Lessons from Five Countries*, research report (Open Society Foundations, 2016).

B NGOs in Court

The previous chapter discussed the capacities in which NGOs engage with the litigation, either as an *amicus curiae* or as direct litigants. Each route has its own advantages and disadvantages. Writing on behalf of the WLC, Martabano and O'Sullivan discuss the strengths of both strategies. They explain that, as litigants, NGOs have more control over the direction of the proceedings, which increases the likelihood of successful litigation. Therefore the role of NGOs as litigators has a stronger impact than their role as advisors (*amici*).[66] On the other hand,

> Amicus interventions seem easier, less costly and more effective... The attorneys for the parties bringing the case have to do all the groundwork of pleadings, founding affidavits, and factual research, and as *amicus* our role is to assist the court by addressing those public interest issues that affect women generally that are not canvassed by the parties.[67]

In comparing both roles, Sandy, from NGO14, explained that the role of NGOs as litigants is limited as they are bound by the facts of the case. As *amicus curiae*, an NGO is able to put broader evidence before the court to demonstrate that the impact of the legal issues goes beyond the litigant, affecting many others.[68] For an NGO, choosing its approach depends on the facts of each case and the litigation strategy.

In both cases, cause lawyering is likely to achieve greater results when 'the client plays an active and engaged role, rather than allowing legal representatives to make key decisions without proper client input'.[69] Also, in all cases, NGOs carry the greatest burden for successful cause lawyering; although South Africa fosters a progressive judiciary, liberal judges still need to be presented with concrete cases that put the legal issues in a strong rights framework.[70]

While NGOs have built strong networks and partnerships to balance each other's services and avoid duplication, there were instances when lack of coordination compromised impact litigation. In the case of *Hoffmann* v. *South African Airways* in which the company refused to employ an HIV positive candidate, communication failure between NGOs caused some delays. While the LRC was litigating this case,

66 Martabano and O'Sullivan, 'Three steps forward', 59.

67 Ibid., 56.

68 Also see Paul M Collins, 'Friends of the court: examining the influence of amicus curiae participation in U.S. Supreme Court litigation court' (2004) 38 *Law and Society Review* 4.

69 Budlender et al. *Public Interest Litigation*, p. 112.

70 Roa and Klugman, 'Considering strategic litigation', 33.

another NGO was litigating the same issue for another candidate against the same company. In this situation, even though the *Hoffmann* case was the first to reach the Constitutional Court, it was lacking important medical information that could have been available if the two NGOs had been collaborating.[71]

C Steering Public Opinion: Media and Publicity

An integral difference between litigation and impact litigation is that the latter is accompanied by strategies to trigger public pressure.[72] The purpose of impact litigation is not only to bring the case before the court, but also before the public, stirring a discussion around important human rights issues, and promoting legal tools with which people can claim their rights. Nongovernmental organisations must therefore de-legalise the legal issue in the case and present it to the people in an attractive and relatable approach. Even if litigation is not successful, a network supporting the litigating NGOs must engage with the public to explain the importance of the legal issues, the purpose of litigation and the remedies suggested.[73] This is done through intensive media and community outreach programmes.

1 The Power of Media Publicity

In the *National Coalition* case, the impact of media publicity was evident, presenting a great example of a successful impact litigation case. The case centred on the constitutionality of the crime of sodomy, which was embodied in several Acts of Parliament and the Sexual Offences Act. Litigation was successful because it was preceded and accompanied by the mobilisation of gays and lesbians and the exertion of political pressure on members of the ruling party, among other advocacy measures. Preemptive pressure meant that litigation did not need to carry the full burden of delivering a favourable judgment, and that lawyers did not need to 'persuade the Constitutional Court to locate such rights under the rubric of privacy, liberty or dignity, as in other jurisdictions'.[74] This publicity can strongly influence society as well. The aggressive media campaign for the legal issues in *Minister of Health*

[71] Ibid., 118.

[72] Kathree, 'Public interest law', 34; also see Scott L Cumming and Deborah L Rhode, 'Public interest litigation: insights from theory and practice' (2009) 36 *Fordham Urban Law Journal*, 4, 603.

[73] Roa and Klugman, 'Considering strategic litigation', 34.

[74] Marcus and Budlender, 'A strategic evaluation', 30.

and Others v. *Treatment Action Campaign and Others* continued to grow in size and power, bringing 'widespread recognition' to matters related to HIV in general, but specifically addressing the stigma linked to the disease and its repercussions on infected people.[75]

Most of the cases discussed in Chapter 5 were heavily covered in the media. *Sonke Gender Justice Network* v. *Julius Malema* was accompanied by an NGO media campaign in which they showed the public the link between the statements of influential figures and how they can perpetuate gender stereotypes. In a news piece, a spokesperson for the Sonke Gender Justice NGO stated, 'instead of perpetuating rape myths, public figures should make it clear that rape can happen anywhere … We need to make sure that women who have been raped are not stigmatised and are not made to feel like the crimes against them were their fault'.[76] Similarly, Lisa Vetten, a women's rights activist in South Africa criticised Malema for contributing to the culture of silence suffered by rape victims, as his conduct is exactly the expectation that deters women from reporting violence.[77]

In some cases, impact litigation explodes an issue that has been silenced for long, and in these cases, the public can be truly involved. The *Levenstein* case discussed in the previous chapter led to a public outcry on sexual violence against children, with adults disclosing unreported sexual harassment and abuse during their childhood through a hashtag campaign #MiniMeToo. 'Piggybacking' on the global #MeToo campaign, which addressed sexual harassment against women, #MiniMeToo shed light on the high possibility of delayed disclosure.[78]

2 *Wide, Deep and Long-term Impact*

The media publicity that accompanied the complaint brought forward by Sonke Gender Justice to the CGE on the underrepresentation of females on the bench (discussed in Chapter 5) continued for years. Furthermore, the publicity included meticulous details on the investigations. For instance, the locations of interviews that the CGE monitored were described as 'drab', and the whole procedure was

[75] Gerntholtz and MacLeod, 'Gender and socio-economic rights', p. 382.

[76] 'ANC youth leader guilty of "hate speech" after rape jibe', *Independent*, 16 March 2010, accessed 20 June 2018 at www.independent.co.uk/news/world/africa/anc-youth-leader-guilty-of-hate-speech-after-rape-jibe-1921836.html

[77] Karyn Maughan, 'Malema in hot water over rape claims', IOL, 26 May 2009, accessed 17 June 2018 at www.iol.co.za/news/politics/malema-in-hot-water-over-rape-claims-444435

[78] Carl Collison, '#MiniMeeToo breaks long silences', Mail & Guardian, 22 June 2018, accessed 14 July 2018 at www.mg.co.za/article/2018-06-22-00-minimetoo-breaks-long-silences

criticised three years into the investigation.[79] In response to the strong publicity that shamed the selection procedure, the JSC held an all-female round of interviews. However, this was still criticised as merely a bandaid on a deep wound; structural discrimination that creates a glass ceiling for female judges could not be 'rectified instantly'. The executive and the judicial committee would have to show consistency and an ongoing commitment to substantial change. Ideally, such commitment should reflect in a constant stream of female candidates being interviewed. Even more importantly, the 'blame game' that the involved stakeholders played in response to the CGE's inquiries was grilled in the media.[80]

Publicity for Unity Dow's case crossed the Botswanan borders and reached faraway places like Toronto; the court hearings were heavily attended by the media and public personnel including visitors from neighbouring countries rooting for gender equality.[81] The government was aware of the negative publicity it was attracting, which expedited the negotiations behind closed doors about changes in the law.[82]

3 *Risks of Public Exposure*

The downside of publicity is the exposure and potential invasion of privacy that may be inflicted on litigants. Sandy explains that media advocacy is a crucial component of impact litigation, and therefore her NGO engages with the media in various ways such as sending press releases. However, they respect the litigants' preference if they want to keep a low profile.

In some cases, such as *Carmichele* and *Dow*, the applicants were aware of the media impact and welcomed the publicity, as it was deemed a positive reinforcement of their cases. Unity Dow was a lawyer, Iris Carmichele was a photographer, and both were determined and activist women, which may have influenced their acceptance of and comfortable attitude towards media exposure.

It is important to be prepared for public discussions to go either way, especially in a socially conservative society such as South Africa. The

[79] Swart, 'Gender reform'.

[80] Gertrude Makhafola, 'Too few women appointed to judiciary', IOL, 7 December 2016, accessed 17 June 2018 at www.iol.co.za/news/politics/too-few-women-appointed-to-judiciary-7119871; also see Roxanne Henderson, 'Gender transformation in the judiciary being addressed in silos': CGE', Times Live, 7 December 2016, accessed 17 June 2018 at www.timeslive.co.za/news/south-africa/2016-12-07-gender-transformation-in-the-judiciary-being-addressed-in-silos-cge/

[81] Freeman, 'Women, law and land', 570.

[82] Ibid.

Teddy Bear Clinic case, which sought to decriminalise teenage sex, was debated in the media.[83] Unsurprisingly, a considerable portion of the general public wanted to avoid a court judgment that may encourage teenagers to engage in sexual activities sooner rather than later.

D Awareness-Raising and Network-Building

Community outreach and awareness-raising are not restricted to media advocacy. In fact, communicating relevant legal matters to local communities is best done through a more direct and engaging approach, working on the ground.[84] This is because 'litigation cannot and should not be the only way in which people are enabled to claim their rights'.[85] This points to the groundwork of grassroots organisations and NGOs, including legal literacy and service provision. In fact, litigation is often seen as 'a complement to social activism' and not as the main pillar around which all other services revolve.[86] Organisations that have only focused on impact litigation in the past have realised the need for wider programmes.[87] These efforts are not necessarily undertaken by the same NGO, but through partnerships and network creation. This was pointed out by Sandy, from NGO14, who confirmed the importance of connections with grassroots organisations.

Some other non-media approaches necessary to accompany strategic litigation include engagement with international organisations, undertaking related research to investigate different dimensions of a problem, political activism in the form of demonstrations or marches, and partnership-building with stakeholders who are interested in the cause, including public figures.[88] NGOs in South Africa employ most of these tools to supplement impact litigation. For instance, in response to the CGE transformative judiciary investigation (discussed in Chapter 5), 22 NGOs launched a coalition to follow up on and monitor the issue, including CALS and Rape Crisis.[89] The coalition contended that the gender transformation of the judiciary should not only be a matter of appointing female judges, but of 'transforming attitudes'.

[83] Rofhiwa Maneta, 'The public weighs in on "adolescent sex" bill', Live South Africa, 6 March 2015, accessed 17 June 2018 at www.livemag.co.za/live-regulars/public-weighs-adolescent-sex-bill/

[84] Budlender et al., *Public Interest Litigation*, p. 99.

[85] Ibid., p. 100.

[86] Guide to strategic litigation, Public Law Project, 13 January 2014, accessed 18 June 2018 at www.publiclawproject.org.uk/resources/guide-to-strategic-litigation/, p. 8.

[87] Ibid.

[88] Lawyers without Borders, *Strategic Litigation*, p. 31.

[89] Korte, 'Judges matter'.

They recounted some cases where judges gave lenient sentences for rape offenders citing apologetic reasons such as the 'rapist's difficult childhood' or that the rape had not caused the child any serious bodily harm.[90] Their aim was to address the topic from another angle – while the CGE was investigating numbers of female judges, the coalition was tackling the feminisation of courts, calling for a profound change in judges' conduct and the elimination of sexism in court sentencing.

E Post-Litigation Phase

More work needs to be done on the post-impact-litigation phase, especially by NGOs. This is not to say that NGOs have completely neglected this work, but their involvement very much depends on the case and the nature of the issue. For instance, in the famous 'mud schools' *Child law* case, the LRC rigorously followed up on the promises made by the Department of Education in 2010, and took the department back to court when severe delays occurred.[91]

There is no specific criteria or roadmap for follow-up. Advice from lawyers working on impact litigation for over a decade specifically mentioned the necessity of a 'plan for post litigation', which should be settled from the ontset.[92] Basically, sufficient attention and resources should be allocated to ensuring that the government is 'translating the legal success into practical benefits for a large number of people on the ground, including those not directly involved in the litigation'.[93]

IV LEGAL REFORM IN COURTS: AN EASY CHOICE?

Legal reform through impact litigation may be easier than lobbying parliament, and sometimes it is the only option available for civil society, especially when constituents who oppose the advancement of women's rights, such as traditional and religious leaders, obstruct or at least prolong the advocacy process in parliament.[94] Nevertheless, its effect is still a matter that is widely discussed and questioned. These debates are not likely to be easily settled.

[90] Ibid.

[91] See Alison Hickey Tshangana, *The Impact of Litigation by the Legal Resources Centre for Adequate Classroom Infrastructure in South Africa*, Case Study Series, Study no 12 (International Budget Partnership, March 2013).

[92] Patel and Ezer, *Advancing Public Health.*

[93] Budlender et al., *Public Interest Litigation*, p. 122.

[94] Martabano and O'Sullivan, 'Three steps forward', 61.

The Constitution is not 'merely the sum of the provisions contained in its text'; it needs to be brought to life, which is the function of the judiciary and the purpose of court judgments.[95] In doing this, courts face ideological challenges when balancing human rights, which need to be highlighted. For instance, the Constitutional Court in *Christian Education South Africa* v. *Minister of Education* was forced to balance between cultural rights and children's rights. This was not an easy decision, one that led Justice Albie Sachs to urge the government to avoid forcing people to choose between their religious beliefs and the obligation to obey the law.[96] Ultimately, impact litigation is not about drawing a fine line between right and wrong; it is about 'striking a balance between competing rights',[97] which the judiciary strives to accomplish.

The criticism directed towards impact litigation is centred on the post-litigation phase, which usually involves other state institutions, specifically parliament and various government departments. It is important to separate roles and responsibilities and to not evaluate impact litigation based on the dereliction of some state organs. In fact, all arms of the state have shortcomings – parliaments have caused severe delays in passing bills, and the police have done a below par job in numerous duties outlined throughout this book. Each party should be held responsible in its own area of work; the judiciary is a key player of a 'coordinated response' to ending gender-based violence,[98] and therefore the practice of impact litigation must be encouraged and celebrated.

Impact litigation is a successful strategy in South Africa because the justice system provides 'an opportunity for legal activists and judges to convene in a democratic debate around a specific case, where they can engage other branches of government, public opinion and specific sectors of the population on how rights should be interpreted and granted'.[99] Nongovernmental organisations, litigants and the public can find and voice their opinions and concerns on legal issues. In this sense, the judiciary meets its role in providing this space. Nongovernmental organisations as well have not only done a great job at securing legal victories for litigants, but they have also improved legal procedures,

[95] Davis and Le Roux, *Precedent and Possibility*, p. 9.

[96] *Christian Education South Africa* v. *Minister of Justice*, para. 50.

[97] Justice D Pillay, 'Public interest Law in South Africa', Oxford Human Rights Hub, 15 May 2013, based on the 11th Victoria and Griffiths Mxenge Memorial Lecture, which Justice Pillay delivered at UKZN in May 2013, accessed 3 June 2018 at http://ohrh.law.ox.ac.uk/public-interest-law-in-south-africa/

[98] Thomas et al., *Working with the Justice Sector*, p. 6.

[99] Roa and Klugman, 'Considering strategic litigation', 31.

making it possible for 'administrators, legislators, and judges to assess the impact of their decision in terms of all affected interests. And, by helping open doors to (the) legal system, they have moved us a little closer to the ideal of equal justice for all'.[100]

V CONCLUSION

Significant resources are poured into cause lawyering every year in South Africa. However, it remains a subject of criticism. This chapter has stressed the importance of highlighting both the direct and indirect benefits of impact litigation.

It is also important to remember that some judgments are easier to implement than others, and so we should not judge the practice of impact litigation based solely on the probability of its non-enforceability. Impact litigation does not provide a conclusive answer, but it ultimately facilitates the flow of information: 'directly and indirectly, the litigation process has proved an invaluable source of information about government policies and practices'.[101] Even more important, the kind of information that flows may shake up cultural rigidness, and ultimately lead to social change. One research study found that strategic litigation has helped challenge stereotypes about litigants.[102] This is one of the key points that this book aims to underscore: the space open and available for NGOs to engage in this 'flow of information' is a responsibility for significant gains in women's rights.

[100] Thurgood Marshall, 'Financing public interest law: the role of the organized bar', Public Interest Law: The Role of the Organised Bar', address at the Award of Merit luncheon of the Bar activities section of the American Bar Association, 10 August 1975, cited in Kathree, 'Public interest law', 40.

[101] Duffy, *Strategic Litigation*, p. 27.

[102] Ibid.

CHAPTER 7

ACCESS TO JUSTICE AND NGOs: AWARENESS, GUIDANCE AND EMPOWERMENT

This book has so far looked at the relationship between NGOs and various state institutions. This chapter will bring the relationship with women (beneficiaries), particularly in their capacity as users of the law, into the discussion.

The chapter will be divided into three parts. After briefly reviewing the main elements of access to justice, Part I will tackle women's sensitive legal journey, identifying the role of NGOs in facilitating women's access to justice. Part II will continue to explore women's pursuit of justice, but will move to informal justice systems. Finally, Part III will reflect on the notion of empowerment, putting it at the centre of the relationship between women and NGOs. Information in this chapter has been gathered through fieldwork in South Africa, as detailed in the methodology section in Chapter 1. This research has used alias names and coded NGOs due to some sensitive information. These are provided in the appendix.

I DEFINING ACCESS TO JUSTICE

'Access to justice' is a key element of various human rights such as the right to equality under the law, the right to legal representation, the right to a fair hearing, the right to effective remedies and the right to fair treatment by law enforcement agents.[1] For simplicity, justice is defined

[1] Ayesha Kadwani Dias, 'International law and sources of access to justice' in Ayesha Kadwani Dias and Gita Honwana Welch (eds.) *Justice for the Poor: Perspectives on Accelerating Access* (Oxford: Oxford University Press, 2009), p. 6.

as fairness in law, meaning the 'exercise of authority in maintenance of rights'; the component of 'fairness' must be applied to both: rules and procedures.[2] As discussed in Chapter 2, legislation in South Africa is progressive and meets the international standards of 'justice'. 'Fairness' in the implementation of rules is a matter of debate, however.

There is general agreement on the components of access to justice; these include physical accessibility to institutions of justice, access to information on legal rights, equality before the law, speedy trials, relevant remedies and affordability.[3] In addition to the 'establishment of institutions and procedural rules granting access to all', access to justice also refers to 'empowerment of individuals to obtain justice'.[4] This is because 'legal empowerment help translate legal guarantees' into actual improvements in personal affairs.[5] Furthermore, 'opportunity cost and trust in the justice system' are strong indicators for people's willingness and ability to resort to the formal justice system.[6]

Social and historical factors can affect the pursuit of justice. For instance, as a result of the racial segregation policies in South Africa during apartheid, 'access to justice' was restricted to specific groups; the Group Areas Act,[7] which grouped people of the same race in the same neighbourhood, meant that access to legal institutions was discriminate. Not surprisingly, black people had limited services in their allocated areas and did not have the freedom of movement to access services elsewhere. By the beginning of the transitional process in 1994, 74 per cent of police stations in the country were located in 'white suburbs

[2] Ghai and Cottrell, *Marginalized Communities and Access to Justice*, p. 3.

[3] See Deborah L Rhode, *Access to Justice* (Oxford: Oxford University Press, 2004); Rebecca L Sanderfur (ed.), *Access to Justice* (Bingley: Emerald Group Publishing, 2009); Deborah L Rhode 'Whatever happened to access to justice' (2008–2009) 42 *Loyola of Los Angeles Law Review*, 869–912; Lillian Artz, 'Violence against women in rural Southern Cape: exploring access to justice through a feminist jurisprudence framework', research thesis (University of Cape Town Institute of Criminology, 1999); UNDP, *Access to Justice*, practice note (2004); Louis Schetzer and Judith Henderson, *Access to Justice and Legal Needs*, research report (Law and Justice Foundation of New South Wales, August 2002); *Access to Justice for Children*, Report of the United Nations High Commissioner for Human Rights (Human Rights Council, 16 December 2013) A/HRC/25/35; Michael J Trebilcock et al. (eds.), *Middle Income Access to Justice* (Toronto: University of Toronto Press, 2012); Asher Flynn and Jacqueline Hodgson (eds.), *Access to Justice and Legal Aid: Comparative Perspectives on Unmet Legal Need* (Oxford and Portland, OR: Hart Publishing, 2017).

[4] Dias, 'International law', p. 5.

[5] *Leveraging the SDGs for Inclusive Growth: Delivering Access to Justice for All*, issue brief (OECD and Open Society Foundation, 11 September 2016), p. 4.

[6] Ibid., p. 7.

[7] Group Areas Act No 41 of 1950 (South Africa).

or business districts'.[8] While apartheid policies restricted black people's access to justice, women specifically suffered due to the 'prohibitive travel costs'.[9]

Today, barriers in access to justice prevail because of persistent social inequalities. Globally, an estimated four billion people do not have access to justice, with women in particular affected by 'legal exclusion'.[10] Children's limited agency puts them also at an increased risk of exclusion from the protection of the law.[11] Social factors associated with vulnerable groups may impede access to justice, such as the lack of childcare facilities, which restrains women from leaving their homestead for long periods of time.[12] One research study in South Africa suggested that the three most prohibitive barriers to access to justice for people with disabilities include the geographic location of equality courts, unsympathetic attitudes of 'front-line workers' as well as fear and that negatively affects individuals' perseverance and agency.[13]

II NGOs MEET WOMEN IN THEIR PURSUIT OF JUSTICE

Serious weaknesses prevail in the justice system in South Africa, particularly relating to sexual violence. Nongovernmental organisations have a significant impact in filling this gap, working on research, awareness-raising, advocacy and service provision, aiming to facilitate women's access to justice.

A Access to Information

1 Lack of Information and Knowledge

A fair and progressive legal framework is useless if people do not claim their rights, putting access to information at the centre of access to justice. There are two important elements of access to information: legal awareness and literacy, and access to information about one's legal affairs. Women may not have access to both, and in addition, they may also lack the incentive to obtain this information.[14]

[8] Vetten, *Addressing Domestic Violence*, p. 6.
[9] Ibid.
[10] *Leveraging the SDGs*, p. 2.
[11] Access to justice for children, Human Rights Council.
[12] Artz, 'Violence against women'.
[13] Willene Holness and Sarah Rule, 'Barriers to advocacy and litigation in the equality courts for persons with disabilities' (2014) 17 *P.E.R.*, 5, 1907–1963.
[14] Dias, 'International law', p. 7.

There is a general low level of awareness of legal rights in South Africa. A 2002 government-funded study found that '62 per cent of South Africans had either not heard of or did not know the purpose of the Bill of Rights'.[15] This included women subjected to VAW who sought to enforce their legal rights. Another study showed that women who sought police services for VAW 'had not received all the services required by law', and they were not aware of these services.[16] For instance, rape victims did not know that they should receive a copy of their statements made to the police;[17] this is a crucial procedure for avoiding future inconsistencies in their statements due to lengthy trials.

2 The Role of NGOs in Information Dissemination

The information gap is usually filled by NGOs. Linda, interviewed for this research, asserted that 'women are not and should not be experts on the law and on their rights'. Women usually have limited knowledge, but they search for help when they need more information, usually from NGOs. Almost all NGOs included in this study either adopt awareness-raising programmes on women's legal rights, or have a policy of informing women of all their legal options at an early stage of their intervention. These efforts incorporate both preventive approaches and remedies available to women.[18]

In fact, most NGOs in South Africa working on VAW are engaged in awareness-raising through either joining campaigns, networks, undertaking community outreach or providing direct advice to women.[19] Furthermore, NGOs also offer individualised advice to women on their legal standing. A holistic legal service is provided to all women as they join Shelters 2 and 3. Upon entry, women speak to a paralegal who evaluates their case and advises them accordingly. NGO5 also offers

[15] Open Society Foundation, *Justice Sector and the Rule of Law* (South Africa: Open Society Foundation, 2005), p. 140. Also see Meokgo Matuba, 'Know your rights – use the law to save a life', Daily Maverick, 8 December 2017, accessed 20 June 2018 at www.dailymaverick.co.za/opinionista/2017-12-08-know-your-rights-use-the-law-to-save-a-life/#.Wy-qWqczbIV

[16] Sanja Bornman et al, Protecting survivors of sexual offences: the legal obligation of the state with regard to sexual offences in South Africa, research report (Rape Crisis and the Women's Legal Centre 2013), p. 26.

[17] Rape survivors' guide to the criminal justice system in South Africa (On in Nine Campaign, 2012), p. 14.

[18] Emily Stanley, 'Engendering change? An analysis of how NGOs work on the problem of violence against women in South Africa' (2012–2013) 8 *Journal of Politics and International Studies*, p. 296.

[19] There are many examples: see People Opposing Women's Abuse campaigns at www.powa.co.za/POWA/projects/campaigns/

advice and support on family law and violence. Similarly, NGO9 runs a law clinic, which provides free advice to women. Shelter 4 organises information sessions on women's constitutional rights.

It is not only the lack of awareness of rights that restricts women's access to justice, but also the understanding of the language of the law. Simplifying the law is another NGO strategy to bridge the gap between women and the law. For example, the Zimbabwean government commissioned a regional NGO group, Women and Law in Southern Africa, to prepare a Family Law Handbook that simplified key legislation in family law, such as the DVA, among others. These handbooks should be used to train paralegals working in local communities so that they can assist the most marginalised and vulnerable women and guide them in the justice system,[20] to guarantee that 'those laws are sufficiently captured and can be widely disseminated'.[21] The continued, automatic and unhindered access to information on women's legal rights is therefore crucial not only to victims, but to the general public.[22]

3 *Media and Information*

There are some permanent as well as seasonal campaigns.[23] In addition, some NGOs use the media to raise awareness. For example, ADAPT, an NGO working on domestic violence, struck a deal with multiple TV and radio channels as well as news sources to advertise on important legal issues such as the DVA and the Recognition of Customary Marriages Act.[24]

While the impact of campaigns and awareness-raising on VAW in South Africa has not been studied, global research indicates that campaigns may be quite effective if they meet specific standards including 'effective strategy and planning, clear immediate objectives on a longer

20 'Targeting paralegals in the drive to improve access to justice for all', UNDP Zimbabwe, 25 September 2012, accessed 20 June 2018 at www.zw.undp.org/content/zimbabwe/en/home/presscenter/articles/2012/09/12/targeting-paralegals-in-the-drive-to-improve-access-to-justice-for-all.html

21 Ibid.

22 Kathleen Dey et al., *The Road to Justice: Victim Empowerment Legislation in South Africa*, research report (Cape Town: the Rape Crisis Cape Town Center and others, 2011), p. 26.

23 An annual campaign runs for 16 days. For the 2017 campaign see the Western Cape Government website at www.westerncape.gov.za/general-publication/what-16-days-activism; also see '16 days of activism against women and children abuse', NGOPulse, 23 November 2017, accessed 20 June 2018 at www.ngopulse.org/article/2017/11/23/16-days-activism-against-women-and-children-abuse

24 See ADAPT website www.adapt.org.za/media.html accessed 20 June 2018; People Opposing Women's Abuse work with the media www.powa.co.za/POWA/projects/raising-her-voice/

term path to change, a thorough understanding of the context and an overwhelming belief and commitment in the campaign. This needs to be supported by timely, accurate research, innovative actions and targeted messages'.[25] Furthermore, research for this book shows that women may make choices based on information they receive either from NGOs or from campaigns run by NGOs. For example, the intake for Shelter 3 and the number of clients for NGO5 increase during the awareness campaign '16 days of activism against VAW' because of the intensive media advertisements. Generally, increased demand for services is expected after running awareness campaigns, and therefore it is important for the organisation responsible to be prepared.[26] A housemother in Shelter 3 explained that 'domestic violence victims that know about the shelter through those campaigns had been subjected to violence for a long time, until they saw the advertisement and were encouraged to move out'. In this way, NGOs offer an exit channel for victims of domestic violence merely by the dissemination of information about legal rights and available channels of support. Ndonsa from Story 2 learned about litigation for domestic violence from the awareness sessions organised by NGO3. When the police tried to direct her to court – a tactic commonly used to turn away domestic violence victims – she resisted and provided comprehensive information about her rights under the DVA. Both her persistent attitude and her legal knowledge surprised the police officer.

4 *Awareness of Personal Legal Affairs*

Women must be aware of their own legal affairs once they are in the justice system. All parties responsible for providing this information are guilty of shortcomings. One study found that women do not receive sufficient information about the progress of their cases through the police or healthcare providers and so are often clueless about their cases; 'the system thus appears as a daunting labyrinth rather than a mechanism for their access to justice'.[27] Not 'knowing how far along their case is', is

[25] Hilary Fisher, *Building Promising Practices: Campaigning, Awareness Raising and Capacity Building to Combat Violence Against Women – A Human Rights Approach*, expert paper (UN Division for the Advancement of Women, Expert Group Meeting, 17–20 May 2005), p 14; also see Ryan Broll and Claire Crooks, *Report on the Evaluation of Violence Against Women Public Education Campaigns* (Center for Research and Education on Violence against Women and Children, December 2012); Tess Kingham and Jim Coe, *The Good Campaigns Guide: Campaigning For Impact*, report (NCVO Publications, 2005).

[26] Michaela Raeba and Jasmin Rocha, *Campaigns to End Violence Against Women and Girls*, research report (UN Women, December 2011), p. 260.

[27] Dey et al., *The Road to Justice*, p. 26.

one of the most common complaints of rape victims in South Africa.[28] This problem affects women's sense of control over their affairs, undermining their ability to make informed decisions on their cases. Making informed decisions requires an understanding of the different choices available at every step in the criminal justice system, including choices of representation, information-sharing and available services.[29]

Data collected for this book confirms the need to share more information with women, even on the part of NGOs. For instance, Fatima, story 7, claimed that legal aid employees were inefficient and did not communicate well. She was frustrated because she was unaware of the status of her case. Most women interviewed in shelters reported that the NGOs did not update them on their cases; some did not even know if they had cases in court. Thobile in Story 1 was supposed to have two cases in court on which she did not have any information except that the NGO was handling them. Zandile from Story 5 also trusted the NGO to follow up on her case but did not have information on it. Nongovernmental organisations must therefore 'maintain their relationships with communities beyond litigation' as there is a need for people to know more information around their cases.[30]

B Cost

Cost is the first concern arising with litigation that may impede access to justice. Banda explains that limited financial resources 'weigh heavily on the mind of most potential litigants and is one of the reasons cited by women for a failure or delay in seeking redress'.[31]

In South Africa, legal representation is provided for criminal offences, pursuant to the Constitution.[32] However, the government has a legal aid scheme for legal counsel in civil cases. The Legal Aid Board determines eligibility through a means test that it regularly revised to account for inflation.[33] The Legal Aid Board (LAB) was established in 1969, setting

[28] Jinel Fourie and Steven Gruzd, 'Battling violence against women: from Africa's top to toe', South African Institute of International Affairs, 20 April 2015, accessed 20 June 2018 at https://saiia.org.za/research/battling-violence-against-women-from-africa-s-top-to-toe

[29] Dey et al., *The Road to Justice*, p. 30.

[30] Socioeconomic Rights Institute of South Africa, Public Interest Legal Services in South Africa, project report (July 2015), p. 86.

[31] Banda, 'Women and access to justice', p. 133.

[32] Constitution, s. 35(2).

[33] For more information about the means test, see McQuoid-Mason, 'Access to justice', 235; Legal Aid Guide, 12th edition, (South Africa Legal Aid Board, 2012), ss. 5.1.4 and 5.1.5; The World Bank, GDP per capita http://data.worldbank.org/indicator/NY.GDP.PCAP.CD

up an aid scheme in 1971.[34] The LAB is 'National Parliament-funds state-run'[35] and its model was inspired by the UK scheme, where the purpose of the Board is 'to render or make available legal aid to indigent persons at state expense'.[36] During apartheid, the LAB focused on civil matters such as divorce; however, with the end of apartheid and under the new Constitution, the demand for legal representation increased dramatically and LAB had to direct significant resources from civil cases to criminal cases.[37] Since 2001, for the purpose of cost reduction, the LAB has been operating 'one-stop shop clinics' known as 'justice centres'.[38] These are comprehensive centres providing 'legal and paralegal advice [and] assistance' to eligible candidates (as determined by the means test) reflecting the 'welfare rights' model of legal aid.[39] The Board also funds and uses the services of NGOs, such as Lawyers for Human Rights and the public-defence programmes in areas where residents do not have access to justice centres.[40] Additionally, there are nongovernmental legal aid resources, for example a 'public interest law community, consisting of both donor-funded NGOs such as the Legal Resources Centre and of pro bono units of commercial law firms, university law clinics and a number of NGOs ... providing free and open access to law ... there is also a network of community advice offices and paralegals providing legal advice'.[41] Some of the NGOs in this study provide legal services to women – one of the most common services among South African women's rights organisations.[42]

C Policing Violence against Women

Evidently, the progressive GBV legislation in South Africa is not sufficient to eradicate this crime, and there is still a significant problem of

[34] Legal Aid Act 22 of 1969 (1969) (South Africa), s. 97.

[35] Markus Weilenmann, 'Legal pluralism: a new challenge for development agencies' in *Access to Justice in Africa and Beyond: Making the Rule of Law a Reality* (National Institute for Trial Advocacy, 2007), p. 98.

[36] Ibid., p. 97.

[37] David J McQuoid-Mason, 'The delivery of civil legal aid services in South Africa' (2000) 24 *Fordham International Law Journal*, 6, 114.

[38] Perelman, 'The way ahead?'

[39] Ibid., 363.

[40] Ibid., 364.

[41] Jonathan Klaaren, 'The cost of justice' (2014) 7 *The Salon*, 21–25, accessed 23 June 2018 at www.jwtc.org.za/resources/docs/salon-volume-7/6_TheSalon_Vol7.pdf, 22.

[42] See activities for the WLC at www.wlce.co.za/about-us/#what-we-do; Tshwaranang Legal Advocacy Centre's legal clinic at www.tlac.org.za/legal-clinic/; and for the Wits Law Clinic family, gender and child unit at www.wits.ac.za/lawclinic/family-gender–child-unit/.

underreporting. For instance, research studies suggest different numbers of unreported rapes, ranging from 1 in 9, to 1 in 15, and for rape by a partner, 1 in 25 rapes is reported.[43] Statistics on gang rape and other forms of sexual violence were also disturbing.[44] The situation is not improving; a 2015 report confirms that the 'proportion of rape victims who report their victimisation to the police decreased by 21% between 2011 and 2014'.[45] The average rate of conviction was between 4 and 8 per cent; in addition, domestic violence is not recorded as a separate crime by SAPS and is 'recorded under a range of different categories such as assault, malicious damage to property, pointing a firearm, murder etc'.[46]

Reporting violence is the first step that officially links women to the formal justice system. However, GBV victims have a lot at stake and the decision to report sexual violation to the police requires an assessment of costs and benefits.[47]

1 *Women's Experience with the Police*

The experience of a woman with the police is a matter of luck, and largely depends on the policeman or policewoman on duty. The first encounter with law enforcement agents either encourages women to pursue legal redress or to abandon it altogether.

Duties and Availability of the Police

Gender-based violence laws are designed to guarantee that women can access formal justice without legal representation, as the guidance and support of the police and court personnel should suffice. For instance, duties of the police under the DVA include 'informing complainants of the rights at their disposal, such as applying for a PO, laying a criminal charge, or both; assisting victims (complainants) in finding suitable shelter and in obtaining medical treatment; explaining the contents of a notice which sets out what complainants must do to enforce their rights under the Act…'[48] Women can also apply for a PO at the court without legal representation. Similarly, the SOA outlines specific duties for the

43 Special Rapporteur report, 2016, p. 6.
44 Ibid., p. 6
45 Lizette Lancaster et al., *Assault and Sexual Offences: Overview of the Official Statistics 2014/15*, research report (Institute for Security Studies September, 2015), p. 4.
46 Fourie and Gruzd, 'Battling violence against women', p. 5.
47 Allen, 'The reporting', 626.
48 Artz, 'Policing the Domestic Violence Act', 6.

police; for instance, keeping hard copies of relevant laws on site such as the Sexual Offences Act, the regulations and forms related to the Sexual Offences Act, 'information about hospitals near to the station that provide Post-Exposure Prophylaxis (PEP)' to rape survivors and 'a list of organisations in the area providing services to rape survivors'.[49]

In many cases, the police do not meet these legal duties. Research conducted during the 16 days of activism on VAW in 2010 showed that on several occasions the person trained to receive cases of GBV was not available at the police station. For example, in the Sophia Town police station, the detective responsible for sexual offences was unavailable on two visits and no one else was able or willing to answer questions. In addition, at Kempton Park station, the two officers responsible for rape victims were on maternity leave and no one else could assist the monitors.[50] The unavailability of trained personnel to receive victims of GBV hinders access to justice at a time when women are most vulnerable. Research also shows that many police stations fell short on their duties under the SOA. In only a meagre 32 per cent of the stations monitored in 2010 did the police have the required documents at hand.[51]

Informing or Misinforming Women on Legal Rights

Law enforcement agents often fail to inform women of their rights. Artz found that domestically abused women usually depend on the information they have previously acquired when they want to file a complaint; it is unclear whether the police was intentionally withholding information or merely being careless. For example, police officers did not inform victims of their full legal rights, leaving them unaware of some forms of violence to which they might have been exposed.[52] In addition, in the first instance, the police directed women to courts to apply for a PO, without explaining the possibility of laying criminal charges.[53] If and when the PO was issued, the police often did not serve it, which meant that women either served it themselves or dropped the domestic violence claim. In Story 13, Winnie summoned the police to her home after a series of domestic violence attacks. In one incident, her husband chased her outside the house when she was almost naked,

[49] Shukumisa, *Monitoring the Implementation*, 2013–2014, p. 20.
[50] Shukumisa, *Monitoring the Implementation*, 2010, p. 8.
[51] Ibid., p. 3.
[52] Artz, 'Policing the Domestic Violence Act', 11.
[53] Ibid., 10.

in front of neighbours and passers-by. When the police showed up, they opted for mediation instead of arresting the husband for assault. The police's response to victims is of the utmost importance as the first step in women's legal journeys, determining their perseverance and their determination to pursue this route.[54]

Intentional Misguidance

Naidoo v. Minister of Police and Others,[55] in which the appellant had tried to lay an assault charge against her husband, demonstrates how the police can intentionally misguide women. The policeman on duty purposely misguided her and when she insisted on her rights, he called her husband to the police station and tried to resolve the matter amicably. When this failed, he advised them both to write claims against each other and arrested them. On the following day, while being transported to court, the police used violence against the woman that caused her physical and psychological harm, which prompted her to file a claim against the police. Similarly, in her 2016 mission, the Special Rapporteur on violence against women found that the police had repeatedly turned away women seeking protection against their abusive partners.[56]

Stories in this research also revealed the police to be careless, non-responsive, lazy or just disinterested. Charlene, interviewed for this research, discusses one strategy used by the police to misinform women of their rights. A common trick to circumvent the PO issued against men is to delegate a third party, such as a girlfriend, to carry out an attack against the ex-partner.[57] In these cases the police generally advise women to apply for a PO against this third party, although the original PO should automatically protect the woman from the abuser and his affiliates.[58]

In several rape cases, the police had released culprits shortly after their arrest. Daya in Story 10 did not have a case in court, and she believed that the legal system had failed her. She was raped in the north of South Africa, where she had been living; the police released her perpetrators after 24 hours. She was forced to move to Johannesburg

[54] Liz Kelly, *Routes To (In)Justice: A Research Review on the Reporting, Investigation and Prosecution of Rape Cases*, research report (London: HMCPSI, 2002), p. 17.

[55] *Naidoo v. Minister of Police* (20431/2014) [2015] ZASCA152 (2 October 2015).

[56] Special Rapporteur report, 2016, p. 18.

[57] Also see Vetten et al., *The Right and the Real*, p. 17.

[58] See Domestic Violence and Abuse www.divorcelaws.co.za/abuse.html

and stay in a shelter because her rapists were 'roaming around the area' and intimidating her, as she explained. Similarly, Story 12 shows how the police neglected their responsibilities to protect Tasneem from violence. Even though she had identified her rapist, the police did not search for him. Her brother, however, tracked the perpetrator down and turned him over to the police, but the latter was shortly released on bail and disappeared afterwards. Five years after the rape, she was still waiting for the trial to resume. During that time, she had completely lost faith in the legal system. In Story 7, Fatima's case was 'lost in the system' shortly after her report because her former partner had moved elsewhere. Thobile from Story 1 reported her rape to the police and expressed a strong suspicion that her husband and sister-in-law had contracted the rapist. However, the police did not open a case for her. Similarly, a resident interviewed in Shelter 3 was raped when travelling from Zimbabwe to South Africa, but the SAPS claimed that this area was not under their jurisdiction. A Human Rights Watch report recounted the similar story of Frances, who was raped in 2008. She had identified the rapist and filed a rape claim, despite the ridicule and harassment she received from the police. While waiting for DNA test results, Frances learned that the perpetrator was serving a 12-year sentence for raping another woman, and had been out on bail when he attacked her.[59] Other issues arising include victims feeling insecure as they were not able to give testimonies in private.[60]

Assessing Police Conduct

Research on police compliance with the DVA from 2002 to 2011 reveals 1403 complaints of non-compliance, with the leading cause as 'failure to arrest the abuser' followed by 'refusal to open criminal cases'.[61] Matters did not improve in the following years. The compliance audit published in 2014 showed that only 1.4 per cent of police stations in the sample were compliant. Compliance was measured by various indicators including record keeping and maintaining a victim-friendly room and using it for its purpose.[62] Other research confirms that the police did not

[59] Human Rights Watch, 'We'll Show You', p. 50.

[60] Bornman et al., *Protecting Survivors*, p. 26.

[61] Lisa Vetten, 'Police accountability and the Domestic Violence Act 1998' (2017) 29 *South African Crime Quarterly*, 10.

[62] SAPS compliance to the Domestic Violence Act, report submitted to the Parliament of the Republic of South Africa, 3 November 2014, accessed 25 June 2018 at http://pmg-assets.s3-website-eu-west-1.amazonaws.com/141105research_unit_dva_compliance.pdf

fulfil their role in preparing victims properly for court, because of poor communication.[63]

Failing to meet their duty to protect women from violence, the police do not only commit a violation of women's rights, but also promote VAW. This was echoed by the Constitutional Court in *Carmichele v. Minister of Safety and Security* discussed in Chapter 5. The Court concurred that the carelessness of the police led to the attack of another woman by the same man. The police incompetence and reluctance to act against GBV left women 'dangerously exposed to their attackers, who moved about freely and terrorized them'.[64]

It is important to remember that the police remain cultural subjects, quite often prejudging victims of violence. For instance, upon receiving a rape report, policemen may look for signs that would fit the stereotypical profile of raped women, and they may be sceptical of the reporter if she does not fit the profile.[65] This means that rape victims may need to 'gain credibility' so as to be believed and not judged by policemen.[66] Similarly, opting for mediation instead of arresting an abusive husband may sometimes reflect ignorance; Mandy explained that the preference of the police for reconciliation stems largely from their flawed judgement rather than their intentions. She stated: 'the police do not understand the cycle of violence; they may believe that they are helping women by encouraging reconciliation'. This becomes even more confusing when they see women sometimes returning to abusive relationships; while it is a normal phase of the cycle of violence, it may be sending conflicting messages to a policeman. The fact that the police were found to be in need of training on GBV especially regarding supporting victims and bringing forward cases is unsurprising.[67]

The state has been trying to address these issues, and NGOs are strongly pushing for strong accountability measures and reform. In fact, in one study with victims of violence who had sought legal redress, the majority of the respondents (60 per cent) reported that they 'felt safe at the police station and were treated with respect'.[68] In a turn of events, the SAPS report for police non-compliance to the DVA for the period

[63] Watson, *The Role of the State*, p. 10.

[64] Human Rights Watch, '*We'll Show You*', p. 50.

[65] Lillian Artz and Dee Smythe, 'Case attrition in rape cases: a comparative analysis' (January 2007) 20 *South African Journal of Criminal Justice* 2, 162.

[66] Jan Jordan, 'Beyond belief: police, rape and women's credibility' (2004) 4 *Criminology and Criminal Justice*, 1, 29–59.

[67] Special Rapporteur report, 2016, p. 18. Also see Lake, *Strong NGOs*, p. 179.

[68] Bornman et al., *Protecting Survivors*, p. 23

April 2015 to March 2016 showed a low level of non-compliance in all South Africa with no serious non-compliance.[69] Lawyers for Human Rights rejected these statistics and Ms Sonja Borman, attorney at the NGO stated, 'the reports we saw today are totally unacceptable. These numbers can't be right. The same problems with the sampling methodology and suspiciously low levels non-compliance are evident year on year, without change'. She further questioned the monitoring system of the SAPS, adding, 'we are also shocked by what appears to be utter failure to properly discipline non-compliant officers'.[70]

From the state's side, the Chairperson of the Portfolio Committee on Police in 2017 proposed measures to improve the police's capacity to respond to gender-based violence including stricter consequences for inadequate responses; training; and an escalated complaint system.[71]

2 *Reporting: NGOs and Women's Perspectives*

'Women will get nowhere without NGOs', stated Linda from NGO9. With the challenges in the implementation of laws, women will undoubtedly meet legal and administrative hurdles if they pursue formal justice unassisted.[72]

Pros and Cons for Women of Reporting Violence

Reporting suggests that women are taking control of their affairs and negotiating the power inequality in a relationship (whether with the abusive partner or the rapist). Mandy from NGO2 shared this opinion, arguing that reporting always empowers women. Similarly, looking at battered women in Hawaii, Merry found that women who resort to the law adopt a 'more powerful self'.[73] However, it is not always an easy choice.

[69] Lizeka Tandwa, 'Police failure to help in domestic violence cases is misconduct – Lawyers for Human Rights', News24, 21 June 2017, accessed 25 June 2018 at www.news24.com/SouthAfrica/News/police-failure-to-help-in-domestic-violence-cases-is-misconduct-lawyers-for-human-rights-20170621

[70] Lawyers for Human Rights, 'Police failure to assist complainants in terms of the Domestic Violence Act is misconduct and a disciplinable offence', press release, 2017, accessed 25 June 2018 at www.lhr.org.za/news/2017/press-release-police-failure-assist-complainants-terms-domestic-violence-act-misconduct-an

[71] Parliament of the Republic of South Africa, 'Police committee chair proposes eight measures to deal with gender violence', press release, 21 November 2017, accessed 25 June 2018 at www.parliament.gov.za/press-releases/police-committee-chair-proposes-eight-measures-deal-gender-violence

[72] See Mauro Cappelletti and Bryant Garth, 'Access to justice: the newest wave in the worldwide movement to make rights effective' (1977–1978) 27 *Buffalo Law Review*, 181–292.

[73] Merry, *Human Rights and Gender Violence*, p. 189.

Looking at the police conduct, it is hardly surprising that many women are still hesitant to report violence. General causes for low reporting levels include economic dependency, isolation from formal legal institutions and dysfunctional administration of justice.[74] Vulnerable groups are even less likely to report. In cases of sexual offences against children, as Sheri from NGO8 explained, mothers and guardians do not report when they are financially dependent on the perpetrator. A low reporting rate is common among children for various other reasons including the risk of stigma and embarrassment, and further victimisation and discrimination; 'many abused children experience a deep sense of shame and guilt. Additionally, there is fear of retaliation from the perpetrators or his/her associates. In other cases abused children may receive little or no support from their families in reporting the abuse'.[75] Sheri added that children are sometimes not ready to report because they are severely traumatised or too young, with some cases involving victims as young as three years old. Those cases are postponed until the victims are ready, usually after they have received therapy or when they grow older. Using an example from a rural area in South Africa, Ewing demonstrated the complications in the justice system, which discourages women from reporting violence. Two girls were raped by a stranger on their way home from school. Their fathers reported the rape and the trial involved:

> Two very brave children, their parents and supporters, 17 witnesses, expert advisers and a few very dedicated professionals in the criminal justice system ... the children had to attend the regional court 20 times and the High Court once. Their family members and supporters attended at least 30 times. Often this meant a round trip of four hours with six hours spent in court for the sake of a five-minute remand.[76]

Linda from NGO9 admitted that 'understanding the legal procedure usually discourages women from reporting as they realise the significant amount of resources they would invest'. Most of the NGO staff members interviewed noted that reporting violence is a difficult choice for women, especially in conservative societies. Nomsa from NGO10, supporting lesbians, strongly emphasised the disadvantages

[74] See Bonnie Fisher et al., 'Reporting sexual victimization to the police and others: results from a national-level study of college women' (2003) 30 *Criminal Justice and Behavior*, 1, 6–38.

[75] Glenford Howe, *Sexual Violence Against Children in the Caribbean: Report 2012* (UNICEF: May 2013); Judy Cashmore, *The Impact of Delayed Reporting on the Prosecution and Outcomes of Child Sexual Abuse Cases*, research report (Commonwealth of Australia, Sydney, 2016), p. 32.

[76] Ewing, 'Rape, gender and the justice system', 55.

of reporting, specifically referring to the prevalence of homophobia. The availability of social support, however, can motivate a woman to 'incur the risk of social recrimination and privacy loss associated with reporting'.[77]

Importance of Reporting for NGOs

Findings of this research reveal the variety of strategies adopted by NGOs on reporting violence. Nongovernmental organisations working with vulnerable groups such as lesbians, sex workers and children are not keen to convince victims to report. However, other NGOs encourage reporting, but support the victim's final decision. NGO12, however, follows a more rigid approach to reporting rape. Joyce explained that staff members try hard to convince the victim to report and finally inform the victim that only the police can manage rape cases. She added that all the rape victims that she had encountered ended up reporting, but some needed more convincing than others. Jabu from NGO13 also had a similar experience with reporting, elaborating that the NGO location on police station premises encouraged victims to report.

Nongovernmental organisations work on causes and so unsurprisingly are more likely to encourage actions that would affect wider groups of people. Reporting violence is important to NGOs because it feeds statistics that can be used in their advocacy and legal reform work, achieving wider impact. Nongovernmental organisations therefore urge women to report, and may even offer incentives. For instance, the American Bar Association Rule of Law Initiative in DRC, offers victims who decide to litigate free medical services, in addition to the free legal representation.[78] Legal aid organisations 'also provide allowances to victims of violence participating in criminal cases so that they can feed and clothe their children' – these incentives may be the only reason women litigate.[79]

Reporting preferences are different for domestic violence. Saccuzzo argues that while a woman should be able to make her own legal decisions, domestic violence presents a special case. He asserts that intervention is necessary for three groups of women who are unable to make legal decisions; 'those women for whom entrapment prevents

[77] Allen, 'The reporting', 627.
[78] Lake, *Strong NGOs*, p. 167.
[79] Ibid., p. 168.

them from expressing a preference, women whose cultural norms make an expression of preference for arrest a betrayal, and women who do not fully understand the risks they face'.[80] Based on the same logic, some NGOs in this study insist on reporting when they fear for a woman's life. Most NGOs and women, however, preferred mediation in domestic violence cases that were not threatening to women's lives. In addition, staff members are usually concerned about the reputation of the NGO if women are harmed. Janet from NGO6 explained that if the victim is in serious danger, staff members directly and firmly make it clear that her life is in danger. If she still refuses to report, she is then required to sign a waiver form, releasing the NGO from responsibility.

3 *Role of NGOs after Reporting*

When the issue of reporting is settled, NGOs fill some gaps in the administration of justice.

Court Preparation Sessions

Court preparation sessions are offered by some NGOs in South Africa, such as PATCH, in recognition of the importance of child preparedness in court, and the awareness of the meagre services provided by the state. Furthermore, PATCH sends a 'court supporter' to accompany the child in court to make them feel at ease, offer snacks and keeps them 'stimulated with videos, music and play while they wait their turn'.[81] Doing research for this book, the author observed some court preparation sessions undertaken by an NGO. In these sessions, the counsellors gave GBV victims realistic expectations of court procedures. Two of the sessions attended were with the two girls in Story 9. The girls had been previously briefed on the procedures and their testimonies were, therefore, clearly prepared. One of the girls pretended to be in front of a judge and recounted the events. The girl spoke eloquently and confidently, the outcome of multiple preparation sessions. In another session, the court preparation officer showed the victim a chart with the design of the court, explained the seating plan, and informed her on court procedures. In this way, NGOs are

[80] Dennis P. Saccuzzo, 'How should the police respond to domestic violence: a therapeutic jurisprudence analysis of mandatory arrest' (1998–1999) 39 *Santa Clara Law Review*, 3, 780.

[81] See PATCH website www.patchhelderberg.co.za/#position

stepping in by providing one key element of access to justice that the state is failing to provide.[82]

Intervention to Overcome Hurdles

NGOs intervene when women meet legal and administrative hurdles. For example, NGO5 appoints volunteers to be based at the magistrate courts so as to assist women in administrative procedures, such as filling in PO applications. In addition, law enforcement agents are more likely to assist women when NGO employees accompany them. Some interviewees reported that the same policeman who was at first unhelpful completely changed his attitude if the woman showed up again with a shelter or NGO staff member. Charlene from NGO2 stressed that 'walk-ins are poorly assisted', and therefore, the police only respond when 'we [NGO2] 'write letters, call and argue'. Similarly, research in Liberia identified one way in which NGOs support women: accompanying them to the police station to 'pressure the police to prioritize reported cases and to follow up on those that are pending', adding that 'NGOs also serve as liaisons between complainants and the police, and their efforts facilitate the investigations'.[83] Human Rights Watch attested to the same problem, citing Nomuula's story; she had filed a rape case in a police station against an acquaintance only to find her rapist walking in her vicinity a few days later. Upon release, he threatened to kill her, but when she returned to the police station her case 'did not exist'; the only reason Nomuula was able to file another claim was because she sought the help of an NGO.[84]

Law enforcement agents respond better to NGOs than to individual women for several reasons. First, the SAPS has implemented monitoring mechanisms, particularly through the Independent Complaints Directory (ICD). While women are unlikely to use this tool, NGOs are more likely to file complaints. Second, Charlene from NGO2 explained that NGOs investigate tactics that police and court clerks use to discourage women from reporting violence. The NGO keeps records of those reports to monitor the police. Third, women are more likely to give up and leave when they face hurdles and the police may take advantage of their hesitation. However, the police know that NGOs will insist on applying the law.

[82] Watson, *The Role of the State*, p. 10.

[83] Peace A Medie, 'Fighting gender-based violence: the women's movement and the enforcement of rape law in Liberia' (2013) 112 *African Affairs*, 448, 390.

[84] Human Rights Watch, '*We'll Show You*', p. 49.

III NGOs AND ACCESS TO JUSTICE IN INFORMAL SETTINGS

Access to justice in rural areas, remote locations and communities living under customary law encompasses an additional set of challenges. Women in these areas find it much harder to access formal legal institutions. They usually have access to magistrate courts in their vicinity as they operate throughout South Africa, but high courts are fewer in number and primarily based in urban areas.[85] The government also operates Circuit Courts, which are mobile High Courts that sit at least twice a year in different rural areas.[86] Artz points to the 'limited availability and high prices of transportation'[87] that hinder women's access to justice. An additional prohibitive expense on NGO staff members in rural areas is the cost of transporting witnesses from remote areas and the costs of their accommodation if needed.[88]

Because of the stratified gender relationships pervasive in areas falling under customary law, as discussed in Chapter 3, NGOs face an incredible set of challenges. Foucault explains that understanding the 'forms of institutionalization' of power is a prerequisite to understanding unequal power relations.[89] Drivers of power inequalities include 'traditional predispositions' and legal structures 'relating to custom or to fashion'.[90] Nongovernmental organisations must therefore understand the complex power relations unique to these areas, untangle the roots of unequal gender power dynamics and subtly present their findings to the community. The community should then be prompted to reject discriminatory norms and develop customary law. In this way, change will emanate from within and will not be viewed as an imposition, ultimately leading to a power shift in favour of women.

Because of their proximity to local communities, NGOs intervene in issues that are 'politically and/or culturally so sensitive that no government wants to touch them with a bargepole'.[91] Their intervention ranges from 'advice' to 'mediation' which 'may appear analytically

85 Open Society Foundation, *Justice Sector*, p. 141.

86 Department of Justice and Constitutional Development website, www.justice.gov.za/about/sa-courts.html

87 Artz, 'Violence against women'.

88 Vetten, *Addressing Domestic Violence*, p.6.

89 Michel Foucault, 'The subject and the power' (1982) 8 *Critical Inquiry*, 777, 792.

90 Ibid.

91 Rica Nagar and Saraswati Raju, 'Women, NGOs and the contradictions of empowerment and disempowerment: a conversation' (2003) 35 *Antipode*, 1, 4.

distinct activities, but in many instances, it is difficult to prise them apart'.[92]

A Successful Intervener

Intervening in conservative societies, specifically those falling under the rule of customary law, requires vigilance and excellent diplomatic skills. Abel discusses successful intervention strategies in small communities. He identifies two important criteria shaping the process and outcomes of the interventions: 'social distance of the intervener' and 'cultural differentiation of the intervener'.[93] Abel adds that:

> social distance and cultural differentiation are likely to be important variables in a developing society, where stratification is replacing egalitarianism and traditional homogeneity giving way to cultural pluralism engendered by changes which are, or at least are seen to be, imitations of an alien competing ideology.[94]

In South Africa's case, NGOs advocate egalitarianism and use the human rights language; both concepts are considered alien to local communities that adopt gender-stratified structures. To challenge such deeply entrenched beliefs and solidified patriarchal systems, Merry suggests that NGOs build and maintain close ties with local institutions in order to bring about 'substantial shifts in beliefs about gender as well as changes in the institutions that govern women's lives'.[95]

Another key element of success with traditional communities is 'working with "insider" agents of change' by 'identifying local citizens who are familiar with the socio-cultural and political contests in a specific locality'.[96] Among the research respondents for this book, NGO3 and NGO12 were the least confrontational and the most diplomatic because they worked in rural and tradition areas that adamantly resisted change. They applied most of the sensitive intervention strategies suggested in this section. For instance, the NGOs trained and hired women from the community to be advocates of human rights, counsellors and mediators in GBV disputes. It is, in fact, a common and successful strategy for NGOs to hire local staff. In their research in

92 Roberts and Palmer, *Dispute Processes*, p. 91.

93 Richard L Abel, 'A comparative theory of dispute institutions in society' (1974) 8 *Law & Society Review*, 2, 255.

94 Ibid., 256. Also see Amy S Tsanga, *Taking Law to the People: Gender, Law Reform, and Community Legal Education in Zimbabwe* (Harare: Weaver Press, 2003).

95 Merry, *Human Rights and Gender Violence*, p. 25.

96 Chopra and Isser, 'Women's access to justice', p. 21.

India, Desai and Howes agree, and as an example, they refer to an NGO working with slum dwellers that hired staff from the community in order to stay in touch with people's needs.[97] This practice echoes Abel's notions of 'social distance and cultural differentiation', in which the distance between the interveners and the community determines the impact of the intervention.

Abel identifies other important characteristics of a successful intervener including different roles an intervener may play in society, the distance that community members have to travel to reach the intervener and the physical setting where dispute resolution takes place.[98] Following a similar strategy, Audrey from NGO3 referred to a coordinator who was also the wife of a chief. Her position encouraged the community to accept her as an intervener, inspired by the chief's approval. Arriera from NGO1 also asserted that she was a successful intervener because of her respected status in the community and her position as an insider. Not only did she know the law, but the community also knew her, trusted her and were able to reach her at the NGO or at her home, anytime.

B Successful Intervention Strategies

NGOs intervene in communities so as to shift the gender power dynamic. Intervention is best done through 'empowerment strategies' that can open spaces for dialogue and discussions on justice, giving traditionally disempowered groups voice and space to be able to question and negotiate traditional power structures.[99] This is the only way 'a serious and meaningful reform' in customs and customary law can come to light, as an outcome of internal critique, debate and engagement that respects the essential attributes of the institution rather than begins from the premise of debunking it and seeking the imposition of an externally defined reality'.[100]

Awareness campaigns organised by NGO5 follow the principle, 'as much as we respect your culture, you have other alternatives; you can choose the law'. Similarly, NGO3 runs workshops for women living

[97] Vandana Desai and Mick Howes, 'Accountability and participation: a case study from Bombay' in Michael Edwards and David Hulme (eds.), *Non-Governmental Organisations: Performance and Accountability* (London: Earthscan, 1996), p. 83. For other examples, see Penal Reform, *Access to Justice*, p. 16.

[98] Abel, 'A comparative theory', 256.

[99] Peter Albrecht et al. (eds.), *Perspectives on Involving Non-State and Customary Actors in Justice and Security Reform* (Rome: International Development Law Organization, 2011), p. 21.

[100] Kane et al., *Reassessing Customary Law*, p. 22.

under customary law, discussing their rights under statutory law. 'Women appreciate this information because many of them face severe violence but fail to stop it because they do not have the tools', explained Audrey. She used Story 2 as an example: Ndonsa was from a prominent family in the community and had been abused by her husband for a long time. After attending the workshop organised by NGO3, she decided to apply for a PO. In this way, NGOs are 'rights translators'; this is a common role in areas falling under customary law, and often the only way women can know their legal rights. Nongovernmental organisations in the DRC similarly run local workshops in which women learn about their rights and possibly meet others who have had similar experiences.[101]

Nongovernmental organisations call attention to customary practices that greatly harm females, stimulating discussions about them in local communities so as to question the necessity for and repercussions of those practices. This is done in an attempt to guide women to make informed decisions on the legal framework they want to follow. In addition, paralegals working with NGO3 represent women in both traditional or magistrate courts. These are all 'promising methods' to achieve real advancements for women's rights in traditional communities falling under customary laws.[102]

Another approach often used by NGOs is focusing on a context that will grab and maintain the attention of the community. For example, NGOs can address GBV issues by linking them to the issues that the community considers more important, including HIV, land rights, education and poverty, among others.[103] This approach is followed by some NGOs in this research; they stress that culture is dynamic and that cultural norms may be negotiated and redefined, encouraging the community to revise customary norms and laws through different publicity techniques. For example, NGO3 links the male privilege of having multiple sex partners to the spread of HIV. Audrey from NGO3 explained that this was a successful campaign because the NGO's involvement was subtle; the community therefore considered the initiative internally driven. In a similar example from Uganda, levirate marriage was customary in the Luo community, where a man had the right to marry the wife of his deceased brother. However, in recent years there had been a surge in HIV/AIDS, which drove the Luo community to recognise the

[101] Lake, *Strong NGOs*, p. 167.
[102] Chopra and Isser, 'Women's access to justice' p. 36.
[103] Britton, 'Organizing against', 160.

connection between levirate marriage and the spread of disease; while the custom was not entirely eliminated, it ceased to be customary. More importantly, a widow who refused this type of marriage received more sympathy from the community.[104]

These examples confirm that the intervention methods of 'the reformer and the activist' who assume that the progressive system of human rights law has self-evident benefits[105] is likely to fail.

C NGOs and Traditional Leaders

Chiefs/traditional leaders enjoy significant legitimacy in their communities, whether or not their judgments are gender discriminatory.

1 Clash of Ideologies

NGOs working in areas falling under customary law must find a channel of communication with traditional leaders. This is usually challenging because of the conflict between the gender inequalities pervasive in communities living under customary law, and the human rights doctrine that is usually adopted by NGOs. The conflict echoes the disagreements between the women's movement and the Council of Traditional Leaders that peaked during the Constitution-drafting process. Not surprisingly, the Council's objection was that 'the commitment to equality at its heart encompassed a commitment to gender equality', which was problematic because 'the legal system over which traditional leaders preside, does not recognize women and men as equals'.[106] While the Constitution endorses the rule of traditional leaders, customary law and adjudication in customary courts are subject to the Bill of Rights, which theoretically limits the power and authority of traditional leaders.[107] Research by Oomen, however, shows that this limitation is merely theoretical because chiefs regularly exceed their jurisdiction with no implications.[108] Working with chiefs in their local communities therefore requires diplomacy, patience and superb negotiation skills from NGOs.

[104] Kane et al., *Reassessing Customary Law*, p. 22.

[105] Nhlapo, ' Cultural diversity, human rights', 217. Also see Makau Mutua, 'Savages, victims and saviors: the metaphor of human rights' (2001) 42 *Harvard International Law Journal*, 1,

[106] Felicity Kaganas and Christina Murray, 'The contest between culture and gender equality under South Africa's Interim Constitution' (1994) 21 *Journal of Law and Society*, 4, 410. Also see Nhlapo, 'International protection'.

[107] Kaganas and Murray, 'The contest', 410.

[108] Oomen, *Chiefs in South Africa*; Gardiol Van Niekerk, *Traditional African Courts* (Cape Town: University of Cape Town, 1993), p. 84.

2 *Moments of Conflict: NGOs, Chiefs and the Police*

The relationship between NGOs and the chiefs varies, as 'some chiefs are altruistic and humane and some of them are stubborn and threatened', as stated by Audrey from NGO3. Oomen similarly reports mixed opinions about chiefs from different South African communities, in which some chiefs are more popular than others.[109] Audrey specified lineage as an important determinant of the popularity of chiefs; descendants of corrupt chiefs who were appointed by the apartheid government to control the native population are unpopular.[110]

It is common for traditional leaders across the continent to consider NGOs as a threat.[111] Introducing formal law and encouraging people to use it in areas that have always fallen under customary law is considered a direct challenge to their authority. Conflict also arises when NGOs are perceived to be interfering in the rulings of customary law. This usually happens when chiefs' judgments are likely to inflict immense suffering upon women and girls. At this point, NGOs may escalate the matter, taking a strong stance against the judgment or referring the matter to formal authorities. For instance, in one case in Afghanistan, payment of financial compensation was imposed on a rapist as a punishment for the rape. The ruling was not even enforced as the perpetrator refused to pay.[112] In these cases, it is necessary to involve the police.

Similarly, in Story 3, NGO3 considered the chief's judgment inadequate, as he had ordered the payment of damages to a girl who had been gang-raped. In response, the NGO summoned the police who showed up, but shortly terminated the investigation due to 'lost evidence'. In Story 2, when Ndonsa attempted to file a claim for assault against her husband, the police discouraged her and failed to provide information about her legal rights. The head of NGO3 explained that the state often does not want to meddle in local politics or question the authority of chiefs, who usually enjoy community recognition. Members of SAPS have previously expressed their utter appreciation and respect for the role of the chiefs,[113] which may jeopardise their neutrality. Furthermore,

[109] Oomen, *Chiefs in South Africa*, pp. 164–165.

[110] For more information on the popularity of chiefs, see Oomen, *Chiefs in South Africa*, pp. 183–186 and 193–198.

[111] For example, see Felix Marco Conteh, 'Chiefs, NGOs and alternative conflict resolution mechanisms in post-conflict Sierra Leone' (2014) 41 *Review of African Political Economy*, 142, 516–529.

[112] UN OHCHR and UNMIT, Report on Human Rights Development in Timor Leste (September 2007–June 2008), p. 11.

[113] Boyane Tshehla, 'Here to stay: traditional leaders' role in justice and crime prevention' (2005) 11 *South Africa Crime Quarterly*, 17.

in one research study, chiefs declared that when they receive reports on matters not under their purview, they call the police; however, the police show up only occasionally.[114]

This research found that even when chiefs cooperate, they expect something in return; this could be assistance with government organisations, drafting documents or, most frequently, financial compensation. Similarly, in one study, both 'large government-sponsored projects and small NGOs' have expressed frustration that financial remuneration is expected by many community elders.[115]

3 Conflict and Cooperation: NGOs and Chiefs

Nongovernmental organisations may not involve the police even if risking unfavourable rulings in customary courts. In this way, they 'pick their battles'. Audrey from NGO3 recounted a dispute between two families over a child whose parents were deceased. The chief ruled that the child should live with his paternal relatives, but the maternal relatives argued that the child was more familiar and comfortable with them. NGO3 represented the maternal relatives in the traditional court proceedings. However, they lost the case. It is not uncommon for customary law to be patrilineal[116] and therefore the issue was more acceptable to the disputants who decided not to proceed to the Magistrate Court so as to maintain harmony in the community. This is an example of failed negotiations on the part of the NGO, demonstrating that customary law prevailed, despite the best interests of the child. However, it also shows how the NGO can compromise on some cases when victims are not seriously harmed or injured.

NGOs have found some room for collaboration with chiefs. Audrey from NGO3 stated, 'the situation has not been favourable for chiefs under the Constitution as they have become politically marginalised. Even though they have rights in the Constitution, they were never taught how to use them'. This was one way for NGOs to win over chiefs. NGO3 helped chiefs to redefine their roles and come up with new

[114] Ibid., 19.

[115] Kate Fearon, 'Pragmatism, proximity and pashtunwali: informal justice at the district level in Helmand Province State' in Peter Albrecht et al. (eds.), *Perspectives on Involving Non-State and Customary Actors in Justice and Security Reform* (Rome: International Development Law Organization, 2011), p. 61.

[116] See Maurice Okechukwu Izunwa, 'A critique of certain aspects of the grounds, procedure and reliefs attaching to customary divorce law in Southern Nigeria' (2015) 7 *Journal of Law and Conflict Resolution* 5, 35; also see Emmanuel Quansah, 'Custody of children: customary principles in Ghana and Nigeria' (1991) 17 *Commonwealth Law Bulletin*, 1.

ways in which they can support women and serve the community. In addition, NGO3 consults chiefs on various issues and resorts to traditional courts for non-serious crimes. This strategy is not only common but inevitable. It has also yielded promising results. Significant success has been reported in Zambia when one NGO collaborated with chiefs on priority issues of gender, human rights, children's rights and HIV/AIDS. Chiefs received training for trainers over seven days on specific issues and then rolled it out to their communities.[117] In South Africa, Sonke Gender Justice brought a campaign against the practice of Ukuthwala to rural communities in the Eastern Cape, with the support of the chiefs. This was a successful intervention as chiefs were on board and have publicly rejected the practice.[118] These examples show that 'working within traditional institutions contributes to the relevance and the legitimacy of changing local decision-making structures to support women's empowerment'.[119]

While areas falling under customary law are perhaps the most challenging for NGOs to work on legal empowerment, they are also the most necessary. Not only are NGOs often the sole source of information for women on their legal rights, NGOs also 'provide an initial point of contact between the legal system and communities otherwise cut off from it'.[120]

D Concluding Remarks on NGOs' Intervention with Informal Justice

Several conclusions can be drawn from the discussion in this section. First, NGOs are willing to work diplomatically and negotiate with all parties. They 'choose their battles', based on the community's desires and preparedness, the sensitivity of the case and the harm it may inflict on the victim. Attempts to develop customary norms and recognise human rights principles must come from within the community. Second, the legitimacy enjoyed by NGOs stems from their cultural and geographic proximity to the served communities. Third, although the

[117] Clare Bishop-Sambrook and Vincent M Akamandisa, *Chiefs and Traditional Leaders, Zambia*, case study (IFAD, November 2014).

[118] Kristin Palitza, *Traditional Leaders Wield the Power, and They Are Almost All Men: The Importance of Involving Traditional Leaders in Gender Transformation*, research report (Sonke Gender Justice Network, October 2010).

[119] Cathy Farnworth et al., *Transforming Gender Relations in Agriculture in Sub-Saharan Africa* (Stockholm: Swedish International Agricultural Network Initiative, 2013), p. 68.

[120] Lake, *Strong NGOs*, p. 188.

police have more legal power than NGOs, they are also more reluctant to intervene in customary matters, leaving the groundwork to NGOs.

While this specific kind of mediation is more common in rural areas, Janet, the social worker in NGO6, confirmed that 'cultural' negotiations with women occur on a daily basis. Their headquarters and satellite offices are all based in socially conservative townships; so social workers constantly try to 'shake up' people's adamant beliefs and values. They push women to question norms and behaviours that have always been taken for granted.

IV NGOs AND EMPOWERMENT

This chapter has shown that NGOs have a strong role in facilitating women's access to justice, whether through formal or informal channels of justice. Consequently, a relationship develops between women and NGOs, which has unique power dimensions. This section will zoom in on this relationship, and will question whether it truly empowers women.

A NGOs and Women Connect

1 Acquaintance

Do women need NGOs or do NGOs look for women? This research suggests that they find each other. Nongovernmental organisations and shelters reported that women find them through word of mouth, walk-ins, referrals and publicity. Referrals come from the police station, courts, hospitals or other NGOs that do not offer the required service. Publicity includes advertisements on television and radio, in magazines and on websites, as mentioned in section II.A of this chapter. While these awareness campaigns cover prevention, rights awareness and general information on violence, some campaigns specifically target women who may be potential beneficiaries. This is because awareness-raising 'of the support available is vital to delivering a cohesive approach to tackling gender-based violence'.[121] These are the most common approaches with which women reach the services they need.[122]

The NGOs' mandate and activities determine the amount of investment in publicity. Of the NGOs that were part of this study, the ones

[121] Stanley, 'Engendering change?' 298.

[122] Eleanor Lyon et al., *Meeting Survivors' Needs: a Multi-state Study of Domestic Violence Shelter Experiences* (National Institute of Justice, October 2008), pp. 52–53.

located on police and court premises do not advertise because they receive many clients due to their location. Moreover, they are usually CBOs working on a limited scale on a specific issue with limited activities so they are not interested in national publicity. On the other hand, NGOs that run awareness-raising and advocacy programmes or work in impact litigation invest more in publicity.

2 *What do Women Want from NGOs?*

When NGOs receive women, they first evaluate their needs. Accordingly, they either assist women or refer them to other organisations that are better able to serve them.

Domestic Violence Services

As is to be expected, abused women look for information and guidance on their options as they come to NGOs in a state of confusion. In a nationwide study on domestic violence shelters in the United States of America, 80 per cent of shelter residents cited 'learning about their options and choices' as one of the main reasons for seeking help.[123] Another study with women in America found that although many women request an emergency restraining order, many do not proceed with a permanent one, citing reasons such as 'attachment to the abusive partner'.[124] Another study found that many women rejected the dominant narrative of domestic abuse, and stayed with their abusive partners after securing a restraining order for a variety of reasons including attachment to the abuser and fear.[125] The indecision is a symptom of the cycle of violence in which many women continue to live.

This research revealed similar trends of confusion. Women want the violence to end and they usually expect NGOs to achieve that. Charlene estimated that 80 per cent of abused women who approach NGO2 do not want to leave their partners. She added that they unrealistically want the law to remedy the relationship. The most common attempt women make to end violence is obtaining a PO so as to scare the abusive partner, hoping to improve their relationship. 'Although they can obtain a PO independently, women usually seek the help

[123] Ibid., p. 62.

[124] Lori A Zoellner et al., 'Factors associated with completion of the restraining order process in female victims of partner violence' (2000) 15 *Journal of Interpersonal Violence*, 10.

[125] Phyllis L Baker, 'And I went back: battered women's negotiation of choice' (1997) 26 *Journal of Contemporary Ethnography* 1; also see Ann Malecha et al., 'Applying for and dropping a protection order: a study with 150 women' (2003) 14 *Criminal Justice Policy Review* 4.

of NGOs for information gathering and support', Linda from NGO9 elaborated.

While many women are trapped in a cycle of violence, others are serious about ending the abusive relationship, especially when the violence becomes unbearable. These women usually want NGOs to help them start over. In Shelter 1, the three women interviewed expressed the desire to move on from their partners. Janet from NGO6 explained that 'women want different things. They mostly need "space to talk"'. She added that many women who approach the NGO neither need legal advice nor ask for it, but just want emotional support. As for NGO7, Jill replied, 'it depends on each woman; some want an end to the violence, others want couple's counselling and space to talk'. A new beginning and a safe future for children was another common answer to the question 'what do women want?' This was mainly the reply from shelter residents as safety was their main concern. Fatima agreed to join Shelter 2 because her ex-husband's family had threatened to kill her. In Story 8, Nelly's most prominent fear was her children's safety.

Generally, there are no roadmaps for NGOs to follow. In a UK report assessing the quality of services victims of domestic abuse are receiving, results reflected the complexity of the crime. For other services, 'more than half of advisers are able to support clients to entirely resolve their cases' but this rate dropped to 4 per cent for domestic abuse cases.[126] Both emotional and practical reasons were responsible for the unfinished business, but in 41 per cent of the cases advisors cited 'client's decision' to not move forward.[127] This is why it is of utmost importance for counsellors to have 'listening skills' and be free from personal judgments, responding with 'empathy, genuineness, respect, acceptance, and caring'.[128]

Rape Victims

Rape victims also want different things. First, Mandy explained that most rape victims who approach the NGO have already filed criminal charges; therefore, they only want moral support and guidance. Second, NGO9 often receives rape victims who just want to gather information and know their options, because they have not made a decision yet

[126] Citizens Advice Bureau UK, *Victims of Domestic Abuse: Struggling for Support*, research report (February 2015), p. 17.

[127] Ibid.

[128] Arizona Coalition against Domestic Violence, *Best Practices Manual for Domestic Violence Programs* (June 2000), p. 15.

regarding legal redress. Third, sometimes rape victims seek the help of NGOs for reinforcement in their legal journey. This was the case with Nasreen in Story 4, who wanted to go to court for her rape despite the low probability of successful litigation.

Linda from NGO9 reported that groups with intersectional vulnerabilities had other needs, giving examples of sex workers who had previously approached NGO9. As she explained, 'sex workers are subjected to violence because of the nature of their jobs and therefore they approached the NGO when they wanted to report. When told that they cannot make anonymous complaints, they withdraw'. This withdrawal is unfortunately expected in a country where sex work is criminalised and sex workers are perceived as criminals.[129] Resorting to NGOs is therefore one of their only options. One study noted the invaluable support provided to sex workers by the NGO SWEAT.[130] Similarly, Nomsa confirmed that lesbians are generally looking for space to express their anger and despair, and to find a support group. It is common for these violent incidents to leave victims questioning their conduct, or for instance, their 'lesbianism', increasing their vulnerability.[131] Nomsa adds that they rarely receive clients who are interested in legal support. Lesbians expect homophobic responses if they seek justice; this is the root of the low reporting rate of corrective, 'curative' rape.[132] Groups with intersectional vulnerability therefore end up resorting to NGOs for moral support.

3 *Terms of Service Provision*

NGOs screen clients who approach them. Screening criteria depend on the NGO mandate and mission. For example, law clinics (such as NGO11) evaluate cases based on the potential success of litigation. In addition to the merits of the case, Legal Aid (the public defence service) accepts cases based on the financial ability of the litigant, which is determined by a means test.[133] This is because they only provide free services to women who are unable to afford a lawyer. NGO11 applies the same criteria. In these cases, staff members have limited discretion to

[129] Ilse Pauw and Loren Brener, '"You are just whores: you can't be raped": barriers to safer sex among women street sex workers in Cape Town' (2003) 5 *Culture, Health and Sexuality* 6, 465.

[130] Ibid., 477.

[131] Katy, *Dealing with Rape as a 'Hate Crime' within the Lesbian Community*, report (Pandora's Aquarium, 2009), accessed 25 June 2018 at www.pandys.org/articles/rapeashatecrime.pdf, p. 3.

[132] Glenn de Swardt, 'The horror of corrective rape', Health24, 11 May 2011, accessed 20 June 2018 at www.health24.com/Sex/Sexual-diversity/The-horror-of-corrective-rape-20120721

[133] Legal Aid Guide, p. 75.

go beyond the threshold that the NGO has set. NGO6 asks women to pay as much as they can afford. On the other hand, NGO4 litigates for impact, and therefore limits its work to cases that are likely to generate meaningful public impact. In these instances, litigation is accompanied by awareness-raising and advocacy campaigns.

Shelters are usually more selective in terms of the women to whom they provide services. This is because shelters use more resources and offer a wider range of services than NGOs. Shelter 2 and Shelter 3 admit women who are in life-threatening situations. They also consider the availability of external networks when they make admission decisions. Shelter 4 has strict rules on women's conduct during their stay. For example, women can only sleep out of the shelter a limited number of times per month because, as Bridget, the manager, questioned, 'if there is family that can support women, then why are they staying in the shelter?' While Bridget imposes this rule to maximise resources, her view is problematic because it fails to capture the impact of violence on women's lives. Victims of domestic violence who were interviewed in shelters had few family members (mostly mothers or maternal grandmothers), to whom they had already resorted and yet were still at risk of violence; the availability of family could be mistakenly considered as networks. 'Good conduct' is necessary for shelters to operate peacefully. All shelters in this study impose strict rules of conduct. In Shelter 1, women are prohibited from swearing and drinking both on and off the shelter premises. The shelter imposes a 7 pm curfew (unless residents have night jobs). Women are allowed to go out every alternate weekend. Beth explained that rules are fundamental to maintaining peace and order, but she confirmed that the rules are often broken. Shelter 1 applied a 'no discrimination' policy, specifically based on race. However, the shelter is 'a Christian home, in which residents can only 'passively' practice their religion. For example, while Muslims are allowed to refrain from eating pork, they are not allowed to pray five times a day (an Islamic ritual). Shelter 4 is also 'a Christian home but does not enforce religion-related rules on residents. This conditionality reflects unequal power relations that will be discussed in the following section.

In fact, all shelters have some entry conditions that may include behavioural aspects such as drinking, taking drugs or having a police record.[134] It is also common for shelters to assess the safety situation of

[134] Lyon et al., *Meeting Survivors' Needs*, pp. 54–55.

women and use this as an admission criteria; for instance whether they have obtained a restraining order against the abuser.[135] It is preferable, however, that women find flexible yet disciplined shelter environments that can help them establish some sense of routine and predictability. One study conducted with residents of domestic violence shelters concludes that collaboration and flexibility in resident–staff relations were most favourable to the women, in addition to transparent enforcement of rules.[136]

4 *Are Women Free to Make Personal Decisions?*

Inflexible Policies

When asked, 'do women always make their decisions in their relationship with NGOs?' Mandy replied, 'Not necessarily'. Women may seek remedies that do not fall within the NGOs' mandates and programmes. When conflict occurs between women and NGOs, the only power that women possess is to 'exit' the programmes.[137] Pelad uses domestic violence as an example to demonstrate the common conflict between NGOs and women. Nongovernmental organisations usually advocate the 'exit' strategy; this is assumed to be the best option based on 'research designed to better understand why women return to the abuser after a stay in a shelter'.[138] Similarly, Baker conducted a study of battered women through in-depth interviews and participant observation. Her findings showed that women initially tried to fight against the 'dominant cultural script' that presents 'exit' as the only solution to domestic violence.[139] Those who decided to stay in abusive relationships found a lack of understanding and support from service providers. When faced with the choice of either ending their relationships or ending their association with the NGO, women chose the latter.[140] Similarly, Tiessen's research in Malawi shows that when conflict occurred with beneficiaries, staff members were unwilling to revise their 'practices, attitudes and behaviours'.[141] This confirms Pelad's argument that conflict

[135] Ibid.

[136] Catherine Glenn and Lisa Goodman, 'Living with and within the rules of domestic violence shelters: A qualitative exploration of residents' experiences' (2015) 21 *Violence against Women* 12.

[137] AlNoor Ebrahim, 'Making sense of accountability: conceptual perspectives for northern and southern nonprofits (2003) 14 *Nonprofit Management and Leadership*, 2, 203.

[138] Pelad et al., 'Choice and empowerment', 12.

[139] Baker, 'And I went back', 56.

[140] Ibid.

[141] Rebecca Teissen, 'Re-inventing the gendered organization: staff attitudes towards women and gender mainstreaming in NGOs in Malawi' (2004) 11 *Gender, Work and Organization*, 6, 701.

between women's choices and the service providers' programmes 'may lead to clients resisting and eventually dropping out of treatment'.[142] It also echoes Ebrahim's scepticism about downward accountability, in which he asserts that the only form of power that beneficiaries have over NGOs is abandoning the programmes.[143]

While most NGOs in this study adopt flexible rules regarding the 'exit' strategy, some exceptions were reported. Janet from NGO6 explained, 'women should pack up their stuff and leave'. She added that women do not share this view because they usually do not have networks or the ability to be financially independent, as previously discussed. Before she joined the shelter, Nelly from Story 8 had tried to access the services of an NGO that provided counselling, but found these services to be restricted to clients who had moved out of the abusive environment. Beth from Shelter 1 did not admit women who have a tendency to return to their partners; she stated, 'before they join the shelter, they know they have to commit to the programme. If there is a possibility that they would change their minds and want to return to their partners, I tell them 'this is not the place for you'. Beth defends her position: 'I invest a lot of time, energy and money into the programme so women must fully commit'.

NGOs cited different reasons for their conditional services; 'concerns for women', 'concern for the NGO's image and reputation', or 'the desire to maximise NGO resources'. Nongovernmental organisations have limited time and resources, and therefore are reluctant to invest in clients who are not likely to benefit.

Power Analysis

Conflict between women's desires and NGOs' policies points to some imbalances in power relations. To analyse social and political relations within communities, it is necessary to assess the power of the parties involved in each relationship. Emerson explains that the nature and extent of the power possessed by a party ascertains that party's value in a social structure. This 'power' also determines the party's level of authority, and it regulates interactions between members of the social structure.[144] This power is determined by the position occupied by an actor whether the actor is aware of this power or not.[145] Marsden also

[142] Pelad et al. 'Choice and empowerment', 12.
[143] Ebrahim, 'Making sense of accountability', 203.
[144] Richard M Emerson, 'Power-dependence relations' (1962) 27 *American Sociological Review*, 1.
[145] Karen S Cook and Richard M Emerson, 'Power, equity and commitment in exchange' (1978) 43 *American Sociological Review*, 5, 721.

links power with position, explaining that actors who exist in the centre of networks 'appear to possess a special prominence in most empirical studies of social networks'.[146] One suggested test to determine the power that each actor possesses is: 'If by removing itself from an exchange, a position could reduce the total resources available in a network, then that position had power'.[147]

Failing to reach a compromise between NGOs and women where the only solution is for women to withdraw from the interaction puts all the power in the possession of NGOs. This approach defeats the purpose of intervention as it prevents women from making decisions and taking control over their affairs, further disempowering them.[148] It is also considered an 'unfair exercise of control'.[149] It is therefore recommended that NGOs strike a balance between the most efficient use of resources and women's freedom of choice.

B Are NGOs Empowering Women?

The mission statements of most NGOs working with women include the term 'empowerment'. Foucault's power analysis provides a useful theoretical framework. Nongovernmental organisations identify the 'system of differentiation'; the means by which men maintain power over women, such as physical threats or economic dependency.[150] This information helps NGOs reach the root of the unequal power dynamic and consequently design relevant programmes to shift power in favour of women. This also means that indiscriminately applied intervention programmes are not likely to be effective. Each case requires a separate evaluation in order to detect the source of power. For example, in a case of domestic violence that is exacerbated by financial dependency, NGOs can assist women in shifting the power dynamic by offering economic empowerment solutions. Likewise, in a rape case, in which a victim is paralysed by fear, the NGO can provide legal or psychological assistance to 'empower' the victim. Nongovernmental organisations therefore redirect power from men to women, giving them agency. This

[146] Peter V Marsden, 'Restricted access in networks and models of power' (1983) 88 *American Journal of Sociology*, 4, 687.

[147] Michael J Lovaglia et al., 'Negotiated exchanges in social networks' (1995) 74 *Social Forces*, 1, 124.

[148] Pelad et al. 'Choice and empowerment', 12.

[149] Connell, 'Understanding victimization', 120.

[150] Foucault, 'The subject', 792.

section will discuss if and how programmes designed for women lead to empowerment.

1 Defining Empowerment

The term 'empowerment' is frequently associated with gender equality; more importantly, it commonly refers to intervention work done by NGOs.[151] 'Empower' is an 'action verb' that carries 'the promise of change, often for the better'.[152] 'Empower' embodies 'power', which is a controversial term in the first place. The most common understanding of 'power' is in its implication of 'obedience' reflecting the concept of 'power over'.[153] This is when:

> A person or a group of people have control over another person or another group of people. This control can either be visible, through physical coercion or hidden through psychological process and it is aimed to restrict the range of options perceived by someone or to lead someone to perceive the desired option as being their own desire.[154]

Empowering one person necessarily means taking power from another person. Mason elaborates: 'people are not empowered or disempowered in a vacuum. Rather, they are empowered or disempowered relative to other people or groups whose lives intersect with theirs and whose interests differ from theirs, at least in part'.[155] The mainstream feminist interpretation of power, based on the verb 'power-over', puts women in a state of 'internalized oppression' that maintains their passive acceptance of power and prevents them from actively making decisions.[156] On the same grounds, Kabeer explains that women often internalise their social value as inferior to men's.[157] This belief can adversely affect women who accept socially constructed roles and obligations. For example, women may be willing to bear children due to social pressure, even at risk to

[151] Pelad et al. 'Choice and empowerment', 12.

[152] Jane L Parpart et al. (eds.), *Rethinking Empowerment: Gender and Development in a Global/Local World* (London and New York: Routledge, 2002), p. 5.

[153] Jo Rowlands, 'Empowerment examined' (1995) 5 *Development in Practice*, 2, 101.

[154] Jo Rowlands, 'A word of the times, but what does it mean? Empowerment in the discourse and practice of development' in Haleh Afshar (ed.), *Women and Empowerment: Illustrations from the Third World* (London: St. Martin's Press, 1998), p. 12.

[155] Karen Oppenheim Mason, 'Measuring women's empowerment: learning from cross-national research' in Deepa Narayan (ed.), *Measuring Empowerment: Cross Disciplinary Perspectives* (Washington, DC: World Bank, 2005), p. 90.

[156] Rowlands, 'Empowerment examined', 102.

[157] Naila Kabeer, 'Resources, agency, achievements: reflections on the measurement of women's empowerment' (1999) 30 *Development and Change*, 3, 440–441.

their health, they accept the minor share of household resources and they are likely to tolerate their husbands' physical and psychological aggression.[158]

Empowerment is achieved by giving power to someone who previously had little or none. Collins described 'internal empowerment' as the ability to create change in the 'private, personal space of an individual woman's consciousness'.[159]

Mahmud adopts a multi-dimensional approach to empowerment, referring to material, cognitive, perceptual and relational empowerment. Material empowerment reflects the expansion of women's resources, while cognitive empowerment is achieved when women can recognise their abilities and skills. This recognition promotes their self-esteem and self-confidence, subsequently elevating their psychological wellbeing. Perceptual empowerment entails an enlightened perception of women by others, which ultimately raises women's social prestige and value. Finally, relational empowerment occurs when women obtain more bargaining power in their relationships, both intimate and community based.[160] Notably, perceptual and relational dimensions of empowerment are concerned with the broader social context rather than merely focusing on the empowerment of a single individual.

The multi-dimensional approach to empowerment was recognised and developed in social sciences when 'self-perception' proved insufficient to measure 'empowerment'. As Pollack notes, 'individualizing social issues can result in blaming individuals for problems that arise from being oppressed in various ways and may be further disempowering to them'.[161] Furthermore, Browne explains that collective and personal empowerments are simultaneously fulfilled: individual empowerment is necessary for group empowerment; and in return, the power of a group empowers individual members.[162] Rowlands asserts that personal and collective empowerments combined enable a person to control the nature of their relationships.[163] Mason's example of a study conducted

[158] Ibid., 440–441.

[159] Patricia Hill Collins, *Black Feminist Thought: Knowledge, Consciousness, and the Politics of Empowerment*, 2nd edition (New York and London: Routledge, 2000), p. 118.

[160] Simeen Mahmud 'Actually how empowering is microcredit?' (2003) 34 *Development and Change*, 4, 585.

[161] Shoshana Pollack, 'Reconceptualising women's agency and empowerment: challenges to self-esteem discourse and women's lawbreaking' (2000) 12 *Women and Criminal Justice*, 1, 77.

[162] Colette V Browne, 'Empowerment in social work practice with older women' (1995) 40 *Social Work*, 3, 359.

[163] Rowlands, 'Empowerment examined', 77.

across five Asian countries reflects the importance of the combination of individual and community empowerment.[164] She found that individual activities that promote a sense of empowerment such as paid employment neither shift decision-making power within the household nor guarantee freedom within the community.[165] She adds that while education, health and employment may reinforce women's empowerment, they do not automatically lead to it. An inclusive approach is therefore necessary, targeting both group and individual empowerment.[166]

The work of NGOs on the macro level demonstrated in this book, such as impact litigation and partnerships with state institutions, aim to change the socio-legal and political environment in the country, whether by enforcing law or by influencing the judiciary's rulings. This work aims to shift the social power in favour of women, working towards collective forms of empowerment that are necessary for individual forms of empowerment to take place. On the other hand, the programmes directly targeting women aim to enhance the individual forms of empowerment.

2 *NGO Programmes Empowering Women*

Empowerment in Counselling and Promoted Self-Esteem

The first step in identifying the needs of GBV victims and providing personalised assistance is counselling, through which NGOs evaluate women's psychological wellbeing and self-perception. All NGOs and shelters in this project offer counselling services, either directly or through partner organisations. Through counselling, NGOs help women to unpack their realities, pushing them with probing questions such as, 'why is this happening to me? Is this what I really want? What can I do to improve my situation?' This activity helps boost women's self-confidence and promote their cognitive empowerment, as identified by Mahmud.[167] For example, Jill from NGO7 helped a client who had been trapped in the cycle of intimate violence by demonstrating the stages that the woman had gone through with drawings and charts. She aimed to push the woman to recognise her abilities and strengths, ultimately enabling her to break the cycle of violence. This is a prerequisite to empowerment; understanding the situation that the victim is in must 'come from her perspective' not the advocates or

[164] The five countries were: India, Malaysia, Pakistan, the Philippines and Thailand.
[165] Mason, 'Measuring women's empowerment', p. 94.
[166] Rowlands, 'Empowerment examined', 103.
[167] Mahmud, 'Actually how empowering', 585.

the NGO worker.[168] Ultimately, successful counselling intervention should lead to 'developing a more positive self-image and being able to make more informed and empowerment choices about life and relationships'.[169] Jill, from NGO7, has been working for decades with victims of intimate violence and has witnessed cases in which women were truly empowered. However, she lamented that she had sometimes failed to influence the decisions of women who stayed in abusive relationships.

Gender-based violence shelters organise activities and programmes aiming to empower residents. Since women who join shelters are shattered and devastated by violence, shelter programmes focus on building women's self-confidence and self-perception. This reflects Mahmud's 'cognitive empowerment', in which women recognise their value and abilities. All shelters aim to provide holistic rehabilitation programmes. However, some programmes are stricter than others. Of the four shelters in the study, those with clearly structured programmes are more successful than those with less regulated ones. This is because women in shelters suffer from a plethora of negative emotions such as apathy and aggression and therefore need strong reinforcement to commit to rehabilitation programmes. Hosting domestic violence victims, Shelter 1 follows a strict rehabilitation programme that includes intensive counselling, therapeutic activities, skills training and support to meet job requirements, such as obtaining a driving licence. Not only is the shelter fulfilling Mahmud's notion of cognitive empowerment, but also material empowerment as they promote women's financial independence. It is, however, a long-term approach, as 'commitment to change … requires a trusting and empathic therapeutic relationship that bolsters ego strengths and powers survivors through positive reinforcement of small changes as well as large ones'.[170]

Empowerment in Access to Information

This chapter has discussed how access to justice for women has been impeded because they do not understand all their legal rights. Acquiring such information is a prerequisite, not only for access to justice, but

[168] Arizona Coalition against Domestic Violence, *Best Practices Manual*, p. 15.

[169] Christiane Sanderson, *Counselling Adult Survivors of Child Sexual Abuse*, 3rd edition (London and Philadelphia: Jessica Kingsley Publishers, June 2006), p. 148.

[170] Albert R Roberts and Sondra Burman, 'National survey on empowerment strategies, crisis intervention and cognitive problem-solving therapy with battered women' in Albert R. Roberts (ed.) *Battered Women and Their Families: Intervention Strategies and Treatment Programs*, 3rd edition (New York: Springer Publishing Company, January 2007), p. 68.

also for empowerment. By offering information and practical tips on legal rights, NGOs provide women with choice. For instance, NGO3 encourages women to decide on the most favourable legal recourse, and sends paralegals to accompany them either to state courts or to traditional courts. Those initiatives reflect Kabeer's perception of empowerment: power is reflected in the ability to make a choice and, for it to be a real choice, 'there must be alternatives – the ability to have chosen differently'. In addition, this alternative 'must be seen to exist'.[171]

When women do not receive the expected services from the police, some NGOs in this research encourage women to go back, be persistent and demand their rights from law enforcement agents and court clerks. This is because putting the theoretical knowledge of legal rights into practice promotes autonomy and self-confidence, and can therefore significantly empower women.[172] This strategy is followed by NGO12; Joyce explained, 'we want to ensure that women do not shift their dependency from their male relatives onto the NGO. This is why we only interfere if access to justice is completely denied'. By acting independently, women challenge the patriarchal gender constructions that are translated into sexist attitudes of law enforcement agents. Women thus improve their bargaining power and consequently promote their relational empowerment as identified by Mahmud.[173] Law enforcement agents do not expect women to be knowledgeable about the law or stubborn about their demands; women with an empowered demeanour 'shake' the stereotype that expects them to be passive. This alters society's view of women, forcing the community to see women's increased bargaining power, fulfilling Mahmud's perceptual empowerment.[174] This also reflects Kabeer's argument that 'agency… implies not only actively exercising choice, but also doing this in ways that challenge power relations'.[175]

Networks for Empowerment

The lack of networks delays women's exit from abusive relationships.[176] After leaving the relationship, building networks is essential for women

[171] Kabeer, 'Resources, agency', 14.
[172] Sanderson, *Counselling Adult Survivors*, p. 147.
[173] Mahmud, 'Actually how empowering', 585.
[174] Ibid.
[175] Kabeer, 'Resources, agency', 14.
[176] SIDA, *Preventing and Responding to Gender-Based Violence: Expressions and Strategies*, research report (2015), p. 10.

to regain their confidence and reclaim control over their lives. These networks pose a major threat to perpetrators of violence as they increase 'the battered women's available resources'.[177] In the absence of personal networks, the relationship between women and NGOs fills this gap in women's lives. Nongovernmental organisations help women through their experiences with violence and give them a sense of protection. For instance, a staff member from Shelter 2 accompanies all new residents to collect their belongings from their houses upon entry, to show women that they have a network – a social power that was missing for a long time. Nongovernmental organisations can also stand up to perpetrators of violence. For example, Rose, in Story 11, was a resident of Shelter 3. Her husband used various tactics, including intimidation and guilt, to pressure her into revealing her location. Since Rose joined the shelter, NGO5 took over and spoke to her husband on her behalf. Marie from Story 6 explained that she used all the services provided by NGO6 including legal advice and a divorce clinic, until she had enough courage to end her relationship. Marie approached NGO6 one year before she ended her marriage. During that year, her abuse had significantly decreased. She explained: '[my husband] knew I can report to the NGO anytime he abused me so he thought twice about it'.

NGOs therefore apply Mahmud's suggested 'cognitive, perceptual and relational' empowerment approach.[178] They work to change gendered perceptions in the community, which eventually improves the perceptions of and attitude towards women; women will not, then, be perceived as minors, but rather as active agents. At the same time, NGOs work on cognitive empowerment, informing women of their rights and offering legal support if women choose to take this route. Taken together, this process will reinforce relational empowerment, in which a gender power shift should occur in women's favour.

3 *NGOs as Gatekeepers*

As reviewed in this chapter, NGOs act as intermediaries between women and the law, often offering the only gateway to formal justice. This research has shown so far that NGOs have the ability and leverage to help women access channels of justice, whether through legal representation, impact litigation or other service provision. In this

[177] Mary Ann Dutton, *Empowering and Healing the Battered Woman: A Model for Assessment and Intervention* (New York: Springer Publishing Company, 2000), p. 90.

[178] Mahmud, 'Actually how empowering'.

sense, they can open or close a gate to formal justice. In this 'intermediary' role, NGOs may possess significant power. This is determined by the role of mediators who act in different capacities. For example, an intermediary can be a 'gatekeeper', who determines 'whether clients can actively pursue benefits', and a gatekeeper has the ability to allow or block access to institutions, services and benefits.[179] Corra and Willer see gatekeeping as a 'structural power condition', giving the following example: 'A' and 'C' have a relationship that involves the exchange of services. 'A' cannot access 'C' without the consent of 'B'. In this case, 'B' has the power to control the relationship.[180] This 'consent' does not need to be official; it is often covert and customary.

Women develop an informal relationship with NGOs. While it can be a productive relationship, the outcome should be based on the consent of both parties, who also have the possibility to take the matter before a formal court.[181] Greatbatch and Dingwall assert that in some cases the 'weaker parties may be pressured into accepting less than they would have gained had they gone through the adversarial process'.[182] When CBOs and NGOs assist women in access to formal justice, they make 'a monumental difference to the fate of the cases'.[183] However, considering the impediments discussed earlier in this chapter, NGO support may often be the only available channel of relief or dispute resolution for many women, eliminating the factor of choice. In addition, as discussed in Chapter 4, the state shifts considerable load onto NGOs in GBV matters and is therefore likely to circle back cases to NGOs, which may also affect women's choice.

On another note, NGO staff members are also subjects of their culture, and therefore, they are not free from prejudgement. This is not a criticism of their intentions, but it is a reflection on the power that NGO employees possess. Nongovernmental organisations' policies may regulate staff's discretion over women's affairs; however, this is difficult

[179] Mamadi Corra and David Willer, 'The gatekeeper' (2002) 20 *Sociological Theory*, 2, 180.

[180] Ibid., 181.

[181] Laurence Boulle and Miryana Nesic, *Mediation: Principles, Process, Practice* (Chatswood: Butterworths, 2001), p. 467.

[182] David Greatbatch and Robert Dingwall, 'Argumentative talk in divorce mediation sessions' (1997) 62 *American Sociological Review*, 1, 152. Also see David Greatbatch and Robert Dingwall, 'Selective facilitation: some preliminary observations on a strategy used by divorce mediators' (1989) 23 *Law and Society Review*, 4: They identify a technique called 'selective facilitation', often used in divorce mediation in the UK, where clients are 'steered' in the direction chosen by the mediator.

[183] Lake, *Strong NGOs*, p. 189.

to control and measure, especially in CBOs, which are too informal to adopt such rules. In this way, NGOs may become gatekeepers. Dunn and Powell-Williams conducted in-depth interviews on domestic violence with advocates working in both the governmental and non-governmental fields. In their responses, respondents repeatedly explained women's behaviour as 'denial', which is 'a social construction that is particularly significant because it implicitly and sometimes explicitly presumes that there is a reality that advocates have 'access to but of which victims are unaware, thereby creating a role for the advocate whose job becomes "breaking through" '.[184] This is a common risk in any intermediary or mediator role, especially when this party is perceived to have more power and perception. Both male and female mediators may exercise gender bias based on their personal perceptions and ideologies; for instance, a sexist mediator 'may believe that behaviour that a woman experiences as sexual harassment is actually good-natured teasing'.[185]

Stories in this research resonate with this possible bias, particularly in interviews with grassroots organisations where monitoring is minimal. Arriera from NGO1 frequently made comments about women such as 'she was lying' or 'she was honest'. The following question was always, 'how did you know?' to which she replied 'I just knew'. Other interviewees, specifically those who worked directly with women as counsellors or social workers, made similar statements, such as 'I knew the relationship would have never worked' or 'the only way to end violence is to break up', among others. After recounting her story to the NGO counsellor, Rose in Story 11 was informed of the danger that she was in and the repercussions of staying in the relationship. The counsellor then asked Rose, 'what do you want to do?' Similarly, NGO5 finally told Nelly from Story 8, who had been regularly counselled for the repeated assault by her ex-partner, 'this is enough; we have a place for you in the shelter. It is up to you whether you want to tolerate the abuse or move on'. Marie from Story 6 wanted to save her marriage. She was surprised when the NGO counsellor advised her to 'move out, get a lawyer and consult a therapist'. In these cases, NGO employees clearly recommended solutions; however, none of them forced women to follow a specific route. On a general note, Jill, a social worker in

[184] Jennifer L Dunn and Melissa Powell-Williams, '"Everybody makes choices": victim advocates and the social construction of battered women's victimization and agency' (2007) 13 *Violence against Women*, 10, 989.

[185] Leigh Goodmark, 'Alternative dispute resolution and potential for gender bias' (2000) 39 *The Judges' Journal*, 21, 25.

NGO7, explained that the cycle of violence is never broken, adding that 'long term counselling for men is the only solution to end intimate abuse, but men rarely agree to go through it'. The danger in making informal decisions is that personal bias, preferences or beliefs could cripple justice.[186]

V CONCLUSION

The importance and impact of NGOs are undeniable. Assuming that the state has the political will to prosecute perpetrators of VAW, it is still unable to ensure that the law will protect women from violence because of the society factors that impede the rule of law. This is where NGOs play a key role.

This chapter has demonstrated the work of NGOs directed towards victims of GBV. Working closely with women allows NGOs to understand their lived realities, as well as their experiences with intersectional vulnerabilities. Furthermore, NGOs understand the social challenges to implementing the law, since they accompany women in their legal journeys, in both formal and informal channels of justice. This knowledge and experience allow NGOs to influence law and policy – a role that has been covered throughout this book. The chapter, therefore, reveals the roots of expertise that enable NGOs to be great advocates for women's rights in South Africa. It is also for this reason that state institutions trust NGOs with advice and support on women's affairs. Furthermore, in all interviews done for this book, NGO staff members expressed the deepest levels of concern for women and significant empathy, despite the few incidents when judgements were passed.

There may remain a few hiccups in the relationship between women and NGOs, emanating from unequal power dynamics. Ideally, women should have an array of choices to pursue their legal affairs. In reality, with the complexity of the legal system, NGOs may offer the only route to justice, significantly limiting women's choices. Nevertheless, they remain the best bet that women can take when they experience violence.

[186] For general guidelines on fair mediation and intervention, see Albie M Davis and Richard A Salem 'Dealing with power imbalances in the mediation of interpersonal disputes' (1984) *Mediation Quarterly*, 6.

CHAPTER 8

DISABLING FACTORS FOR SOCIO-LEGAL DEVELOPMENT: INSIGHTS FROM EGYPT

This chapter will move the lens towards Egypt, and the comparison with South Africa cannot be starker – one can clearly see the impact of the political environment on the ability of NGOs to work on women's legal rights.

Despite the persistently high levels of gender-based violence in South Africa, there has been undeniable progress on all fronts: putting gender matters on the public agenda, providing adequate services for women who need and choose to use them, as well as gender-sensitising laws and policies. These achievements would not have been possible without strong and fruitful partnerships between NGOs and state institutions with the understanding that they share the same goal: eliminating gender-based violence in South Africa. A constructive relationship can include road bumps, but it must be founded on the mutual understanding that women's rights are a non-negotiable priority, and that each party has essential and valuable input on the matter. This book has shown the various fronts of cooperation between NGOs and states in South Africa, demonstrating that a plural legal and social system can lead to a win-win situation.

The ability of NGOs to thrive is mostly dependent on the circumstances in which they are allowed to work – decided upon by law and policymakers.[1] Thus, the state has a responsibility to foster an amicable relationship with NGOs. States have more power to adopt

[1] Jennifer N Brass, *Allies or Adversaries: NGOs and the State in Africa* (Cambridge: Cambridge University Press 2016), p. 2.

and implement laws and policies, direct resources towards priorities and maintain an open socio-legal dialogue with the community. States that adopt a pluralist approach in general are more 'apt to create a space for NGOs'.[2] While South Africa demonstrates a great example of a pluralist approach to engaging with NGOs, this chapter will discuss the opposite example, Egypt.

The choice to exemplify Egypt stems from the deteriorating state of women's rights in the country, accompanied by a shrinking space for women's rights NGOs to work. Sexual violence laws are outdated and undeveloped, outrageous gender stereotypes dominate public dialogue, religious interpretations of ultra-conservative institutions primarily determine women's affairs, and customs and traditions take precedence over law and the Constitution. Nongovernmental organisations are the only actors willing and able to change perceptions and behaviours about gender through law and policymaking, as well as engagement in the public sphere. Yet they are strangled socially, legally and politically. Their struggle, therefore, becomes one of survival rather than one of protecting and promoting women's rights, as the following arguments will show.

The comparison between South Africa and Egypt in this matter strictly looks at the stance of a plural and liberal system towards women's rights NGOs, in contrast to a restrictive and conservative system. There are certain limitations in this comparison including the social composition, which is much more racially and ethnically diverse in South Africa than in Egypt, as well as the different forms of political transition in the recent history of both countries. The arguments will therefore centre on the relationship between NGOs and the state so as to provide insights on this comparative matter. In this regard, interviews with Egyptian NGOs will be referenced.

This chapter will start with some theoretical foundations of the relationship between state and NGOs that underpin the power struggle evident in autocratic and non-pluralist states. It will go on to provide an overview of relevant domestic laws in Egypt, in addition to a discussion of the status of women's rights in both law and society. A brief history of the women's movement in Egypt will be discussed next. To demonstrate how the socio-political environment can severely compromise the work of NGOs, the chapter will examine the lived realities of women's rights organisations including the legal, administrative,and security threats.

[2] Ibid., p. 50.

Finally, an overview of their survival strategies and coping mechanisms will be presented.

I NGOs AND THE STATE: RELATIONSHIPS DEFINED

Dynamism is a fundamental characteristic of the relationship between states and NGOs. Numerous factors affect the nurture or demise of this relationship. The two are fundamentally different kinds of institution and their disagreements (whether occasional or constant) are rooted in their conflicting foundations. In fact, NGOs are defined as 'non-state' actors, indicating an opposite spectrum to state ideology and conduct.[3] As Bratton accurately states, 'governments and NGOs are separate species of organization. Crudely stated, the organizational imperative of the State is administrative command and control, whereas NGOs seek to inculcate autonomous and participatory action'.[4] NGOs are supposed to be issue-based, neutral organisations, without submitting allegiance to any political faction. Even when they fail to deliver, they often provide a more promising outcome 'to entrenched and bureaucratic methods of doing development'.[5] Unlike states, NGOs are 'mobilisational', engaging with communities on social issues, and are more likely to provide care and attention for people who may feel marginalised by the state.[6]

A NGO–State Relationship Parameters

Coston identifies the two most extreme forms of relationship between state and NGOs: complementarity and rivalry, and then the wide spectrum of possibilities in between. These are grouped into eight different forms of relations which can develop between the two parties depending on competition, collaboration, power asymmetry and perceptions of roles.[7] While a lot of external factors affect the relationship, as a general rule, multi-party and pluralist systems are more likely to be 'hospitable to NGOs than governments which are still in the process of consolidating power in a single-party state'.[8]

[3] Kendra E Dupuy et al., 'Who survived? Ethiopia's regulatory crackdown on foreign-funded NGOs' (2015) 22 *Review of International Political* Economy, 2, 421.

[4] Michael Bratton, *The Politics of Government – NGO Relations in Africa*, Working paper no. 456 (Nairobi: Institute for Development Studies, University of Nairobi, 1987), p. 10.

[5] Ibid., p. 12.

[6] Ibid., p. 12.

[7] Jennifer M Coston, 'A model and typology of government-NGO relationships' (1998) 28 *Nonprofit and Voluntary Sector Quarterly*, 3, 358–382.

[8] Bratton, *The Politics*, p. 14.

1 Conflict and Competition

The most severe forms of state–NGOs relationship are that of repression and rivalry, in which the balance of power falls almost completely in favour of the state, fuelled by repressive laws aiming to control civil society, and consequently leading to a total absence of collaboration between the two parties.[9] This relationship is most likely to develop between NGOs in a struggling civil society and insecure states, as their governments have a fragile 'sense of political legitimacy' and therefore lack confidence in their power.[10]

Conflict emanates from the will to survive and the urge to destroy any possible threats from NGOs. Competing over funding is a common reason for states to exercise power and control over NGOs in order to weaken the competition.[11] NGOs and states can also compete over reputation and criticism,[12] for instance, spreading rumours through media outlets. Nongovernmental organisations' activities and areas of interest determine the level of resistance they are likely to receive from power-hungry states; advocacy and policymaking, for example, are red flags.[13] In Jordan, human rights NGOs, unlike other NGOs, have faced crackdowns from the government when they 'seem to threaten the regime'.[14] Grassroots organisations, however, can survive under the radar, especially when the state is fragmented and has difficulty in acquiring information about them. They are even encouraged to operate by avoiding politics and, instead, focusing on the social needs and necessities that the state is struggling to provide.[15] It is inevitable, and even necessary, for governments to design and strictly enforce regulations for NGOs' accountability. However, there is a fine line between regulation and abuse of legal requirements 'to keep tabs on organisations, particularly those suspected of subversive activity'.[16]

One notable NGO strength that is a source of worry for states is their ability to reach people, including vulnerable and remotely located

[9] Coston, 'A model', 364.

[10] Bratton, *The Politics*, p. 17.

[11] Quintan Wiktorowica, 'The political limits to nongovernmental organizations in Jordan' (2002) 30 *World Development*, 1, 81.

[12] Coston, 'A model', 365.

[13] Kamat S, 'The privatization of public interest: theorizing NGOs discourse in a neoliberal era' (2004) 11 *Review of International Political Economy*, 1, 155–176.

[14] Wiktorowica, 'The political limits', 83.

[15] Anthony J Spires, 'Contingent symbiosis and civil society in an authoritarian state: understanding the survival of China's Grassroots NGOs' (2011) 117 *American Journal of Sociology*, 1, 1.

[16] Ebrahim, 'Making sense of accountability', 816.

people, much more easily than public institutions. Working on African NGOs, Marcussen summarises the role of NGOs based on several reports by multilateral and aid agencies. This includes, 'a capacity to reach the poorest, and "outreach" to remote areas; a capacity to promote local participation and to implement projects in direct collaboration with target beneficiary groups; a capacity to operate on low costs; a capacity to be innovative, experimental, adaptive and flexible; a capacity to strengthen local institutions/organisations and to empower marginal groups'.[17] If successful, these activities may disturb the status quo for states who have a tight grip on power and states that do not keep their citizens economically 'satisfied'. These relationships are likely to worsen if the organisations provide services in territories under dispute, border areas and locations with security threats.[18]

2 *Amicability*

Coston's typology moves to the next level of amicability – a relationship in which the state and NGOs recognise the importance of their said roles and find grounds for collaboration. These relationships can take several forms including contracting, where the state 'remains an essential actor but operational activities are devolved to other organizations';[19] third-party government, in which government contracts NGOs but uses different methods and more flexibility than in contracting;[20] and finally cooperation, in which the two parties act jointly and mutually, with the state still holding significant power, although it does not intentionally use it to sabotage NGOs.[21]

This relationship is also shaped by the level of stability of confidence enjoyed by the political regime – the more stable the regime is, the more amicable the relationship will become. In despotic regimes, this relationship is more attainable for service based or welfare NGOs, especially in states with ailing economies that depend on NGOs for basic services. This was handy for the Ethiopian government when it allowed NGOs to expand their work in the 1990s as the Ethiopia-Eritrea war dramatically increased the demand for relief assistance. While still under strict government regulations, and by no means seen as 'equal'

[17] Henrik Secher Marcussen, 'NGOs, the state and civil society' (1996) 23 *Review of African Political Economy*, 69, 408.

[18] Brass, *Allies or Adversaries*, p. 48.

[19] Coston, 'A model', 368.

[20] Ibid., 369.

[21] Ibid., 370.

to the state, this period saw an exponential increase in the number of Ethiopia-based NGOs that prevailed past the crisis, 'from 70 in 1994 to 368 in 2000, and to 2275 in 2009'.[22] On a similar note, relationships of cooperation coupled with some control were mostly common after the neoliberal austerity measures 'shocked' economies into 'efficient capitalism' – a time when service delivery NGOs were integral to state survival.[23] Similarly, in a country notorious for state security control, most peacefully operating NGOs in Jordan are on the 'supply' side, focusing on services much needed by people in response to state cuts in aid.[24]

3 *Completion and Complementarity*

Coston then moves to complementarity – an ideal situation in which NGOs and the state recognise their comparative advantages and invest their resources in these areas with the full understanding that they are cooperating towards the same goals;[25] and finally, collaboration, which is a positive relationship between the two parties identifying their strengths and limitations. This relationship entails 'NGOs participation in planning, and – at minimum – consideration of NGO input in policy making'.[26] It is important to note, however, that at the core of these relationships is a realisation of both parties that they have conflicting interests, but these are used as a 'source of creative interaction', especially when neither party has dominant power over the other.[27]

After a decade working on state–NGOs relations, Brass concludes that, in favourable circumstances, NGOs can be a huge benefit to the state in developing countries. They are not necessarily threatening, and can even strengthen state legitimacy in the eyes of doubtful citizens; she adds that 'nongovernmental organizations have come to comprise part of the de facto organizational makeup of the state in many developing countries of the world… they have become part and parcel of public service administration through interpenetration with government'.[28] In

[22] Dupuy et al. 'Who survived', 425.
[23] Darin Christensen and Jeremy M. Weinstein, 'Defunding dissent: restrictions on aid to NGOs' (2013) 24 *Journal of Democracy*, 2, 80.
[24] Wiktorowica, 'The political limits', 83.
[25] Coston, 'A model', 372.
[26] Ibid., 375.
[27] Ibid.
[28] Brass, *Allies or Adversaries*, p. 39; see also Susan Pick et al., 'NGO-Government partnerships for scaling-up: sexuality education in Mexico' (2008) 18 *Development in Practice*, 2, 164–175. This article discusses an example of a successful upscaling project in Mexico in a fruitful partnership between state and NGOs.

this scenario, collaborative work on an equal power basis will yield positive outcomes, also offering new learning opportunities. Cooperation between the two parties can educate the state on some new methodologies as NGOs are by nature more experimental than state institutions. In this way, NGOs take the risk of 'testing innovative solutions' and inspiring and educating states with new methods.[29] Brass also exemplifies this relationship model with participatory development and civic education that has remarkably helped various government employees and divisions with new and creative tools to serve constituents.[30]

B NGOs, Donors and States

NGO affairs are not solely dependent on states and political circumstances; NGOs must secure other strategic partnerships with donors, civil society actors and other state and non-state stakeholders.[31] These relationships may expedite or impede operations for NGOs.

As mentioned earlier, competition over funds between NGOs and governments is a concern for states, but fear of meddling in domestic affairs is the strongest drive behind adopting a repression and rivalry approach towards NGOs, especially through imposing strict regulations, most commonly related to funding. The social and political space granted to NGOs is therefore politically determined, with minimal regard to the economic or social benefit that NGOs may generate.[32] Fear of political upheaval sets the stage for this relationship. It stems from the possibility of foreign states partnering with domestic NGOs that are able to mobilise and influence people.[33] Foreign states can meddle in domestic affairs either directly, or through funding local initiatives to implement specific agendas.

This makes donors an important player in the relationship between states and NGOs. Hearsay and covert political agendas may tempt states to restrict funding altogether. Donors, on the other hand, often require governments to work with NGOs[34] – a condition that is usually rooted in the belief in the value of NGOs, but perceived by receiving

[29] Carolyn Hsu, 'Beyond civil society: an organizational perspective on state–NGO Relations in the People's Republic of China' (2010) 6 *Journal of Civil Society*, 3, 273.

[30] Brass, *Allies or Adversaries*, p. 39.

[31] Hsu, 'Beyond civil society'; Iveta Silova, 'Contested alliances: international NGOs and authoritarian governments in the era of globalization' (2007–2008) 10 *Current Issues in Comparative Education*, 1/2, 26–31

[32] Bratton, *The Politics*, p. 17.

[33] Christensen and Weinstein, 'Defunding dissent', 81.

[34] Brass, *Allies or Adversaries*, p. 52.

states as intrusive and controlling. Some donors take it a step further by cutting funding for states or making funding conditional on loosening restrictions on NGOs. However, this strategy is not always successful and strongly dependent on the funding strategies in each country. For donors who direct funding towards implementing partners rather than the government, threatening to cut off funding ultimately means fewer resources to third parties such as local and international NGOs.

The state's bargaining power in international politics can also determine its response to conditionality imposed by donors: does the state 'fear that the potential costs of retaliation by donor countries and multilateral organizations will outweigh whatever domestic benefits it hopes to gain by restricting civil society's access to foreign resources?'.[35] Countries like Russia, Ethiopia and Egypt are strong and strategic enough to have political bargaining power, allowing them to not succumb to international donor pressure on domestic affairs.[36] In this way, it is important to highlight donors as third parties that often affect state–NGO power relations, but in some circumstances, it may not be an effective tool for state pressure.

C Shifting the Parameters of State–NGO Relationships

States-NGOs relationships can change over time, in response to external developments in the socio-political environment. A relationship between NGOs and the state may start as hostile, but can gradually develop into a series of constructive interactions that allows relationships of familiarity and trust to develop between NGO leaders and state officials, as they realise the interconnectivity of their work and mutual dependence.[37] Even strained relationships can mellow with time, through the process of 'social learning'.[38] The change in a relationship and the loosening of restrictions may also be politically driven – NGOs are summoned when needed. The Ethiopian government encouraged NGO activity after the Eritrean war when their contribution was needed. With fluctuations over the years, 'state–NGO relations again soured in the wake of Ethiopia's contested national

[35] Ibid., p. 82.

[36] Ibid.

[37] Claire Mcloughlin, 'Factors affecting state-non-governmental organization relations in service provision: key themes from the literature' (2001) 31 *Public Administration and Development*, 4, 206.

[38] Brass, *Allies or Adversaries*, p. 11.

elections'.[39] These relationships may therefore improve or deteriorate, depending on various factors.

II FOCUSING ON EGYPT: RELEVANT LAWS

The relationship between the state and NGOs in Egypt falls under the 'conflict and competition' component of the typology. In fact, along with Russia, Egypt is perhaps the most famous example of repressive NGO laws,[40] which has severely affected the work on women's rights in the country. This has been exacerbated since the revolution in 2011. At the same time, the state of women's affairs in the country is quite worrisome, both in law and in society. The current reality leaves women's rights NGOs with tied hands: they know the desperately needed legal reforms to women's rights, but they are unable to efficiently work on these issues.

The remainder of the chapter will focus on Egypt, exploring the relevant laws, history and contemporary state–NGO relations.

A Regulating Nongovernmental Organisations

Bratton identifies regulatory means with which states can control NGOs, such as monitoring the birth and operations of organisations,[41] as well as the threat of dissolution,[42] both of which are incorporated in Egyptian law regulating NGOs.

1 Law 84/2002

Nongovernmental organisations in Egypt function pursuant to law 84, passed in 2002 under President Mubarak. Initially, the law was regarded as severely restrictive; it required all groups interested in social work to register with the Ministry of Social Solidarity (MOSS – previously known as Ministry of Social Affairs). This condition was regarded as repressive as it provided state leaders with updated insights and details on NGOs, including any newly registered organisation – a common method of controlling NGOs that is often implemented by one-party regimes.[43]

[39] Dupuy et al. 'Who survived', 425.

[40] Ibid., 423.

[41] Bratton, *The Politics*, p. 20.

[42] Ibid., p. 24.

[43] Christopher Heurlin, 'Governing civil society: the political logic of NGO–state relations under dictatorship' (2010) 21 *Voluntas: International Journal of Voluntary and Nonprofit Organizations*, 2, 226.

Law 84/2002 identifies two kinds of organisation: nongovernmental organisations (NGOs) and foundations. They both adhere to the same rules and restrictions. However, foundations are treated as private entities because they deposit capital funds at the time of registration, and they have looser regulations regarding board selection and resignation. With both types of organisation, the law imposes unrealistic operational conditions. For instance, NGOs must have an office or headquarters to register, and groups are not allowed to operate from a member's home or office.[44] This requirement puts a financial burden on new NGOs, which must find the capital to secure rent and overheads before registration. This is exacerbated by the funding restrictions imposed on NGOs that will be discussed later in this section. Nongovernmental organisations, therefore, have to meet the paradox of finding money to launch the NGO and commence activities with severe restrictions on fundraising. Other than finding an office, and a means to pay for it, 'the licensing process itself is time-consuming and tedious',[45] and the success of its application is random, based on the discretion of MOSS staff, and arguably security. For instance, the law obliges NGOs to submit their registration requests to MOSS, and if they do not hear back within 60 days, their registration is confirmed and they are allowed to operate.[46] Rejection of an application is at the discretion of the state, pursuant to Article 11 of the law, which is vaguely interpreted, and is often used to ban organisations who may be politically threatening to the regime.[47]

2 *Law 70/2017*

Compared to the NGO law passed in 2017, law 84/2002 is quite lenient. In 2014, an Egyptian parliamentarian put forward a bill that triggered public outrage, domestically and internationally. The bill lingered for a few years, with occasional mentions in public debates until it was approved by parliament and ratified by the Egyptian President in May 2017. To date, the bylaws have not yet been published, which keeps law 84/2002 in effect. The 2017 law is generally problematic, but it has serious red flags that prompted the United Nations High Commissioner for Human Rights, Zaid Al-Hussein, to say that it was 'muzzling' NGOs

[44] Bylaws to law 178/2002 (Arab Republic of Egypt).

[45] Kareem Elbayar, 'NGO laws in selected Arab states' (2005) 7 *International Journal of Not-for-Profit Law*, 4, 18.

[46] Law regulating non-governmental organisations, 84/2002 (Arab Republic of Egypt) Article 6.

[47] James McGann, 'Pushback against NGOs in Egypt' (2008) 10 *International Journal of Not-for-Profit Law*, 4, 35.

when they were already operating under a severely repressive law.[48] The law was also opposed by various rights groups,[49] the National Council for Human Rights[50] and some parliamentarians.[51]

To circumvent restrictions imposed by law 84/2002, numerous human rights organisations had registered as companies, law firms or medical clinics. Consequently, they did not report to MOSS, and instead, reported to other less restrictive authorities such as the lawyers' syndicate or the Ministry of Investment. This has impeded the state's control over the operations of these organisations, especially regarding funding. Law 70/2017 gave these organisations a one-year grace period to 'rectify' their legal status and register with the MOSS so that they fall under the new law; otherwise they faced dissolution.[52]

Law 70/2017 calls for the establishment of a 'Committee' tasked with regulating all matters related to foreign entities, managing relations between domestic NGOs and foreign entities, and ruling on all funding matters for domestic NGOs.[53] Practically, the Committee will have veto power over foreign and local NGO affairs.[54] This Committee is under the auspices of the Prime Minister; its Director is appointed by the Egyptian President and its ten members are appointed by their respective institutions; these include the Ministry of Interior Affairs, the Central Bank, General Intelligence Authority, Money-Laundering Unit, Administrative Control Authority, Ministry of Justice, Ministry of International Cooperation, Ministry of Foreign Affairs, Ministry of Defence and any other ministry relevant to the project requesting funding.[55]

48 'UN human rights chief urges repeal of repressive NGO law in Egypt', UN News, 1 June 2017, accessed 30 June 2018 at https://news.un.org/en/story/2017/06/558522-un-human-rights-chief-urges-repeal-repressive-ngo-law-egypt

49 AFP, 'Rights groups denounce Egypt NGO Law' Al-Monitor, 2 June 2017, accessed 17 July 2018 at www.al-monitor.com/pulse/afp/2017/06/egypt-politics-rights-law.html

50 Hagar Hosny, 'George Ishak yotaleb bi3adet el nazar fi qanoun el gamaet el ahleyya' (George Ishaak demands the reconsideration of the NGO law), Maswawy, 3 October 2017, accessed 17 July 2018 at www.masrawy.com/news/news_egypt/details/2017/10/3/1165387/

51 'Parliamentary 25–30 bloc calls on Sisi not to ratify new "restrictive" NGO Law', Ahram Online, 1 December 2016, accessed 17 July 2018 at http://english.ahram.org.eg/NewsContent/1/0/251089/Egypt/0/-Parliamentary--bloc-calls-on-Sisi-not-to-ratify-n.aspx

52 Law regulating non-governmental organisations, 70/2017 (Arab Republic of Egypt), Article 2.

53 Ibid., Article 70.

54 Todd Ruffner, *Under Threat: Egypt's Systematic Campaign Against NGOs*, research report (POMED: Project on Middle East and Democracy, March 2015), p. 3.

55 Law 70/2017, Article 72. For instance, if the project is related to education, the Ministry of Education will be involved. If the project crosses over different ministries such as school meals, then both ministries should be involved – in this case, the health and education ministries.

The law severely restricts NGO activities; their goals and objectives should align with the 'national plan, and the state's developmental needs and priorities'.[56] It ensures that advocacy and human rights organisations are not eligible to register as they do not provide the needed developmental services. Furthermore, it prohibits NGOs from working on matters that they deem urgent, so long as these issues are not recognised as a priority by the state; this may significantly limit the work on women's rights, which has traditionally been sidelined. Furthermore, Article 14 prohibits NGOs from conducting research or opinion polls without approval. In fact, a permit from the Central Agency for Public Mobilization and Statistics is already required to conduct research in Egypt. The new law additionally obliges NGOs to seek approval from the Committee on any research twice, once before the research commences and once before the results are publicised; this is a means for the Committee to ensure that the results are 'accurate and neutral'.[57] The same Article requires Committee approval before finalising or amending any agreement with foreign organisations based in Egypt or abroad, even if the agreement does not include a financial element.

The new law empowers MOSS to shut down NGOs for a variety of reasons including violating funding regulations, failing to inform the Ministry of moving office, or cooperating with a foreign entity without the necessary approvals.[58] Finally, Article 87 of Law 70/2017 outlines the list of penalties: violating the funding guidelines, cooperating with a foreign organisation without approval, and undertaking the work of an NGO under a different legal framework leads to imprisonment from one to five years and a fine of between 50,000 to one million Egyptian Pounds (EGP).[59] Article 88 provides more lenient penalties, also including imprisonment and a fine, to NGO members and trustees who do not fully cooperate with the administrative authority, move the NGO office without informing MOSS or conduct field research without securing the necessary approvals.

Funding under Law 70/2017

The core problem with law 70/2017 lies in its restrictions on funding, which guarantee the end of NGOs in Egypt. This is the most common

[56] Law 70/2017, Article 14.
[57] Law 70/2017, Article 14.
[58] Ibid., Article 42.
[59] Equivalent to US$2,800–55,000.

strategy for states to control NGOs. Governments often 'insist on the sovereign right to act as gatekeepers between organizations within their borders and agencies from the outside world'.[60] The desire to control the flow of funds usually overrides any economic benefits that may result from these funds.[61]

Imposing strict funding regulations is recurrent in history. One research study looked at a set of 98 countries, collecting and analysing their laws regarding foreign funding. The study found that 51 countries either prohibit[62] or restrict[63] foreign funding channelled to civil society.[64] In 2005, Ethiopia's Prime Minister expelled several foreign-funded civil society groups confirming that there will be no 'Rose Revolution' in Ethiopia after the elections; four years later, his government passed a law prohibiting civil society groups involved in political activities from receiving more than 10 per cent of their funding from foreign donors.[65] Ethiopia restricts human rights and democracy work to NGOs that are based in the country and locally funded. However, all NGOs are prohibited from receiving anonymous donations and must abide by strict administrative procedures.[66] India's Foreign Contribution Regulation Act of 1976 has been used for decades to provide federal oversight of NGOs receiving foreign funds; the Act was a survival mechanism originally enacted to monitor the flow of foreign funds to NGOs during a state of emergency.[67] In Kenya, the government used the NGO Coordination Act, passed in 1996, to monitor and control the activities of NGOs. This Act was the focal point of NGO resistance in the following two years, eventually forcing the government to loosen the restrictions.[68]

Egypt's 84/2002 law allows NGOs to collect domestic funding with the approval of the administrative authority.[69] To receive foreign funds, NGOs must submit a request with detailed working plans for a project

60 Bratton, *The Politics*, p. 9.

61 Ibid.

62 Christensen and Weinstein, 'Defunding dissent', 80, defining prohibition: 'the law places a strict upper limit on the receipt of foreign funds for at least a subset of NGOs'.

63 Ibid., defining restriction: 'if the law places at least one restriction on the receipt of foreign funds' (e.g., requires prior approval or the routing of funds through a state bank or ministry).

64 Ibid.

65 Dupuy et al. 'Who survived'.

66 Ibid., 426.

67 Ebrahim, 'Making sense of accountability', 816.

68 Stephen N. Ndegwa, *The Two Faces of Civil Society: NGOs and Politics in Africa* (West Hartford, CN: Kumarian Press, 1996), 31.

69 Law 84/2002, Article 17.

and wait for 60 days to receive a reply from MOSS. Silence on the part of MOSS should mean approval of the grant.[70] The implementation of this law is a different matter, however, as will be discussed in the following section. Law 70/2017 took funding restrictions to a new level. It allows NGOs to fundraise from domestic sources, with the approval of the Committee 30 days in advance – the Article then refers to the impending bylaws for details and conditionality regarding domestic fundraising.[71] NGOs are also allowed to receive foreign funding directly to their bank accounts. They should inform the Committee once the money is deposited into their accounts, but they are prohibited from spending it before the Committee approves the project. The Committee should give an answer in 60 days from the date of the request; however, silence on the foreign funding matter automatically means a rejection.[72] The administrative authority has the right to shut down the NGO for one year, shut it down permanently or depose of the trustees with a court order if funding rules are violated.[73]

Rationale of the Law and Further Restrictions

Law 70/2017 centres on knowledge – the state seeks detailed information on NGO affairs. Bratton sees power in knowledge. Reduced and quiet NGO activity does not attract state attention, and even if it does, the government turns a blind eye. However, growth, and especially uncontrollable growth, alerts the state radar and triggers the desire to acquire 'full official knowledge.[74] In 2017, an Egyptian parliamentarian stressed the need to monitor and watch foreign funding of some NGOs, adding that law 70/2017 does not restrict NGO activity but guarantees national security.[75] In a preemptive measure to prevent NGO staff from circumventing the NGO law, in September 2014, the penal code was amended to sentence individuals receiving foreign funds with the purpose of 'disturbing general peace' to life in prison, in addition to fines of at least 500,000 EGP (28,000 USD).[76] There are no guidelines defining

[70] Ibid., Article 58.
[71] Ibid., Article 23.
[72] Ibid., Article 24.
[73] Law 70/2017, Articles 26 and 41.
[74] Bratton, *The Politics*, p. 15.
[75] Mohamed Magdy Al Sisi, 'Saad Gamal to the doubters of the NGO law: we will not leave our country to turmoil', Parlamany, 23 August 2017, accessed 18 July 2018 at www.parlmany.com/
[76] Presidential Decree No. 128 of 2014 (Arab Republic of Egypt); Amnesty International, *Circles of Hell: Domestic Public and State Violence Against Women in Egypt*, report (Amnesty International, 2015).

the 'disturbing general peace' clause and therefore the court has discretion. While the MOSS was assured by the judiciary that this law would only be used to target terrorists, NGO leaders disagree and contend that this Article has 'very effectively discouraged numerous rights NGOs from working for fear of reprisals'.[77]

While the law was met with domestic and international scrutiny, it is to no avail. The development of civil society is not a domestic interest. This is because 'the likelihood and effectiveness of international pressure hinge on the nature of the strategic relationship between the offending country and its donors'.[78] The Egyptian state is powerful enough to shut off international criticism and deflect global pressure due to its pivotal strategic security and political role in the region.

B Gender in Egypt: A Need for Socio-legal Reforms

It is not the purpose of this book to provide a critique of gender in Egyptian law and society. However, a brief review is necessary to demonstrate the dire need for reform in this area. Hope of this reform slowly withers with the deteriorating relationship between the state and NGOs in Egypt. For relevance, this section will review the main laws used to address gender-based violence, as well as some social stereotypes that maintain the unequal gender power dynamic.

1 Gender in the Constitution and Penal Code

The Egyptian Constitution puts Sharia law as the primary source of legislation.[79] This guarantees that all laws will be in line with Islam – as primarily interpreted by one of the most conservative and patriarchal institutions globally, Al-Azhar.[80] The Egyptian Constitution nevertheless includes an Article obliging the state to protect women from all forms of violence.[81]

Sexual violence is treated under the Penal Code. Article 267 defines rape as sexual intercourse with a woman without her consent, setting the sentence at aggravated imprisonment or imprisonment with hard

[77] Ruffner, *Under Threat*, p. 8.

[78] Christensen and Weinstein, 'Defunding dissent', 82.

[79] Constitution of the Republic of Egypt, 2014. Preamble. For information about women's historical role in constitutional development, see Hala Kamal, 'Inserting women's rights in the Egyptian Constitution: personal reflections' (2015) 19 *Journal for Cultural Research*, 2, 150–161.

[80] Peter Madsen, 'Rebellious women – discourses and tests: Shari'a, civil rights and penal law' in Lisbet Christoffersen and Jørgen S. Nielson (eds.), *Shari'a as Discourse: Legal Traditions and the Encounter with Europe* (London and New York: Routledge, 2016), p. 235.

[81] Constitution of the Arab Republic of Egypt, Article 11.

labour, possibly for life.[82] Articles 268 and 269 address acts of sexual assault, but refers to them as 'indecent assault'. The acts considered under this article are not specified;[83] however, in practice, they include anal rape, rape with a sharp object and any kind of forced sexual activity that does not include penetration.[84]

Sexual harassment is defined and punished under Article 306(a) and (b) of the penal code, which was lauded as a positive legal development in 2014. The definition includes actions, words, signals, insinuation or hints of a sexual nature including pornography. These actions are considered sexual harassment whether undertaken through personal, wired or wireless communications. The sentence for this crime is either at least six months imprisonment, a 3000 EGP fine, or both. The sentence is doubled for repeated offences. In 2011, when in power, the Supreme Council of Armed Forces amended these laws with the following: rape is always punished by life in prison; if the victim is vulnerable[85] or has a power relation with the offender[86], the sentence increases to death penalty; for sexual assault and harassment, the punishments have been increased under the same conditions as the rape law.[87]

Positive legislative developments are miniscule, most notably such as the adoption of the first sexual harassment law in 2014 and the amendment of the law criminalising FGM to include harsher punishment.[88] However, there is strong criticism on how the legal system treats VAW.

2 *Critiques of Gender-based Violence Laws*

The abovementioned laws are responsible for trying most gender-based violence cases. The holes in these laws are numerous. For instance, the definition of rape is quite narrow as it includes only vaginal penetration and it is gender specific. 'Indecent assault' is vaguely interpreted by the judiciary, because there is no official definition for it in the Penal Code.

82 A life sentence in the Egyptian Penal Code is treated as 25 years in prison.

83 N Marroushi, *Violence Against Women in Egypt: Prospects for Improving Police Response*, report (Saferworld, June 2015), p. 6.

84 Katie Booth and Salma El Husseiny, *Keeping Women out: Sexual Violence Against Women in the Public Sphere*, report number 630a (FIDH and others, 2014), p. 38.

85 If she is less than 18 years or was kidnapped.

86 If the offender is a blood relative, caregiver, domestic worker, or has other power over the victim.

87 Presidential Decree Promulgating Law no 11/2011 (Arab Republic of Egypt).

88 'Egypt: events of 2016', Human Rights Watch, accessed 1 June 2018 at www.hrw.org/world-report/2017/country-chapters/egypt#6e1aab

Furthermore, the term 'indecent assault' stigmatises the victim rather than the offender, and therefore discourages women from reporting the crime.[89] Nongovernmental organisations have therefore been pushing for a definition of the term 'indecent assault'.[90] In December 2017 a parliamentarian proposed an amendment to the law to consider the act of anal and oral rape legally as 'rape' rather than 'indecent assault'[91] – a welcome development, but it leaves huge possibilities of sexual violence scenarios falling out of the definition of rape.

The abovementioned provisions are not the only gender problems in Egyptian law. Personal status laws are quite sexist.[92] While these are not at the core of this book, as a brief reference, divorce law is unequivocally in favour of men, 'honour' is still accepted in courts as an excuse for a man to exercise violence against his wife to the extent of murder, and there is a gendered bias in the provisions penalising adultery.[93] Most importantly, a domestic violence law is notably missing from the Penal Code, and the crime is instead treated under general law.[94] These shortcomings are not surprising considering the lack of public dialogue and the exclusion of civil society from the process of legal developments.

3 *Gender Stereotypes and Gender-based Violence: An Expected Outcome*

Not only are gender stereotypes that maintain the status quo rampant in society, they are also echoed by government. For instance, the General appointed to combat VAW at the Ministry of Interior Affairs has urged women to not laugh or speak loudly, and to dress modestly so as to avoid sexual harassment in public spaces.[95] And the research report *Understanding Masculinity* revealed shocking information on

[89] Booth and El Husseiny, *Keeping Women out*, p. 19.

[90] Marroushi, *Violence Against Women*, p. 6.

[91] 'Parliamentarian calls for toughening penalties of anal rape', Egypt Today, 17 December 2017, accessed 1 June 2018 at www.egypttoday.com/Article/2/37218/Parliamentarian-calls-for-toughening-penalties-of-anal-rape

[92] Marwa Sharafeldin, 'Personal status law reform between Islamic and international human rights law' in Ziba Mir-Hosseini et al. (eds.), *Gender and Equality in Muslim Family Law: Justice and Ethics in the Islamic Legal Traditions* (London and New York: I B Tauris, 2013); Azza Soliman, 'Personal status law – feminist testimonies from Egypt', Mada Masr, March 14 2017, accessed 2 June 2018 at www.madamasr.com/en/2017/03/14/feature/society/personal-status-laws-feminist-testimonies-from-egypt/; Lisa Hajjar, 'Religion, state power, and domestic violence in Muslim societies: a framework for comparative analysis' (2004) 29 *Law and Social Inquiry*, 1, 1–38.

[93] Rana Allam, 'In Egypt, the Law itseld is an Enemy of Women's Rights', Informed Comment, 24 February 2015, accessed 5 June 2018 at www.juancole.com/2015/02/itself-womens-rights.html

[94] Kathryn M Yount, 'Women's "justification" of domestic violence in Egypt' (2009) 71 *Journal of Marriage and Family*, 5, 1125–1140.

[95] 'Egypt: events of 2016'.

gender expectations and stereotypes. For instance, two thirds of the male respondents believed that marriage is more important for women than a career. Even more alarming, more women than men share this view; they also support the idea of prioritising work opportunities for men if employment is scarce.[96] Emphasising the role of women to maintain the institution of marriage and the family, 'more than half of male respondents believe that women deserve to be beaten on occasion and 90 percent assert that women should accept such treatment in order to preserve family life', while only 33 per cent of women agree to that statement.[97] In a similar study done in 2008, one-third of the sample (of women 18–45) agreed that wife beating is acceptable in at least one of many situations that the survey suggested.[98] This indicates that gender stereotypes on VAW have not changed in almost a decade.

With poor legislation and rampant gender stereotypes, it is expected that rates of GBV including violence in both the public[99] and the private spheres[100] will grow faster than the current rates, which are already alarming. Endemic sexual harassment keeps women out of the public sphere, and their social acceptance and image is often tied to their conservative attire symbolised by the head cover.[101] In a 2017 survey, more than half of male respondents reported using physical violence and more than 80 per cent of men who had been married before reported using emotional abuse against their wives.[102]

This section has briefly reviewed the urgent need for reform on the social and legal fronts. Nongovernmental organisations are usually the most active actors interested in implementing such change, which takes significant time and effort. Their work is, however, severely restricted in Egypt, as this chapter aims to demonstrate.

[96] Shereen El Feki et al., *Understanding Masculinities: Results from the International Men and Gender Equality Survey*, report (UN Women and Promundo-US, 2017), p. 51.

[97] Ibid., p. 80.

[98] Hanan Mosleh et al., *Advancing Egyptian Society by Ending Violence Against Women*, policy brief (Population Reference Bureau, May 2015), p. 3.

[99] See UN Women, 'Ending violence against women: gender profile Egypt', May 2018, accessed 1 June at http://egypt.unwomen.org/en/digital-library/publications/2018/05/ending-violence-against-women-gender-profile-egypt-may-2018

[100] Ibid., p. 3.

[101] Maha Shahin and Yasmeen El-Ghazaly, 'The impact of notions of nationalism on women's rights in Egypt' (2017) 17 *Studies in Ethnicity and Nationalism*, 2, 178–179.

[102] El Feki et al., *Understanding Masculinities*, p. 80.

III WOMEN'S MOVEMENTS IN EGYPT – PAST AND PRESENT PERSPECTIVES

The challenges faced by women's rights NGOs in Egypt today are similar to some of the upheavals found in the last century. This section will move away from the law, and provide a brief overview of women's activism in recent history, particularly in relation to the state.

A History of Women's Movement in Egypt

Activists in the earlier half of the twentieth century were quite politicised. The first notable feminist movement was under the leadership of Huda Sha'arawi's Egyptian Feminist Union in 1923. It was established in close ties with the political movement of 1919 to challenge British colonial power.[103] Sha'arawi's activism had substantial influence in the region; she was followed by several feminists, such as Doria Shafiq, mostly associated with the liberal political movement.[104] However, one notable feminist who had roots in Islamic thought was Zaynab al-Ghazali.[105]

The association between the women's movement and politics continued. For instance, with the 1952 national revolution, Doria Shafik transformed her feminist organisation Bint El Nil into a political party.[106] This was also the time when the movement made significant legal gains under the leadership of Abdel Nasser. These included the right to work and a general increase in female participation in the education and economic sectors, in addition to female representation in parliament.[107] However, these gains were accomplished against the backdrop of an authoritarian regime[108] and therefore there was no space for organised feminism, just as there was no space for any other political organisation.[109]

[103] Nadine Sika and Yasmine Khodary, "One step forward, two steps back? Egyptian women within the confines of authoritarianism' (2012) 13 *Journal of International Women's Studies*, 5, 92; Mervat Hatem, 'In the shadow of the state: changing definitions of Arab women's "developmental" citizenship rights' (2005) 1 *Journal of Middle East Women's Studies*, 3, 20–45.

[104] Nawla Darwiche, 'Women in Arab NGOs: a publication of the Arab network for non-governmental organisations' (2001) 69 *Feminist Review*, 16.

[105] Sika and Khodary, 'One step forward', 92.

[106] Nadje Al-Ali, *Secularism, Gender and the State in the Middle East: The Egypt Women's Movement* (Cambridge: Cambridge University Press, 2004), pp. 64–65.

[107] Hatem, 'In the shadow', 25.

[108] Sika and Khodary, 'One step forward', 92.

[109] Al-Ali, *Securalism, Gender*, pp. 69–70.

The following era, starting in 1970 under the leadership of Al-Sadat, moved the women's rights movement under the sponsorship of the regime in a 'state-centric approach',[110] another approach to tying gender to politics. Al-Sadat's wife supported most of the legal gains; the involvement of the ruling family in the gender movement was paralleled by a decrease in the number of independent women's rights advocates, and since then women's rights have become a state business used to garner international support.[111] At this point, there was a notable absence of women's 'independent representative organizations' and instead, they depended on the regime, which 'lacked an overall programme to ensure women's rights and did not encourage independent feminist activism'.[112] This decade also saw the peak of one of the most influential feminists in Egypt's history, Al Saadawi, who led one of the most organised yet radical feminist organisation: the Arab Women Solidarity Association. It was banned in 1990,[113] but Al Saadawi remains one of the most prominent feminists in Egyptian history.

The practice of involving the first lady in gender politics continued throughout Mubarak's era. At that point, Egypt sought international approval linked with aid, and therefore it carefully considered its global image. As a result, the state passed a significant number of laws promoting women's rights, perhaps the fastest boost in Egyptian history. Some of these gains included the right to divorce in court, the right to pass nationality on to a woman's children from a non-Egyptian man, repealing the required husband approval prior to a woman's travel, and custody laws were amended in favour of women.[114] Mubarak's era also saw the birth of the National Council for Women (NCW), created by a Presidential decree in 2010. The Council was set up to follow the direction of the presidency, operating nationwide but sitting in Cairo. It was tasked with clear duties including policy recommendations, setting up national plans, arranging trainings, conferences and public events on pressing women's issues, monitoring and evaluating policies pertaining to women, representing Egyptian women before relevant international

[110] Sika and Khodary, 'One step forward', 93.

[111] Al-Ali, *Securalism, Gender*, pp. 72–74.

[112] Ibid.

[113] Ibid., p. 79.

[114] Aliaa Dawoud, 'Why women are losing rights in the post-revolutionary Egypt' (2012) 13 *Journal of International Women's Studies*, 5, 160–169; B K Rutherford, *Egypt after Mubarak: Liberalism, Islam, and Democracy in the Arab World* (Princeton University Press, 2008).

bodies, producing relevant publications, and responding to any other request made by the presidency.[115]

This period saw fragmentation and conflict between women's activists, rooted in political differences that had persisted since Sadat's reforms to personal status laws. This conflict surfaced when leftist feminists who were originally against Sadat's open-door policy and allegiance with Israel, sided with the opposition, including Islamists and Al Azhar – two of the most conservative parties in Egypt.[116] Other disagreements, rooted in the different social and educational backgrounds of activists, ensued. Al-Ali recounts some problems between the founders of The New Women Foundation based on preferences on the organisation's direction and priorities,[117] pointing to the elite background to which most of the leaders of the movement belonged. Such conflicts emanate from the three vastly different foundations that feed the thought on women's rights: Islamic and cultural traditions; Western liberal ideologies; and national law and policy.[118] Because of these differences, 'women's organizations never developed into a full-fledged feminist movement'.[119]

B Contemporary History of Egypt's Women's Movement

1 *Formalising the Women's Movement in Egypt*

In the 1990s, the Egyptian women's movement started to find its footing in civil society. The 'NGOisation' of the women's movement, 'the spread of a different form of structure for women's activism, one which limits the participation of women at the local level to "their" organization',[120] took place in the whole region. Nongovernmental organisations in Egypt were generally becoming popular platforms for social and developmental reform. Their numbers reached 15,000 in the 1990s[121] and exploded during the Mubarak era, with some differences in reported numbers of registered NGOs. According to one estimate, NGOs had reached 30,000 at the time of Mubarak's ousting in 2011,[122]

[115] Presidential Decree 90 of 2000 (Arab Republic of Egypt), Article 3.

[116] Al-Ali, *Securalism, Gender*, p. 76.

[117] Ibid., p. 189.

[118] Nagwa Meghahed and Stephen Lack, 'Colonial legacy, women's rights and gender-educational inequality in the Arab World with particular reference to Egypt and Tunisia' (2011) 57 *International Review of Education*, 3/4, 397–418

[119] Sika and Khodary, 'One step forward', 94.

[120] Islah Jad, 'The 'NGOization' of the Arab women's movements' (2003) 11 *Al-Raida*, 44.

[121] Hatem, 'In the shadow', 30.

[122] Catherine E Herrold, 'NGO policy in pre- and post-Mubarak Egypt: effects on NGOs' roles in democracy promotion' (2016) 7 *Nonprofit Policy Forum*, 2, 195.

and 36,724 by 2012.[123] This trend, in addition to international influence on NGO structure, was behind the move to formalise women's rights by setting up NGOs.[124] This made it possible for women to have a career in the field of women's rights and activism[125] without linking it to other political and charitable activities.

Despite the exponential growth of NGOs during Mubarak's era, this was the time when the state started using the law to interfere in civil society operations. Granted, female activists have had to struggle with all regimes, but the 1990s and 2000s saw the formal changes in the legal system that would guarantee long-term control of NGOs.[126] Nongovernmental organisations were allowed to operate under the supervision of the Ministry of Social Affairs, as discussed in the previous section, and this enabled the state to maintain the needed level of control.[127]

2 *The Women's Movement and the 2011 Revolution*

The last few years, particularly since the 2011 revolution, have seen a surge in youth activism, peaking right after the revolution. Some of these groups started as informal initiatives and eventually died down, but others have formalised and sought fruitful partnerships, even with the state. A few have even reached out to the Supreme Council of Armed Forces to form coalitions to advance human rights at this important time in history.[128] The political events right after the 2011 revolution rapidly developed, with many hopes and dreams hanging on the final political scene to be set by elections.

The regime that followed was dominated by the Muslim Brotherhood who held the majority of parliament seats, as well as the presidency. This time was not promising for women's rights activists.

> Despite the economic and political turmoil in Egypt, the first post-Mubarak elected parliament deemed it more urgent to curb women's rights, seeking to annul the meagre legal and political gains they had

[123] Ayman Abdel Wahab, 'Al Gamaet Al Ahleyya fi Masr: ikhtilalat el dor' (NGOs in Egypt: role disorder) Al Ahram Center for Political and Strategic Studies, 30 May 2017, accessed 25 June 2018 at http://acpss.ahram.org.eg/News/16307.aspx

[124] Naima Sakr, 'Seen and starting to be heard: women and the Arab media in a decade of change' (2002) 69 *Social Research*, 3, 827

[125] Al-Ali, *Securalism*, *Gender*, p. 81.

[126] Hamdy A Hassan, 'Civil society in Egypt under the Mubarak regime' (2011) 2 *Afro Asian Journal of Social Sciences*, 2.2; Sakr, 'Seen and starting to be heard'.

[127] Al-Ali, *Securalism*, *Gender*, p. 80.

[128] Herrold, 'NGO policy', 202.

made during Mubarak's era. Parliamentarians discussed regressive legal amendments suggesting the repeal of unilateral divorce, the restriction on women's movements, and the legalization of female genital mutilation.[129]

3 *Current Status and Forms of NGOs*

Women's organisations have prevailed, and continue to operate in one of the toughest periods in Egyptian history. With a quick scan of organisations in Egypt, one will find that NGOs are formed in various sizes and adopt different ideologies. The older generation of feminists and women's rights organisations who made it through the previous few decades include The Association for the Development and Enhancement of Women (ADEW), the New Women Foundation and the Women and Memory Forum. They provide some developmental services like the micro-credit programme run by ADEW; they also conduct research and advocacy, and offer legal support and other services. Some organisations have incorporated feminist work within their broader agendas such as the Nadeem Centre for Rehabilitation of Victims of Violence. The centre primarily works on all kinds of violence and torture, but also addresses severe sexual violence cases, including gang rape and political VAW.

Newer organisations are too many to mention, but one can draw some trends from their missions and focus. Some service-based organisations work on various issues ranging from economic empowerment programmes to free legal representation. Others are charities and often serve the general population but may run special assistance programmes for female heads of households and may offer development services to women such as training. However, many of the newer and more visible organisations are rights-based and are focused on research and advocacy, sometimes also offering some legal and psychological support for victims/survivors of violence. One example is Nazra for Feminist Studies, which was active on all fronts until the recent legal impediments to be discussed in the next section. Some organisations have a special unit for women under the wider umbrella of human rights such as the Egyptian Initiative for Personal Rights. These rights-based organisations adopt varying levels of confrontational strategies with the

[129] Reem Mohamed, 'Women and the Arab Spring: tough choices to make', Open Democracy, 25 October 2013, accessed 25 June 2018 at www.opendemocracy.net/arab-awakening/reem-mohamed/women-and-arab-spring-tough-choices-to-make; also see Rutherford, *Egypt after Mubarak*.

state; some have always been critical of state conduct and others have sought partnerships with different arms of the state. The only other important group to mention is Islamists – feminists/women's rights activists who seek to find gender equality and justice in the Islamic discourse. Karam divides these into two main sub-groups: those who criticise the need to see men and women as equal because this would ignore the biological difference and therefore be disadvantageous to women; and those who 'try to steer a middle course between interpretations of socio-political and cultural realities according to Islam and a human rights discourse'.[130]

There is limited NGO work done on impact litigation, primarily focused on human rights. Human Rights Legal Aid, set up in 1994, was the most 'aggressive' of these groups, joined by the Centre for Women's Legal Aid in 1995 and the Land Centre for Human Rights in 1996, and others.[131] This strategy was becoming more popular by 1997 because it offered easier legal gains when the alternative was mobilising the public under Mubarak's regime.[132] However, this is not a well-researched area, and court proceedings are not publicly available for research.

C Reflections on Sidelining the Women's Movement

Following a global trend in history, the Egyptian women's movement has had to endure unforgiving attacks and backlashes as it found its footing in Egyptian civil society. Women's issues are always expected to take a backseat to national liberation and national security, and activists have to constantly respond to accusations of selfishness and treason[133] – perhaps the motivation for earlier feminists to engage in politics was to 'sell' women's agendas. Both the regime and national liberation movements throughout the history of Egypt have used women's issues to serve their own agendas.[134] For instance, Al Ali quotes Al Saadawi's daughter recounting the reasons for the closure of her organisation in 1991, 'we were accused of separating men and women; of not focusing

[130] Azza Karam, *Women, Islamisms and the State: Contemporary Feminisms in Egypt* (London: Palgrave MacMillan, 1998). p. 10.

[131] Tamer Moustafa, 'Law versus the state: the judicialization of politics in Egypt' (2003) 28 *Law and Society Inquiry*, 4, 898.

[132] Ibid., 894.

[133] Darwiche, 'Women in Arab NGOs'; Lina Suneri, 'Moving beyond the feminism versus nationalism dichotomy' (2000) 20 *Canadian Women's Studies*, 2, 143–148; Sahar Khamis, 'The Arab "feminist" spring?' (2011) 37 *Feminist Studies*, 3, 692–695, Reem Wael, 'Betrayal or realistic expectations? Egyptian women revolting' (2014) 6 *Interface*, 1, 478–491.

[134] See Shahin and El-Ghazaly, 'The impact of notions', 180.

on the national issue and class aspect … and being influenced by the west. We were called Islamists. We were accused of obscenity, immorality and westernization'[135] – similar to the contemporary narratives to be discussed in the following section.

IV UNPACKING 'REPRESSION AND RIVALRY' BETWEEN THE STATE AND NGOs IN EGYPT

This section will zoom in on the current relationships between NGOs and the state in Egypt. There is some limited literature on this topic, and therefore, interviews with four staff members in different rights-based organisations in Egypt will give deeper insights into their lived realities.

A State Perception of NGOs

The restrictive laws imposed on NGO activities are indicative of the state's perception of NGOs. The state does not see NGOs as equal partners in social, political and economic development, but rather a 'helping hand' to respond to the economic demands of the public that the state is unable to provide. In fact, in reference to the aforementioned NGO law 70/2017, one parliamentarian (who is also the Chairman of the Committee on Arab Affairs in parliament) explained that the law in fact welcomed the work of NGOs – but only those that provide services to fill the gaps that the state treasury cannot afford.[136]

This position does not only limit the role of NGOs to service provision, but it even limits the services on which NGOs can work. Nejima calls this the 'infrastructural dimension' in which the state determines its ability to supply specific resources, and this 'determines the areas of activities available to NGOs'.[137] For Egypt, these areas are mainly healthcare provision, food assistance, and to a lesser extent, other financial support such as microcredit. Nongovernmental organisations running these programmes have huge fundraising campaigns and seem unbothered with the new NGO law; in fact, they were invited by

[135] Al-Ali, *Securalism, Gender*, p. 79.

[136] Al Sisi, 'Saad Gamal'.

[137] Susumu Nejima, 'Pakistan: regulations and potentiality in a fragmented society' in Shinichi Shigetomi (ed.), *The State and NGOs: Perspective from Asia* (Singapore: ISEAS–Yusof Ishak Institute, 2002), p. 9.

parliament to discuss it.[138] They also have great relationships with the state. The NGO giants include Hospital 57357[139] treating childhood cancer; several other cancer hospitals for adults; Dar El Orman for community development;[140] Ahl Masr Hospital specialised in treating burn victims;[141] and the Misr El Kheir foundation running various charity and development programmes.[142]

There are other NGOs that provide services, but they are the 'wrong' kind of services. Three of the NGOs interviewed for this book provide free legal services to women, as well as psychological support to victims of violence. They all face closure and have dramatically reduced their services because of the legal and political hurdles discussed in this chapter. While the services provided by these NGOs are not available in public institutions, they are still not a priority because they do not fall within the gaps identified by the state treasury. Ingy, an NGO staff member who was interviewed for this research, recounts her conversation with a MOSS employee following the rejection of a grant that she had applied for. Her NGO wanted to use the grant to offer free legal services to women for family law matters, while the ministry employee hinted that they should direct it towards charity, such as 'distributing blankets to the poor in the winter'. This is echoed by another NGO founder, Azza Kamel, in an interview. She described the stance of the state as: 'they want civil society to be reduced to Ramadan bags, charity, and the cycle of begging'.[143]

The state therefore limits the role of NGOs to what it sees necessary; while law 84/2002 'vaguely' banned political activities, law 70/2017 more specifically limits NGOs to 'social care, development, and awareness raising of communities'.[144] This preference extends across the NGO spectrum. For instance, feminist organisations who criticise law and policy related to women 'have also been on the list of security targets' while women's organisations who focus on charity and harmless activities such as offering literacy classes are not targeted.[145]

[138] Lina Attalah, 'While a bad year for civil society, all vow to find ways to continue', Mada Masr, 26 December 2016, accessed 17 July 2018 at www.madamasr.com/en/2016/12/26/feature/politics/while-a-bad-year-for-civil-society-all-vow-to-find-ways-to-continue/

[139] www.57357.com/

[140] www.dar-alorman.com/

[141] www.ahl-masr.org

[142] www.misrelkheir.org/en/

[143] Attalah, 'While a bad year'.

[144] Herrold, 'NGO policy', 206.

[145] Mariz Tadros, 'The securitisation of civil society: a case study of NGOs–state security investigations (SSI) relations in Egypt' (2011) 11 *Conflict, Security & Development*, 1, 89.

It is important to note, however, that all NGOs must follow law 70/2017 with the same legal and administrative hurdles, and therefore 'not targeted' merely means that they are not likely to face additional security threats such as imprisonment, travel bans or asset freezes. Strict regulations under the law are usually waived for the aforementioned giant NGOs, as will be discussed later.

B Perceptions of NGOS' Relationship with the State

Interviews for this book and the limited available literature show that NGOs do not see themselves as state rivals or competitors. On the contrary, a certain amount of collaboration is desired. Herrold conducted some interviews with NGO leaders and staff to convey their perspective:

> The important role of NGOs is providing a model… we can't substitute the government but we can be creative and provide a catalog and technical expertise to the government. We can serve as consultants between civil society and the government. Civil society provides ideas and technicians. We can also mobilize local communities and link the grassroots and the government. We can help the governing authorities come down to the ground. We should build bridges, create ideas and models, provide links, and catalyze.[146]

Interviews conducted for this research revealed similar sentiments. Ingy reiterates the strength of 'working on the ground' and explains that this position enables organisations like her NGO to understand the lived realities of women and girls, and consequently, to give accurate and relevant insights on laws and policies. She cites a few legal reforms on women's rights that have been under parliament review in the last four years. She viewed these as problematic, but civil society was not part of the said dialogue. She concludes 'we always welcome any social discussion that we are invited to'. Invitations, however, are rarely received.

Arwa, also interviewed for this research, is a lawyer like Ingy and runs an NGO that provides legal services to women. Her NGO has put forward various bills before parliament throughout the years, usually followed by a summons to discuss the suggestions. It still happens occasionally with the current government; however, the summons informally asks for specific people to not attend as they are politically controversial 'activists'. Ingy's organisation has only been summoned once to parliament, also to discuss a bill they had suggested in 2013. They put forward other bills in the following years, but never received

[146] Confidential Interview on 2 April 2012, as quoted in Herrold, 'NGO policy', 202.

an invitation to discuss. All NGOs interviewed for this book work on women's rights, but their experiences are likely to be similar to those of other human rights organisations. State conduct may be different towards other NGOs that are charity or development based.

This resonates with the importance of the role of NGOs as liaisons between the state and the community that has been discussed throughout this book. The strength of NGOs is their closeness to local communities, which gives them a unique perspective of women's lived realities. The South African state, as this book has shown, realises this strategic position, as evident in the numerous partnerships and fruitful collaborations between NGOs and state institutions.

C Replacing NGOs with State-sponsored Institutions

Conflict and competition are likely to prompt the state to exclude and shun NGOs from the public scene[147] and find a replacement. The Palestinian National Authorities for instance set up a network of NGOs deemed loyal to the state so as to secure the development funds coming to the Palestinian Territories, totalling 15 million USD from the World Bank. This was in addition to a set of legal and administrative hurdles placed on unfavourable NGOs.[148] Another possible form of exclusion by the state is 'to supplant the work of existing NGOs with state institutions'.[149] Bratton refers to this practice as co-optation and exemplifies it with the National Councils of Social Service that exist in Kenya, Uganda and Zambia,[150] while Wiktorwica calls it 'state feminist apparatus'.[151]

Most interview respondents in Egypt mentioned the National Council for Women (NCW) as taking this role. Its work overlaps with a lot of NGOs, but because it was an extension to the state (it was set up by the former president and reports to the Presidency), it is more visible. The public often groups all 'women's organisations' together, and therefore may not be able to differentiate between the NCW and NGOs. Fatma, interviewed for this research, worked in an NGO providing psychological support to victims of violence. She recounts an incident in which her NGO supported women subjected to gang violence. They accompanied the women until they received medical help, and the NCW was

[147] Heurlin, 'Governing civil society', 223.
[148] Wiktorowica, 'The political limits', 81.
[149] Heurlin, 'Governing civil society', 223
[150] Bratton, *The Politics*, p. 23.
[151] Wiktorowica, 'The political limits', 81.

following up by phone. When the said women went on television afterwards to tell their stories, they gave all the credit to the NCW.

There is consensus among interviewees that the work on women's rights is being centralised through the NCW, especially with the legal impediments facing NGOs. Abdel Rahim and Fracolli question whether the NCW can and will replace women's rights organisations in Egypt, and they also look at how the Council reshapes the women's agenda to align with the state's interests. This has been observed since 2013 as the Council has repeatedly spoken against terrorism – a national security issue which is not directly related to women, raising 'questions regarding state influence on the council's agenda'.[152] The politicising of the NCW has been observed through its statements, media interviews and campaigns.[153] Even more alarming is the perpetuation of gender stereotypes through this dialogue, which diverts attention away from the violence that women face, and towards their roles in preventing terrorism as wives and mothers. For instance, in September 2017, the NCW held several press conferences across the country to announce that Egyptian women stand against terrorism, stressing the role of women in fighting terrorism as peacemakers and as mothers of future generations, being the main source of internal stability in society.[154] In aligning with national security concerns, this position promotes the stereotype that 'as mothers and wives', women are responsible for their family's wellbeing, their children's behaviour and that women bear the burden of social stability. While the NCW addresses important issues occasionally, such as sexual harassment, it is selective in its choice and approach, with a general exclusion of women's NGOs. For instance, there was minimal involvement by civil society on a number of laws brought forward to parliament by NCW.[155] When NGOs were invited, it was purely for show.[156]

[152] Sara Abdel Rahim and Erin Fracolli, 'Egypt's National Council for Women: a substitute for civil society?' The Tahrir Institute for Middle East Policy, 15 July 2016, accessed 26 May 2018 at www.timep.org/commentary/egypts-national-council-for-women-a-substitute-for-civil-society/

[153] See Arwa Ibrahim, 'Head of Egyptia's council for women slams detained female activists', Middle East Eye, 17 November 2014, accessed 17 July 2018 at www.middleeasteye.net/news/head-egypt-council-women-slams-detained-girls-1879918577; also see Manar Mohsen, 'No reconciliation with terrorists', Daily News Egypt, 21 August 2013, accessed 17 July 2018 at https://dailynewsegypt.com/2013/08/21/no-reconciliation-with-terrorists-ncw/

[154] Nagwa Derdeery, 'Al mar'a saneat al salam' (The woman is a Peacemaker), Al Ahram, 18 September 2017, accessed 20 June 2018 at http://gate.ahram.org.eg/News/1584718.aspx

[155] Abdel Rahim and Fracolli, 'Egypt's National Council'.

[156] Dalia Abd El-Hamid, 'The National Council for Women: state feminism seeking to contain revolutionary feminism', Egyptian Initiative for Personal Rights, 2 October 2013, accessed

D Administrative, Legal and Security Hurdles Facing NGOs in Egypt

Legal and administrative hurdles threatening the survival of NGOs in Egypt have reinforced the exclusion strategy; consequently, some NGOs have closed down and others are struggling to stay afloat after adopting some coping mechanisms.

1 *Fluid Application of the Law*

Stability, clarity and transparency are success-enabling factors. Vagueness, uncertainty and secrecy foster an environment of fear and distrust. Applying this to a regulatory and legal environment,[157] one can conclude that favourable environments for NGOs to grow must offer an easy and straightforward registration process, clear reporting requirements and incentives (rather than force) to work on state priority areas.[158] For instance, NGOs in Pakistan have the option to register. They *choose* to register because it is beneficial to them; in addition to gaining credibility with donors, registration gives them rights to land acquisitions as well as tax exemptions.[159] This is not the case in Egypt.

The random implementation of repressive laws is even more unsettling, where the 'law will ultimately be used against those the authorities want to target'.[160] This randomness gives significant power to the implementers of the law. In Egypt's case, law 84/2002 is currently enforced until the bylaws for law 70/2017 are released. MOSS are the implementers of law 84/2002, which is in fact 'not so much restrictive as it is discretionary'.[161] This discretion is the root of the problem, and it is the source of fear for one interviewed staff member of an NGO working on VAW, Ayman. He states, 'it is the uncertainty that scares me the most. What if we are doing something wrong and we do not know? I ask ten different lawyers and MOSS staff before I take a step, and usually I get different answers'.

This uncertainty starts from the registration phase and continues throughout operations. For registration, both NGO laws (84/2002 and

26 May 2018 at www.eipr.org/en/blog/dalia-abd-el-hameed/2013/10/national-council-women-state-feminism-seeking-contain-revolutionary

[157] McLoughlin, 'Factors affecting'.

[158] Batley, 'Engaged or divorced?'

[159] Nejima, 'Pakistan: regulations', p. 102.

[160] Attalah, 'While a bad year for civil society'.

[161] Elbayar, 'NGO laws', 8.

70/2017) require NGOs to 'inform' the ministry of registering and wait 60 days for a response. Silence 60 days after the application date is an automatic approval. In practice, the process is tedious, time consuming and a 60-day wait does not guarantee registration. Applicants may not hear back for many months and they are usually not given a 'proof of application' so as to track their papers and prove that they have waited for 60 days.[162] The ministry can also reject applications without reason under the provision of 'violating public order', which is also applied randomly.[163] Even after a successful registration, a long complicated administrative journey awaits NGOs only to consume their valuable resources.[164] The law is therefore not in line with NGOs' needs and lived realities. This is unsurprising considering the absence of consultation with affected stakeholders while drafting the law[165] – only a few NGOs that are 'friends of the state' were consulted.[166]

Another matter of confusion causing delays and hesitation is having two laws in effect. One year after the President's ratification of the 70/2017 law, the bylaws have not yet been published. This means that the 84/2002 law is still applied, but technically this should not be the case. Both NGOs and MOSS staff are in limbo; none of the NGOs interviewed had received any funding approvals in the last three years since the conversation about the law started in 2014/2015. All participants interviewed assumed that MOSS staff are also scared and confused so they prefer the status quo. In fact, instilling fear among state employees is a commonly used tactic globally to curb NGO activities. Employees are generally easier to control than NGO staff members, and are more likely to be scared and risk averse.[167] They have nothing to lose by impeding NGO businesses, but they have a lot to lose by going against the state. It is therefore fairly common for one-party states to put decisions at the discretion of state employees.[168] Ingy recounts some

[162] Ruffner, *Under Threat*, p. 5.

[163] Elbayar, 'NGO laws', 9.

[164] McGann, 'Pushback', 36; Rutherford, *Egypt After Mubarak*, p. 94; Hassan, 'Civil society in Egypt'.

[165] Kristina Kausch, *Defenders in Retreat: Freedom of Association and Civil Society in Egypt*, working paper (Madrid: Fride, April 2009), p. 15; Mohamed Agati, 'Undermining standards of good governance: Egypt's NGO law and its impact on the transparency and accountability of CSOs' (2006–2007) 9 *International Journal of Nonprofit Law*, 2, 56–85.

[166] Attalah, 'While a bad year for civil society'.

[167] Heurlin, 'Governing civil society', 226.

[168] Yayoi Tanaka, 'Singapore: subtle NGO control by a developmentalist welfare sate' in Shinichi Shigetomi (ed.), *The State and NGOs: Perspectives from Asia* (Singapore: Institute of South Asian Studies, 2002), p. 209.

project rejections that her NGO received from the MOSS; the reasons for rejection were unclear so she sought a connection with an upper level authority in the MOSS to appeal the decision. They went back and forth with the ministry employees in what she called 'a power game' and up until the time of the interview, their issue was not resolved. Arwa similarly explains that MOSS staff follow the same 'discretionary' rule, finding comfort in keeping information fluid and unconfirmed. She had previously received verbal approvals from MOSS staff, which they refused to support with written confirmation.

The fear embedded in uncertainty is a push factor for people working in the NGO sector. One of Herrold's research participants states, 'I can't imagine anyone who would want to set up an NGO'.[169]

2 Funding Uncertainties and Randomness

The fastest way to end rights-based NGOs is banning their funding – they will simply not be able to survive. Funding regulations under both laws 84/2002 and 70/2017 have been previously discussed. Not only have these laws put severe restrictions on funding, their fluid implementation creates additional impediments. For instance, the 2002 law allows NGOs to raise funds domestically from 'anyone';[170] however, in practice, NGOs are only allowed to accept donations from known and identified individuals. Anonymous donations require an additional permit to be considered by the MOSS within 15 days of the application date.[171] Permission is rarely granted to NGOs, except to huge charitable organisations, and well-connected ones. 'We applied for the permit to collect donations about two years ago and never received a reply, whether positive or negative. We do not understand why', stated Ayman. Prohibiting anonymous donations means that NGOs are not allowed to fundraise online, through media or at public events.

Both laws give the state 60 days to review requests for foreign funding submitted by NGOs – silence under law 84/2002 means approval, but silence under law 70/2017 means rejection. In practice, NGOs almost never get a reply after 60 days, and they do not expect to.[172] Usually MOSS does not give a reason for rejection even for apolitical and non-controversial projects.[173] Sometimes it does not even give a rejection,

[169] Herrold, 'NGO policy', 206.
[170] Law 84/2002, Article 18.
[171] Bylaws to law 178/2002, Article 57, Egypt.
[172] McGann, 'Pushback', 37.
[173] Herrold, 'NGO policy', 268.

but keeps the request lingering forever, explained Fatma. The only action an NGO can take in this case is going to court; however, court impartiality is questionable and therefore most NGOs do not choose this option.[174] Arwa, for the first time in decades, has received four rejections for funding since 2014, all citing 'security concerns' with no further details. Since then, her NGO has not had any grants approved.

But can such laws be beneficial? The same funding laws apply to all NGOs, even the giants that help the government deliver necessary services. In this case, randomness in legal application can be positive, where specific NGOs are granted shortcuts and exceptions. Some of the most well-known service provision NGOs were invited to meet with parliamentary members and 'it was reportedly explained that the new legislation will not target them, but other threatening groups, particularly those receiving foreign funding'.[175] This is similar to China's case, where the government had placed strong regulations on NGOs' fundraising with private donations. These were commonly 'loosened or waived' for NGOs favourable to the government, whether based on their activities or their influential connections.[176]

3 *Security Forces 'Informally' Reaching out to NGOs*

One reason for the random silence of MOSS staff regarding registration and funding applications from NGOs is their powerlessness. Registration papers are delivered to various security divisions requiring the approval from all of them,[177] which takes matters out of the control of MOSS staff. Ayman recalls that when they registered their NGO, their lawyer mentioned five different security divisions to which their papers were sent. It is impossible to confirm this information as there are no guidelines to such procedures; even communication between MOSS staff and security occurs over the phone and is not documented.[178] In fact, beyond the 60-day registration waiting period, the law is silent on the procedure and applicants only deal with MOSS.

After registration, state security keeps a close eye on NGO activities – the most dangerous kind of power. Nongovernmental organisation boards and staff may be kept in the dark on legal and security

[174] Ibid. 196.
[175] Attalah, 'While a bad year'.
[176] Hsu, 'Beyond civil society', 268.
[177] Agati, 'Undermining standards'.
[178] Tadros, 'The securitisation', 87.

issues concerning them.[179] However, they are sometimes summoned by security intelligence to conduct informal interviews regarding funding applications.[180] This has increased in the last decade as state security is in direct contact with NGOs, asking informal questions, making threats and even prohibiting some meetings from happening in public places, like hotels.[181] They also send out 'signals and cues to actors and their organisations about what they see as inappropriate or unacceptable behaviour'.[182] Eventually, NGO staff members developed the sense to understand covert procedures[183] and read between the lines to know where they stand.

While the involvement of security was a customary practice under law 84/2002, law 70/2017 formalises its role in managing NGO affairs,[184] as previously discussed.

E Politicising the Law against NGOs

Randomness in applying the law essentially makes the law threatening. Even if these laws are merely disciplinary tools and are not commonly implemented, they still serve as a scarecrow for NGOs. For instance, the law in Jordan allows the state to monitor and control NGOs with the possible threat of closure. In this way, it keeps NGOs at bay through 'self-censorship'.[185] Similarly, in Egypt, the discretionary law of 84/2002 is only applied to NGOs when they are considered a threat to the state, whereas most NGOs in Egypt are apolitical, focusing on noncontroversial developmental issues and therefore are usually allowed to operate.[186]

The NGO law is not the only legal tool used against NGOs. Since 2011, legal action has been used in an unprecedented manner to curb their activities. It started with a trial in 2011 when the Ministry of Justice established a fact-finding committee to investigate NGOs receiving foreign funding in Egypt. Details of the committee were published in a newspaper soon afterwards, listing 39 organisations operating without licence and 28 NGOs receiving illegal foreign funds.[187]

[179] Ibid., 88.
[180] Ruffner, *Under Threat*, p. 7.
[181] Kausch, *Defenders in Retreat*, p. 12.
[182] Tadros, 'The securitisation', 87.
[183] Ibid. 91.
[184] Hassan, 'Civil society in Egypt'.
[185] Wiktorowica, 'The political limits', 84.
[186] Elbayar, 'NGO laws', 8.
[187] 'UN human rights chief'; Herrold, 'NGO policy', 203.

Following this, the offices of some organisations were raided,[188] and this was the beginning of the ongoing legal war against civil society in Egypt.[189] While activists have always been targeted by the state, this is an exceptional level of utilising the law for political pressure. The case has been ongoing since 2011, prevailing through three different regimes – starting with the Supreme Council of the Armed Forces, sentences were passed during the rule of the Muslim Brotherhood and implemented during the current regime.[190]

Since the trial in 2011, several other activists have been arrested, charged, interrogated and subjected to a travel ban and asset freeze; this involves some of the most important organisations working on women's rights advocacy and service provision: Nazra for Feminist Studies, which provides free legal representation and emotional support to victims of violence, in addition to research and advocacy work; the Centre for Egyptian Women's Legal Assistance (CEWLA), which focuses on litigation and legal representation, but also runs a domestic violence shelter and provides other direct services;[191] and the Nadeem Centre for Rehabilitation of Victims of Violence.[192] Trials have not officially started, but activists are summoned occasionally for questioning. Meanwhile, their organisations have been struggling to stay afloat.

The legal basis of the charges is also confusing. For instance, Azza Soliman, head of CEWLA, is accused of 'slandering Egypt's image by claiming that women in the country face rape'.[193] At the same time, the NCW has prepared a national plan 'to safeguard the dignity of women and protect them from acts of violence'[194] – a clear indication of the

[188] 'UN human rights chief'.

[189] For a background on the events, and on the organisations, see Jenny O'Connor, '"NGO": the guise of innocence' (2012) 5 *Irish Foreign Affairs*, 1, 5–8.

[190] Harris Setzer, 'Civil society on trial in Egypt: revisiting the NGO workers case', The Washington Institute, 30 January 2018, accessed 15 June 2018 at www.washingtoninstitute.org/policy-analysis/view/civil-society-on-trial-in-egypt-revisiting-the-ngo-workers-case

[191] Liz Ford, 'Egypt court ruling upholds decision to freeze assets of women's rights activists', *The Guardian*, 12 January 2017, accessed 17 July 2018 at www.theguardian.com/global-development/2017/jan/12/egypt-court-ruling-upholds-decision-freeze-assets-womens-rights-activists

[192] 'Co-founder of anti-torture NGO Al-Nadeem prevented from traveling', Mada Masr, 18 October 2017, accessed 17 July 2018 at www.madamasr.com/en/2017/10/18/news/u/co-founder-of-anti-torture-ngo-al-nadeem-prevented-from-traveling/

[193] 'Speak out for women's rights defender Azza Soliman', Amnesty International Petition, accessed 29 May 2018, www.amnesty.org/en/get-involved/take-action/speak-out-for-egypt-womens-rights-defender-azza-soliman/

[194] Lowla Reda, 'Introducing Egypt's strategy to combat violence against women', Egypt Today, 3 December 2017, accessed 20 June 2018 at www.egypttoday.com/Article/2/35200/Introducing-Egypt%E2%80%99s-strategy-to-combat-violence-against-women

existence of VAW in the country. Therefore, Azza faces a charge for stating an obvious problem in Egypt, one on which the NCW is working. Some of the other charges that Azza faces because of law 70/2017[195] include the 'establishment of an entity that conducts activities similar to that of associations' activities'.[196] This is confusing because the implementation of the new law is supposed to be pending the release of its bylaws. It is unclear why Azza is charged under a law that is not enforced yet; this is another example of the randomness in the implementation of the law.

Using the law as a political tool to trigger fear and curb civil society activity[197] is a trend that has been recently spreading on a global level, including in countries such as India, Russia, China, Uganda and Cambodia.[198]

F Steering Public Opinion

Public opinion can strongly reinforce the legal war against civil society. This starts with scrutinising the connection between NGOs and international organisations and donors,[199] in an attempt to tarnish the reputation of NGOs by raising public concerns about their patriotism and allegiance.[200] This is an old technique[201] used by autocratic regimes globally when they feel threatened by NGOs. In 2012, Ecuador's President launched a campaign against NGOs with various accusations such 'colluding with rebels and working to replace or destabilize the government', which ended with the shutting down of 16

[195] Larice Schuurbiers, 'Women's rights activist Azza Soliman faces charges to possible 15 years of prison', The international Angle, 20 November 2017, accessed 15 June 2018 at www.theinternationalangle.com/index.php/2017/11/20/womens-rights-activist-azza-soliman-faces-charges-to-possible-15-years-of-prison/

[196] FIDH, 'Egypt: Arrest and release on bail of Azza Soliman', urgent appeal, International Federation for Human Rights, 8 December 2016, accessed 18 June 2018 at www.fidh.org/en/issues/human-rights-defenders/egypt-arrest-and-release-on-bail-of-azza-soliman

[197] 'Egypt: escalating judicial harassment of human rights NGOs', Frontline Defenders, 21 March 2016, accessed 17 July 2018 at www.frontlinedefenders.org/en/statement-report/egypt-escalating-judicial-harassment-human-rights-ngos. This is a common practice in many countries. See David M. Moore, *Civil Society Under Threat: Common Legal Barriers and Potential Responses*, report (European Parliament, 2006) EP/ExPol/B/2006/30.

[198] Harriet Sherwood, 'Human rights groups face global crackdown "not seen in a generation"', *The Guardian*, 26 August 2015, accessed 2 June 2018 at www.theguardian.com/law/2015/aug/26/ngos-face-restrictions-laws-human-rights-generation

[199] Bratton, *The Politics*, p. 9.

[200] Schuurbiers, 'Women's rights activist'.

[201] Ibid.

NGOs that had received foreign funding, and imposing a ban on further foreign funding.[202] These campaigns actually work well on public opinion and may severely impede NGOs' work, their impact possibly lasting for years. Ingy mentions an NGO in the area where they work and explains how community members still remember that this NGO used to receive foreigners in their office 10 to 15 years ago. This information is remembered although the NGOs is no longer operating. Nejima warns of underestimating the impact of public opinion on the work of NGOs, arguing that communities also have a 'despotic dimension'.[203] She compares NGOs in Pakistan and Bangladesh and shows that, even though the former has more need for NGO support, the non-profit sector is remarkably limited and weak as it is undermined by social resistance.[204]

The current civil society crisis in Egypt also started with a campaign in 2011 'to frame NGOs as tools of foreign agents',[205] accusing activists of treason and espionage so as to discredit them and undermine their work.[206] Despite the lack of evidence, these rumours have 'manufactured a real and dangerous public suspicion of the NGO community'.[207] This has even affected the perceptions of some of the most vulnerable victims of violence and other beneficiaries who receive free services from the NGOs they criticise. Fatma remembers some of the comments she heard in 2012 when she was trying to provide psychological support to victims of sexual violence, during their most difficult times; victims asked her about funding and questioned whether her NGO was really planning to destabilise Egypt. She adds that some women refused to receive help from the NGO because of these campaigns; however, they always came back because they did not have a choice, considering the minuscule number of organisations providing such services in Egypt. Ingy also recounts an incident when they accompanied a client to the police station to make a report on a VAW case. The policemen privately warned the client not to hire a human rights organisation that lacks nationalism. Since then, Ingy and her lawyer colleagues do not identify themselves as 'human rights lawyers' when they accompany victims to the police station so as not to negatively affect their cases.

202 Christensen and Weinstein, 'Defunding dissent', 81.
203 Nejima, 'Pakistan: regulations', p. 13.
204 Ibid.
205 Herrold, 'NGO policy', 202.
206 Tadros, 'The securitisation', 87.
207 Ruffner, *Under Threat*, p. 13.

V OUTCOMES OF REPRESSION AND RIVALRY

A Impact on NGOs

With the open and liberal political space enjoyed by NGOs in South Africa, they can focus on advancing women's rights; the legal and policy developments referenced throughout this book are good examples. It is counter-productive to work on human rights when activists are personally targeted. Even activists who are not under a travel ban or asset freeze in Egypt still feel the impact of the deteriorating image and reputation of NGOs[208] on two levels: psychologically and professionally, often overlapping.

Respondents in this research conveyed some of their deeply troubled thoughts and feelings. 'Every time I go through airport security I wonder if this will be the time I receive the news of my travel ban. I am not even sure why. We do not do any political work, we work quietly to help women and yet we always feel that they will find something wrong with our work', explained Fatma. Arwa moves to the relationship with MOSS: 'they consume your time and make you vigilant because you always feel that you are a thief and somehow you are breaking the law. You are always arranging your papers to avoid the tiniest mistakes so that you do not end up going to jail. You do a lot of things that seem illogical to avoid conflict'. Ingy sees this as the price they pay for the choices they make. They choose to work on women's rights as independent organisations, and unfortunately, in Egypt, this is the price of this choice.

While psychological wellbeing is important of itself, it can also strongly affect these women's jobs. Fatma explains that she quit her job when her tiredness overcame any sense of accomplishment and eventually destroyed her passion. Initially, she was a full-time staff member working on research and providing psychological support. With shrinking public space, research became too dangerous, so the organisation terminated research activities and Fatma ended up only working on psychological support. She elaborates, 'the research was where I learned new things. It inspired me the most. When it was gone, the burnout, pressure and fear took over and I quit'. Ingy explains that for the last two years, disappointment and low morale have taken over the whole

[208] See Ernesto Londono, 'In Egypt, NGO crackdown and draft law have chilling effect', *The Washington Post*, 11 February 2012, accessed 17 July 2018 at www.washingtonpost.com/world/middle_east/in-egypt-ngo-crackdown-and-draft-law-have-chilling-effect/2012/02/11/gIQANO9b6Q_story.html?noredirect=on&utm_term=.c41b1cdbca8c

organisation. For instance, they usually draft the organisation's strategic plan as a team, in a workshop setting, where they discuss the most urgent needs, then approach donors to fundraise. Currently, they have a few funds approved by donors but pending ministry approval; Ingy continues, 'it has been two years now since we set our strategy and were enthusiastic to start, but now everyone is hopeless that these activities will ever be implemented. This is not comprehensible because all our activities are consistent with the priorities of the state, and the elements of the strategy coincide with the national plan to combat VAW prepared by the NCW.'

The complicated and vague administration process forces organisations to dedicate significant resources towards administrative issues. Arwa spends a lot of time when submitting new projects to MOSS making sure all the requirements are met. Similarly, Ingy communicates with MOSS staff 2–3 times a week – a considerable amount of time to spend on unfunded work without achieving any progress for women's rights. It specifically gets tedious when there is a rejection for a grant and she has to follow up consistently and submit new papers as requested. She explains, 'the documents requested are sometimes simple but the staff are not at their offices so we have to go multiple times to catch them at the right time – this is repeated with every single document'. Another notable waste of resources in addition to time and effort is financial resources. Some organisations spent a lot of money on digital security, as Ayman explained.

As is to be expected, downsizing work means downsizing staff, and whether in the case of an asset freeze or lack of funds, employees do not have access to their salaries.[209] Also, in 2018, Nazra for Feminist Studies had to shut down its offices, resort to volunteerism instead of hired staff, and adopt a 'work from home' policy.[210]

B Impact on Services

The inability of states to cover all service sectors leaves space for NGOs to work. In economic terms, this is called the 'economic space for NGOs'.[211] In Egypt, this is not applicable beyond the direct service sector: NGOs are only free to work on social services that are needed

[209] Schuurbiers, 'Women's rights activist'.

[210] 'Nazra bids farewell to its office and continues its work', press release, Nazra for Feminist Studies, 16 March 2018, accessed 17 July 2018 at www.nazra.org/en/2018/03/nazra-bids-farewell-its-office-and-continues-its-work

[211] Nejima, 'Pakistan: regulations', p. 11.

by the state but fall outside the state budget, as discussed earlier in this chapter.

Looking at state services available to victims and survivors of violence, one will see a void. There are neither adequate direct services for women nor programmes, such as campaigns, aiming to change perceptions and attitudes towards VAW.[212] NGOs are the only stakeholders providing services for victims of VAW. In addition to the legal, psychological and medical services that will end with NGOs, these unfortunate circumstances will leave a void in documentation, awareness-raising and meaningful legal reform.[213] A number of reports have warned about the gap in services as a result of the deteriorating civil society conditions in Egypt,[214] including traditional charitable services.[215] However, interviewees for this research give deeper insights and intricate details on their lived realties.

Interviews show that services have definitely been affected to date. Arwa's organisation shut down their shelter and downsized their direct services including legal support. Ingy's NGO started charging women for legal services. She explains, 'we try to provide free services to women who cannot afford to pay, and many of our lawyers volunteer their time as they understand our circumstances. It is still hard to operate with significantly decreased overhead cost after the downsizing when we do not have any funding approvals coming through'. Paying customers are also not covering a lot of the NGO's costs, as Ingy adds, 'in the last two months, we brought 45 cases to court, with only three women able to pay'. The most serious problem for Ayman's NGO lies in the strong censorship of the organisation and staff. After so much wasted time trying to obtain security permits for various activities including research, the NGO eliminated all programmes that need any kind of legal permit because they could not afford the administrative resources needed to secure such permits, which usually fail anyway. As for Fatma, her organisation cut out all legal services and closed the legal department. However, they still have one lawyer who volunteers to guide women in pursuing their own legal battles. Fatma's organisation was one of the first to downsize; initially they used to refer cases to partner NGOs

[212] Euromed Rights, *Report on Violence against Women, Egypt* (9 December 2016).

[213] Amnesty International, *Circles of Hell*, p. 23.

[214] See Marroushi, *Violence Against Women*, p. 15; Attalah, 'While a bad year'.

[215] Hossam Al-Hindi, 'Qanun al gameat al ahleya' (NGO law), SAS Post, 1 December 2016, accessed 17 July 2018 at www.sasapost.com/ngos-law-in-egypt/

who still provided legal services. However, eventually, they eliminated this service as all their partner organisations also downsized. Another notable change mentioned by Fatma is the decrease in the number of refugees seeking emotional and legal support. They used to get referrals by organisations working with refugees, but these have also closed, or are currently closing down. Refugees were specified as additionally vulnerable in a statement issued by a coalition of NGOs concerning the shrinking space for NGOs.[216]

The value of advocacy in Egypt is not well studied. Nongovernmental organisations have taken different approaches such as working with parliament or some ministries to lobby for laws and policies. This involvement is definitely not as intense as it is in South Africa, but there has still been a voice bringing gender matters to the table even if the state has not been attentive. The demise of NGOs means that this voice will be lost.

C Coping Strategies Adopted by NGOs

Women's rights activists work under extreme levels of pressure. Throughout the years they have learned to cope, not only to circumvent administrative hurdles, but also to push the women's rights agenda towards positive political opportunities.

Some global surviving techniques include 'minimizing, avoiding, or trying to defeat new rules… Survival strategies can involve attempts to change the organization (internal transformation), the environment (external transformation), or both'.[217] Bratton identifies some organisations which deem the government incompetent and therefore choose to work completely independently from it.[218] This may be done in two ways: by keeping a close 'behind the scenes' relationship with senior officials or 'concentrating on relatively less controversial areas of rights representation, such as consumer and environmental affairs'.[219] Other organisations survive by having family and friends donate to running costs.[220] Others invest time and resources in building relationships with different arms of the state[221] so as to achieve maximum political gains;

[216] 'Egypt: new law will crush civil society', Human Rights Watch, 2 June 2017, accessed 17 July 2018 at www.hrw.org/news/2017/06/02/egypt-new-law-will-crush-civil-society

[217] Dupuy et al., 'Who survived', 429.

[218] Bratton, *The Politics*, p. 28.

[219] Ibid., p. 29.

[220] Herrold, 'NGO policy', 194.

[221] Pick et al., 'NGO-Government'.

it is important to remember that 'even "bad" governments often have "good" departments with which NGOs can work'.[222] This can be done by sharing information with state officials, working on joint projects with relevant public institutions or supporting state staff through capacity building or other training.[223] Even organisations who choose to work on advocacy can succeed. However, the leaders must have a high level of sophistication when 'managing a dialogue with the state'.[224]

Women's rights NGOs in Egypt have tried some of these coping strategies. One popular approach that worked for many years was to avoid MOSS altogether and register under another official authority, such as a law firm or a company. This strategy is now unfeasible as it can lead to prison and a fine, as per the 70/2017 NGO law. Currently organisations are trying to stay afloat until they either pass this stage or completely die. They are keeping a low profile and cutting down on activities, as previously mentioned.

Some of the abovementioned coping strategies were mentioned in the interviews. For instance, Fatma explains that staff members at the NGO now operate from their homes. Ingy personally funds her organisation's overheads. Ayman similarly notes that they often work from home, and they also try to find innovative ways of fundraising, while avoiding foreign grants. Generally, organisations started avoiding any foreign funds with even a 'hint of a rights component'.[225]

While at the time of writing collaboration with the state is quite difficult, NGOs have previously worked with state agencies when there were political opportunities and the impact was promising. These were not coping strategies for survival, but rather strategies for bringing forward the women's rights agenda. Arwa, for example, has previously worked with judges on incorporating international law into domestic legislation. Fatma explains that they learned to spot the cooperative employees in the system. For instance, when they worked with the victims of sexual violence, they found the forensics division quite aware of the psychological trauma inflicted on victims, and therefore the experience of women was much better there than in other departments in the healthcare system. Ayman notes that they take any chance they

[222] John Clark, 'Democratising development: NGOs and the state' (1992) 2 *Development in Practice*, 3, 153, as quoted in Brass, *Allies or Adversaries*, p. 11.
[223] Brass, *Allies or Adversaries*, p. 55.
[224] Bratton, *The Politics*, p. 32.
[225] Ruffner, *Under Threat*, p. 9.

find to build relations with state departments – it helps with legitimacy and connections. Nongovernmental organisations have seen these opportunities and have capitalised on them. It is now a difficult time to implement any of these strategies and reap any benefits from them, but they may be relevant for future possibilities, depending on how events unfold.

VI REFLECTIONS ON THE POSITION OF NGOs IN EGYPT

The state's actions towards NGOs is based on the 'perceived ability of NGOs to destabilize the government, along with the perceived costs of transparency'.[226] The measures taken by the Egyptian state towards civil society are truly baffling. Nongovernmental organisations, including human rights organisations, are not threatening by any means to the longevity of the state. Their impact is quite limited and they are already stigmatised by the aforementioned campaigns. Adopting and implementing repressive NGO legislation is equally confusing. As of 2017, out of more than 35,000 registered NGOs in Egypt, 239 organisations were characterised as working on human rights; the rest are either working on culture and religion or local development.[227]

Where will this take women's legal rights in Egypt? There is so much work that needs to be done on gender, both socially and legally. Ingy states, 'I do not want to close down but I do not know what else to do. I feel like I have accomplished a lot and I can do more. However, I am depressed, we have never been attacked this way before. My projects are not approved, I cannot run the office, and we have no more staff. I cannot see the light at the end of the tunnel. Maybe because this is not the time for civil society'.

The question remains: who is going to carry the burden of fighting violence against women now? There is little hope for the next generation of feminists. Ayman explains that young feminists found this unfortunate reality as they were taking their first steps in civil society; 'they have no tools and no money. They cannot carry the burden'.

One possible area of work on which interviewees have disagreed is impact litigation. Ingy believes that there is space for it, and they are

[226] Christensen and Weinstein, 'Defunding dissent', 84.
[227] Abdel Wahab, 'Al Gamaet'.

eager to work on the persistent ban of females from the State Council.[228] This issue has stirred public discussions for a few years. Several applicants have submitted complaints and attempted litigation before the Supreme Administrative Court, to no avail. The case was struck down on a technicality.[229] Arwa, on the other hand, asserts that in the current legal and political environment, impact litigation is not a possibility. In addition, compared to other countries where impact litigation is commonly used, Egypt's judicial system is not plural – unorthodox resources are not sought and the judge's opinion and sentence are not usually contested by the public.

VII CONCLUSION

A pluralist state not only sees the value in NGOs, but strives to provide favourable working conditions for NGO staff who undertake such demanding work, especially regarding perceptual and behavioural change. This only happens when both parties believe in complementarity. Rights-based NGOs are mostly concerned with the doctrine of human rights, and states usually have other priority issues, which revolve around economic development and security. The two parties will inevitably clash and may not be able to compromise on every issue; however, they should move on to the next issue, and keep engaging. This is the example provided by South African civil society – incessant diligence to work together to reach common goals.

Eliminating dissent may work well for autocratic states in the short term. But gender problems, if left unattended, will create serious social imbalances that will affect generations to come. Egypt desperately needs gender to be at the forefront of public debate. It needs courageous activists who are not afraid to challenge religious and conservative institutions on the principles of equality and discrimination. There are activists willing to take on this fight, but they need state support. The only hope for eliminating VAW and promoting gender equality is for the state and civil society to work together.[230]

[228] Ahmed Aleem, 'Egyptian women fight for right to top judicial positions', Al-Monitor, 7 May 2018, accessed 15 June 2018 at www.al-monitor.com/pulse/originals/2018/05/egypt-appointment-female-judges-state-councils-controversy.html

[229] Nihal Samir, 'State Council postpones reviewing challenge to female judge ban', Daily News Egypt, 15 November 2017, accessed 15 June 2018 at www.dailynewsegypt.com/2017/11/15/state-council-postpones-reviewing-challenge-female-judge-ban/

[230] For a list of recommendations, see Mosleh, *Advancing Egyptian Society*, p. 6.

This chapter came after discussions on South Africa to provide a contrasting example. Public space can be opened or closed for NGOs. This includes space in courts to litigate, in society to shift social attitudes and behaviours, and with various government and private institutions to implement policies and create gender sensitive environments.

CHAPTER 9

CONCLUSION

What does it take to move local communities to take action to end violence against women? The question that Andrew Harding asked in 2013 about South Africa[1] does not offer simple answers. Attempting to investigate the rampant rate of VAW in South Africa, its causes, prevention and remedies, one must look at the core of the relationship between law and society: how does the state view VAW? How does society treat it? What is the relationship between the two?

To bring this issue to the forefront of public dialogue, there needs to be constant constructive conversation about it, centred on gender-sensitive perspectives. State responsibility, service provision and dedicated resources to end VAW is an important, yet limited, part of the discussion. Efforts need to be dedicated to the legal and political messages reaching the public on VAW; and critical attention must be given to the actual impact of the progressive laws and policies that aim to protect women from violence. In other words, one must look at closing the gap between the state (with all its institutions) and the public. This is where NGOs play an indispensable role.

This book has explored some of the most important areas where NGOs engage with stakeholders and beneficiaries to implement the progressive rights discourse enshrined in the Constitution and legislation, in an attempt to gender-sensitise the law and, at the same time, make it more accessible to women. To assume this essential role, NGOs need significant space to work with women on a micro level and engage

[1] Harding, 'Will South Africans'.

with the state on a macro level. The South African state, as this book has shown, succeeds in providing a platform for dialogue on human rights issues with different stakeholders, moving towards a common goal: eradicating gender-based violence.

This concluding chapter will recap the arguments in this book, and will make some recommendations for further research.

I RATIONALE OF THE RESEARCH AND METHODOLOGY

The strong contradiction between the progressive gender laws and persistent risk of violence faced by South African women was the trigger for the initial research, which was the subject of a doctoral dissertation. The availability of the socio-legal and political space to constructively discuss gender issues was the inspiration behind developing the research into a book.

Nongovernmental organisations in South Africa have written numerous reports on VAW, and have reported on their work in the field. However, information about the internal operations, partnerships and external engagements of these organisations is either missing, or quite scattered. In other words, NGOs have conducted a lot of research, but have not been the subjects of research that conclusively looks at their multifaceted activities, as well as the web of relationships and engagements they undertake to bring women's rights alive. Looking at NGOs through this lens is particularly important in a socio-legal environment that recognises the importance of NGOs and utilises their expertise. It sheds light on the abilities and capacities of organisations to bring people and the law closer.

II AN OVERVIEW OF THE RESEARCH IN THIS BOOK

This research looked at the socio-legal and political space available in South Africa, where multiple stakeholders can engage in the negotiation of human rights and state responsibility. While this space is available for all kinds of activism and not restricted to NGOs, it provides a conducive environment for nonprofit organisations to grow and flourish, and this space has been effectively used by NGOs.

This book has explored the grounds on which negotiations on women's rights occur between NGOs, states and various stakeholders. This entailed an investigation of NGOs' work in relation to women and state institutions, an analysis of the power dynamics developing between the three parties and an evaluation of the strategies used to bring forward socio-legal change for women subjected to violence. The book zoomed in on some NGO activities, such as advocacy, service provision and awareness-raising. Achieving significant gains has been a product of a long history of social and political negotiations to situate gender at the core of the human rights discourse in South Africa. It is therefore difficult to imagine the movement against GBV without talking about NGOs.

III KEY FINDINGS: ENABLING FACTORS FOR BRINGING FORWARD SOCIO-LEGAL CHANGE

The progressiveness of the South African legal system is undeniable; however, gaps and problems with laws are still found The *Levenstein* case discussed in this book is a case in point. It was not until 2018 that a group of women decided to disclose the sexual abuse they had faced as children, but they were unable to litigate because of a time limitation set by the law. They therefore challenged the constitutionality of this law. Other problems and loopholes in the law are likely to surface. In addition, gender stereotypes that perpetuate GBV and excuse offenders of violence are more challenging to reform. Therefore, there is a long way to go for South Africa, and NGOs are determined to achieve this change. This work will not be possible without some enabling factors and conditions.

This book has discussed these factors and this section will summarise them. They include: a legal system based on a rights-based approach; public institutions that understand their limitations and pull together the resources needed to eliminate a social problem or crime; a diverse range of non-state actors undertaking specialised roles that complement each other; and a public system that realises these requirements and strives to create change.

A Rights-based Framework

In addition to the progressive Constitution that includes a Bill of Rights incorporating the core international human rights principles, South Africa has adopted almost comprehensive legislation to address GBV, which received limited critique, as discussed in Chapter 2.

Furthermore, the Constitution recognises the value of expertise and therefore calls for the establishment of various institutions, such as the

Commission for Gender Equality, to oversee matters related to gender in the country. The book has also shown that the international human rights doctrine plays an important role in court judgments and in the arguments brought forward by NGOs to courts. The legal framework is therefore not only progressive, but also open to further development and change.

B Progressive Public Institutions

South Africa fosters a remarkably progressive judiciary that strives to reach the most implementable and fairest interpretation of Constitutional rights, balanced with state responsibility. It is even open to self-criticism and has engaged with the CGE in the investigation of the complaint brought forward by the NGO, Sonke, to question the speed with which female judges are joining the bench. It is also impressive how an NGO is able to challenge an institution so fundamental to the state, and put it under investigation not only in law, but also before the public eye. These engagements are reflective of the state's diligence in achieving equality and fulfilling human rights.

Other institutions, such as the CGE and the Equality Courts, have been pivotal to the women's rights movement, either in an adjudicative, investigative or advisory role. The state has also established specialised service provision through centres, such as the Thuthuzela, discussed in Chapter 2, in an attempt to improve the experiences of victims of violence with the law.

A noted strength in South Africa's institutional capacity is diversity and plurality. This book has reviewed instances when courts took over law-making in urgent situations due to severe delays in Parliament. Courts are also more courageous in challenging customary law systems that the police may be hesitant to face.

C Specialised Non-state Actors

Globally, NGOs are the most specialised and interested party in social development and human rights. The South African state is fully aware of this expertise and actually strives to include NGOs, not only in the implementation of programmes, but also in planning and decision-making. The book has covered many of these instances. For example, NGOs have contributed to drafting the DVA and the SOA, they frequently provide submissions to courts either of their own accord or as requested by courts and they regularly provide insights on legal amendments and evaluations of the law.

Even more importantly for the state, NGOs are flexible and adaptable enough to work with informal institutions of justice in areas falling under customary law. This is a field or work that most governments are hesitant to penetrate. Throughout this book, women living under customary law have been identified as vulnerable,and NGOs are often their only resort to relief. In this way, NGOs are carrying a significant burden away from the state and, at the same time, the state is recognising the advantageous position enjoyed by NGOs that allows them to engage with these communities. In addition, in many instances, the state facilitates the work of NGOs in these areas, such as hosting them on police station premises, or sharing resources.

At the micro level, NGOs oversee the implementation of laws protecting women from violence. They provide legal counselling and legal representation to women. In addition, they monitor the conduct of government institutions, holding the state accountable for violations in its duty to respect, protect, ensure and fulfil the rights of women. While the work of NGOs is generally recognised and appreciated by the government, there are some hiccups in this relationship, especially when it relates to the state's failure to deliver.

The book has also reviewed how the state truly respects the specialisation of NGOs, whether as experts working with a specific vulnerable group or in a specialised field. Most importantly, the state recognises the proximity of NGOs to local communities, and therefore expects them to bring the voices of women into the legal sphere, either through contributions to court proceedings or through cooperative partnerships with state institutions. This can be seen in the frequent requests for NGOs to provide expert opinions or in the invitations to monitor and evaluate laws. This is one of the most important enabling factors to the growth of NGOs.

D An Open and Engaging Public System

To allow for reform in law and society, there must be space for conversations and negotiations. Providing this space is the responsibility of the state. State departments must accept criticism and welcome reform. Parliament and the justice system should encourage different voices and opinions.

This book has demonstrated some examples of these negotiations and discussions taking place between states and NGOs, whether regarding housing rights or the state responsibility to protect women from violence. In this area, South Africa is fairing quite well; Chapter 5 showed how NGOs are not the only external voices in the system. In fact, courts diversify their resources so as to profoundly understand core issues before them and make informed judgments; this includes calling for expert opinions or resorting to global and academic research.

The value of this space cannot be overemphasised. It is the focus of this book, as it is the prerequisite to any social and legal reforms that the state hopes to make. The previous chapter in this book provided the opposite example of Egypt to demonstrate the catastrophic consequences when NGOs are regarded as a threat.

IV REMAINING CHALLENGES

A Reforming Public Opinion

Nongovernmental organisations have been remarkably successful in numerous areas, most notably, connecting victims of violence with the law and in return, gender-sensitising the law; however, 'activists and NGOs have struggled to significantly shift the legal culture' around VAW.[2] Sexism and homophobia are still rampant in South Africa, as repeatedly mentioned through the book. This area is understandably the most challenging for NGOs and the state to reform. While NGOs can lobby for laws and convince the court to pass gender-sensitive judgments, changing the perceptions of a critical mass of people takes time, innovative strategies and unique monitoring and evaluation tools.

It is imperative to measure the impact of public awareness initiatives, whether campaigns or legal education activities. This is a noted area of improvement, without which legal reform will always be limited. NGOs undertake various awareness-raising activities and, in partnership with the state, they run regular campaigns. While these campaigns may increase the number of women who respond to violence and seek assistance from NGOs, it is unclear how much they shake pervasive gender stereotypes that plague South African society. NGOs realise the importance of social development, complementing legal reform to combat VAW. In fact, they have previously addressed public officials who make sexist statements and have criticised court judgments that perpetuate gender stereotypes. However, new and innovative tools are required to address the general public, who can seem unbothered by strict laws and therefore continue to exercise and tolerate violence.

[2] Lake, *Strong NGOs*, p. 173.

B Identifying Accountability

Most intervention strategies developed by the state require the collaboration of multiple state actors. This is likely to lead to a deflection of responsibility, making it difficult to locate any dereliction of duty. This issue has come up several times in the book. In Chapter 5, for example, when the CGE was investigating a complaint regarding the number of females on the bench, it expressed concern over the finger-pointing approach adopted by the stakeholders responsible. Similarly, Chapter 2 discussed the difficulties in implementing the SOA, identifying a challenge in the number of different state institutions responsible for the implementation of the Act. Because of the complexity of the power relations behind GBV, interventions will always be multidimensional, requiring the contribution of multiple public institutions and nonprofit organisations. It is therefore imperative to develop adequate accountability measures to catch the multidimensional element of GBV.

V CONCLUSION

It is the hope of this book to demonstrate the South African model as an imperfect functioning relationship between state and NGOs, where both parties strive to fight VAW and promote women's rights. When NGO work is curtailed, women are mostly likely to suffer, as shown by Egypt's example. This is because states are not experts on women's rights; also, women's issues are still, unfortunately, sidelined. NGOs therefore must come at the forefront of the movement to respect, protect, ensure and fulfil women's human rights.

APPENDIX

ETHNOGRAPHIC DATA

Table A.1 Introducing the NGOs included in the study

NGO	Contact Person	Activities
NGO1	Arriera - mediator and court preparation officer	This is a victim support centre based on the premises of a police station in a township. It is based on volunteer work and provides multiple services to the community, which include mediation, as well as urgent assistance such as housing or financial help to members of the community. The NGO runs court preparation sessions for victims of rape and sexual abuse, and supports abused women accessing formal justice.
NGO2	Charlene - a legal officer in Cape Town branch Mandy - a legal officer in the Johannesburg branch	This is a nationwide legal centre that specialises in advocacy and provides legal assistance in civil cases. Gender is only one of their many areas of focus. Their offices are urban-based, but they also work in collaboration with community-based organisations in rural areas when needed.
NGO3	Audrey - programme officer Katrina - the head of the organisation	The headquarters are based in Pietermaritzburg, but the NGO runs satellite offices in rural areas subject to customary law in KZN. The NGO's mission is to assist women in making choices about the law. They work closely with traditional leaders, but also coordinate with the police when necessary.

(continued)

Table A.1 (*Cont.*)

NGO	Contact Person	Activities
NGO4	Joylene - legal officer	This NGO specialises in public interest litigation as well as counselling and referrals to other organisations for specialised assistance.
NGO5	Sibongile - head of legal unit	Based in Johannesburg, this NGO provides psychosocial counselling and paralegal services to victims of GBV. In addition, the NGO offers capacity-building and specialised training to other organisations, and works in partnerships for advocacy. NGO5 also runs GBV shelters.
NGO6	Janet - social worker and mediator	Provides services to women in abusive relationships. It mediates between family members and runs a divorce clinic. This NGO has many offices around South Africa.
NGO7	Jill - social worker	Works with women and children who are victims of GBV. It has a Head Office in Johannesburg as well as satellite offices. Its activities include training, research, advocacy and running a shelter.
NGO8	Sheri - court preparation officer	Focuses on children, offering a wide variety of services tackling issues of child physical and sexual abuse.
NGO9	Linda - head of legal unit	Specialises in advocacy and lobbying. In addition, the NGO offers paralegal counselling, provides training to other organisations and runs a legal clinic.
NGO10	Nomsa - gender-based violence specialist	This is an NGO supporting homosexual people and is based in Pietermaritzburg. The NGO fights hate crime in law and society. It undertakes awareness activities and offers training. The NGO also runs a legal clinic for sexual violence and a rehabilitation programme for victims of violence.
NGO11		A law clinic that offers free services to underprivileged women.
NGO12	Joyce - satellite programme	A research centre based in Pietermaritzburg that launched an outreach programme for empowering community members to be victim support officers, providing legal and psychosocial support to the community in cases of violence.

Table A.1 (*Cont.*)

NGO	Contact Person	Activities
NGO13	Jabu - officer and mediator	This is one of the satellite offices for NGO12. They are based in a rural area in KZN.
NGO14	Sandy - gender specialist	Works on various areas of the law, including impact litigation, legal representation and advocacy. It has offices across South Africa.

Table A.2 Introducing the shelters included in the study

Shelter 1	Beth - the manager	The shelter is based in Johannesburg with capacity for 54 women, who are allowed to stay up to one year. The shelter provides housing and life necessities and follows a programme of rehabilitation based on psychological and economic empowerment
Shelters 2 and 3	The heads of the shelters, housemothers and counsellors	Shelter 2 and Shelter 3 are run by NGOs also included in this research. They are both based in Johannesburg and have capacity for about ten residents. They provide counselling and referrals to organisations that provide legal services. Women are allowed to stay up to one year, but most women stay between three to six months.
Shelter 4	Bridget - shelter manager	The shelter is based in Pietermaritzburg. Bridget set it up ten years ago through a church. It has a crisis centre for non-serious and temporary cases, and a safe house in an undisclosed location out of town for more serious cases. The shelter has capacity for 50 women, but is only licensed for 35. Shelter 4 does not have a maximum stay policy.

Table A.3 Introducing interview participants

Code	Name	Story
Story 1	Thobile	Thobile was interviewed in Shelter 2. She was married for 21 years and was constantly abused by her husband and sister-in-law. Thobile did not have access to her marriage certificate, she did not have any income and was not allowed to make any financial or material demands on her husband.
Story 2	Ndonsa	Ndonsa was from a prominent family in a rural community subject to customary law. She was repeatedly physically and emotionally abused by her husband.
Story 3	Lindiwe	A staff member at NGO3 recounted Lindiwe's story. Lindiwe was gang-raped in a rural community. The chief ordered the payment of minor damages. The NGO later intervened and summoned the police.
Story 4	Nasreen	Nasreen was a 19-year-old Muslim woman, who was repeatedly raped by her manager. She returned to work without reporting it. The rape was discovered after she broke down and was sent by her family for psychological counselling. At the time of the interview, she had two cases in court, a criminal case and a labour case. An NGO in this study was supporting the labour case and monitoring the criminal one.
Story 5	Zandile	Zandile was married to a policeman for years. She was a foreigner and therefore did not have a support network in South Africa. Physical, sexual and emotional abuse had persisted for a long time until she decided to move to the shelter where she was interviewed.
Story 6	Marie	Marie's husband was an alcoholic and addicted to gambling. He was therefore emotionally abusive. In addition, he gambled with her money and put her in debt. She was in the relationship for 11 years and had two children. Marie used multiple services provided by NGO6.
Story 7	Fatima	Fatima, who was interviewed in Shelter 2, is Nigerian. She was married to a Nigerian man. He tricked Fatima into leaving South Africa temporarily and leaving her daughter with his mother. He took her passport and would not let her re-enter South Africa or contact her child. Fatima was back in South Africa at the time of the interview, attempting to gain custody of her child.

Table A.3 (*Cont.*)

Code	Name	Story
Story 8	Nelly	Nelly was interviewed in Shelter 2. She was abused for 12 years by her partner, physically and emotionally. She moved out from their house a few months before the interview to a shack on the same street, but he chased her there. She had moved to a shelter a few weeks before the interview. She has two children.
Story 9	Sindiso and Nokthula	Sindiso and Nokthula were both teenagers who were raped by the same boy. Their court case was about to start at the time of the interview.
Story 10	Daya	Daya was interviewed in Shelter 3. She was gang-raped near the Zimbabwean border. She was later introduced to an NGO that referred her to the shelter, where she had been for about a year.
Story 11	Rose	Rose was interviewed in Shelter 3. She had three children from a relationship that had turned abusive over the last three years. She read about one of the NGOs in a magazine, which linked her up with the shelter where she was interviewed.
Story 12	Tasneem	Tasneem's case was sponsored by one of the NGOs in the study. She was 50 years old and was raped five years ago by a security guard in her compound.
Story 13	Winnie	Winnie was interviewed in Shelter 1. She had just moved in when the interview took place. Her husband started abusing her when she lost her job, as he did not want to support her.

Table A.4 Introducing research participants and NGOs in Egypt

Interviewee	NGO
Arwa	Arwa runs an NGO working on women's legal rights in Cairo, which has been operating for many years. She provides legal support to women, but also engages in some advocacy work.
Fatma	A former employee of an NGO, and now a volunteer. The NGO provides legal and psychological support to victims of violence, and also works on advocacy.
Ingy	Her NGO works on free legal representation in both civil and criminal cases for women, in addition to some advocacy, training and community awareness.
Ayman	A staff member at an NGO that works on sexual violence, focusing on policy and awareness-raising.

BIBLIOGRAPHY

PRIMARY SOURCES AND REPORTS

African Commission on Human and People's Rights, Concluding Observations and Recommendations on the Combined Second Periodic Report under the African Charter on Human and People's Rights and Initial Report under the Protocol to the African Changer on the Rights of Women in Africa (Adopted by the African Commission on Human and Peoples' Rights at its 20th Extra-Ordinary Session held from 9 to 18 June 2016, Banjul)

African National Congress, Freedom Charter (Adopted at the Congress of the People at Kliptown, 26 June 1955)

African National Congress, Women's Charter (Adopted in Johannesburg, 17 April 1954)

Briefing by Commission for Gender Equality to the Women in the Presidency Committee on CEDAW and Beijing +20 report to UN by South Africa: 3 March 2015, accessed 20 July 2018 at https://pmg.org.za/committee-meeting/20098/

Combined Second Periodic Report under the African Charter on Human and People's Rights and Initial Report under the Protocol to the African Changer on the Rights of Women in Africa, South Africa (August 2015), accessed 20 July 2018 at http://www.achpr.org/files/sessions/58th/state-reports/2nd-2002-2015/staterep2_southafrica_2003_2014_eng.pdf

Commission for Gender Equality (CGE), Lack of gender transformation in the judiciary, investigative report, Complaint Ref No: WC/DRGU and Sonke/2012/KL (2016) http://pmg-assets.s3-website-eu-west-1.amazonaws.com/docs/080311nhtl.htm

Invitation for public comments, draft regulations relating to sexual offences courts: criminal law (sexual offences and related matters) amendment Act, 2007 (Act No. 32 of 2007), General Notice, (Department of Justice and Constitutional Development, 2017), accessed 20 July 2018 at https://juta.co.za/media/filestore/2015/10/Draft_Regulations_relating_to_Sexual_Offences_Courts_2015.pdf

Justice and Constitutional Development Portfolio Committee, Meeting Report, 18 May 2007, Criminal Law (Sexual Offences) Amendment Bill: Adoption of Report, Chairperson, Ms F Chohan-Khota

Legal Aid Guide, 12th edition (South Africa Legal Aid Board, 2012)
Ministerial Advisory Task Team on the Adjudication of Sexual Offence Matters, Report on the Re-establishment of Sexual Offences Courts (Department of Justice and Constitutional Development, August 2013)
National House of Traditional Leaders, Budget Review Report 2007–2008, accessed 20 July 2018 at http://pmg-assets.s3-website-eu-west-1.amazonaws.com/docs/080311nhtl.htm
Rules of the Constitutional Court, 460 Regulation Gazette (Department of Justice and Constitutional Development, 31 October 2003)
SAPS compliance to the Domestic Violence Act, report submitted to the Parliament of the Republic of South Africa, 3 November 2014, accessed 25 June 2018 at http://pmg-assets.s3-website-eu-west-1.amazonaws.com/141105research_unit_dva_compliance.pdf
Shadow Report on the South Africa State Report on the African Charter on Human and People's Rights and the Maputo Protocol by a Coalition of South African NGOs, 31 March 2016 (58th Ordinary Session of the ACHPR)
South African Law Commission, Harmonisation of the Common Law and the Indigenous Law: (Issue Paper 4 1999)
Harmonisation of the Common Law and the Indigenous Law: The Application of Customary law: Conflict of personal Laws
Harmonisation of the Common Law and Indigenous Law: Traditional Courts and the Judicial Function of Traditional Leaders (Discussion Paper 82, 1999)
Sexual Offences: The Substantive Law (Discussion Paper 85, 1999)
South African Law Reform Commission, Project 107 on Sexual Offences: Adult Prostitution (2017)

UN DOCUMENTS AND REPORTS

Access to justice for children, Report of the United Nations High Commissioner for Human Rights (16 December 2013) A/HRC/25/35
CEDAW Committee, General Recommendation No 12 on Violence Against Women (1989) UN Doc A/44/38
General Recommendation No 19 on Violence Against Women, (1992), UN Doc A/47/38
General Recommendation No 23 on Political and Public Life (1997), UN Doc A/52/38
General Recommendation No 25 on Article 4 paragraph 1 on temporary special measures (2004), UN Doc A/59/38
General Recommendation No 27 on older women and protection of their human rights (2010), UN Doc C/GC/27

General Recommendation No 28 on the core obligations of States parties under article 2 of the Convention on the Elimination of All Forms of Discrimination against Women, UN Doc C/GC/28 2010

Concluding Observations of the Committee on the Elimination of Discrimination against Women (5 April 2011) C/ZAF/CO/4

General Statement on the Elimination of Discrimination against Women on Rural Women (Adopted on 19 October 2011 during the 50th session)

Committee on Economic, Social and Cultural Rights, General Comment 3 on the Nature of States Parties' Obligations (1990) UN Doc E/1991/23

Committee on the Rights of the Child, General Comment No 13 on The Right of the Child to Freedom from all Forms of Violence (2011) CRC/C/GC/13

Coomaraswamy R, Report by the Special Rapporteur on Violence Against Women, its Causes and Consequences (4 January 1996) UN Doc E/CN.4/1996/53

Ertürk Y, Report by the Special Rapporteur on the Promotion and Protection of all Human Rights (27 May 2009) UN Doc A/HRC/11/6/Add.5.

Human Rights Council, Discriminatory Laws and Practices and Acts of Violence against Individuals based on their Sexual Orientation and Gender Identity (17 November 2011) UN Doc A/HRC/19/41

Resolution on Human Rights, Sexual Orientation and Gender Identity (15 June 2011) Res HRC/17/L.9/Rev.1

Nowak M, Report of the Special Rapporteur on Torture and other Cruel, Inhuman or Degrading Treatment or Punishment (5 February 2010) UN Doc A/HRC/13/39/Add.5

Report to the CEDAW Committee, South Africa, (25 February 1998) CEDAW/C/ZAF/1

Report to the CEDAW Committee, South Africa, (24 March 2010) CEDAW/C/ZAF/2–4

Report of the Special Rapporteur on violence against women, its causes and consequences on her mission to South Africa (14 June 2016) A/HRC/32/42/Add.2

South African Shadow Report submitted to the CEDAW Committee, 48th Session (17 January–4 February 2011)

UN Department on Economic and Social Affairs, Handbook for the Legislation on Violence against Women (New York, 2010) UN Doc ST/ESA/329

Supplement to the Handbook for Legislation on Violence against Women (New York, 2011) ST/ESA/331

UNGA, Report of the Independent Expert for the United Nations Study on Violence against Children (2006) UN Doc A/61/299

UNHCR, Gender, equality, nationality laws and statelessness, background note, (UNHCR, 7 March 2014)

United Nations, Report of the World Conference of the International Women's Year, (Mexico, 19 June–2 July 1975) UN Doc A/CONF.66/34

Report of the World Conference of the United Nations Decade for Women: Equality, Development and Peace, (Copenhagen, 14–30 July 1980) UN Doc A/CONF.94/35

World Conference to review and appraise the achievements of the United Nations Decade for Women: Equality, Development and Peace, (Nairobi, 15–26 July 1985) UN Doc A/CONF.116/28/Rev.

Report of the Fourth World Conference on Women, (Beijing, 4–15 September 1995) UN Doc A/CONF.177/20/Rev.1

SECONDARY SOURCES

Abd El-Hamid D, 'The National Council for Women: state feminism seeking to contain revolutionary feminism', Egyptian Initiative for Personal Rights, 2 October 2013, accessed 26 May 2018 at www.eipr.org/en/blog/dalia-abd-el-hameed/2013/10/national-council-women-state-feminism-seeking-contain-revolutionary

Abdel S and Fracolli E, 'Egypt's National Council for Women: a substitute for civil society?' The Tahrir Institute for Middle East Policy, 15 July 2016, accessed 26 May 2018 at www.timep.org/commentary/egypts-national-council-for-women-a-substitute-for-civil-society/

Abdel Wahab A, 'Al Gamaet Al Ahleyya fi Masr: ikhtilalat el dor' (NGOs in Egypt: role disorder), Al Ahram Center for Political and Strategic Studies, 30 May 2017, accessed 25 June 2018 at http://acpss.ahram.org.eg/News/16307.aspx

Abel R, 'A comparative theory of dispute institutions in society' (1974) 8 *Law and Society Review*, 2, 217–347

Politics by Other Means: Law in the Struggle Against Apartheid, 1980–1994 (New York and London: Routledge, 1995)

Abrahams H, *Rebuilding Lives after Domestic Violence: Understanding Long-term Outcomes* (London and Philadelphia, PA: Jessica Kingsley Publishers, 2010)

Supporting Women after Domestic Violence: Loss Trauma and Recovery (London and Philadelphia, PA: Jessica Kingsley Publishers, 2007)

Ackermann L and De Klerk G, 'Social factors that make South African women vulnerable to HIV infection' (2002) 23 *Health Care for Women International*, 2, 163–172

Adams R, 'Violence against women and international law: the fundamental rights to state protection from domestic violence' (2007) 20 *New York International Law Review*, 57, 104–129

Adams S, 'Court finds men can't be raped', The Mercury, 11 May 2007, cited in the Committee meeting of Justice and Correctional service, accessed 20 June 2018 at https://pmg.org.za/committee-meeting/8049/

Adeleye-Fayemi B, 'Creating and sustaining feminist space in Africa' in Luciana Ricciutelli et al. (eds.), *Feminist Politics, Activism and Vision: Local and Global Challenges* (London: Inanna Publications, 2004), pp. 100–121

AFP, 'Rights groups denounce Egypt NGO Law' Al-Monitor, 2 June 2017, accessed 17 July 2018 at www.al-monitor.com/pulse/afp/2017/06/egypt-politics-rights-law.html

Afshar H and Maynard M (eds.), *The Dynamics of Race and Gender: Some Feminist Interventions* (London: Taylor and Francis, 1994)

Afsharipour A, 'Empowering ourselves: the role of women's NGOs in the enforcement of the women's convention' (1999) 99 *Columbia Law Review*, 1, 129–172

Agati M, 'Undermining standards of good governance: Egypt's NGO law and its impact on the transparency and accountability of CSOs' (2006–2007) 9 *International Journal of Nonprofit Law*, 2, 56–85

Ahmed A, 'Criminalising consensual sexual behaviour in the context of HIV: consequences, evidence, and leadership' (2011) 6 *An International Journal for Research, Policy and Practice*, 3, 357–369

Al Sisi M, 'Saad Gamal lel moshakeken fi qanun el gameat el ahleyya: lan natruk belandna lel takhreeb' (Saad Gamal to the doubters of the NGO law: we will not leave our country to turmoil), Parlamany, 23 August 2017, accessed 18 July 2018 at www.parlmany.com

Al-Ali N, *Secularism, Gender and the State in the Middle East: The Egypt Women's Movement* (Cambridge: Cambridge University Press, 2004)

Al-Hindi H, 'Qanun al gameat al ahleya' (NGO law), SAS Post, 1 December 2016, accessed 17 July 2018 at www.sasapost.com/ngos-law-in-egypt/

Albertyn C, 'Women and the transition to democracy in South Africa' (1994) *Acta Juridica* 39

Albrecht P et al. (eds.), *Perspectives on Involving Non-State and Customary Actors in Justice and Security Reform* (Rome: International Development Law Organization, 2011)

Aleem A, 'Egyptian women fight for right to top judicial positions', Al-Monitor, 7 May 2018, accessed 15 June 2018 at www.al-monitor.com/pulse/originals/2018/05/egypt-appointment-female-judges-state-councils-controversy.html

Algero M G, 'The sources of law and the value of precedent: a comparative and empirical study of a civil law state in a common law nation' (2005) 65 *Louisiana Law Review*, 2, 775–822

Allam R, 'In Egypt, the Law itself is an Enemy of Women's Rights', Informed Comment, 24 February 2015, accessed 5 June 2018 at www.juancole.com/2015/02/itself-womens-rights.html

Allen D, 'Ethnomethodological insights into insider–outsider relationships in nursing ethnographies of healthcare settings' (2004) 11 *Nursing Inquiry*, 1, 14–24

Allen W, 'The reporting and underreporting of rape' (2007) 73 *Southern Economic Journal*, 3, 623–641

Alliance for Rural Democracy, 'Traditional courts bill is dead!' Land and Accountability Research Centre, 21 February 2014, accessed 30 June 2018 at www.customcontested.co.za/traditional-courts-bill-dead/

Allott A, *The Limits of Law* (London: Butterworths, 1980)

Amien W, 'A South African case study for the recognition and regulation of Muslim family law in a minority Muslim secular context' (2010) 24 *Law, Policy and the Family*, 3, 361–396

Amin H, *Research Methods in Law* (Glasgow: Royston Publishers, 1992)

Amit R, 'Winning isn't everything: courts, context, and the barriers to effecting change through public interest litigation' (2011) 27 *South African Journal on Human Rights*, 1, 8–38

Amnesty International, *Circles of Hell: Domestic Public and State Violence Against Women in Egypt*, report (Amnesty International, 2015)

An-Na'im A, 'State responsibility under international human rights law to change religious and customary law' in Rebecca Cook (ed.), *Human Rights of Women: National and International Perspectives* (Pennsylvania: University of Pennsylvania Press, 1994), pp. 167–189

'ANC youth leader guilty of "hate speech" after rape jibe', *Independent*, 16 March 2010, accessed 20 June 2018 at www.independent.co.uk/news/world/africa/anc-youth-leader-guilty-of-hate-speech-after-rape-jibe-1921836.html

Anderson K L and Umberson D, 'Gendering violence: masculinity and power in men's accounts of domestic violence' (2001) 15 *Gender and Society* 3, 358–380

Anderson M, 'Rape in South Africa' (1999–2000) 1 *Georgetown Journal of Gender and the Law*, 789

Andrew K and Nyirenda S, 'The role of the judiciary in protecting the rights of vulnerable groups in Malawi' in Anneke Meerkotter (ed.), *Using the Courts to Protect Vulnerable People: Perspectives from the Judiciary and Legal Profession in Botswana, Malawi, and Zambia* (Southern Africa Litigation Centre and others, 2015), pp. 1–10

Andrews P, 'From gender apartheid to non-sexism: the pursuit of women's rights in South Africa' (2001) 26 *North Carolina Journal of International Law and Commercial Regulation*, 693–716

'Violence against women in South Africa: the role of culture and the limitations of law' (1998–1999) 8 *Temple Political and Civil Rights Law Review*, 425–457.

Anaeme F O, 'Reducing gender discrimination and violence against women through library information services' (2012) *Library Philosophy and Practice*, 765

'Anger at South Africa woman trouser "ban"', BBC News, 26 July 2007, accessed 28 June 2018 at http://news.bbc.co.uk/2/hi/africa/6917332.stm

Anglin M, 'Feminist perspectives on structural violence' (1998) 5 *Identities: Global Studies in Culture and Power*, 2, 145–151.

Arizona Coalition against Domestic Violence, *Best practices manual for domestic violence programs* (June 2000)

Armstrong A, *Culture and Choice: Lessons from Survivors of Gender Violence in Zimbabwe* (Harare: AKA Distributer, 1998)

'Evidence in rape cases in four Southern African countries' (1989) 33 *Journal for African Law* 2, 172–184

Struggling over Scarce Resources: Women and Maintenance in Southern Africa (Harare: University of Zimbabwe Publications, 1992)

Artz L, 'Policing the Domestic Violence Act: teething troubles or system failure' (2001) 47 *Agenda*, 47, 4–13

'Shelter in the Southern Cape: gender violence undermines development' (1999) 15 *Agenda*, 42, 55–59

'Violence against women in rural Southern Cape: exploring access to justice through a feminist jurisprudence framework', research thesis (University of Cape Town Institute of Criminology, 1999)

Artz and Smythe D (eds.), *Should We Consent? Rape Law Reform in South Africa* (Cape Town: Juta, 2008)

'Case attrition in rape cases: a comparative analysis' (January 2007) 20 *South African Journal of Criminal Justice*, 2, 158–181

Arup C J, 'Educating cause lawyers in Australia after South Africa' in Stephen Ellman et al. (eds.), *For Martin Chanock: Essays on Law and Society* (Annandale, NSW: The Federation Press, 2010), pp. 107–125

Asimow M, 'Administrative law under South Africa's Interim Constitution' (1996) 44 *American Journal of Comparative Law*, 3, 393–420

Attalah L, 'While a bad year for civil society, all vow to find ways to continue', Mada Masr, 26 December 2016, accessed 17 July 2018 at www.madamasr.com/en/2016/12/26/feature/politics/while-a-bad-year-for-civil-society-all-vow-to-find-ways-to-continue/

Aucamp L et al., 'A critical analysis of legislation pertaining to the sexual abuse of children' (2012) 13 *Child Abuse Research: A South African Journal*, 1–10

Bachar G and Hensler D, 'Does alternative dispute resolution facilitate prejudice and bias? We still don't know' (2017) 70 *SMU Law Review*, 4, 817–836

Bader W and Cleveland D, 'Precedent and justice' (2011) 49 *Duquesne Law Review*, 56, 35–60

Baker P, 'And I went back: battered women's negotiation of choice' (1997) 26 *Journal of Contemporary Ethnography*, 1, 55–74

Banda F, 'Protocol to the African Charter on the Rights of Women in Africa' in Malcolm Evans and Rachel Murray (eds.), *The African Charter on Human and Peoples' Rights: The System in Practice, 1986–2006*, 2nd edition (Cambridge: Cambridge University Press, 2008), pp. 441–474

'Women and access to justice' in Ayesha Kadwani Dias and Gita Honwana Welch (eds.), *Justice for the Poor: Perspectives on Accelerating Access* (Oxford: Oxford University Press, 2009), pp. 129–153

'Women, law and human rights in Southern Africa' (2006) 32 *Journal of Southern African Studies*, 13, 13–27.

Barfield T et al., *Clash of Two Goods: State and Non-State Dispute Resolution in Afghanistan*, report (United States Institute of Peace, 2006)

Batley R, 'Engaged or divorced? Cross-service findings on government relations with non-state service-providers' (2006) 26 *Public Administration and Development*, 3, 241–251

Bauer G and Dawuni J (eds.), *Gender and the Judiciary in Africa: From Obscurity to Parity?* (New York: Routledge, 2015)

Bekker J et al. (eds.), *Introduction to Legal Pluralism in South Africa*, 2nd edition (Durban: LexisNexis Butterworths, 2006)

Belluck P, 'Shelters for women disclosing their locations, in spite of risks', *The New York Times*, 10 August 1997, accessed 20 July 2018 at www.nytimes.com/1997/08/10/us/shelters-for-women-disclosing-their-locations-in-spite-of-risk.html

Benedek W et al. (eds.), *The Human Rights of Women: International Instruments and African Experiences* (London: Zed Books, 2002)

Bennett T, *Customary law in South Africa* (Juta, 2004)

'The equality clause and customary law' (1994) 10 *South African Journal on Human Rights*, 1, 122–130

Human Rights and African Customary Law under the South African Constitution (Cape Town: Juta, 1995)

Benninger-Budel C (ed.), *Due Diligence and Its Application to Protect Women from Violence* (Leiden and Boston, MA: Martinus Nijhoff Publishers, 2008)

Beyani C, 'Toward a more effective guarantee of women's rights in the African human rights system' in Rebecca J Cook (ed.), *Human Rights of Women: National and International Perspectives* (Pennsylvania: University of Pennsylvania Press, 1994), pp. 285–307

Bijl C and Rumney P, 'Attitudes, rape and law reform in South Africa' (2010) 13 *New Criminal Law Review: An International and Interdisciplinary Journal*, 4, 826–840

Bishop-Sambrook C and Akamandisa V, *Chiefs and traditional leaders, Zambia*, case study (IFAD, November 2014)

Booth K and El Husseiny S, *Keeping Women Out: Sexual Violence Against Women in the Public Sphere*, report number 630a (FIDH and others, 2014)

Boonzaier F and La Rey C, '"He's a man, and I'm a woman": cultural constructions of masculinity and femininity in South African women's narratives of violence' (2003) 9 *Violence Against Women*, 8, 1003–1029

Bornman S et al., *Protecting Survivors of Sexual Offences: The Legal Obligation of the State with Regard to Sexual Offences in South Africa*, research report (Rape Crisis and the WLC, 2013)

Boulle L, *South Africa and the Consociational Option: A Constitutional Analysis* (Johannesburg: Juta, 1984)

Boulle L and Nesic M, *Mediation: Principles, Process, Practice* (Chatswood: Butterworths, 2001)

Bourke-Martignoni J, 'The history and development of the due diligence standard in international law and its role in the protection of women against violence' in Benninger-Budel C (ed.), *Due Diligence and Its Application to Protect Women from Violence* (Leiden and Boston, MA: Martinus Nijhoff Publishers, 2008), pp. 47–62

Brass J, *Allies or Adversaries: NGOs and the State in Africa* (Cambridge: Cambridge University Press, 2016)

Bratton M, *The Politics of Government – NGO Relations in Africa*, Working paper no. 456 (Nairobi: Institute for Development Studies, University of Nairobi, 1987)

Briggs C, *Learning How to Ask* (Cambridge: Cambridge University Press, 1986)

Britton H, 'Organising against gender-based violence in South Africa' (2006) 32 *Journal of Southern African Studies*, 1, 145–163

Broll R and Crooks C, *Report on the Evaluation of Violence Against Women Public Education Campaigns*, research report (Center for Research and Education on Violence against Women and Children, December 2012)

Browne C, 'Empowerment in social work practice with older women' (1995) 40 *Social Work*, 3, 358–364

Brownmiller S, *Against Our Will: Men, Women and Rape* (New York: Ballantine Books, 1994)

Brownstein B E, 'Private practice and cause lawyering: a practical and ethical guide' (2009) 31 *University of Arkansas at Little Rock Law Review*, 4, 601–608

Bryden D and Lengnick S, 'Rape in the criminal justice system' (1997) 87 *Journal of Criminal Law and Criminology*, 4, 1194–1384

Budlender G, 'Access to justice, lessons from South Africa land reform program' in Yash Ghai and Jill Cottrell (eds.), *Marginalized Communities and Access to Justice* (Abingdon and New York: Routledge, 2010), pp. 23–37

Budlender S et al., *Public Interest Litigation and Social Change in South Africa: Strategies, Tactics and Lessons*, research report (The Atlantic Philanthropies, 2014)

Bunch C, 'Women's rights as human rights: toward a re-vision of human rights' (1990) 12 *Human Rights Quarterly*, 4, 486–498

Burgess R, *In the Field: An Introduction to Field Research* (London and New York: Routledge, 1984)

Burman S, 'Fight a two-pronged attack: the changing legal status of women in Cape-ruled Basutoland, 1872–1884' in Cherryl Walker (ed.), *Women and Gender in Southern Africa to 1945* (Cape Town and London: David Philip Publisher, 1990), pp. 48–76

Burton M, 'Failing to protect: victims' rights and police liability' (2009) 72 *The Modern Law Review*, 2, 283–295

Burton R et al., 'Prevention of mother-to-child transmission in South Africa: an ever-changing landscape' (2015) 8 *Obstet Med*, 1, 5–12

Buss D and Manji A (eds.), *International Law: Modern Feminist Approaches* (Oxford: Hart, 2005)

Byrnes A and Connors J, 'Enforcing the human rights of women: a complaints procedure for the women's convention?' (1995–1996) 21 *Brooklyn Journal of International Law*, 3, 679–797

Byrnes B, 'The Convention on Elimination of all forms of Discrimination against Women' in Wolfgang Benedek et al. (eds.), *Human Rights of Women: International Instruments and African Experiences* (London: Zed Books, 2002), pp. 119–172

Calmore J, 'A call to context: the professional challenges of cause lawyering at the intersection of race, space and poverty' (1998–1999) 67 *Fordham Law Review*, 5, 1927–1957

Calnan S, *The Effectiveness of Domestic Human Rights NGOs: A Comparative Study* (Leiden and Boston, MA: Martinus Nijhoff Publishers, 2008)

CALS, Submission to the Director-General: Justice and Constitutional Development on the Draft Regulations Relating to Sexual Offences Courts: Criminal Law (Sexual Offences and Related Matters) Amendment Act, 2007 (Act No. 32 of 2007) (January 2018)

Cappelletti M and Garth B, 'Access to justice: the newest wave in the world-wide movement to make rights effective' (1977–1978) 27 *Buffalo Law Review*, 181–292

Cantrell D J, 'Sensational reports: the ethical duty of cause lawyers to be competent in public advocacy' (2007) 30 *Hamline Law Review*, 3, 568–585

Cashmore J, *The Impact of Delayed Reporting on the Prosecution and Outcomes of Child Sexual Abuse Cases*, research report (Sydney: Commonwealth of Australia, 2016)

Center for the Study of Reconciliation and Development, *Mapping Local Gender-based Violence Prevention and Response Strategies in South Africa*, research report (April 2016)

Center for Women's Global Leadership (ed.), *Gender Violence and Women's Human Rights in Africa* (Douglas College: Center for Women's Global Leadership, 1994)

Centre for Child Law, *Strategic Impact Litigation for Children's Rights*, research report (2011)

Chabalala J, 'Shock at moves to "spread resources" for sexual offences courts', News24, 18 May 2017, accessed 3 June 2018 at www.news24.com/SouthAfrica/News/shock-at-moves-to-spread-resources-for-sexual-offences-courts-20170518

Chanock M, 'Law, state and culture: thinking about 'customary law' after apartheid' (1991) *Acta Juridica*, 52–70

The Making of South African Legal Culture 1902–1936 (Cambridge: Cambridge University Press, 2001)

Charlesworth H, "Talking to ourselves? feminist scholarship in international law' in Sari Kouvo and Zoe Pearson (eds.), *Feminist Perspectives on Contemporary International Law* (Oxford: Hart, 2011), pp. 17–32

Charlesworth H and Chinkin C, 'The gender of jus cogens' (1993) 15 *Human Rights Quarterly*, 1, 63–76

Charlesworth H et al., 'Feminist approaches to international law' (1991) 85 *American Journal of International Law*, 4, 613–645

Chayes A, 'The role of the judge in public law litigation' (1976) 89 *Harvard Law Review*, 7, 1281–1316

Chiba M, *Legal Pluralism: Toward a General Theory through Japanese Legal Culture* (Tokyo: Tokai University Press, 1989),

Chinkin C, 'Violence against women' in Marsha A. Freeman et al. (eds.), *The UN Convention on the Elimination of all Forms of Discrimination against Women: A Commentary* (Oxford: Oxford University Press, 2012), pp. 444–475

Chopra T and Isser D, 'Women's access to justice, legal pluralism and fragile states' in Peter Albrecht et al. (eds.), *Perspectives on Involving Non-State and Customary Actors in Justice and Security Reform* (Rome: International Development Law Organization, 2011), pp. 23–36

Christensen D and Weinstein J, 'Defunding dissent: restrictions on aid to NGOs' (2013) 24 *Journal of Democracy*, 2, 77–91

Christofide N et al., *The State of Sexual Assault Services: Findings from a Situation Analysis of Services in South Africa*, research report (The South African Gender-based Violence and Health Initiative, 2003)

Citizens Advice Bureau UK, *Victims of Domestic Abuse: Struggling for Support*, research report (February 2015)

Claassens A, 'What's wrong with the Traditional Courts Bill', Mail & Guardian, 2 June 2008, accessed 30 June 2018 at www.mg.co.za/article/2008-06-02-whats-wrong-with-the-traditional-courts-bill.

Clark J, 'Democratising development: NGOs and the state' (1992) 2 *Development in Practice*, 3, 151–162

Clear S, '2018 must be the year that we reimagine judicial diversity', The Conversation, 3 January 2018, accessed 2 June 2018 at www.theconversation.com/2018-must-be-the-year-that-we-reimagine-judicial-diversity-89593

'Co-founder of anti-torture NGO Al-Nadeem prevented from traveling', Mada Masr, 18 October 2017, accessed 17 July 2018 at www.madamasr.com/en/2017/10/18/news/u/co-founder-of-anti-torture-ngo-al-nadeem-prevented-from-traveling/

Cock J, 'Engendering gay and lesbian rights: the equality clause in the South African Constitution' (2002) 26 *Women's Studies International Forum*, 1, 35–45

Women and War in South Africa (London: Open Letters, 1992)

Cock J and Fi D, 'The impact of globalisation on environmental politics in South Africa, 1990–2002' (2001) 5 *African Sociological Review*, 2, 15–35

Collins P, *Black Feminist Thought: Knowledge, Consciousness, and the Politics of Empowerment*, 2nd edition (New York and London: Routledge, 2000)

'Friends of the court: examining the influence of amicus curiae participation in U.S. Supreme Court litigation court (2004) 38 *Law and Society Review* 4, 807–832

Collison C, '#MiniMeeToo breaks long silences', Mail & Guardian, 22 June 2018, accessed 14 July 2018 at www.mg.co.za/article/2018-06-22-00-minimetoo-breaks-long-silences

'ConCourt ruling offers sexual abuse survivors opportunity of "getting justice"', Mail & Guardian, 14 June 2018, accessed 28 June 2018 at www.mg.co.za/article/2018-06-14-concourt-ruling-offers-sexual-abuse-survivors-opportunity-of-getting-justice

'"I didn't want to die" – queers battle prison', Mail & Guardian, 18 January 2018, accessed 11 July 2018 at www.mg.co.za/article/2018-01-18-i-didnt-want-to-die-queers-battle-prison-wardens

Comaroff J and Roberts S, *Rules and Processes: The Cultural Logic of Dispute in an African Context* (Chicago: University of Chicago Press, 1981)

Combrinck H, 'Positive state duties to protect women from violence: recent South African developments' (1998) 20 *Human Rights Quarterly*, 3, 666–690

Connell D, 'Strategies for change: women and politics in Eritrea and South Africa' (1998) 25 *Review of African Political Economy*, 76, 189–206

Connell P, 'Understanding victimization and agency: considerations of race, class and gender' (2008) 20 *Political and Legal Anthropology Review*, 2, 115–143

Connolly S, *Assessing the Successes of and Challenges Facing Civil Society Organizations in South Africa, in Influencing Gender-Based Violence Policy*, research report (SIT Graduate Institute, 2017)

Connors J, 'Optional Protocol' in M Freeman et al. (eds.), *The UN Convention on the Elimination of all Forms of Discrimination against Women: A Commentary* (Oxford: Oxford University Press, 2012), pp. 607–681

Conteh F, 'Chiefs, NGOs and alternative conflict resolution mechanisms in post-conflict Sierra Leone' (2014) 41 *Review of African Political Economy*, 142, 516–529

Cook R (ed.), *Human Rights of Women: National and International Perspectives* (Pennsylvania: University of Pennsylvania Press, 1994)

Cook R and Emerson R, 'Power, Equity and Commitment in Exchange' (1978) 43 *American Sociological Review*, 5, 721–739

Corra M and Willer D, 'The gatekeeper' (2002) 20 *Sociological Theory*, 2, 180–207

Coston J, 'A model and typology of government-NGO relationships' (1998) 28 *Nonprofit and Voluntary Sector Quarterly*, 3, 358–382

Cote D and Garderen J, 'Challenges to public interest litigation South Africa: external and internal challenges to determining the public interest' (2011) 27 *South African Journal on Human Rights*, 1, 167–182

Cowan R, 'Do women on South Africa's Courts make a difference', Courting Justice, June 2011, accessed 20 June 2018 at www.courtingjustice.com/DoWomen-MD.html

Cowan R B, 'Women's representation on the courts in the Republic of South Africa' (2006) 6 *The University of Maryland Law Journal of Race, Religion, Gender and Class*, 291–318

Cumming S and Rhode D, 'Public interest litigation: insights from theory and practice' (2009) 36 *Fordham Urban Law Journal*, 4, 615–619

Curran E and Bonthuys E, 'Customary law and domestic violence in South African communities' (2005) 21 *South African Journal on Human Rights*, 4, 607–635

Cusack S and Timmer A, 'Gender stereotyping in rape cases: The CEDAW Committee's decision in *Vertido v The Phillipines*' (2011) 11 *Human Rights Law Review*, 2, 329–342

Dagnino F, 'Expanding access to justice in Africa' in Ayesha Kadwani Dias and Gita Honwana Welch (eds.), *Justice for the Poor: Perspectives on Accelerating Access* (Oxford: Oxford University Press, 2009), pp. 419–448

Daly K, *Conventional and Innovative Justice Responses to Sexual Violence*, research report no 12 (Australian Center for the Study of Sexual Assault, 2011)

Daly K and Bouhours B, 'Rape and attrition in the legal process: a comparative analysis of five countries' (2010) 39 *Crime and Justice*, 1, 565–650

Danish Institute for Human Rights, *Informal Justice System: Charting a Course for Human Rights Based Engagement* (UN Women, UNICEF and UNDP, 2012)

Darwiche N, 'Women in Arab NGOs: a publication of the Arab network for non-governmental organisations' (2001) 69 *Feminist Review*, 15–20

Davis A and Salem R 'Dealing with power imbalances in the mediation of interpersonal disputes' (1984) 6 *Mediation Quarterly*, 19–26

Davis D and Le Roux M, *Precedent and Possibility: The (ab)use of Law in South Africa* (Cape Town: Juta and Company Ltd, 2009)

Dawoud A, 'Why women are losing rights in the post-revolutionary Egypt' (2012) 13 *Journal of International Women's Studies*, 5, 160–169

Dawuni J, 'To 'mother' or not to 'mother': The representative roles of women judges in Ghana' (2016) 60 *Journal of African Law*, 3, 419–440

Dembowski H, *Taking the State to Court: Public Interest Litigation and the Public Sphere in Metropolitan India* (Oxford: Oxford University Press, 2001)

De Vos P, 'Male rape: what were the judges smoking?', Constitutionally Speaking, 10 May 2007, accessed 20 June 2018 at www.constitutionallyspeaking.co.za/male-rape-what-were-the-judges-smoking

Derdeery N, 'Al mar'a saneat al salam' (The woman is a peacemaker), Al Ahram, 18 September 2017, accessed 20 June 2018 at http://gate.ahram.org.eg/News/1584718.aspx

Desai V and Howes M, 'Accountability and participation: a case study from Bombay' in Michael Edwards and David Hulme (eds.), *Non-Governmental Organisations: Performance and Accountability* (London: Earthscan, 1996), pp. 83–95

Deva S, 'Public interest litigation in India: a critical review' (2009) 28 *Civil Justice Quarterly*, 19–40

Devi K (ed.), *Violence against Women: Human Rights Perspectives* (New Delhi: Serials Publications, 2005)

Dey K et al., *The Road to Justice: Victim Empowerment Legislation in South Africa*, research report (Cape Town: the Rape Crisis Cape Town Center and others, 2011)

Di Silvo L, 'Correcting corrective rape: *Carmichele* and developing South Africa's affirmative obligations to prevent violence against women' (2011) 99 *Georgetown Law Journal*, 5,1469–1516

Dias A, 'International law and sources of access to justice' in Ayesha Kadwani Dias and Gita Honwana Welch (eds.), *Justice for the Poor: Perspectives on Accelerating Access* (Oxford: Oxford University Press 2009), pp. 3–73

Dias A and Welch G (eds.), *Justice for the Poor: Perspectives on Accelerating Access* (Oxford: Oxford University Press, 2009)

Dingwall R and Eekelaar J (eds.), *Divorce Mediation and the Legal Process* (Oxford: Clarendon Press, 1988)

Dissel A and Ngubeni K, *Giving Women Their Voices: Domestic Violence and Restorative Justice in South Africa*, research report (Center for the Study of Violence and Reconciliation, 2003)

Du Bois F, 'Judicial selection in post-apartheid South Africa' in Kate Malleson and Peter H Russell (eds.), *Appointing Judges in an Age of Judicial Power – Critical Perspectives from Around the World* (Toronto: University of Toronto Press, 2006), pp. 280–312

Duffy H, *Strategic Litigation Impacts Torture in Custody*, research report (Open Society Foundations, 2017)

Dunn J and Powell-Williams M, '"Everybody makes choices": victim advocates and the social construction of battered women's victimization and agency' (2007) 13 *Violence against Women*, 10, 977–1001

Dupuy K et al., 'Who survived? Ethiopia's regulatory crackdown on foreign-funded NGOs' (2015) 22 *Review of International Political Economy*, 2, 419–456

Dutton M, *Empowering and Healing the Battered Woman: A Model for Assessment and Intervention* (New York: Springer Publishing Company, 2000)

Ebrahim A, 'Accountability in practice: mechanisms for NGOs' (2003) 31 *World Development*, 5, 813–829

'Making sense of accountability: conceptual perspectives for northern and southern nonprofits' (2003) 14 *Nonprofit Management and Leadership*, 2, 191–212

NGOs and Organizational Change: Discourses, Reporting, and Learning (Cambridge: Cambridge University Press, 2003)

Edwards A, 'Violence against women as sex discrimination: judging the jurisprudence of United Nations human rights treaty bodies' (2008) 18 *Texas Journal of Women and the Law*, 1–44

Violence Against Women under International Human Rights Law (Cambridge: Cambridge University Press, 2011)

Edwards M and Hulme D (eds.), *Making a Difference: NGOs and Development in a Changing World* (UK and USA: Earthscan Publication, 1992)

Non-Governmental Organisations: Performance and Accountability (London: Earthscan Publications, 1996)

Eekelaar J, 'From multiculturalism to cultural voluntarism: a family-based approach' (2010) 81 *The Political Quarterly*, 3, 344–355

'Egypt: escalating judicial harassment of human rights NGOs', Frontline Defenders, 21 March 2016, accessed 17 July 2018 at www.frontlinedefenders.org/en/statement-report/egypt-escalating-judicial-harassment-human-rights-ngos

'Egypt: events of 2016', Human Rights Watch, accessed 1 June 2018 at www.hrw.org/world-report/2017/country-chapters/egypt#6e1aab

El Feki S et al., *Understanding Masculinities: Results from the International Men and Gender Equality Survey*, report (UN Women and Promundo-US, 2017)

Elbayar K, 'NGO laws in selected Arab states' (2005) 7 *International Journal of Not-for-Profit Law*, 4, 3–27

Elias T, *The Nature of African Customary Law* (Manchester: Manchester University Press, 1956)

Ellman S et al. (eds.), *For Martin Chanock: Essays on Law and Society* (Annandale, NSW: The Federation Press, 2010)

Emerson R, 'Power-dependence relations' (1962) 27 *American Sociological Review*, 1, 31–41

Emerton R et al. (eds.), *International Women's Rights Cases* (New York: Routledge, 2016)

Enyew E L, 'Ethiopian customary dispute resolution mechanisms: forms for restorative justice?' (2014) 14 *African Journal on Conflict Resolution*, 1, 125–155

Ernberg E et al., 'Court evaluations of young children's testimony in child sexual abuse cases', Legal and Criminological Psychology, 7 February 2018, accessed 6 June 2018 at www.onlinelibrary.wiley.com/doi/epdf/10.1111/lcrp.12124

Esack F, 'Three Islamic strands in the South African struggle for justice' (1998) 2 *Islam and politics*, 2, 473–498

Etienne M, 'The ethics of cause lawyering: an empirical examination of criminal defense lawyers as cause lawyers' (2005) 95 *Journal of Criminal Law and Criminology*, 4, 1195–1260

Euromed Rights, Report on Violence against Women, Egypt (9 December 2016)

Ewing D, 'Rape, gender and the justice system' (2003) 56 *Agenda*, 54–60

Ezer T and Patel P, 'Being strategic about strategic litigation: four things we've learned from a public health context', Human Rights Funders Network, 28 July 2016, accessed 11 July 2018 at www.hrfn.org/community-voices/being-strategic-about-strategic-litigation-four-things-weve-learned-from-a-public-health-context/

Faedi B, 'Domestic violence as a human rights violation: the challenges of a regional human rights approach in Africa' in Emily Burrill et al. (eds.), *Domestic Violence and the Law in Colonial and Postcolonial Africa* (Ohio: Ohio University Press, 2010), pp. 256–277

Falola T, *Colonialism and Violence in Nigeria* (Bloomington and Indianapolis, IN: Indiana University Press, 2009)

Farnworth C et al., *Transforming Gender Relations in Agriculture in Sub-Saharan Africa* (Stockholm: Swedish International Agricultural Network Initiative, 2013)

Faundez J, 'Community, justice institutions and judicialization: lessons from rural Peru' in Ayesha Kadwani Dias and Gita Honwana Welch (eds.),

Justice for the Poor: Perspectives on Accelerating Access (Oxford: Oxford University Press, 2009), pp. 106–128

Fearon K, 'Pragmatism, proximity and pashtunwali: informal justice at the district level in Helmand Province State' in Peter Albrecht et al. (eds.), *Perspectives on Involving Non-State and Customary Actors in Justice and Security Reform* (Rome: International Development Law Organization, 2011)

Fedler J, 'Lawyering domestic violence through the Prevention of Family Violence Act 1993 – evaluation after a year in operation' (1995) 112 *South African Law Journal* 231

Felstiner W, 'Influences of social organization on dispute processing' (1974) 9 *Law and Society Review*, 1, 63–94

FIDH, 'Egypt: Arrest and release on bail of Azza Soliman', urgent appeal, International Federation for Human Rights, 8 December 2016, accessed 18 June 2018 at www.fidh.org/en/issues/human-rights-defenders/egypt-arrest-and-release-on-bail-of-azza-soliman

Fife W, *Doing Fieldwork: Ethnographic Methods for Research in Developing Countries and Beyond* (USA: Palgrave Macmillan, 2005)

Fine S, 'Sexual assault myths at centre of important Supreme Court case', The Globe and the Mail, 8 Febraury 2018, accessed 6 June 2018 at www.theglobeandmail.com/news/national/sexual-assault-myths-at-centre-of-important-supreme-court-case/article37916188/

Fisher B et al., 'Reporting sexual victimization to the police and others: results from a national-level study of college women' (2003) 30 *Criminal Justice and Behavior*, 1, 6–38

Fischer K et al., 'The Culture of Battering and the Role of Mediation in Domestic Violence Cases' (1992–1993) 46 *Southern Methodist University Law Review*, 2117–2174

Fisher H, *Building Promising Practices: Campaigning, Awareness Raising and Capacity Building to Combat Violence Against Women – A Human Rights Approach*, expert paper (UN Division for the Advancement of Women, Expert Group Meeting, 17–20 May 2005)

Fitzpatrick P, 'Law and societies' (1984) 22 *Osgoode Hall Law Journal*, 1, 115–138

Flynn A and Hodgson J (eds.), *Access to Justice and Legal Aid: Comparative Perspectives on Unmet Legal Need* (Oxford and Portland, OR: Hart Publishing, 2017)

Foa E et al., 'Psychological and environmental factors associated with partner violence' (2000) 1 *Trauma, Violence and Abuse*, 1, 67–91

Ford L, 'Egypt court ruling upholds decision to freeze assets of women's rights activists', *The Guardian*, 12 January 2017, accessed 17 July 2018 at www.theguardian.com/global-development/2017/jan/12/egypt-court-ruling-upholds-decision-freeze-assets-womens-rights-activists

Foucault M, 'The subject and the power' (1982) 8 *Critical Inquiry*, 777

Fourie J and Gruzd S, 'Battling violence against women: From Africa's top to toe', South African Institute of International Affairs, 20 April 2015, accessed 20 June 2018 at www.saiia.org.za/opinion-analysis/battling-violence-against-women-from-africas-top-to-toe

Fourie R, 'South Africa' in K Malley-Morrison (ed.), *International Perspectives on Family Violence and Abuse: A Cognitive Ecological Approach* (New York: Routledge, 2004), pp. 243–261

Freeman M, 'Women, law and land at the local level: claiming women's human rights in domestic legal systems' (1994) 16 *Human Rights Quarterly*, 3, 559–575

Freeman M et al. (eds.), *The UN Convention on the Elimination of all Forms of Discrimination against Women: A Commentary* (Oxford: Oxford University Press, 2012)

Frenkel R, 'Feminism and contemporary culture in South Africa' (2008) 67 *African Studies*, 1, 1–10

Fritz N, 'Crossing Jordan: constitutional space for (un)civil sex' (2004) 20 *South African Journal on Human Rights*, 2, 230–248

Fuchs G, 'Using strategic litigation for women's rights: political restrictions in Poland and achievements of the women's movement' (2013) 20 *European Journal of Women's Studies*, 1, 21–45

Gallinetti J and Kassan D, 'Children and sexual offences' victims' in Lillian Artz and Dee Smythe (eds.), *Should We Consent? Rape Law Reform in South Africa* (Cape Town: Juta, 2008), pp. 144–173

Garcia-Moreno C et al., *Global and Regional Estimates of Violence against Women: Prevalence and Health Effects of Intimate Partner Violence and Nonpartner Sexual Violence* (World Health Organization, 2013)

Gasa N, 'Let them build more goals' in Gasa N (ed.), *Women in Southern African History: They Remove Boulders and Cross Rivers* (Cape Town: Human Science Research Council, 2007), pp. 129–152

Women in Southern African History: They Remove Boulders and Cross Rivers (Human Science Research Council, 2007)

Geisler G, 'Parliament is another terrain of struggle: women, men and politics in South Africa' (2000) 38 *The Journal of Modern African Studies*, 4, 605–630

Gender Equality Commission, *Balanced Participation of Women and Men in Decision-making*, analytical report (Council of Europe, 2016)

Gerntholtz L and MacLeod J, 'Gender and socio-economic rights "the case of gender-based violence and health"' in Malcolm Langford et al. (eds.), *Socio-economic Rights in South Africa: Symbols or Substance* (Cambridge: Cambridge University Press, 2014), pp. 365–388

Ghai Y and Cottrell J (eds.), *Marginalized Communities and Access to Justice* (Abingdon and New York: Routledge, 2010)

Gibbons, K and Johnson T, *Integrated Approaches to Eliminate Gender Based Violence* (London: Commonwealth Secretariat, 2003)

Glenn C and Goodman L, 'Living with and within the rules of domestic violence shelters: A qualitative exploration of residents' experiences' (2015) 21 *Violence against Women*, 12, 1481–1506

Goetz A, 'Women in politics and gender equity in policy: South Africa and Uganda' (1998) 25 *Review of African Political Economy*, 76, 241–262

'Women's political effectiveness: a conceptual framework' in Anne Marie Goetz and Shireen Hassim (eds.), *No Shortcuts to Power: African Women in Politics and Policy Making* (London and New York: Zed Books, 2003), pp. 29–80

Goetz A and Hassim S (eds.), *No Shortcuts to Power: African Women in Politics and Policy Making* (London and New York: Zed Books, 2003)

Goldfarb S F, 'Reconceiving civil protection orders for domestic violence: Can law help end the abuse without ending the relationship?' (2008) 29 *Cardozo Law Review*, 4, 1487–1551

Goodman G et al., 'Testifying in criminal court: emotional effects of child sexual assault victims' (1992) 57 *Monographs of the Society for Research in Child Development*, 5

Goodmark L, 'Alternative dispute resolution and potential for gender bias' (2000) 39 *The Judges' Journal*, 21

Gordon N, 'Human rights, social space and power: why do some NGOs exert more influence than others?' (2008) 12 *The International Journal of Human Rights*, 1, 23–39

Gouws A, 'The state of national gender machinery: structural problems and personalised politics' in Sakhela Buhlungu et al. (eds.), *State of the Nation: South Africa 2005–2006* (Cape Town: HSRC Press, 2006)

Govender M, 'Domestic violence: is South Africa meeting its obligations in terms of the women's convention?' (2003) 19 *South African Journal on Human Rights*, 4, 663–687

Govender V and Killean R, *Lawyers, Conflict and Transition: South Africa*, research report (Economic and Social Research Council, December 2016)

Gqirana T, 'New traditional courts bill "everyone can live with"', News24, 23 January 2017, accessed 30 June 2018 at www.news24.com/SouthAfrica/News/new-traditional-courts-bill-everyone-can-live-with-20170123

Grant E, 'Human rights, cultural diversity and customary law in South Africa' (2006) 50 *Journal of African Law*, 1, 2–23

Greatbatch D and Dingwall R, 'Argumentative talk in divorce mediation sessions' (1997) 62 *American Sociological Review*, 1, 151–170

'Selective facilitation: some preliminary observations on a strategy used by divorce mediators' (1989) 23 *Law and Society Review*, 4, 613–642

Green D, *Gender Violence in Africa: African Women's Responses* (London: Palgrave Macmillan, 1999)

Grey S and Sawer M (eds.), *Women's Movements: Flourishing or in Abeyance* (London: Routledge, 2008)

Griffin R, 'The Traditional Courts Bill: Are they getting it right?', Helen Suzman Foundation, 14 February 2017, accessed 30 June 2018 at www.hsf.org.za/publications/hsf-briefs/the-traditional-courts-bill-are-they-getting-it-right

Griffiths A, *In the Shadow of Marriage: Gender and Justice in the African Community* (Chicago, IL: University of Chicago Press, 1997)

Grossman N, 'Sex on the bench: do women judges matter to the legitimacy of international courts' (2011–2012) 12 *China Journal of International Law*, 2, 647–683

Grubb A and Turner E, 'Attribution of blame in rape cases: a review of the impact of rape myth acceptance, gender role conformity and substance use on victim blaming' (2012) 17 *Aggression and Violent Behaviour*, 5, 443–452

Guide to Strategic Litigation, Public Law Project, 13 January 2014, accessed 18 June 2018 at www.publiclawproject.org.uk/resources/guide-to-strategic-litigation/

Habib, A, 'State-civil society relations in post-apartheid South Africa' (2005) 72 *Social Research*, 3, 671–692

Habib A and Taylor R, 'South Africa: anti-apartheid NGOs in transition' (1999) 10 *Voluntas: International Journal of Voluntary and Nonprofit Organizations*, 1, 73–82.

Hague G et al., *Is Anyone Listening?: Accountability and Women Survivors of Domestic Violence* (London: Routledge, 2003)

Hajjar, L, 'Religion, state power, and domestic violence in Muslim societies: a framework for comparative analysis' (2004) 29 *Law and Social Inquiry*, 1, 1–38

Hallward-Driemeier M and Hasan T, *Empowering Women: Legal Rights and Economic Opportunities in Africa* (Washington, DC: World Bank, 2012)

Harding A, 'Will South Africans ever be shocked by rape?', BBC World News, 10 January 2013, accessed 17 July 2018 at www.bbc.co.uk/news/world-africa-20971240

Hassan H A, 'Civil society in Egypt under the Mubarak regime' (2011) 2 *Afro Asian Journal of Social Sciences*, 2, 2

Hassim S, '"A conspiracy of women": the women's movement in South Africa's transition to democracy' (2002) 69 *Social Research*, 3, 693–732

Hatem M, 'In the shadow of the state: changing definitions of Arab women's "developmental" citizenship rights' (2005) 1 *Journal of Middle East Women's Studies*, 3, 20–45

Henderson R, '"Gender transformation in the judiciary being addressed in silos": CGE', Times Live, 7 December 2016, accessed 17 June 2018 at www.timeslive.co.za/news/south-africa/2016-12-07-gender-transformation-in-the-judiciary-being-addressed-in-silos-cge/

Herrold C, 'NGO policy in pre- and post-Mubarak Egypt: effects on NGOs' roles in democracy promotion' (2016) 7 *Nonprofit Policy Forum*, 2, 189–212

Heurlin C, 'Governing civil society: the political logic of NGO–state relations under dictatorship' (2010) 21 *Voluntas: International Journal of Voluntary and Nonprofit Organizations*, 2, 220–239

Himonga C and Bosch C, 'The application of African customary law under the Constitution of South Africa: problems solved or just beginning?' (2000) 117 *South African Law Journal*, 306

Hoffman-Wanderer Y, 'Sentencing and management of sexual offenders' in Lillian Artz and Dee Smythe (eds.), *Should We Consent? Rape Law Reform in South Africa* (Cape Town: Juta, 2008), pp. 224–262

Holness W and Rule S, 'Barriers to advocacy and litigation in the equality courts for persons with disabilities' (2014) 17 *P.E.R.*, 5, 1907–1963

Holtmaat R, 'Article 5' in Marsha A Freeman et al. (eds.), *The UN Convention on the Elimination of all Forms of Discrimination against Women: A Commentary* (Oxford: Oxford University Press, 2012), pp. 141–167

'Preventing violence against women: the due diligence standards with respect to the obligation to banish gender stereotypes on ground of Article 5(a) of the CEDAW Convention' in Carin Benninger-Budel (ed.), *Due Diligence and Its Application to Protect Women from Violence* (Leiden and Boston, MA: Martinus Nijhoff Publishers, 2008), pp. 63–90

Honemann B and Heywood M, 'A judgment that saved a million lives', The Star, 5 July 2012, accessed 17 June 2018 at www.iol.co.za/the-star/a-judgment-that-saved-a-million-lives-1334636

Hooks B, *Feminist Theory: From Margin to Center*, 3rd edition (New York and London: Routledge, 2014)

Horowitz R, 'Remaining an outsider: membership as a threat to research rapport' (1986) 14 *Journal of Contemporary Ethnography*, 4, pp. 409–430

Hosny H, 'George Ishak yotaleb bi3adet el nazar fi qanoun el gamaet el ahleyya' (George Ishaak demands the reconsideration of the NGO law), Maswawy, 3 October 2017, accessed 17 July 2018 at www.masrawy.com/news/news_egypt/details/2017/10/3/1165387/

Hossain S and Welchman L (eds.), *Honour: Crimes, Paradigms, and Violence Against Women* (London and New York: Zed Books, 2005)

Howe G, *Sexual Violence Against Children in the Caribbean: Report 2012* (UNICEF, May 2013)

Hsu C, 'Beyond civil society: an organizational perspective on state–NGO relations in the People's Republic of China' (2010) 6 *Journal of Civil Society*, 3, 259–277

Hulme D and Edwards M, (eds.), *NGOs, States and Donors: Too Close for Comfort?* (UK: Palgrave Macmillan, 1997)

Human Rights Watch, 'Egypt: new law will crush civil society', Human Rights Watch, 2 June 2017, accessed 17 July 2018 at www.hrw.org/news/2017/06/02/egypt-new-law-will-crush-civil-society

Hated to Death: Homophobia, Violence and Jamaica's HIV/AIDS Epidemic, research report (Human Rights Watch, 2004)

The State Response to Domestic Violence and Rape, research report (Human Rights Watch, 1995)

Violence Against Women in South Africa: State Response to Domestic Violence and Rape, research report (Human Rights Watch, 1996)

'We'll Show You You're a Woman': Violence and Discrimination Against Black Lesbians and Transgender Men in South Africa, research report (Human Rights Watch, 2011)

Hund J (ed.), *Law and Justice in South Africa* (Rondebosch: Centre for Intergroup Studies, 1988)

'Husband killer loses bid for appeal' IOL, 22 September 2010, accessed 20 June 2018 at www.iol.co.za/news/south-africa/western-cape/husband-killer-loses-bid-for-appeal-680850

Hutchinson T, *Researching and Writing in Law* (Pyrmont, NSW: Lawbook, 2006)

Hweshe F, 'Call for faster delivery after Irene's death', IOL, 5 August 2008, accessed 10 June 2018 at www.iol.co.za/news/south-africa/call-for-faster-delivery-after-irenes-death-411161

Ibrahim A, 'Head of Egypt's council for women slams detained female activists', Middle East Eye, 17 November 2014, accessed 17 July 2018 at www.middleeasteye.net/news/head-egypt-council-women-slams-detained-girls-1879918577

International Council on Human Rights, *When Legal Worlds Overlap: Human Rights, State and Non-State Law* (Versoix: International Council on Human Rights, 2009)

International Standards of Judicial Independence (International Association of Judicial Independence and World Peace, 2008)

Izunwa M, 'A critique of certain aspects of the grounds, procedure and reliefs attaching to customary divorce law in Southern Nigeria' (2015) 7 *Journal of Law and Conflict Resolution*, 5, 31–38

Jad I, 'The "NGOization" of the Arab women's movements' (2003) 11 *Al-Raida*, 38–47

Jankie D, 'Tell me who you are: problematizing the construction and positionalities of "insider"/"outsider" of a "native" ethnographer in a postcolonial context' in Kagendo Mutua and Beth Blue Swadener (eds.), *Decolonizing Research in Cross-Cultural Context: Critical Personal Narratives* (New York: State University of New York Press, 2004), pp. 87–104

'JASA assembles experts to oppose bid to lower age of sexual consent', Gateway News, 14 December 2011, accessed 2 June 2018 at www.gatewaynews.co.za/jasa-assembles-experts-to-oppose-bid-to-lower-age-of-sexual-consent/

Jayawardena K, *Feminism and Nationalism in the Third World* (London: Zed Books, 1986)

Jegede A, 'From military rule to constitutional government: the case of Nigeria' in Morris Kiwinda Mbondenyi and Tom Ojienda (eds.), *Constitutionalism and Democratic Governance in Africa: Contemporary Perspectives from Sub-Saharan Africa* (Pretoria: Pretoria University Law Press, 2013), pp. 337–353

Jewkes R et al., *He Must Give Me Money, He Mustn't Beat me': Violence Against Women in Three South African Provinces* (Pretoria: Medical Research Council, 1999)

Joachim J, 'Framing issues and seizing opportunities: the UN, NGOs, and women's rights' (2003) 47 *International Studies Quarterly*, 2, pp. 247–274

John V, 'Sadtu warns it will go after NGOs', Mail & Guardian, 2 November 2012, accessed 7 July 2018 at www.mg.co.za/article/2012-11-02-sadtu-warns-it-will-go-after-ngos

Johnson K, 'Lawyering for social change: what's a lawyer to do?' (1999) 5 *Michigan Journal of Race and Law*, 1, 201–228

Jonas O, 'The participation of the amicus curiae institution in human rights litigation in Botswana and South Africa: a tale of two jurisdictions' (2015) 59 *Journal of African Law*, 2, 329–354

Jones L, 'The haves come out ahead: how cause lawyers frame the legal system for movements' in Austin Sarat and Stuart Scheingold (eds.), *Cause Lawyering, Political Commitments and Professional Responsibilities* (Oxford: Oxford University Press, 1998), pp. 182–196

Jordan J, 'Beyond belief: police, rape and women's credibility' (2004) 4 *Criminology and Criminal Justice*, 1, 29–59

Joubert P, 'Grootboom dies homeless and penniless', Mail & Guardian, 8 August 2008, accessed 10 June 2018 at www.mg.co.za/article/2008-08-08-grootboom-dies-homeless-and-penniless

Kabeer N, 'Resources, agency, achievements: reflections on the measurements of women's empowerment' (1999) 30 *Development and Change*, 3, 435–464

Kaersvang D, 'Equality courts in South Africa: legal access for the poor' (2008) 15 *The Journal of the International Institute*, 2, 4–9

Kaganas F and Murray C, 'The contest between culture and gender equality under South Africa's Interim Constitution' (1994) 21 *Journal of Law and Society*, 4, 409–433

'Law and women's rights in South Africa: an overview' (1994) 1 *Acta Juridica*, 1–38

'Rape in marriage – conjugal right or criminal wrong' (1983) *Acta Juridica*, 125–143

Kamal H, 'Inserting women's rights in the Egyptian Constitution: personal reflections' (2015) 19 *Journal for Cultural Research*, 2, 150–161

Kamat S, 'The privatization of public interest: theorizing NGOs' discourse in a neoliberal era' (2004) 11 *Review of International Political Economy*, 1, 155–176

Kamau W, 'Law, culture and dispute resolution: prospects for alternative dispute resolution in Africa' (2009) 15 *East African Journal of Peace and Human Rights*, 2, 336–360

'Women judges and magistrates in Kenya: challenges, opportunities and contributions' in Ulrike Schultz and Gisela Shaw (eds.), *Gender and Judging* (Oxford: Hart Publishing, 2013)

Kane M et al., *Reassessing Customary Law Systems as a Vehicle for Providing Equitable Justice for the Poor*, research paper (New Frontiers of Social Policy, Arusha, December 2005)

Karam A M, *Women, Islamisms and the State: Contemporary Feminisms in Egypt* (London: Palgrave MacMillan, 1998)

Kathree F, 'Public interest law: its continuing role in South Africa' (2002) 15 *Advocate*, 3, 32–40

Katy, *Dealing with Rape as a 'Hate Crime' within the Lesbian Community*, report (Pandora's Aquarium, 2009), accessed 25 June 2018 at www.pandys.org/articles/rapeashatecrime.pdf

Kausch K, *Defenders in Retreat: Freedom of Association and Civil Society in Egypt*, working paper (Madrid: Fride, April 2009)

Keck M and Sikkink K, *Activists Beyond Borders: Advocacy Networks in International Borders* (Ithaca, NY: Cornell University Press, 1998)

Keehn E, *The Equality Courts as a Tool for Gender Transformation* (Cape Town: Sonke Gender Justice Network, 2010)

Kelly L, *Routes to (In)Justice: A Research Review on the Reporting, Investigation and Prosecution of Rape Cases*, research report (London: HMCPSI, 2002)

Kenney S, *Gender and Justice: Why Women in the Judiciary Really Matter* (New York: Routledge, 2013)

Kerber K et al., 'South African child deaths 1990–2011: have HIV services reversed the trend enough to meet Millennium Development Goal 4?' (2013) 27 *AIDS*, 16, 2637–2648

Kettel B, 'Challenging the margin: gender equality and the UN reform process' (2007) 28 *Third World Quarterly*, 5, 871–886

Khamis S, 'The Arab "feminist" spring?' (2011) 37 *Feminist Studies*, 3, 692–695

Kholofelo M, 'Challenges and achievement with regard to woman and child abuse prevention by the South African Police Services' (2016) 4 *Sociology and Anthropology*, 1, 6–10

Kim J and Motsei M, '"Women enjoy punishment": attitudes and experiences of gender-based violence among PHC nurses in rural South Africa' (2002) 54 *Social Science and Medicine*, 8, 1243–1254

Kimble J and Unterhalter E, '"We opened the road for you, you must go forward": ANC women's struggles, 1912–1982' (1982) 12 *Feminist Review*, 11–35

Kingham T and Coe J, *The Good Campaigns Guide: Campaigning for Impact*, report (NCVO Publications, 2005)

Klaaren J, 'The cost of justice' (2014) 7 *The Salon*, 21–25, accessed 23 June 2018 at www.jwtc.org.za/resources/docs/salon-volume-7/6_TheSalon_Vol7.pdf

Klug H, *The Constitution of South Africa: A Contextual Analysis* (UK: Hart Publishing, 2010)

Korte M, 'Judges matter: transforming the judiciary', GroundUp,15 July 2014, accessed 20 June 2018 at www.groundup.org.za/article/judges-matter-transforming-judiciary_1999/

Krishnan J K, 'Lawyering for a cause and experiences from abroad' (March 2006) 94 *California Law Review*, 2, 575–616

Kruger R, 'Sex work from a feminist perspective: a visit to the Jordan case' (2004) 20 *South African Journal on Human Rights*, 1, 138–150

Kruger T et al., *Making South Africa Safe: A Manual for Community-based Crime Prevention*, research report (The Council for Scientific and Industrial Research, 2016)

Kuumba M, *Gender and Social Movements* (Jaipur: Rawat Publications, 2003)

Lake M, *Strong NGOs and Weak States: Pursuing Gender Justice in the Democratic Republic of Congo and South Africa* (Cambridge: Cambridge University Press, 2018)

Lamble L, 'UN Women report: access to justice in Botswana', The Guardian, 6 July 2011, accessed 3 June 2018 at www.theguardian.com/global-development/poverty-matters/2011/jul/06/un-women-justice-botswana

Lancaster L et al., *Assault and Sexual Offences: Overview of the Official Statistics 2014/15*, research report (Institute for Security Studies, September 2015)

Lawyers for Human Rights, 'Police failure to assist complainants in terms of the Domestic Violence Act is misconduct and a disciplinable offence', press release, 2017, accessed 25 June 2018 at www.lhr.org.za/news/2017/press-release-police-failure-assist-complainants-terms-domestic-violence-act-misconduct-an

Lawyers without Borders, *Strategic Litigation of Human Rights Abuses: A Guidebook for Legal Practitioners from the Commonwealth Caribbean* (Quebec City and Kingston: Lawyers without Borders, 2014)

Lea J and Stemson K, 'Security, sovereignty and non-state governance "from below"' (2007) 22 *Canadian Journal of Law and Society*, 2, 9–27

Lehnert W, 'The role of the courts in the conflict between African customary law and human rights' (2005) 21 *South African Journal on Human Rights*, 2, 241–277

Lemaire K L et al., 'Labelling sexual victimization experiences: the role of sexism, rape myth acceptance and tolerance for sexual harassment' (2016) 31 *Violence and Victims*, 2, 332–346

Leonard L, 'Characterising civil society and its challenges in post-apartheid South Africa' (2014) 40 *Social Dynamics*, 2, 371–391

Leveraging the SDGs for Inclusive Growth: Delivering Access to Justice for All, issue brief (OECD and Open Society Foundation, 11 September 2016)

Liamputtong P, *Doing Cross-Cultural Research: Ethical and Methodological Perspectives* (Dordrecht: Springer, 2008)

Logan T et al., 'Protective orders in rural and urban areas: a multiple perspective study' (2005) 11 *Violence Against Women*, 7, 876–911

Londono E, 'In Egypt, NGO crackdown and draft law have chilling effect', The Washington Post, 11 February 2012, accessed 17 July 2018 at www.washingtonpost.com/world/middle_east/in-egypt-ngo-crackdown-and-draft-law-have-chilling-effect/2012/02/11/gIQANO9b6Q_story.html?noredirect=on&utm_term=.c41b1cdbca8c

Longwe S, 'Breaking the patriarchal alliance: governments, bi-laterals, and NGOs' (1994) 2 *Gender and Development*, 3, 62–69

'Case study: legal action to stop hotels discriminating against women in Zambia' (2011) 15 *Feminist Africa*, 83–104

Lovaglia M et al., 'Negotiated exchanges in social networks' (1995) 74 *Social Forces*, 1, 123–155

Lyon E et al., *Meeting Survivors' Needs: A Multi-state Study of Domestic Violence Shelter Experiences* (National Institute of Justice, October 2008)

Mabandla B, 'Women in South Africa and the Constitution-making process' in Julie Peters and Andrea Wolper (eds.), *Women's Rights, Human Rights: International Feminist Perspectives* (New York: Routledge 1995), pp. 67–71

Maboe M, 'Strategies to tackle rape and violence against women in South Africa' in Center for Women's Global Leadership (ed.), *Gender Violence and Women's Human Rights in Africa* (New Brunswick, NJ: Douglass College, Center for Women's Global Leadership, 1994), pp. 30–37

MacCrate R, '"The lost lawyer" regained: the abiding values of legal profession' (1996) 100 *Dickinson Law Review*, 587

Mackinnon C, *Toward a Feminist Theory of the State* (Cambridge, MA: Harvard University Press, 1991)

Women's Lives Men's Laws (Cambridge, MA: Harvard University Press, 2005)

Maclean M and Eekelaar J, *Family Law Advocacy: How Barristers Help the Victims of Family Failure* (Oxford and Portland, OR: Hart Publishing, 2009)

Madlingozi T, 'Post-apartheid social movements and legal mobilisation' in Malcolm Langford et al. (eds.), *Socio-economic Rights in South Africa: Symbols or Substance* (Cambridge: Cambridge University Press, 2014), pp. 92–130

Madsen, Peter, 'Rebellious women – discourses and tests: Shari'a, civil rights and penal law' in Lisbet Christoffersen and Jørgen S. Nielson (eds.),

Shari'a As Discourse: Legal Traditions and the Encounter with Europe (London and New York: Routledge, 2016), pp. 217–236

Mahmud S, 'Actually how *empowering* is microcredit?' (2003) 34 *Development and Change*, 4, 577–605

Makhafola G, 'Too few women appointed to judiciary', IOL, 7 December 2016, accessed 17 June 2018 at www.iol.co.za/news/politics/too-few-women-appointed-to-judiciary-7119871

Malecha A et al., 'Applying for and dropping a protection order: a study with 150 women' (2003) 14 *Criminal Justice Policy Review*, 4, 486–504

'Malema pays R50 000 fine for rape remark', News24, 8 August 2011, accessed 20 June 2018 at www.news24.com/SouthAfrica/Politics/Malema-pays-R50-000-fine-for-rape-remark-20110808

Malleson K and Russell P H (eds.), *Appointing Judges in an Age of Judicial Power – Critical Perspectives from Around the World* (Toronto: University of Toronto Press, 2006)

Maneta R, 'The public weighs in on "adolescent sex" bill', Live South Africa, 6 March 2015, accessed 17 June 2018 at www.livemag.co.za/live-regulars/public-weighs-adolescent-sex-bill/

Manji A, 'Imagining women's "legal world": towards a feminist theory of legal pluralism in Africa' (1999) 8 *Social Legal Studies*, 4, 435–455

Manjoo R, 'Case study: the Commission for Gender Equality, South Africa: promotion and protection of gender equality – are separate structures necessary?' (July 2005) 14 *Griffith Law Review*, 2, 268–279

Marcus G and Budlender S, *A Strategic Evaluation of Public Interest Litigation in South Africa*, research report (The Atlantic Philanthropies, 2008)

Marcussen H, 'NGOs, the state and civil society' (1996) 23 *Review of African Political Economy*, 69, 405–423

Margulies P, 'Political lawyering, one person at a time: the challenge of legal work against domestic violence for the impact litigation/client service debate' (1996) 3 *Michigan Journal of Gender and Law*, 2, 493–514

Marroushi N, *Violence Against Women in Egypt: Prospects for Improving Police Response*, report (Saferworld, June 2015)

Marsden P, 'Restricted access in networks and models of power' (1983) 88 *American Journal of Sociology*, 4, 686–717

Martabano A and O'Sullivan M, '"Three steps forward, two steps back": legal activism for women's rights in South Africa' (2004) 60 *Agenda*, 55–61

Mason K, 'Measuring women's empowerment: learning from cross-national research' in Deepa Narayan (ed.), *Measuring Empowerment: Cross Disciplinary Perspectives* (Washington, DC: The World Bank, 2005), pp. 89–102

Mashele P, 'Traditional leadership in South Africa's new democracy' (2004) 31 *Review of African Political Economy*, 100, 349–354

Mathews S et al., *Every Six Hours a Woman Is Killed by her Intimate Partner*, Policy Brief (Medical Research Centre, 2004)

Matuba M, 'Know your rights – use the law to save a life', Daily Maverick, 8 December 2017, accessed 20 June 2018 at www.dailymaverick.co.za/opinionista/2017-12-08-know-your-rights-use-the-law-to-save-a-life/#.Wy-qWqczbIV

Maughan K, 'Malema in hot water over rape claims', IOL, 26 May 2009, accessed 17 June 2018 at www.iol.co.za/news/politics/malema-in-hot-water-over-rape-claims-444435

May C, 'Substantive gender equality, sex work and the assumptions of S v Jordan: in pursuit of equality in South Africa' in Mandivavarira Mudarikwa et al. (eds.), *Pursuit of Equality in South Africa* (Johannesburg: Synergetic Fast Services, 2017).

Mbondenyi M and Ojienda T (eds.), *Constitutionalism and Democratic Governance in Africa: Contemporary Perspectives from Sub-Saharan Africa* (Pretoria: Pretoria University Law Press, 2013)

McClintock A, 'No longer in a future heaven: women and nationalism in South Africa' (1991) 51 *Transition*, 104–123

McGann J, 'Pushback against NGOs in Egypt' (2008) 10 *International Journal of Not-for-Profit Law*, 4, 29–42

McKaiser E, 'Not white enough, not black enough', The New York Times, 15 February 2012, accessed 20 July 2018 at https://latitude.blogs.nytimes.com/2012/02/15/in-south-africa-after-apartheid-colored-community-is-the-big-loser/?_r=0

Mcloughlin C, 'Factors affecting state-non-governmental organization relations in service provision: key themes from the literature' (2001) 31 *Public Administration and Development*, 4, 240–251

McNeely N and Robinson-Simpson G, 'The truth about domestic violence: a falsely framed issue' (1987) 32 *Social Work*, 6, 485–490

McNeely R L and Robinson-Simpson G, 'The truth about domestic violence: a falsely framed issue' (1987) 32 *Social Work*, 6, 485–490

McQuoid-Mason D, 'Access to justice in South Africa' (1999) 17 *The Windsor Yearbook of Access to Justice*, 230–246

'The delivery of civil legal aid services in South Africa' (2000) 24 *Fordham International Law Journal*, 6, 111–142

'Delivery of legal aid services in developing countries' in Ayesha Kadwani Dias and Gita Honwana Welch (eds.), *Justice for the Poor: Perspectives on Accelerating Access* (Oxford: Oxford University Press, 2009), pp. 449–482

Medie P, 'Fighting gender-based violence: the women's movement and the enforcement of rape law in Liberia' (2013) 112 *African Affairs*, 448, 377–397

Meerkotter A (ed.), *Using the Courts to Protect Vulnerable People: Perspectives from the Judiciary and Legal Profession in Botswana, Malawi, and Zambia* (Southern Africa Litigation Centre and others, 2015)

Meghahed N and Lack S, 'Colonial legacy, women's rights and gender-educational inequality in the Arab World with particular reference to Egypt and Tunisia' (2011) 57 *International Review of Education*, 3/4, 397–418

Meintjes S, 'The politics of engagement: women transforming the police process – domestic violence legislation in South Africa' in Anne Marie Goetz and Shireen Hassim (eds.), *No Shortcuts to Power: African Women in Politics and Policy Making* (London and New York: Zed Books, 2003), pp. 110–139

'The women's struggle for equality during South Africa's transition to democracy' (1996) 30 *Transformation*, 47–63

Menkel-Meadow C, 'The causes of cause lawyering' in Austin Sarat and Stuart Scheingold (eds.), *Cause Lawyering, Political Commitments and Professional Responsibilities* (Oxford: Oxford University Press, 1998), pp. 31–61

Menski W, *Comparative Law in a Global Context: the Legal Systems of Asia and Africa* (London: Platinum, 2000)

Mercer C, 'Reconceptualizing state-society relations in Tanzania: are NGOs "making a difference"?' (1999) 31 *Area*, 3, 247–258.

Merry S, *Human Rights and Gender Violence: Translating International Law into Local Justice* (Chicago, IL: University Of Chicago Press, 2006)

'Rights, religion, and community: approaches to violence against women in the context of globalization' (2003) 35 *Law and Society Review*, 1, 39–88

Merten M, 'Parliament: national minimum wage bill will not be rushed', The Daily Maverick, 23 March 2018, accessed 6 June 2018 at www.dailymaverick.co.za/article/2018-03-23-parliament-national-minimum-wage-bill-will-not-be-rushed/#.Wx_snkiFPIU

'Parliament: Opt-out, Traditional Courts Bill supports "most hated clause"', Daily Maverick, 19 March 2018, accessed 30 June 2018 at www.dailymaverick.co.za/article/2018-03-19-parliament-opt-out-traditional-courts-bill-supporters-most-hated-clause/#.WzhCmNIzbIU

Meyer M, 'The plaintiff as person: cause lawyering, human subject research, and the secret agent problem' (15 July 2012) 119 *Harvard Law Review*, 5, 1510–1532

Meyer M and Prugal E (eds.), *Gender Politics in Global Governance* (Lanham, MD: Rowman and Littlefield Publishers, 1999)

Michaels R, 'Re-statement of non-state law: the state, choice of law and the challenge from global legal pluralism' (2005) 51 *Wayne Law Review*, 1209–1259

Mikell G, *African Feminism: The Politics of Survival in Sub-Saharan Africa* (Pennsylvania: University of Pennsylvania Press, 1997)

Miller S, 'Consent and coercion in the law of rape in South Africa: a feminist transformative approach' (2010) 28 *Canadian Women's Studies*, 1, 81–89

'Reforming the law of rape in South Africa' in Clare McGlynn and Vanessa E Munro (eds.), *Rethinking Rape Law: International and Comparative Perspectives* (London: Routledge 2010)

Victims as Offenders: The Paradox of Women's Violence in Relationships (New Brunswick, NJ and London: Rutgers University Press, 2005)

Mills S, *Language and Sexism* (Cambridge: Cambridge University Press, 2010)

Milton J, *South African Criminal Law and Procedure*, 3rd edition (South Africa: Juta, 1996)

Mkhize S, 'A victory for the rights of women in rural South Africa', Open Society Foundations, 7 May 2014, accessed 30 June 2018 at www.opensocietyfoundations.org/voices/victory-rights-women-rural-south-africa

Moffett H, 'These women, they force us to rape them: rape as narrative of social control in post-apartheid South Africa' (2006) 32 *Journal of Southern African Studies*, 1, 129–144.

Moghadam V, *Globalizing Women: Transnational Feminist Networks* (Baltimore, MD and London: The Johns Hopkins University Press, 2005)

Mohamed R, 'Women and the Arab Spring: tough choices to make', Open Democracy, 25 October 2013, accessed 25 June 2018 at www.opendemocracy.net/arab-awakening/reem-mohamed/women-and-arab-spring-tough-choices-to-make

Mohsen M, 'No reconciliation with terrorists', Daily News Egypt, 21 August 2013, accessed 17 July 2018 at www.dailynewsegypt.com/2013/08/21/no-reconciliation-with-terrorists-ncw/

Moore D, *Civil Society Under Threat: Common Legal Barriers and Potential Responses*, report (European Parliament, 2006) EP/ExPol/B/2006/30

Moore S, *Law as Process, an Anthropological Approach*, 2nd edition (Oxford: James Curreys, 2000)

Morabe B, 'The equality court explained', Polity, 19 May 2011, accessed 28 June 2018 at www.polity.org.za/article/the-equality-court-explained-2011-05-19

Morris H and Read J (eds.), *Indirect Rule and the Search for Justice* (Oxford: Clarendon Press, 1972)

Mosleh H et al., *Advancing Egyptian Society by Ending Violence Against Women*, policy brief (Population Reference Bureau, May 2015)

Moult K, 'Providing a sense of justice: informal mechanisms for dealing with domestic violence' (2005) 12 *South Africa Crime Quarterly*, 1, 19–24

Moustafa T, 'Law versus the state: the judicialization of politics in Egypt' (2003) 28 *Law and Society Inquiry*, 4, 883–930

Moyo, 'Regulation or strangulation? NGO laws in Africa, part 1: South Africa', Mail & Guardian, 5 October 2008, accessed 20 July 2017 at www.thoughtleader.co.za/bhekinkosimoyo/2008/10/05/regulation-or-strangulation-ngo-laws-in-africa-part-1-south-africa

Mubangizi J, *The Protection of Human Rights in South Africa: A Legal and Practical Guide* (Lansdowne: Juta, 2004)

Muholi Z, 'Thinking through lesbian rape' (2004) 61 *Agenda: Empowering Women for Gender Equity*, 61, 116–125

Mujuzi J, 'Protocol to the African Charter on Human and People's Rights on the Rights of Women in Africa: South Africa's reservations and interpretative declarations' (2008) 12 *Law, Democracy and Development*, 2, 41–62

Mulugeta Y, 'Public interest litigation as practiced by South African human rights NGOs: any lessons for Ethiopia', LLM Thesis (University of Pretoria, 2005)

Munger F, 'The cause lawyer's cause' in Stephen Ellman, Heinz Klug and Penelope Andrews (eds.), *For Martin Chanock: Essays on Law and Society* (Annandale, NSW: The Federation Press, 2010), pp. 95–106

Mushota L, *International Law, Women's Rights and the Courts: A Zambian in Using Courts to Protect Vulnerable People*, research paper (Southern Africa Litigation Centre and others, 2004)

Mutua M, 'Savages, victims and saviors: the metaphor of human rights' (2001) 42 *Harvard International Law Journal*, 1, 201–246

Myers J, *Indirect Rule in South Africa: Tradition, Modernity and the Costuming of Political Power* (New York: University of Rochester Press, 2008)

Nagar R and Raju S, 'Women, NGOs and the contradictions of empowerment and disempowerment: a conversation' (2003) 35 *Antipode*, 1, 1–13

Naidu E and Mkhiz N, 'Gender-based violence: the lesbian and gay experience' (2005) 19 *Agenda*, 66, 34–38

'Nazra bids farewell to its office and continues its work', press release, Nazra for Feminist Studies, 16 March 2018, accessed 17 July 2018 at www.nazra.org/en/2018/03/nazra-bids-farewell-its-office-and-continues-its-work

Ndegwa S, *The Two Faces of Civil Society: NGOs and Politics in Africa* (West Hartford, CT: Kumarian Press, 1996)

Ndulo M, 'African customary law, customs, and women's rights' (2011) 11 *Indiana Journal of Global Legal Studies*, 1, 87–120.

Nejima S, 'Pakistan: regulations and potentiality in a fragmented society' in Shinichi Shigetomi (ed.), *The State and NGOs: Perspective from Asia* (Singapore: ISEAS-Yusof Ishak Institute, 2002), pp. 94–109

Nell D, 'The rainbow nation and its strange racial terminology', MacMillan Dictionary Blog, 28 June 2010, accessed 20 July 2018 at www.macmillandictionaryblog.com/bastaard

NGOPulse, '16 days of activism against women and children abuse', NGOPulse, 23 November 2017, accessed 20 June 2018 at www.ngopulse.org/article/2017/11/23/16-days-activism-against-women-and-children-abuse

Nhlapo T, 'Cultural diversity, human rights and the family in contemporary Africa: lessons from the South African Constitutional debate' (1995) 9 *International Journal of Law and the Family*, 2, 208–225

'Customary law in post-apartheid South Africa: The vexed question of cultural diversity, women's rights, "living law", and appropriate law reform' (2014) New York Law Review, accessed 20 July 2018 at www.nylslawreview.com/wp-content/uploads/sites/16/2014/11/Nhlapo.pdf

'Indigenous law and gender in South Africa: taking human rights and cultural diversity seriously' (1995) 13 *Third World Legal Studies*, 49–71

'International protection of human rights and the family: Africa variations on a common theme' (1989) 3 *International Journal of Law and Family*, 1, 1–20

Nicolson G, 'Gender-based violence: concerns raised over reduction in funding for sexual offences courts', Daily Maverick, 19 May 2017, accessed 4 June 2018 at www.dailymaverick.co.za/article/2017-05-19-gender-based-violence-concerns-raised-over-reduction-in-funding-for-sexual-offences-courts/#.WxlDj0iFPIU

Nielsen M L, 'From practice to police, and back: emerging lessons from working with community-based justice mechanisms in Helmand, Afghanistan' in Peter Albrecht et al. (eds.), *Perspectives on Involving Non-State and Customary Actors in Justice and Security Reform* (Rome: International Development Law Organization, 2011), pp. 159–177

Nolde J, 'South African women under apartheid: domestic service and forms of resistance to promote change' (1991) 10 *Third World Legal Studies*, 203–223

Nullis C, 'New rape laws to help protect victims', The Mail & Guardian, 14 December 2007, accessed 6 June 2018 at www.mg.co.za/article/2007-12-14-new-rape-laws-to-help-protect-victims

Nutley S et al., *Using Evidence: How Research Can Inform Public Services* (Bristol: Policy Press, 2007)

Nzegwu N, *Family Matters: Feminist Concepts in African Philosophy of Culture* (New York: State University of New York Press, 2006)

O'Connor J, '"NGO": the guise of innocence' (2012) 5 *Irish Foreign Affairs*, 1, 5–8

O'Neill A, 'Strategic litigation before the European Courts' (2015) 16 *ERA Forum*, 4, 495–509

Oagile B and Dingake J, 'The role of the judiciary and the legal profession in protecting the rights of 18 vulnerable groups in Botswana' in Anneke Meerkotter (ed.), *Using the Courts to Protect Vulnerable People: Perspectives from the Judiciary and Legal Profession in Botswana, Malawi, and Zambia* (Southern Africa Litigation Centre and others, 2015), pp. 18–24

Okharedia A, 'The emergence of alternative dispute resolution in South Africa: a lesson for other African countries', 6th IIRA African Regional Congress of Industrial Relations, Lagos, Nigeria (January 2011)

Oloka-Onyango J, 'Modern-day missionaries or misguided miscreant? NGOs, the women's movement and the promotion of human rights in Africa' in Wolfgang Benedek et al. (eds.), *Human Rights of Women: International Instruments and African Experiences* (London: Zed Books, 2002), pp. 286–294

One in Nine Campaign, *Rape Survivors' Guide to the Criminal Justice System in South Africa* (2012)

Onyejekwe C, 'The interrelationship between gender-based violence and HIV/AIDS in South Africa' (2004) 6 *Journal of International Women's Studies*, 1, 34–40

Oomen B, *Chiefs in South Africa: Law, Power and Culture in the Post-Apartheid Era* (USA: Palgrave, 2005)

Open Society Foundation, *Justice Sector and the Rule of Law* (South Africa: Open Society Foundation, 2005)

Osório C, 'The justice delivery system: a crossroads', WLSA, July 2003, accessed 30 June 2018 at www.wlsa.org.mz/article-the-justice-delivery-system-a-crossroads/

Oyewumi O, *The Invention of Women: Making an African Sense of Western Gender Discourses* (Minneapolis, MN and London: University of Minnesota Press, 1997), pp. 21–157

Pagelow M, *Family Violence* (New York, Westport, CT and London: Greenwood Publishing Group, 1984)

Palitza K, *Traditional Leaders Wield the Power, and They Are Almost All Men: The Importance of Involving Traditional Leaders in Gender Transformation*, research report (Sonke Gender Justice Network, October 2010)

'Pants ban prohibited in Umlazi', News24, 9 April 2008, accessed 18 June 2018 at www.news24.com/SouthAfrica/News/Pants-ban-prohibited-in-Umlazi-20080409

Parliament of the Republic of South Africa, 'Police committee chair proposes eight measures to deal with gender violence', press release, 21 November 2017, accessed 25 June 2018 at www.parliament.gov.za/press-releases/police-committee-chair-proposes-eight-measures-deal-gender-violence

'Parliamentarian calls for toughening penalties of anal rape', Egypt Today, 17 December 2017, accessed 1 June 2018 at www.egypttoday.com/Article/2/37218/Parliamentarian-calls-for-toughening-penalties-of-anal-rape

'Parliamentary 25–30 bloc calls on Sisi not to ratify new "restrictive" NGO Law', Ahram Online, 1 December 2016, accessed 17 July 2018 at http://english.ahram.org.eg/NewsContent/1/0/251089/Egypt/0/-Parliamentary--bloc-calls-on-Sisi-not-to-ratify-n.aspx

Parpart J et al. (eds.), *Rethinking Empowerment: Gender and Development in a Global/Local World* (London and New York: Routledge, 2002),

Parry-Williams J, 'Scaling-up via Legal Reform in Uganda' in Edwards M and Hulme D (eds.), *Making a Difference: NGOs and Development in a Changing World* (London: Earthscan Publications, 1992), pp. 89–98

Patel P, 'Realising the full potential of civil and political rights for marginalized populations in African Countries' in Anneke Meerkotter (ed.), *Using the Courts to Protect Vulnerable People: Perspectives from the Judiciary and Legal Profession in Botswana, Malawi, and Zambia* (Southern Africa Litigation Centre and others, 2015), pp. 39–46

Patel P and Ezer T, *Advancing Public Health Through Strategic Litigation: Lessons from Five Countries*, research report (Open Society Foundations, 2016)

Patton M, *Qualitative Research and Evaluation Methods* (USA: Sage Publications, 2002)

Pauw I and Brener L, '"You are just whores: you can't be raped": barriers to safer sex among women street sex workers in Cape Town' (2003) 5 *Culture, Health and Sexuality*, 6, 465–481

Pelad E et al., 'Choice and empowerment for battered women who stay: toward a constructive model' (2000) 45 *Social Work*, 1, 9–25

Penal Reform International, *Access to Justice in Sub-Saharan Africa: The Role of Traditional and Informal Justice Systems* (UK: Penal Reform International, 2000)

Perelman J, 'The way ahead? Access-to-justice, public interest lawyering and the right to legal aid in South Africa' (2005) 41 *Stanford Journal of International Law*, 2, 357–400

Pick S et al., 'NGO-Government partnerships for scaling-up: sexuality education in Mexico' (2008) 18 *Development in Practice*, 2, 164–175

Pickup F et al., *Ending Violence against Women* (Oxford: Oxfam, 2001)

Pillay D, 'Public interest Law in South Africa', Oxford Human Rights Hub, 15 May 2013, based on the 11th Victoria and Griffiths Mxenge Memorial Lecture, delivered at UKZN in May 2013, accessed 3 June 2018 at http://ohrh.law.ox.ac.uk/public-interest-law-in-south-africa/

Pithey B et al., 'Gender-based violence in South Africa: a submission to the Universal Periodic Review' (Shukumisa, 2016)

'Police, NGO team up to fight human trafficking', News24, 4 October 2016, accessed 7 July 2018 at www.news24.com/SouthAfrica/News/police-ngo-team-up-to-fight-human-trafficking-20161004

Pollack S, 'Reconceptualising women's agency and empowerment: challenges to self-esteem discourse and women's lawbreaking' (2000) 12 *Women and Criminal Justice*, 1, 75–89

Pollard A and Court J, 'How civil society organizations use evidence to influence policy processes' in Anthony Bebbington et al. (eds.), *Can NGOs Make a Difference? The Challenge of Development Alternatives* (London and New York: Zed Books, 2008), pp. 133–153

POWA, *Breaking the Silence, Stories from the Other(ed) Women*, research report (POWA Women's Writing Project, 2009)

Priaulx N, 'Testing the margin of appreciation: therapeutic abortion, reproductive "rights" and the intriguing case of *Tysiąc v. Poland*' (2008) 15 *European Journal of Health Law*, 4, 361–379

Ptacek J (ed.), *Restorative Justice and Violence against Women* (Oxford: Oxford University Press, 2009)

Quansah E, 'Custody of children: customary principles in Ghana and Nigeria' (1991) 17 *Commonwealth Law Bulletin*, 1, 347–355

Rackley E, *Women, Judging and the Judiciary: From Difference to Diversity* (Oxon: Routledge, 2013)

Raeba M and Rocha J, *Campaigns to End Violence Against Women and Girls*, research report (UN Women, December 2011)

Ramotsho K, 'Sexual Offences Act reviewed', De Rebus: Law Society of South Africa, 1 February 2018, accessed 25 June 2018 at www.derebus.org.za/sexual-offences-act-reviewed/

Randell M, 'Refugee law and state accountability for violence against women: a comparative analysis of legal approaches to recognizing asylum claims based on gender persecution' (2002) 25 *Harvard Women's Law Journal*, 281–318

Rani R, Bonu S and Diop-Sidibe N, 'An empirical investigation of attitudes towards wife-beating among men and women in seven Sub-Saharan African Countries' (2004) 8 *African Journal of Reproductive Health*, 3, 116–136

Reda L, 'Introducing Egypt's strategy to combat violence against women', Egypt Today, 3 December 2017, accessed 20 June 2018 at www.egypttoday.com/Article/2/35200/Introducing-Egypt%E2%80%99s-strategy-to-combat-violence-against-women

Redman R, 'Litigating for gender equality: the amicus curiae role of the sex discrimination commissioner' (2004) 27 *University of New South Wales Law Journal*, 3, 849–957

Regan L and Kelly L, *Rape: Still a Forgotten Issue*, briefing document (Europe: Rape Crisis Network, 2003)

Reid G, 'The Traditional Courts Bill threatens LGBT South Africans', Human Rights Watch, 29 May 2012, accessed 30 June 2018 at www.hrw.org/news/2012/05/29/traditional-courts-bill-threatens-lgbt-south-africans

Rhode D, *Access to Justice* (Oxford: Oxford University Press, 2004)

'Whatever happened to access to justice?' (2008–2009) 42 *Loyola of Los Angeles Law Review*, 869–912

Ricciutelli L et al. (eds.), *Feminist Politics, Activism and Vision: Local and Global Challenges* (London: Inanna Publications, 2004)

Riskin L, 'Mediation and lawyers' (1982) 43 *Ohio State Law Journal*, 29–60.

Rittenhouse R, *The Due Diligence Obligation to Prevent Violence Against Women: The Case of Pakistan*, legal report (New York: Human Rights Foundation, 22 December 2011),

Roa M and Klugman B, 'Considering strategic litigation as an advocacy tool: a case study of the defence of reproductive rights in Colombia' (2014) 22 *Reproductive Health Matters*, 44, 31–41

Roberts A and Burman S, 'National survey on empowerment strategies, crisis intervention and cognitive problem-solving therapy with battered women' in Albert R. Roberts (ed.) *Battered Women and Their Families: Intervention Strategies and Treatment Programs*, 3rd edition (New York: Springer Publishing Company, 2007)

Roberts S, 'Law and the study of social control in small-scale societies' (1976) 39 *The Modern Law Review*, 6, 663–679

'Three models of family mediation' in Robert Dingwall and Jon Eekelaar (eds.), *Divorce Mediation and the Legal Process* (Oxford: Oxford University Press, 1988), pp. 144–149

Roberts S and Palmers M, *Dispute Processes: ADR and the Primary Forms of Decision-Making*, 2nd edition (Cambridge: Cambridge University Press, 2005)

Roehrs S, 'Half-hearted HIV-related services for victims' in Lillian Artz and Dee Smythe (eds.), *Should We Consent? Rape Law Reform in South Africa* (Cape Town: Juta, 2008), pp. 175–197

Ross R, *A Concise History of South Africa* (Cambridge: Cambridge University Press, 1999)

Rowe C J, 'Cyberfeminism inaction' in Sandra Grey and Marian Sawer (eds.), *Women's Movements: Flourishing or in Abeyance* (London: Routledge, 2008), pp. 128–140

Rowlands J, 'Empowerment examined' (1995) 5 *Development in Practice*, 2, 101–107

'A word of the times, but what does it mean? Empowerment in the discourse and practice of development' in Haleh Afshar (ed.), *Women and Empowerment: Illustrations from the Third World* (London: St. Martin's Press, 1998), pp. 11–34

Ruffner T, *Under Threat: Egypt's Systematic Campaign Against NGOs*, research report (POMED: Project on Middle East and Democracy, March 2015)

Rutherford, B K, *Egypt after Mubarak: Liberalism, Islam, and Democracy in the Arab World* (Princeton, NJ: Princeton University Press, 2008)

Saccuzzo D, 'How should the police respond to domestic violence: a therapeutic jurisprudence analysis of mandatory arrest' (1998–1999) 39 *Santa Clara Law Review*, 3, 765–787

Sachs A, 'Concluding comments on the panel discussion' (2007) 8 *ESR Review*, 1, 17–20

The Strange Alchemy of Life and Law (Oxford: Oxford University Press, 2009)

Sakr N, 'Seen and starting to be heard: women and the Arab media in a decade of change' (2002) 69 *Social Research*, 3, 821–850

Samir N, 'State Council postpones reviewing challenge to female judge ban', Daily News Egypt, 15 November 2017, accessed 15 June 2018 at www.dailynewsegypt.com/2017/11/15/state-council-postpones-reviewing-challenge-female-judge-ban/

Samodien L, '"Black widow" wins appeal against sentence', IOL, 23 December 2011, accessed 20 June 2018 at www.iol.co.za/capetimes/black-widow-wins-appeal-against-sentence-1203843

Sanderfur R (ed.), *Access to Justice* (Bingley: Emerald Group Publishing, 2009)

Sanderson C, *Counselling Adult Survivors of Child Sexual Abuse*, 3rd edition (London and Philadelphia, PA: Jessica Kingsley Publishers, 2006)

Santos B, 'Law: a map of misreading: toward a postmodern conception of law' (1987) 14 *Journal of Law and Society*, 3, 279–302

SAPS, 'Victim empowerment service in the South African police service', SAPS website, accessed 7 July 2018 at www.saps.gov.za/resource_centre/women_children/amended_victim_empo_service.pdf

Sarat A and Scheingold S, 'Cause lawyering and the reproduction of professional authority: an introduction' in Austin Sarat and Stuart Scheingold (eds.), *Cause Lawyering, Political Commitments and Professional Responsibilities* (Oxford: Oxford University Press, 1998), pp. 3–30

Sarat A and Scheingold S (eds.), *Cause Lawyering, Political Commitments and Professional Responsibilities* (Oxford: Oxford University Press, 1998)

Schärf W, 'Community justice and community policing in post-apartheid South Africa' (2001) 32 *IDS Bulletin*, 1, 74–82

Schetzer L and Henderson J, *Access to Justice and Legal Needs*, research report (Law and Justice Foundation of New South Wales, August 2002)

Schneider E, 'Feminism and the false dichotomy of victimization and agency' (1993) 38 *New York Law School Law Review*, 387

'Lesbians, gays and feminists at the bar: translating personal experience into effective legal argument – a symposium' (1987–1988) 10 *Women's Rights Law Reporter*, 2, 107–142

Schultz U and Shaw G (eds.), *Gender and Judging* (Oxford: Hart Publishing, 2013)

Schuurbiers L, 'Women's Rights activist Azza Soliman faces charges to possible 15 years of prison', The International Angle, 20 November 2017, accessed 15 June 2018 at www.theinternationalangle.com/index.php/2017/11/20/womens-rights-activist-azza-soliman-faces-charges-to-possible-15-years-of-prison/

Segar S, 'Parliament may face court challenge if it delays language bill', IOL, 19 January 2012, accessed 6 June 2018 at www.iol.co.za/dailynews/news/parliament-may-face-court-challenge-if-it-delays-language-bill-1215868

Seidman G, 'Institutional dilemmas: representation versus mobilization in the South African Gender Commission' (2003) 29 *Feminist Studies*, 3, 541–563

'"No freedom without the women": mobilization and gender in South Africa, 1970–1992' (1992) 18 *Signs* 2, 291–320

Setzer H, 'Civil society on trial in Egypt: revisiting the NGO workers case', The Washington Institute, 30 January 2018, accessed 15 June 2018 at www.washingtoninstitute.org/policy-analysis/view/civil-society-on-trial-in-egypt-revisiting-the-ngo-workers-case

'Sexual Offences Courts to Open Soon', News24, 18 April 2013, accessed 20 July 2018 at www.news24.com/SouthAfrica/News/Sexual-offences-courts-to-open-soon-20130418

Shah H, 'Brutality by acid: utilizing Bangladesh as a model to fight acid violence in Pakistan' (2008–2009) 26 *Wisconsin International Law Journal*, 1172–1199

Shahin M and El-Ghazaly Y, 'The impact of notions of nationalism on women's rights in Egypt' (2017) 17 *Studies in Ethnicity and Nationalism*, 2, 178–179

Sharafeddine F, 'Discrimination against women in the nationality law: its impact on Lebanese families and issues of national integration' (December 2017) 17 *The Peace Building in Lebanon*, 15

Sharafeldin M, 'Personal status law reform between Islamic and international human rights law' in Ziba Mir-Hosseini et al. (eds.), *Gender and Equality in Muslim Family Law: Justice and Ethics in the Islamic Legal Traditions* (London and New York: I B Tauris 2013), pp. 57–81

Sheldon K, 'Women and revolution in Mozambique' in Tetreault M (ed.), *Women and Revolution in Africa, Asia and the New World* (Columbia, SC: University of South Carolina Press, 1994), pp. 33–61

Sherwood H, 'Human rights groups face global crackdown "not seen in a generation"', The Guardian, 26 August 2015, accessed 2 June 2018 at www.theguardian.com/law/2015/aug/26/ngos-face-restrictions-laws-human-rights-generation

Shukumisa, *Monitoring the Implementation of Sexual Offences Legislation and Policy*, research report (Tshwaranang Legal Advocacy Centre and others, 2010)

Shukumisa, *Monitoring the Implementation of Sexual Offences Legislation*, research report (Tshwaranang Legal Advocacy Centre and others, 2013–2014)

Shukumisa, *Sexual Violence, Calling the System to Account*, research report (Tshwaranang Legal Advocacy Centre and Others, 2010)

SIDA, *Preventing and Responding to Gender-Based Violence: Expressions and Strategies*, research report (2015)

Sika N and Khodary Y, 'One step forward, two steps back? Egyptian women within the confines of authoritarianism' (2012) 13 *Journal of International Women's Studies*, 5, 91–100

Silova I, 'Contested alliances: international NGOs and authoritarian governments in the era of globalization' (2007–2008) 10 *Current Issues in Comparative Education*, 1/2, 26–31

Simmons B A, *Mobilizing for Human Rights: International Law in Domestic Politics* (Cambridge: Cambridge University Press, 2009)

Simpson R M, 'Un-ringing the bell: McGowan on oppressive speech and the asymmetric pliability of conversations' (2013) 91 *Australasian Journal of Philosophy*, 3, 555–575

Skard T, *Continent of Mothers Continent of Hope* (London and New York: Zed Books, 2003)

Skelton A, 'The role of the courts in ensuring the right to a basic education in a democratic South Africa: a critical evaluation of recent education case law' (2014) 46 *De Jure*, 1, 1–23

Slye R, 'International law, human rights beneficiaries and South Africa: some thoughts on the utility of international human rights law' (2001) 2 *Chicago Journal of International Law*, 1, 59–79

Smart C, *Feminism and the Power of Law* (New York: Routledge, 1998)

Smith D, 'South Africa searches for solution after teenage girl's gang rape and murder', The Guardian, 13 February 2013, accessed 20 July 2018 at www.guardian.co.uk/world/2013/feb/13/south-africa-rape-murder

Smyth R, 'Academic writing and the courts: a quantitative study of the influence of legal and non-legal periodicals in the High Court' (1999) 166 *University of Tasmania Law Review*, 2, 165–185

Smythe D, 'South Africa's response to domestic violence' in Carin Benninger-Budel (ed.), *Due Diligence and Its Application to Protect Women from Violence* (Leiden and Boston, MA: Martinus Nijhoff Publishers, 2008), pp. 161–172

Socioeconomic Rights Institute of South Africa, *Public Interest Legal Services in South Africa*, project report (July 2015)

Sokoloff N and Dupont I, 'Domestic violence at the intersections of race, class, and gender' (2005) 11 *Violence Against Women*, 1, 38–64

Soliman A, 'Personal status law – feminist testimonies from Egypt', Mada Masr, March 14 2017, accessed 2 June 2018 at www.madamasr.com/en/2017/03/14/feature/society/personal-status-laws-feminist-testimonies-from-egypt/

Solomon M, 'Claim that 58 sexual offences courts ready in South Africa by September looks untrue', Africa Check, 7 May 2013, accessed 4 June 2018 at www.africacheck.org/reports/claim-that-58-sexual-offences-courts-ready-by-september-looks-untrue/

Sonke Gender Justice, 'Wits-Sonke study reveals alarming levels of women's violence against women in Diepsloot', press release, 28 November 2016, accessed 17 July 2018 at http://genderjustice.org.za/news-item/wits-sonke-study-reveals-alarming-levels-mens-violence-women-diepsloot/

'South Africa looking for innovative ways to work with NGOs – interview with minister', Open Government Partnership, 12 September 2012, accessed 5 July 2018 at www.opengovpartnership.org/stories/south-africa-looking-innovative-ways-work-ngos-interview-minister

Southern African Research and Documentation Centre, *Beyond Inequalities: Women in South Africa* (Zimbabwe: Southern African Research and Documentation Centre, 1997)

'Speak out for women's rights defender Azza Soliman', Amnesty International Petition, accessed 29 May 2018 at www.amnesty.org/en/get-involved/take-action/speak-out-for-egypt-womens-rights-defender-azza-soliman/

Spies A, 'The importance and relevance of amicus curiae participation in litigating on the customary law of marriage' (2016) 16 *African Human Rights Law Journal*, 247–264

Spires A, 'Contingent symbiosis and civil society in an authoritarian state: understanding the survival of China's Grassroots NGOs' (2011) 117 *American Journal of Sociology*, 1, 1–45

Stanley E, 'Engendering change? An analysis of how NGOs work on the problem of violence against women in South Africa' (2012–2013) 8 *Journal of Politics and International Studies*, 279–321

Steady F, *Women and Collective Action in Africa* (USA: Palgrave Macmillan, 2005)

Stefiszyn K, 'The African regional response to gender-based violence' in Centre for Human Rights (ed.), *Gender Based Violence in Africa: Perspectives from the Continent* (Pretoria: University of Pretoria, 2010), pp. 17–30

Stewart J, 'Arenas of anguish – tracking multiple perpetuation trauma in HIV/AIDS and gender-based violence intersections' in Centre for Human Rights (ed.), *Gender Based Violence in Africa: Perspectives from the Continent* (Pretoria: University of Pretoria, 2010), pp. 105–126

'Strategic litigation with strong data drives better implementation of right-to-education ruling in South Africa', ESCR, 15 December 2017, accessed 4 June 2018 at www.escr-net.org/news/2017/strategic-litigation-strong-data-drives-better-implementation-right-education-ruling-south

Strauss A, *Qualitative Analysis for Social Scientists* (Cambridge: Cambridge University Press, 1987)

Stuart L, 'The South African nonprofit sector: struggling to survive, needing to thrive', NGOPulse, 9 April 2013, accessed 7 July 2018 at www.ngopulse.org/article/south-african-nonprofit-sector-struggling-survive-needing-thrive

Suarez R, 'Reporter's notebook: South African society shaped by racial identity, apartheid', PBS Newshour, 20 February 2009, accessed 20 July 2018 at www.pbs.org/newshour/health/health-jan-june09-sa4_0220

Suneri L, 'Moving beyond the feminism versus nationalism dichotomy' (2000) 20 *Canadian Women's Studies*, 2, 143–148

Suttner R, 'The ideological role of the judiciary in South Africa' in John Hund (ed.), *Law and Justice in South Africa* (Rondebosch: Centre for Intergroup Studies, 1988), pp. 81–102

Swanson M, 'The fight to criminalize violence against women in Lebanon' Open Society Foundations, 6 May 2011, accessed 6 June 2018 at

www.opensocietyfoundations.org/voices/fight-criminalize-violence-against-women-lebanon
Swardt G, 'The horror of corrective rape', Health24, 11 May 2011, accessed 20 June 2018 at www.health24.com/Sex/Sexual-diversity/The-horror-of-corrective-rape-20120721
Swart M, 'Gender reform in the judiciary is still skin deep', Mail & Guardian, 24 July 2015, accessed 20 June 2018 at www.mg.co.za/article/2015-07-23-gender-reform-in-the-judiciary-is-still-skin-deep
Swemmer S and Mntonintshi V, *Response to the South African Law Reform Commission's Report on 'Sexual Offences: Adult Prostitution'* (Centre for Applied Legal Studies, 26 February 2018)
Sword R and Zimbardo P, 'The Trump effect: an update: The toxicity is spreading', Psychology Today, 30 January 2018, accessed 20 June 2018 at www.psychologytoday.com/us/blog/the-time-cure/201801/the-trump-effect-update
Tadros M, 'The securitisation of civil society: a case study of NGOs–state security investigations (SSI) relations in Egypt' (2011) 11 *Conflict, Security and Development*, 1, 79–103
'Taking stock of the Sexual Offences Bill', University of Cape Town News, 4 June 2007, accessed 6 June 2018 at www.news.uct.ac.za/article/-2007-06-04-taking-stock-of-the-sexual-offences-bill
Tamale S, *African Sexualities* (Cape Town, Dakar, Nairobi and Oxford: Pambazuka Press 2011)
'Alternative leadership in Africa' in Luciana Ricciutelli et al. (eds.), *Feminist Politics, Activism and Vision: Local and Global Challenges* (London: Inanna Publications, 2004), pp. 313–328
Tanaka Y, 'Singapore: subtle NGO control by a developmentalist welfare state' in Shinichi Shigetomi (ed.), *The State and NGOs: Perspectives from Asia* (Singapore: Institute of South Asian Studies, 2002), pp. 200–221
Tandwa L, 'Police failure to help in domestic violence cases is misconduct-Lawyers for Human Rights', News24, 21 June 2017, accessed 25 June 2018 at www.news24.com/SouthAfrica/News/police-failure-to-help-in-domestic-violence-cases-is-misconduct-lawyers-for-human-rights-20170621
'Targeting paralegals in the drive to improve access to justice for all', UNDP Zimbabwe, 25 September 2012, accessed 20 June 2018 at www.zw.undp.org/content/zimbabwe/en/home/presscenter/articles/2012/09/12/targeting-paralegals-in-the-drive-to-improve-access-to-justice-for-all.html
Taylor J, 'Struggles against systems that impoverish: South African civil society at the crossroads' (2013) 23 *Development in Practice*, 5/6, 617–630
Terblanche S, 'Case reviews; sentencing' (2005) 18 *South African Journal of Criminal Justice*, 3, 385–400

Teubner G, 'Autopoiesis in law and society: a rejoinder to Blankenburg' (1984) 18 *Law and Society Review*, 2, 291–301

Thomas A, 'Whatever happened to reciprocity? Implications of donor emphasis on 'voice' and 'impact' as rationales for working NGOs in development' in Anthony J Bebbington et al. (eds.), *Can NGOs Make a Difference? The Challenge of Development Alternatives* (London and New York: Zed Books, 2008), pp. 90–111

Thomas C et al., *Working with the Justice Sector to End Violence Against Women and Girls*, research report (UN Women, December 2011)

Tiessen R, 'Re-inventing the gendered organization: staff attitudes towards women and gender mainstreaming in NGOs in Malawi' (2004) 11 *Gender, Work and Organization*, 6, 689–708

Trebilcock M et al. (eds.), *Middle Income Access to Justice* (Toronto: University of Toronto Press, 2012)

Tripp A M, 'Women's movements and constitution making after civil unrest and conflict in Africa: the cases of Kenya and Somalia' (2016) 12 *Politics and Gender*, 1, 78–106

True J, 'Gender specialists and global governance' in Sandra Grey and Marian Sawer (eds.), *Women's Movements: Flourishing or in Abeyance* (London: Routledge, 2008), pp. 91–104

Tsanga A, *Taking Law to the People: Gender, Law Reform, and Community Legal Education in Zimbabwe* (Harare: Weaver Press, 2003).

Tshangana A, *The Impact of Litigation by the Legal Resources Centre for Adequate Classroom Infrastructure in South Africa*, Case Study Series, Study no 12 (International Budget Partnership, March 2013)

Tshehla B, 'Here to stay: traditional leaders' role in justice and crime prevention' (2005) 11 *South Africa Crime Quarterly*, 15–20

'Twists and turns in Traditional Courts Bill proceedings', Sonke Gender Justice, 1 November 2012, accessed 30 June 2018 at www.genderjustice.org.za/article/sordid-twist-to-traditional-courts-bill-proceedings/

UN OHCHR and UNMIT, *Report on Human Rights Development in Timor Leste* (September 2007–June 2008)

UNDP, *Access to Justice*, practice note (2004)

Ulrich J, 'Confronting gender-based violence with international instruments: is a solution to the pandemic within reach?' (2000) 7 *Indiana Journal of Global Legal Studies*, 2, 629–654

'UN human rights chief urges repeal of repressive NGO law in Egypt', UN News, 1 June 2017, accessed 30 June 2018 at www.news.un.org/en/story/2017/06/558522-un-human-rights-chief-urges-repeal-repressive-ngo-law-egypt

Usdin S et al., 'The value of advocacy in promoting social change: implementing the new Domestic Violence Act in South Africa' (2000) 8 *Reproductive Health Matters*, 16, 55–65

Valters C and Jahan F, *Getting to Grips with Power: Can NGOs Improve Justice in Bangladesh?* Research Report (Overseas Development Institute, March 2017)

Van Der Spuy P and Clowes L, 'Accidental feminists? Recent histories of South African women' (2007) *Kronos*, 33, 211–235

Van Niekerk G, *Traditional African Courts* (Cape Town: University of Cape Town, 1993)

Vetten L, *Addressing Domestic Violence in South Africa: Reflections on Strategy and Practice* (UN Division for the Advancement of Women in collaboration and UN Office on Drugs and Crime, 2005)

It Sucks' / 'It's a Wonderful Service': Post-Rape Care and the Micro-Politics of Institutions, research report (Actionaid/Shukumisa, 2015)

'Paradox and policy in post-apartheid South Africa' in Nicole Westmarland and Geetanjali Gangoli (eds.), *International Approaches to Rape* (UK: The Policy Press, 2012), pp. 147–169

'Police accountability and the Domestic Violence Act 1998' (2017) 29 *South African Crime Quarterly*, 7–19

Vetten L et al., *The Right and the Real: A Shadow Report Analysing Selected Government Departments' Implementation of the 1998 Domestic Violence Act and 2007 Sexual Offences Act*, Research Report, (Tshwaranang Legal Advocacy Centre to End Violence Against Women, 2010)

Wael R, 'Betrayal or realistic expectations? Egyptian women revolting' (2014) 6 *Interface*, 1, 478–491

Wahlquist C, 'Court system is unfair and traumatic for child sexual abuse victims, inquiry chair says', The Guardian, 2 August 2017, accessed 6 June 2018 at www.theguardian.com/australia-news/2017/aug/02/court-system-is-unfair-and-traumatic-for-child-sexual-abuse-victims-inquiry-chair-says

Walker C, *Women and Resistance in South Africa* (Cape Town and Johannesburg: David Philip Publishers, 1991)

Walker C (ed.), *Women and Gender in Southern Africa to 1945* (Cape Town: New Africa Books, 1990)

Walker L, *The Battered Women's Syndrome*, 3rd edition (New York: Springer, 2009)

Walker L et al., 'Beyond the juror's ken: battered women' (1982) 7 *Vermont Law Review*, 1, 1–14

Walker S and Louw D, 'The court for sexual offences: perceptions of the victims of sexual offences' (May–June 2005) 28 *International Journal of Law and Psychiatry*, 3, 231–245

'The court for sexual offences: perceptions of the families of the victims of sexual offences' (July–August 2005) 28 *International Journal of Law and Psychiatry*, 4, 418–429

'The court for sexual offences: perceptions of the perpetrators of sexual offences' (July–August 2006) 29 *International Journal of Law and Psychiatry*, 4, 306–315

Walsh D, 'The liberal movement: women and just debate in South Africa 1994–1996' (2006) 32 *Journal of Southern African Studies*, 1, 85–105

Warioba C and Luhanga A, 'SADC initiatives aimed at combatting gender-based violence' in Centre for Human Rights (ed.), *Gender-based Violence in Africa: Perspectives from the Continent* (Pretoria: University of Pretoria 2010), pp. 31–50

Watson J, *The Role of the State in Addressing Sexual Violence: Assessing Policing Service Delivery Challenges Faced by Victims of Sexual Offences*, Policy Brief (Cape Town: APCOF, 13 August 2015)

Waylen G, *Engendering Transitions: Women's Mobilization, Institutions, and Gender Outcomes* (Oxford: Oxford University Press, 2007)

Weeks S M, 'South Africa's Traditional Courts Bill 2.0: improved but still flawed', The Conversation, 4 April 2017, accessed 30 June 2018 at www.theconversation.com/south-africas-traditional-courts-bill-2-0-improved-but-still-flawed-74997

Weilenmann M, 'Legal pluralism: a new challenge for development agencies' in *Access to Justice in Africa and Beyond: Making the Rule of Law a Reality* (National Institute for Trial Advocacy, 2007), pp. 87–96

Weir J, 'Chiefly women and women's leadership in pre-colonial Southern Africa' in Nomboniso Gasa (ed.), *Women in Southern African History: They Remove Boulders and Cross Rivers* (Cape Town: Human Science Research Council, 2007), pp. 3–20

Weiss E and Berg R, 'Child victims of sexual assault: impact of court procedures' (1982) 21 *Journal of the American Academy of Child Psychiatry*, 5, 513–518

Weiss E et al., 'Gender, sexuality and HIV: making a difference in the lives of young women in developing countries' (2000) 15 *Sexual and Relationship Therapy*, 3, 233–245

Weldon S, *Protest, Policy, and the Problem of Violence Against Women: A Cross-National Comparison* (Pittsburg, PA: University of Pittsburgh Press, 2002)

Wells H and Polders L, 'Anti-gay hate crimes in South Africa: prevalence, reporting practices, and experiences of the police' (2006) 2 *Agenda* 3, 20–28.

Wendoh S and Wallace T, 'Re-thinking gender mainstreaming in African NGOs and communities' (2005) 13 *Gender and Development*, 2, 70–79

Wiktorowica Q, 'The political limits to nongovernmental organizations in Jordan' (2002) 30 *World Development*, 1, 77–93

Winick B, 'Applying the law therapeutically in domestic violence cases' (2000–2001) 69 *University of Missouri-Kansas City Law Review*, 1, 3–91

Wittkopp S, 'Article 8' in Marsha A Freeman et al. (eds.), *The UN Convention on the Elimination of all Forms of Discrimination against Women: A Commentary* (Oxford: Oxford University Press 2012), pp. 221–233

Wojcicki J, 'She drank his money: survival sex and the problem of violence in taverns in Gauteng Province, South Africa' (2002) 16 *Medical Anthropology Quarterly*, 3, 267–293

Wojkowska E, *Doing Justice: How Informal Justice System Can Contribute*, research report (Oslo: United Nations Development Programme, 2006)

Wolf D (ed.), *Feminist Dilemmas in Fieldwork* (Boulder, CO: Westview Press, 1996)

Women's Legal Centre Newsletter, volume 1 (Women's Legal Centre, 2008)

Wood K and Jewkes R, 'Violence, rape and sexual coercion: everyday love in a South African Township' (1997) 5 *Gender and Development*, 2, 41–46

Woolford A and Ratner R, *Informal Reckonings: Conflict Resolution in Mediation, Restorative Justice and Reparations* (London: Routledge-Cavendish, 2008)

Worden N, *The Making of Modern South Africa: Conquest, Apartheid, Democracy* (Oxford: Blackwell, 2007)

World Health Organization, *Global and Regional Estimates of Violence Against Women: Prevalence and Health Effects of Intimate Partner Violence and Nonpartner Sexual Violence*, report (World Health Organization, 2013)

Wyttenbach J, 'Violence against women, cultural/religious traditions and the international standards of due diligence' in Benninger-Budel C (ed.), *Due Diligence and Its Application to Protect Women from Violence* (Leiden and Boston, MA: Martinus Nijhoff Publishers, 2008), pp. 225–240

Yang Q, 'Eradicating "mud schools" in South Africa' (2015) 54 *Columbia Journal of Transnational Law Bulletin*, 1, 1–12

Yount K M, 'Women's 'justification' of domestic violence in Egypt' (2009) 71 *Journal of Marriage and Family*, 5, 1125–1140

Zoellner L et al., 'Factors associated with completion of the restraining order process in female victims of partner violence' (2000) 15 *Journal of Interpersonal Violence*, 10, 1018–1099

WEBSITES

ADAPT, www.adapt.org.za/media.html

Ahl Masr hospital, Egypt, www.ahl-masr.org

Black Sash 'Our History', www.blacksash.org.za/index.php/our-legacy/history-of-the-black-sash

Center for Applied Legal Studies, www.wits.ac.za/cals/about-us/

Center for Gender and Refugee Studies, https://cgrs.uchastings.edu/our-work/matter-kasinga-1996

Center for Gender and Refugee Studies, 'Matter of Kasinga', https://cgrs.uchastings.edu/our-work/matter-kasinga-1996

Da El Orman, NGO, Egypt, www.dar-alorman.com/

Department of Justice and Constitutional Development, www.justice.gov.za/about/sa-courts.html

Domestic Violence and Abuse, www.divorcelaws.co.za/abuse.html

'Facts and figures: ending violence against women' UN Women, www.unwomen.org/en/what-we-do/ending-violence-against-women/facts-and-figures

Global Campaign for Equal Nationality Rights, https://equalnationalityrights.org

Hospital 57357, Egypt, www.57357.com/

Independent Police Investigative Directorate Website (IPID), www.ipid.gov.za/

Judges Matter, www.judgesmatter.co.za/

Misr El Kheir foundation, Egypt, wwwmisrelkheir.org/en/

PATCH, www.patchhelderberg.co.za/#position

People Opposing Women's Abuse (POWA) campaigns, www.powa.co.za/POWA/projects/campaigns/

POWA, Raising her voice, www.powa.co.za/POWA/projects/raising-her-voice/

South Africa Government Information: Traditional Leadership, www.gov.za/about-government/government-system/traditional-leadership

SWEAT NGO, www.sweat.org.za/

Thuthuzela Care Centre: Turning Victims into Survivors (The National Prosecuting Authority of South Africa), www.npa.gov.za/UploadedFiles/THUTHUZELA%20Brochure%20New.pdf

Thuthuzela Care Centres, UNICEF, www.unicef.org/southafrica/hiv_aids_998.html

Tshwaranang Legal Advocacy Centre's legal clinic, www.tlac.org.za/legal-clinic/

UN Women, Ending violence against women country gender profile, May 2018, accessed 1 June 2018 at http://egypt.unwomen.org/en/digital-library/publications/2018/05/ending-violence-against-women-gender-profile-egypt-may-2018

Western Cape Government, www.westerncape.gov.za/general-publication/what-16-days-activism

Wits Law Clinic family, gender and child unit, www.wits.ac.za/lawclinic/family-gender--child-unit/

Women's Legal Centre, www.wlce.co.za/about-us/#what-we-do

The World Bank, GDP per capita, http://data.worldbank.org/indicator/ny.gdp.pcap.cd

VIDEO MATERIAL

'I am a Woman', Lauren Groenewald and Miki Redelinghuys of Plexus films, Season 1 episode 19, act 2 (5 August 2012).

INDEX

CAMBRIDGE STUDIES IN LAW AND SOCIETY

Books in the Series

Diseases of the Will: Alcohol and the Dilemmas of Freedom
Mariana Valverde

The Politics of Truth and Reconciliation in South Africa: Legitimizing the Post-Apartheid State
Richard A. Wilson

Modernism and the Grounds of Law
Peter Fitzpatrick

Unemployment and Government: Genealogies of the Social
William Walters

Autonomy and Ethnicity: Negotiating Competing Claims in Multi-Ethnic States
Yash Ghai

Constituting Democracy: Law, Globalism and South Africa's Political Reconstruction
Heinz Klug

The Ritual of Rights in Japan: Law, Society, and Health Policy
Eric A. Feldman

Governing Morals: A Social History of Moral Regulation
Alan Hunt

The Colonies of Law: Colonialism, Zionism and Law in Early Mandate Palestine
Ronen Shamir

Law and Nature
David Delaney

Social Citizenship and Workfare in the United States and Western Europe: The Paradox of Inclusion
Joel F. Handler

Law, Anthropology, and the Constitution of the Social: Making Persons and Things
Edited by Alain Pottage and Martha Mundy

Judicial Review and Bureaucratic Impact: International and Interdisciplinary Perspectives
Edited by Marc Hertogh and Simon Halliday

Immigrants at the Margins: Law, Race, and Exclusion in Southern Europe
Kitty Calavita

Lawyers and Regulation: The Politics of the Administrative Process
Patrick Schmidt

Law and Globalization from Below: Toward a Cosmopolitan Legality
Edited by Boaventura de Sousa Santos and Cesar A. Rodriguez-Garavito

Public Accountability: Designs, Dilemmas and Experiences
Edited by Michael W. Dowdle

Law, Violence and Sovereignty among West Bank Palestinians
Tobias Kelly

Legal Reform and Administrative Detention Powers in China
Sarah Biddulph

The Practice of Human Rights: Tracking Law between the Global and the Local
Edited by Mark Goodale and Sally Engle Merry

Judges beyond Politics in Democracy and Dictatorship: Lessons from Chile
Lisa Hilbink

Paths to International Justice: Social and Legal Perspectives
Edited by Marie-Bénédicte Dembour and Tobias Kelly

Law and Society in Vietnam: The Transition from Socialism in Comparative Perspective
Mark Sidel

Constitutionalizing Economic Globalization: Investment Rules and Democracy's Promise
David Schneiderman

The New World Trade Organization Knowledge Agreements: 2nd Edition
Christopher Arup

Justice and Reconciliation in Post-Apartheid South Africa
Edited by François du Bois and Antje du Bois-Pedain

Militarization and Violence against Women in Conflict Zones in the Middle East: A Palestinian Case-Study
Nadera Shalhoub-Kevorkian

Child Pornography and Sexual Grooming: Legal and Societal Responses
Suzanne Ost

Darfur and the Crime of Genocide
John Hagan and Wenona Rymond-Richmond

Fictions of Justice: The International Criminal Court and the Challenge of Legal Pluralism in Sub-Saharan Africa
Kamari Maxine Clarke

Conducting Law and Society Research: Reflections on Methods and Practices
Simon Halliday and Patrick Schmidt

Planted Flags: Trees, Land, and Law in Israel/Palestine
Irus Braverman

Culture under Cross-Examination: International Justice and the Special Court for Sierra Leone
Tim Kelsall

Cultures of Legality: Judicialization and Political Activism in Latin America
Javier Couso, Alexandra Huneeus, and Rachel Sieder

Courting Democracy in Bosnia and Herzegovina: The Hague Tribunal's Impact in a Postwar State
Lara J. Nettelfield

The Gacaca Courts, Post-Genocide Justice and Reconciliation in Rwanda: Justice without Lawyers
Phil Clark

Law, Society, and History: Themes in the Legal Sociology and Legal History of Lawrence M. Friedman
Edited by Robert W. Gordon and Morton J. Horwitz

After Abu Ghraib: Exploring Human Rights in America and the Middle East
Shadi Mokhtari

Adjudication in Religious Family Laws: Cultural Accommodation, Legal Pluralism, and Gender Equality in India
Gopika Solanki

Water on Tap: Rights and Regulation in the Transnational Governance of Urban Water Services
Bronwen Morgan

Elements of Moral Cognition: Rawls' Linguistic Analogy and the Cognitive Science of Moral and Legal Judgment
John Mikhail

Mitigation and Aggravation at Sentencing
Edited by Julian V. Roberts

Institutional Inequality and the Mobilization of the Family and Medical Leave Act: Rights on Leave
Catherine R. Albiston

Authoritarian Rule of Law: Legislation, Discourse and Legitimacy in Singapore
Jothie Rajah

Law and Development and the Global Discourses of Legal Transfers
Edited by John Gillespie and Pip Nicholson

Law against the State: Ethnographic Forays into Law's Transformations
Edited by Julia Eckert, Brian Donahoe, Christian Strümpell and Zerrin Özlem Biner

Transnational Legal Ordering and State Change
Edited by Gregory C. Shaffer

Legal Mobilization under Authoritarianism: The Case of Post-Colonial Hong Kong
Waikeung Tam

Complementarity in the Line of Fire: The Catalysing Effect of the International Criminal Court in Uganda and Sudan
Sarah M. H. Nouwen

Political and Legal Transformations of an Indonesian Polity: The Nagari from Colonisation to Decentralisation
Franz von Benda-Beckmann and Keebet von Benda-Beckmann

Pakistan's Experience with Formal Law: An Alien Justice
Osama Siddique

Human Rights under State-Enforced Religious Family Laws in Israel, Egypt, and India
Yüksel Sezgin

Why Prison?
Edited by David Scott

Law's Fragile State: Colonial, Authoritarian, and Humanitarian Legacies in Sudan
Mark Fathi Massoud

Rights for Others: The Slow Home-Coming of Human Rights in the Netherlands
Barbara Oomen

European States and Their Muslim Citizens: The Impact of Institutions on Perceptions and Boundaries
Edited by John R. Bowen, Christophe Bertossi, Jan Willem Duyvendak, and Mona Lena Krook

Environmental Litigation in China: A Study in Political Ambivalence
Rachel E. Stern

Indigeneity and Legal Pluralism in India: Claims, Histories, Meanings
Pooja Parmar

Paper Tiger: Law, Bureaucracy and the Developmental State in Himalayan India
Nayanika Mathur

Religion, Law and Society
Russell Sandberg

The Experiences of Face Veil Wearers in Europe and the Law
Edited by Eva Brems

The Contentious History of the International Bill of Human Rights
Christopher N. J. Roberts

Transnational Legal Orders
Edited by Terence C. Halliday and Gregory Shaffer

Lost in China? Law, Culture and Society in Post-1997 Hong Kong
Carol A. G. Jones

Security Theology, Surveillance and the Politics of Fear
Nadera Shalhoub-Kevorkian

Opposing the Rule of Law: How Myanmar's Courts Make Law and Order
Nick Cheesman

The Ironies of Colonial Governance: Law, Custom and Justice in Colonial India
James Jaffe

The Clinic and the Court: Law, Medicine and Anthropology
Edited by Ian Harper, Tobias Kelly, and Akshay Khanna

A World of Indicators: The Making of Government Knowledge through Quantification
Edited by Richard Rottenburg, Sally Engle Merry, Sung-Joon Park, and Johanna Mugler

Contesting Immigration Policy in Court: Legal Activism and Its Radiating Effects in the United States and France
Leila Kawar

The Quiet Power of Indicators: Measuring Governance, Corruption, and Rule of Law
Edited by Sally Engle Merry, Kevin Davis, and Benedict Kingsbury

Investing in Authoritarian Rule: Punishment and Patronage in Rwanda's Gacaca Courts for Genocide Crimes
Anuradha Chakravarty

Contractual Knowledge: One Hundred Years of Legal Experimentation in Global Markets
Edited by Grégoire Mallard and Jérôme Sgard

Iraq and the Crimes of Aggressive War: The Legal Cynicism of Criminal Militarism
John Hagan, Joshua Kaiser, and Anna Hanson

Culture in the Domains of Law
Edited by René Provost

China and Islam: The Prophet, the Party, and Law
Matthew S. Erie

Diversity in Practice: Race, Gender, and Class in Legal and Professional Careers
Edited by Spencer Headworth and Robert Nelson

A Sociology of Constitutions: Constitutions and State Legitimacy in Historical-Sociological Perspective
Chris Thornhill

A Sociology of Transnational Constitutions: Social Foundations of the Post-National Legal Structure
Chris Thornhill

Shifting Legal Visions: Judicial Change and Human Rights Trials in Latin America
Ezequiel A. González Ocantos

The Demographic Transformations of Citizenship
Heli Askola

Criminal Defense in China: The Politics of Lawyers at Work
Sida Liu and Terence C. Halliday

Contesting Economic and Social Rights in Ireland: Constitution, State and Society, 1848–2016
Thomas Murray

Buried in the Heart: Women, Complex Victimhood and the War in Northern Uganda
Erin Baines

Palaces of Hope: The Anthropology of Global Organizations
Edited by Ronald Niezen and Maria Sapignoli

The Politics of Bureaucratic Corruption in Post-Transitional Eastern Europe
Marina Zaloznaya

Revisiting the Law and Governance of Trafficking, Forced Labor and Modern Slavery
Edited by Prabha Kotiswaran

Incitement on Trial: Prosecuting International Speech Crimes
Richard Ashby Wilson

Criminalizing Children: Welfare and the State in Australia
David McCallum

Global Lawmakers: International Organizations in the Crafting of World Markets
Susan Block-Lieb and Terence C. Halliday

Duties to Care: Dementia, Relationality and Law
Rosie Harding

Insiders, Outsiders, Injuries, and Law: Revisiting "The Oven Bird's Song"
Edited by Mary Nell Trautner

Hunting Justice: Displacement, Law, and Activism in the Kalahari
Maria Sapignoli

Injury and Injustice: The Cultural Politics of Harm and Redress
Edited by Anne Bloom, David M. Engel, and Michael McCann

Ruling Before the Law: The Politics of Legal Regimes in China and Indonesia
William Hurst

The Powers of Law: A Comparative Analysis of Sociopolitical Legal Studies
Mauricio García-Villegas

A Sociology of Justice in Russia
Edited by Marina Kurkchiyan and Agnieszka Kubal

Constituting Religion: Islam, Liberal Rights, and the Malaysian State
Tamir Moustafa

The Invention of the Passport: Surveillance, Citizenship and the State, Second Edition
John C. Torpey

Law's Trials: The Performance of Legal Institutions in the US "War on Terror"
Richard L. Abel

Law's Wars: The Fate of the Rule of Law in the US "War on Terror"
Richard L. Abel

Transforming Gender Citizenship: The Irresistible Rise of Gender Quotas in Europe
Edited by Eléonore Lépinard and Ruth Rubio-Marín

Muslim Women's Quest for Justice: Gender, Law and Activism in India
Mengia Hong Tschalaer

Children as 'Risk': Sexual Exploitation and Abuse by Children and Young People
Anne-Marie McAlinden

The Legal Process and the Promise of Justice: Studies Inspired by the Work of Malcolm Feeley
Jonathan Simon, Rosann Greenspan, Hadar Aviram

Sovereign Exchanges: Gifts, Trusts, Reparations, and Other Fetishes of International Solidarity
Grégoire Mallard

Measuring Justice: Quantitative Accountability and the National Prosecuting Authority in South Africa
Johanna Mugler

Printed in the United Kingdom by TJ Clays Ltd.